P9-DEP-394

ANTIQUE TRADER BOOKS

American & European Decorative & Art Glass Price Guide

Edited by
Kyle Husfloen

Special Art Glass Feature by Bob Rau

An illustrated comprehensive price guide to all types of
decorative & art glass.

Antique Trader Books
P.O. Box 1050
Dubuque, IA 52004

STAFF

Assistant Editor . . . . .Marilyn Dragowick

Production Coordinator/Editorial Assistant . . . .Louise Paradis

Production Assistant/Editorial Assistant . . . . .Ruth Willis

Cover Design . . . . .Jaro Sebek

Subscription Manager . . . . .Bonnie Rojemann

Copyright © 1994 by The Antique Trader. All rights reserved. No part of this publication may be reproduced, stored in a retrieval system, or transmitted in any form or by any means, electronic, mechanical, photocopying, recording or otherwise, without prior permission in writing from the publisher.

ISBN: 0-930625-10-2
Library of Congress Catalog Card No. 94-79662

Other books and magazines published by Antique Trader Publications:

American Pressed Glass & Bottles Price Guide
The Antique Trader Weekly
Toy Trader
Postcard Collector
Discoveries
Antiques & Collectibles Annual Price Guide

Ceramics Price Guide
Collector Magazine & Price Guide
Big Reel
Baby Boomer Collectibles
Military Trader

To order additional copies of this book or other publications listed above, contact:

Antique Trader Publications
P.O. Box 1050
Dubuque, Iowa 52004
1-800-334-7165

Introduction

In the spring of 1994 Antique Trader Books began an expanded program of publishing price guides and reference books for collectors. Building on our twenty-five years experience in the price guide publishing field, highlighted by our *ANNUAL ANTIQUES & COLLECTIBLES PRICE GUIDE*, we launched our new efforts with the release of *ANTIQUE TRADER BOOKS POTTERY AND PORCELAIN - CERAMICS PRICE GUIDE*, a comprehensive survey of all types of American and foreign ceramic wares from the 18th century through the 20th. This successful release was followed up in fall 1994 with a book of similar size and format dealing with collectible glassware - *ANTIQUE TRADER BOOKS AMERICAN PRESSED GLASS & BOTTLE PRICE GUIDE*. The book you now hold is a sequel to this glass reference and covers all types of American and European decorative and Art glasswares of the 19th and 20th centuries.

ANTIQUE TRADER BOOKS AMERICAN & EUROPEAN DECORATIVE & ART GLASS PRICE GUIDE offers you a truly comprehensive guide to the finest glasswares produced since the mid-19th century. It was in that era that glassmakers in Europe, England and America began to produce very ornate and decorative glass pieces to appeal to the tastes of the 'carriage trade' as well as the increasingly prosperous middle class who wished to emulate the tastes and fashions of the elegant elite. Popular magazines and newspapers of the day helped spread the word about what was new and chic and large international expositions, beginning with England's Crystal Palace exposition of 1851, served as an ideal venue for glass manufacturers to spotlight their newest and most elegant wares. With hundreds of thousands of visitors during the course of such World Fairs, a great demand was spurred among all levels of society for glasswares (and many other products) which people had seen on display. To help serve this demand some glass companies actually set-up small factories right on the exposition grounds to produce and sell souvenir glass items, a prime example being Gillinder & Sons display at the 1876 Philadelphia Centennial Exposition.

By the last decades of the 19th century every glass factory of any size or pretension was striving to produce new and novel lines of glass to attract a wider buying public. Several American glassmakers lead the way in this field by designing and patenting a number of unique and quite expensive glass lines such as Amberina, Burmese and Crown Milano. Today collectors refer to these and related colorful wares as "Art Glass," since they were always meant more for artful show than for everyday use. Although some of these exclusive products were beyond the pocketbooks of average buyers, glassmakers saw to it that less expensive but still colorful and showy wares were available to fit their budgets and yet still provide at least the illusion of taste and style.

The demand for elegant glasswares in colorful Art glass or "Brilliant Period" fine cut glass continued right through the turn of the 20th century. As new styles evolved, like the Art Nouveau movement of the 1890s, designers and tastemakers such as Louis Comfort Tiffany came forward to provide a new range of elegant and choice glasswares. This Victorian era interest in the elegant, exotic and ornate seemed to scarcely abate until the hard realities of the first World War made such frivolousness seem outdated and unimportant.

From the 1920s onward for many years there was a strong reaction against all things Victorian, including glassware. Some elegant lines continued to be produced by firms such as Steuben, but the sparkling excess of the 1880-1910 era was well over. When the great Depression of the 1930s hit, the production of expensive, elegant glass took another hit and since that era only a handful of makers have attempted to revive the look and style of the 19th century's rarest glasswares. Today there is evolving a

Studio Glass movement where glass artisans design and hand-produce fine pieces, some inspired by earlier lines, but many of unique modernist style. Fewer and fewer glassmakers in this country and abroad can afford to develop, produce and market the wonderfully diverse range of hand-crafted glass which was available to our ancestors a century ago. That, of course, is why those increasingly rare and unique Victorian examples are so much in demand today.

I hope you'll find our new guide to these decorative and Art glasswares of great assistance. We feel we're providing an excellent introduction to this realm of collecting beginning with a special introductory feature by noted writer, appraiser and television personality Bob Rau. In addition to our price listings, we provide a brief introductory paragraph about each line we list and, in many instances, we include a copy of the mark or markings which may be found on typical examples. We also are offering a series of sketches which highlight typical forms used in antique Art glass. And to round out our text we are offering a Glossary of Terms, a Selected Bibliography and Appendices covering Clubs for collectors and Museums which feature glass collections.

My staff and I have worked hard to gather a wide range of pricing information from many sources which should provide an accurate and in-depth gauge of current collecting trends. We have also expanded the number of illustrations we are including to show as many unique examples as possible. After all, a picture *is* worth a thousand words, especially when a unique piece of glass is being considered.

I hope you'll find our new guide interesting and informative and I'll look forward to hearing your comments. We're always interested in reader input and we strive to meet your needs whenever possi-ble. Let me know what you think after you've had a chance to sit back and peruse the world of colorful and elegant glass encased in the following pages.

Kyle Husfloen, Editor

Please note: Though listings have been double-checked and every effort has been made to insure accuracy, neither the compilers, editors nor publisher can assume responsibility for any losses that might be incurred as a result of consulting this guide, or of errors, typographical or otherwise.

Photography Credits

Photographers who have contributed to this issue include: Edward Babka, East Dubuque, Illinois; Stanley L. Baker, Minneapolis, Minnesota; Donna Bruun, Galena, Illinois; Jeff Grunewald, Chicago, Illinois; and Louise Paradis, Galena, Illinois.

For other photographs, artwork, data or permission to photograph in their shops, we sincerely express appreciation to the following auctioneers, galleries, museums, individuals and shops:

The Burmese Cruet, Montgomeryville, Pennsylvania; Christie's, New York, New York; Garth's Auctions, Delaware, Ohio; Grunewald Antiques, Hillsborough, North Carolina; Vicki Harmon, San Marcos, California; Gene Harris Antique Auction Center, Marshalltown, Iowa; the late William Heacock, Marietta, Ohio; Agnes Koehn Antiques, Cedar Rapids, Iowa; James Lehnhardt, Galena, Illinois; Joy Luke Gallery, Bloomington, Illinois; Dr. James Measell, Berkley, Michigan; Virginia Mills, Peabody, Massachusetts; Jane Rosenow, Galva, Illinois; Skinner, Inc., Bolton, Massachusetts; Sotheby's, New York, New York; Temples Antiques, Minneapolis, Minnesota; Lee Vines, Hewlett, New York; Wolf's Fine Arts Auctioneers, Cleveland, Ohio; and Woody Auctions, Douglass, Kansas.

ON THE COVER: . Upper left - A white cut to emerald green mantel lustre decorated with enameled flowers & gilt scroll trim, 9" h., ca. 1860; Lower left - Daum Nancy signed cameo vase, 11½ h.; Lower right - Victorian bride's bowl in shaded pink cased with white, hand-painted gilt leafy vines & flowers with a butterfly, 11" d., ca. 1890.

Cover design by Jaro Sebek. Cover photographs by Greta Wallace.

Special Feature

The Evolution of Art Glass 1880-1930

by Bob Rau

For years crystal clear glass had been the standard for buyers of the best glasswares in Europe and America, but by the mid-nineteenth century the public was growing tired of colorless wares, even those with beautiful cut designs. They wanted color and more flair in design, and these elements became paramount in satisfying the tastes of the glass-buying public.

Glass industry innovations in colored glass began in earnest around 1850 in England and elsewhere in Europe and soon there were tremendous advances. In England, especially, there were offerings by many great glass designers and technicians. The first true 'world's fair,' the Great Exhibition of 1851 at the Crystal Palace in London, showed just how inventive were the major British glasshouses, which were determined to maintain their traditional excellence in deep cut crystal but also determined to challenge and excel the famous French and Bohemian makers of colored, cased and enamel-painted products. During the 1850s and 1860s, some of the most sophisticated glassware was crystal enhanced by engraving, often done by immigrant Bohemians. In the following decades, Venetian-inspired creations (especially ornate table centerpieces) were developed and quickly gave rise to a craving for fancy colors and shapes in glassware.

Thomas Webb & Sons signed cameo vase. It features a frosted yellow ground layered with red and white opal and cut and carved with a bouquet of wild geranium blossoms, buds and leaves and linear border above and below. 9" h. Photo courtesy Skinner, Inc., Bolton, Massachusetts.

Soon glass firms in Stourbridge, a major English glass center, introduced cameo glass, which required extensive etching and carving through a white glass casing to a dark colored ground. Most designs in English cameo were classically inspired and soon rivaled the Italian shell cameos.

By the 1870s and 1880s, names like Thomas Webb and Sons, Stevens and Williams, the Northwood Family, the Richardsons, George Woodall and

Joseph Locke were well established as leaders in the production of some of the most exciting glasswares ever developed. Although widely appreciated in this country, you would be fortunate in visiting a museum in England to find many of these pieces on display today.

This "Silveria" vase is an example of a lesser known line produced by the Stevens and Williams firm early in the 20th century. It features clear glass internally decorated with foil and overlaid with transparent molten glass in spring green, pink, yellow, and cobalt blue and randomly applied with green vertical threading. It features an etched mark "S&W - 107." 11⅜" h. Photo courtesy of Sotheby's, New York, New York.

During the mid-nineteenth century in France, Bohemia, Austria and Germany, glasshouses were producing significant amounts of deep-cut crystal in imitation of English wares and experimental and innovative colored products similar to those that were associated with earlier Bohemian artisans. Opaline, often with elaborate painted or gilded decorations, was especially favored by the public. French paperweights with artistic colored designs became famous worldwide, while the large factories of Baccarat and St. Louis moved to satisfy the ever-growing demand for glass artifacts. Individual French artists, however, rather than the large companies experimented in decorative glass work. Joseph Brocard and Eugene Rousseau were two such glass artists. The most famous, though, was Emile Gallé, a newcomer who arrived on the scene around 1885 and eventually established his own school in Nancy, France.

Gallé soon became a true master of glass, lending his talents to the carving of glass with exotic botanical themes. Although the English had earlier revived the ancient cameo glass technique, it was Gallé who originated a multicolored cameo ware featuring many unique

This large 16¼" d. charger is a choice example of Gallé's cameo work. It features a slightly opalescent lemon yellow ground shading to amber at the rim and overlaid in amber and rhododendron pink and cut with lotus blossoms, pads and foliage. Ca. 1900. Photo courtesy of Sotheby's, New York, New York.

A cameo inkwell by Daum, Nancy. The squared body and matching lid are in amber, overlaid in lavender and cut with a continuous landscape scene. 5" h. Photo courtesy of Wolf's Fine Art Auctioneers, Cleveland, Ohio.

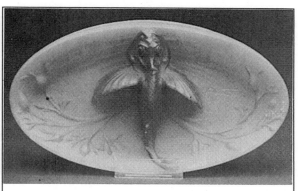

An interesting *pâté de verre* oval tray molded with a realistic dark green fish on a lighter green ground highlighted with molded seaweeds. Signed "A. Walter Nancy," one of the major French producers of this type of glass. 5½ x 9¼". Photo Courtesy of Skinner, Inc., Bolton, Massachusetts.

designs and hues. Later, when the Daum Brothers of France became interested in glass, they received help and advice from Gallé. Their combined talents developed new and different techniques for interior and intaglio work on cameo glass. It is not surprising that the finer pieces of Daum rank very close to those of Emile Gallé in desirability and value.

Pâté de verre (literally "paste of glass"), was another glassmaking technique popular with the French. Unlike cameo, with its cut-back layers of various colors, *pâté de verre* involved building up layers of colored glass with a compound that created unique and often life-like designs.

While the French focused on cameo, enameled and *pâté de verre* Art glasswares, the English and Americans continued to develop a broad range of colorful lines in the period from 1885 to 1900.

Some English wares, such as Rainbow, Pull-up and Silveria, are rarely found on the open market today and may go unrecognized except by a few experts. Many American-made lines are much more readily recognized and available.

By the middle of the nineteenth century many American glass companies were employing European craftsmen and designers, though the standard glasswares were pressed glass, sometimes in patterns to imitate cut glass. By the time of the Centennial Exhibition in 1876, crystal glass produced in the United States was comparable in quality to most produced overseas. One of the most celebrated companies of the era was the New England Glass Company of East Cambridge, Massachusetts, which later became the Libbey Glass Company and was re-located to Toledo, Ohio. This firm patented several color-ful Art glass lines including Amberina, Peach Blow, Pomona, and Agata. Other notable glass companies producing Art glass were the Mt. Washington Glass Company of New Bedford, Massachusetts

A rare variation of Amberina is Plated Amberina, which is a cased glass. It features the same coloring as Amberina but pieces always have molded ribbing around the sides. This lovely pitcher has an applied amber handle.

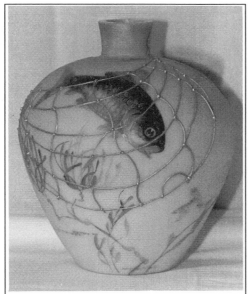

Burmese was another heat-reactive glass patented by the Mount Washington Glass Company. Pieces shade from a deep peach pink to a pale yellow and some, such as this 7½" h. vase, are further decorated with lovely enameled scenes of florals, birds, or fish. The colorful fish in this scene is being snared by a hand-painted heavy gilt enamel net. Photo courtesy of DuMouchelle's, Detroit, Michigan.

One of the most ornate lines produced by the Mount Washington Glass Company was Crown Milano. Pieces featured a creamy or white opal body decorated with florals, scenes, or heavy gilt trim. This 15½" h. vase is highlighted with an elaborate Venetian gondola scene in polychrome enamels and further gilt scrolling frames. It is marked on the base with the "CM" in wreath mark. Photo courtesy of Skinner, Inc., Bolton, Massachusetts.

(Burmese, Crown Milano, Royal Flemish) and Hobbs, Brockunier & Company of Wheeling, West Virginia (Wheeling Peach Blow, pressed Amberina and Opalescent lines.)

In the 1890s one of the greatest proponents of a new style of Art glass was Louis Comfort Tiffany. Tiffany had been born into a notable mercantile family, and his father, Charles Tiffany, was a man

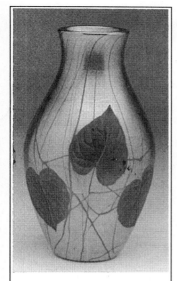

A handsome Tiffany baluster-form vase with a golden amber iridescent finish with green inclusions which are wheel-cut as broad naturalistic leaves. Marked on the base "L.C. Tiffany Favrile - 3403L." 8⅝" h. Photo courtesy of Skinner, Inc., Bolton, Massachusetts.

of considerable wealth and business experience and founder of the premier jewelry firm, Tiffany and Company, of New York City.

Louis Comfort worked long and hard in the jewelry trade while growing up, and perhaps it was this experience which developed his interest in art. It must have been a shock to his father, however, when, at age 19, Louis announced his desire to study art rather than attend college. Not only did he study art but he became a leading interior designer of the Gilded Age and then evolved an interest in designing and producing stunning leaded glass windows, lamps, and, of course, unique decorative glass-wares. Tiffany's Favrile glass, with its lustrous, shimmering metallic effects in a rainbow of colors, was one of his most startling creations. Most frequently encountered are gold and blue, but there are also impressive examples with brown, green, red and black lustre finishes. A leading designer in the Art Nouveau style of the 1890s (his works were first publicly exhibited in 1893), Tiffany also developed other glass lines with exotic names such as Lava, Tel El Amarna, Agate and Cypriote. These wares are rare and much sought after.

Tiffany's genius guided the development of other glass artists including Kimble, Durand, Nash and many others, some of whom went on to open their own glass firms.

The one glass artist who closely rivaled Tiffany in creativity was the transplanted Englishman, Frederick Carder, who came to this country in 1903 and helped found the Steuben Glass Works in Corning, New York Over his long career (he lived for nearly a century), Carder developed and promoted iridescent glass as a true art form and built a studio known for its many talented artists.

The many glass creations of Louis

One of Louis Tiffany's unique and innovative glass lines was called "Lava." This pitcher in Lava features rough-hewn navy blue iridescent sides decorated with controlled amber iridescent hourglass devices, the interior and applied C-scroll handle also in amber iridescence. It is signed "L.C. Tiffany 4586C." Ca. 1908. 6⅞" h. Photo courtesy of Sotheby's, New York, New York.

Frederick Carder developed the iridescent Aurene line for Steuben. These baluster- and ring-turned candlesticks feature an overall gold Aurene iridescent finish. One is marked "Aurene 3100," 8¼" h. Photo courtesy of Skinner, Inc., Bolton, Massachusetts.

Among the many interesting types of glass developed by Frederick Carder was Jade. This three-prong tree-trunk vase in green Jade features realistic thorns. 3¾" d., 6⅛" h. Photo courtesy of Temples Antiques, Minneapolis, Minnesota.

Tiffany and Frederick Carder remain as monuments to the vivid imaginations and skills of these glass artists. Both of these men served as a bridge between the ornate and fussy Art glass of the 1880s, the Art Nouveau era of the turn-of-the-century, and the dawning of the modern era of glass design.

Tiffany had his "Favrile" glass and Carder developed a similar line he called "Aurene," but other glassmakers followed their lead and also produced iridized glasswares.

A. Douglas Nash, who had worked for Tiffany for many years, purchased the Tiffany glass furnaces in 1928 and started his own company which began producing lines which closely resembled Tiffany's earlier work. He also developed his own unique lines, such as Chintz and Cluthra. Later, in 1931, when his company failed, he went to work for the Libbey Glass Company of Toledo, where he designed the Libbey-Nash line.

Martin Bach, another former employee of Tiffany, established the Quezal Art Glass & Decorating Company, Brooklyn, New York, in 1901. His glasswares are so similar to Tiffany's that they can prove confusing to today's collector. Of course, his old master, Tiffany, was both amazed and angered by

The best known line of glass developed by A. Douglas Nash was Chintz. This tall vase in Chintz features green and blue draped stripes. Ca. 1930. 17⅝" h. Photo courtesy of Skinner, Inc., Bolton, Massachusetts.

This Durand vase in the so-called King Tut pattern features green walls decorated with iridescent cobalt blue, opaque white and gold pulled and trailed overall designs. 6½" h. Photo courtesy of Wolf's Fine Art Auctioneers, Cleveland, Ohio.

Closely resembling the iridescent wares of Tiffany, this simple Quezal glass vase features blue swirled designs on a gold iridescent ground. It is signed on the bottom. 6½" h. Photo courtesy of Wolf's Fine Art Auctioneers, Cleveland, Ohio.

Bach's overt opportunism in producing a rival glass.

The Vineland Flint Glass Works of Vineland New Jersey, was opened by Victor Durand, Jr. in 1897 and became another well-known glass factory at the turn of the century. About 1920 Martin Bach developed a gold lustre glass decorated with random threading for the Vineland firm and this line eventually won first prize at the Sesquicentennial International Exposition in Philadelphia in 1926. Most of Durand's glass was signed "V. Durand" or just "Durand." After his death in 1931, Evan F. Kimble took over the Vineland factory and started the Kimble Glass Company, today best remembered for its version of Cluthra glass. Kimble glass was produced for only a short time, and the few marked pieces found today can bring high prices.

The Union Glass Works of Somerville, Massachusetts, established in 1851, today is best known for the production of the Art Nouveau era line of glass called Kew Blas. This iridized glass of the 1890s derives its name

Another type of iridescent glass closely resembling Tiffany is "Kew Blas." This Kew Blas pitcher features a white ground decorated with green and gold iridescent pulled-feather designs. It has a scrolled and ribbed applied gold handle and gold interior. Ca. 1900. 4⅛" h. Photo courtesy of Skinner, Inc., Bolton, Massachusetts.

This dresser box with a ornate molded square form decorated with large daisies on a dark background is an example of the Kelva line from the C.F. Monroe Company. Photo courtesy of Doris Johnson, Rockford, Illinois.

Beautifully decorated with the bust portrait of a Victorian lady, this large round dresser box is an example of the Nakara line from C.F. Monroe. 8" d., 5½" h. Private collection.

from an anagram of the name of the plant manager of that time, W(illiam) S. Blake.

Not all turn-of-the-century Art glass was iridized, of course. Several famous lines of decorated white opal glass with molded designs and painted decoration were released by the C.F. Monroe Company of Meriden, Connecticut. Wave Crest ware was their most famous and abundant line, but

An ornate Wave Crest dresser box with gilt-metal hinged rim fittings and base band with scroll feet. The body features black and white banding with delicate hand-painted florals and heavy gilt trim. 6¾" w., 6" h. Photo courtesy of Joy Luke Gallery, Bloomington, Illinois.

Scarce white opal wares with colored decoration were also produced by the Handel Glass Decorating Co. This humidor, marked "Tobacco" on the lid, has a drinking scene on the side on a shaded russet to green background with gilt trim. 7½" w., 7¾" h. Courtesy of Lee Vines, Hewlett, New York.

A selection of American Victorian Art Glass. Left to right: a New England Glass Company Amberina lily-form vase, 7" h.; a New England Amberina angular pitcher in the Inverted Thumbprint pattern, 4¾" h.; a New England Amberina finger bowl, 5½" d., 2½" h.; a New England Peach Blow Tumbler, a Burmese tumbler, a Green Opaque tumbler and (back) a Coralene-decorated tumbler in the seaweed design.

similar pieces were marked with the names Nakara and Kelva. The Handel Glass Decorating Company, Meriden, Connecticut, famous for their decorative lamps, also produced a limited line of decorated white opal wares and a frosted clear line with a chipped ice effect and painted decoration which they called Teroma.

This brief discussion can't possibly cover all the diverse and colorful glasswares of the Art glass era, but you will find many others touched upon in the following pages. We hope this will inspire you to study further to learn all you can about this unique era in glass production. Whatever color or form of glass is your favorite, there is undoubtedly an Art glass ware that will appeal to you. Although the rarest examples can bring astronomical prices, with care, study, and diligence, most collectors can still locate and afford pieces which they can display with pride.

ABOUT THE AUTHOR

Bob Rau is a well-known writer, lecturer and appraiser who is familiar to many antiquers as host of the popular PBS television series, "The Collectors."

Bob has been a frequent contributor to *The Antique Trader Price Guide* and authored our 1989 Special Focus feature, 'The Art of Steuben Glass.' In addition he authored the book, "The Collectors," published by the Graphic Arts Center Publishing Company in 1989.

TYPICAL FORMS
BASKETS & BOWLS

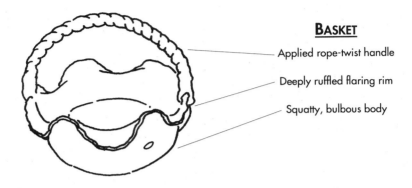

BASKET

Applied rope-twist handle

Deeply ruffled flaring rim

Squatty, bulbous body

BOWL

Incurved, ruffled rim

Squatty, bulbous body

Applied feet

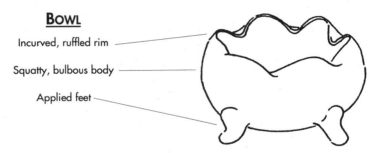

BOWL

Flat rim

Pressed overall pattern

Deep rounded body

BOWL

Scalloped, rolled rim

Deep rounded body

Footring

TYPICAL FORMS
CRUETS & DECANTERS

CRUETS

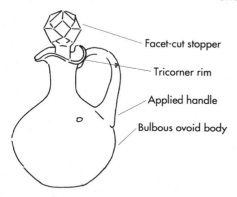

Facet-cut stopper

Tricorner rim

Applied handle

Bulbous ovoid body

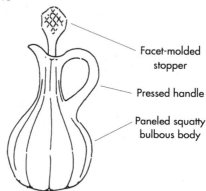

Facet-molded stopper

Pressed handle

Paneled squatty bulbous body

DECANTERS

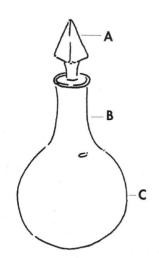

A

B

C

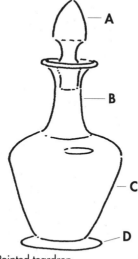

A

B

C

D

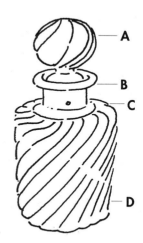

A

B

C

D

A. Cut, paneled & pointed stopper

B. Cylindrical neck with flat rim

C. Spherical body

A. Pointed teardrop stopper

B. Waisted cylindrical neck with flared rim

C. Tapering ovoid body

D. Applied foot

A. Ball stopper with molded & swirled ribs

B. Short cylindrical neck with rolled rim

C. Flat shoulder

D. Cylindrical body with molded & swirled ribs

TYPICAL FORMS
PITCHERS & EWERS

EWERS

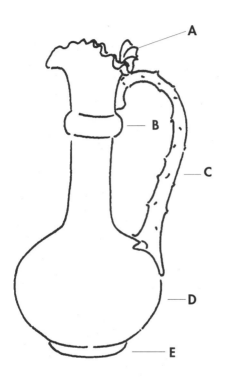

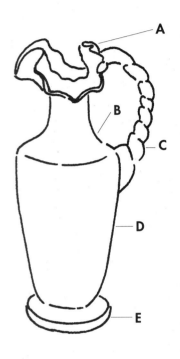

A. Tricorner crimped & ruffled rim

B. Molded neck ring on tall neck

C. Applied 'thorn' handle

D. Bulbous body

E. Molded footring

A. Tricorner ruffled rim

B. Tapering shoulder

C. Applied rope-twist (braided) handle

D. Tapering ovoid body

E. Cushion foot

PITCHERS (continued)

PITCHERS

Tricorner rim

Applied rope-twist (braided) handle & neck ring

Tapering ovoid body

Flat rim with pinched spout

Applied handle, sometimes "reeded" (ribbed)

Tankard-style cylindical body

PITCHERS (continued)

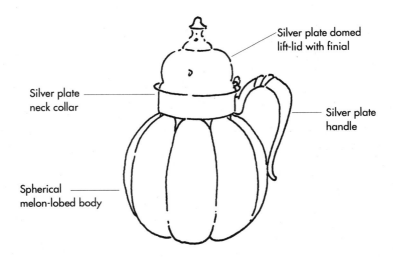

Silver plate domed
lift-lid with finial

Silver plate
neck collar

Silver plate
handle

Spherical
melon-lobed body

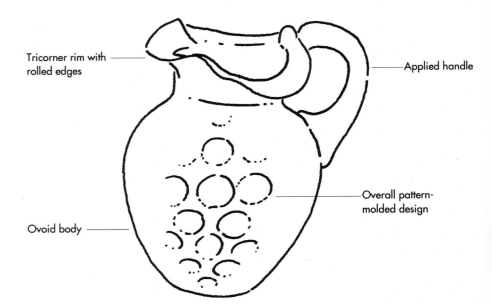

Tricorner rim with
rolled edges

Applied handle

Overall pattern-
molded design

Ovoid body

TYPICAL FORMS
VASES

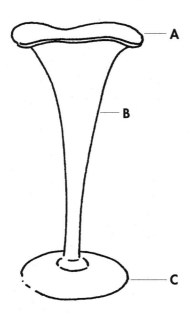

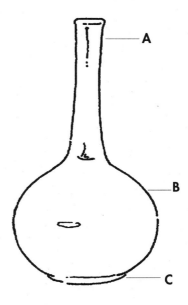

LILY-FORM VASE

BOTTLE-FORM VASE

A. Widely flaring, lightly ruffled rim

B. Slender trumpet-form body

C. Applied disc-form foot

A. Tall slender 'stick' neck with flat rim

B. Spherical body

C. Molded footring

VASES (continued)

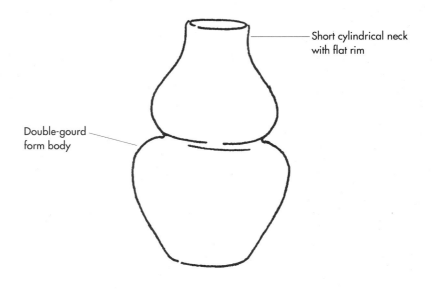

Short cylindrical neck
with flat rim

Double-gourd
form body

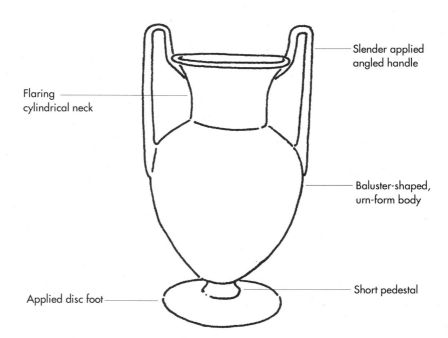

Slender applied
angled handle

Flaring
cylindrical neck

Baluster-shaped,
urn-form body

Applied disc foot

Short pedestal

VASES (continued)

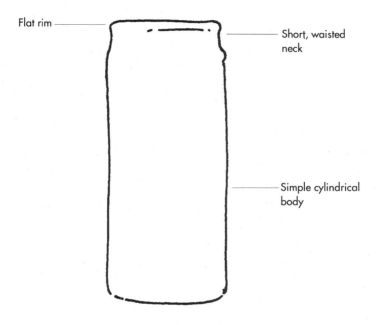

Flat rim

Short, waisted neck

Simple cylindrical body

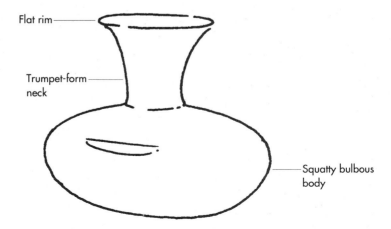

Flat rim

Trumpet-form neck

Squatty bulbous body

VASES (continued)

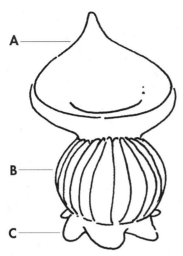

A. Jack-in-the Pulpit rim

B. Spherical body with molded ribs

C. Applied 'petal' feet

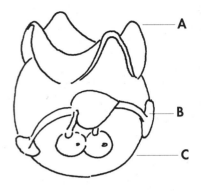

A. Four-lobed ruffled rim

B. 'Appliqued' decoration of fruit

C. Spherical body

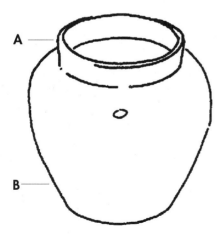

A. Short, wide cylindrical neck

B. Wide ovoid body

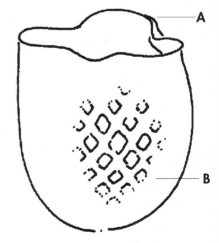

A. Lobed, flat rim

B. Egg-shaped body with overall pattern-molded design

AGATA

Green Opaque Agata Tumbler

Agata, in production only a short time, was one of a number of unique Art glass wares brought out by the New England Glass Company. Patented by Joseph Locke in 1887, Agata wares were decorated with an application of mineral stain which left a mottled effect on the surface. The stain was most often applied to Wild Rose (Peach Blow) items, but sometimes it was used as a border on pale opaque green objects. The items listed below are of the Wild Rose line unless otherwise noted

Bowl, 5" d., 2½" h., flaring cylindrical
sides w/deep ruffling $770.00

Celery vase, bulbous base tapering
slightly w/a gently flaring rim, green
opaque ground decorated w/lacy
gold trim on the rim & shoulder,
6⅞" h.. 985.00

Celery vase, green opaque 750.00

Toothpick holder, green opaque,
squatty ovoid body tapering to a
widely flaring rim, decorated around
the rim w/a band of blue mottled
stain w/a gold border band,
2¼" h. 770.00

Toothpick holder, squatty ovoid base
tapering to a flaring rim, green
opaque ground decorated w/lacy
gold trim on the rim & shoulder 1,150.00

Toothpick holder, tri-cornered rim....1,600.00

Tumbler, cylindrical, oily mottling
w/blue spotting, 2½" d., 3⅞" h. 695.00

Tumbler, cylindrical, deep raspberry
shading to creamy pink, decorated
w/oily mottling & blue spotting,
2½" d., 3⅞" h. 695.00

Tumbler, cylindrical, green opaque, oil
spot band at the rim (ILLUS.)............300.00

Tumblers, deep color w/excellent
spotting, 3¼" h., set of 6 ....2,530.00

Vase, 4½" h., cylindrical body
w/squared scalloped rim, fine
coloring 880.00

Vase, 7¾" h., lily-form w/tricorner
rim, glossy finish 1,265.00

ALEXANDRITE

Inspired by the gemstone of the same name, Alexandrite is a decorative glass shading from yellow-green to rose to blue. It was produced by Thomas Webb & Sons and Stevens & Williams of England in the late 19th century. The Moser firm of Karlsbad, Bohemia made a similar line.

Bowl, 8½" d., free-form w/outswept
rim, molded ribbed sides, attributed
to Moser..$125.00

Goblet, large bell-form bowl w/tiny
optic honeycomb design, plain stem
& round foot, Thomas Webb &
Sons, 4½" h. 747.50

Punch cup, barrel-shaped w/applied citron
handle, 2¼" d., 2¾" h.......................550.00

Small Alexandrite Vase

Vase, 3" h., squatty bulbous base

Alexandrite Trumpet-form Vase

tapering to an upright hexagonal neck, molded Diamond Quilted patt. (ILLUS.) 450.00

Vase, 4¼" h., Honeycomb patt. 765.00

Vase, 8¼" h., trumpet-shaped, round foot, swirl-molded compressed base (ILLUS. bottom previous page) 2,800.00

Alexandrite Wine Glass

Wine glass, deep rounded Diamond Quilted patt. bowl on a slender stem & round foot, 4½" h. (ILLUS.) 1,100.00

Wine, Optic patt., 4½" h. 950.00

AMBERINA

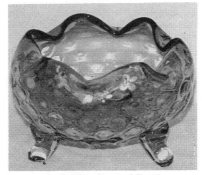

Amberina Footed Bowl

Probably the most popular of late 19th century Art glasswares, Amberina was developed in the 1880s by the New England Glass Company. Patented by Joseph Locke in 1883, this heat-reactive glass shaded from amber to deep red or fuchsia. A similar line, which they called Rose Amber, was brought out by the Mt. Washington Glass Company about the same time. Both Amberina and Rose Amber were produced in a myriad of free-blown and mold-blown forms. A related ware, today called Plated Amberina *(which see), was lined with a creamy white interior layer. The New England Glass Company licensed Hobbs, Brockunier & Company of Wheeling, West Virginia to make a pressed version of Amberina. The Libbey Glass*

Company, successor to the New England Glass Company, revived a blown line of Amberina, using modern shapes, in 1917.

Amberina Label

Bar bottle w/original amber facet-cut stopper, Swirled Rib patt., 8" h. $350.00

Basket, footed w/serrated rim, decorated w/h.p. pink & blue flowers, applied ruffled amber handle, six applied amber feet, berry pontil 480.00

Bonbon, shape No. 3029, Libbey Glass Co., signed 350.00

Bowl, ice cream, individual, 5" d., pressed Daisy & Button patt. 90.00

Bowl, 2½ x 5½ " rectangle, Libbey Glass Co. 295.00

Bowl, 5¾" d., 3¾" h., squatty bulbous body w/incurved six-crimp rim, Inverted Thumbprint patt., raised on three applied amber scroll feet, decorated around the rim w/gold florals (ILLUS.) 325.00

Bowl, 10" oval, pressed Daisy & Button patt. 350.00

Bowl, 11" d., shape No. 3026, Libbey Glass Co., signed 450.00

Bowl, 6½ x 11¾" oval, 6½" h., Swirl patt., footed, applied amber handles, rim edging & feet.............................325.00

Bowl-vase, Plated Amberina, waisted cylindrical twelve-ribbed body, New England Glass Co., 3½" h. 3,960.00

Butter dish, cov., Diagonal Block patt. 235.00

Butter pat, petal-shaped, pressed Daisy & Button patt., 3" d. 115.00

Carafe, Reverse Amberina, Inverted Thumbprint patt., 7½" h. 275.00

Celery vase, pressed Daisy & Button patt., Hobbs, Brockunier & Co. 150.00

Celery vase, square top w/ruffled rim, Diamond Quilted patt. 445.00

Celery vase, Inverted Thumbprint patt., 6¾" h.....................................135.00

Cheese dish, cov., twelve-paneled cover w/cut finial, Optic patt., 9½" d., 7" h...345.00

Cologne bottle w/original facet-cut stopper, Inverted Thumbprint patt., New England Glass Co., 5" h. 275.00

Cologne bottle w/original stopper,
bulbous, Swirl patt., 5¼" h. 475.00

Cologne bottle w/original stopper,
shape No. 3040, Libbey Glass Co.,
signed, 2 oz. 450.00

Compote, open, 6½" d., 8" h., shape
No. 3017, Libbey Glass Co.,
signed 800.00

Compote, open, 10" h., ruffled rim,
ball connector, flat disc base,
shape No. 3016, Libbey Glass Co.,
signed 2,310.00

Creamer, Inverted Thumbprint patt.,
4¾" h..275.00

Creamer, globular base, slender neck
w/flaring rim & pinched lip, applied
angular amber handle, Swirl patt.,
3⅜" d., 5" h. 135.00

Creamer w/applied amber handle,
Reverse Amberina, Diamond
Quilted patt. 165.00

Cruet w/original amber bubble
stopper, spherical body w/slender
cylindrical neck & tricorner rim,
Inverted Thumbprint patt., applied
amber handle, 3⅜" d., 6" h. 275.00

Amberina Cruet

Cruet w/facet-cut amber stopper,
bulbous ovoid body w/lightly molded
ribbing, slender cylindrical neck
w/tricorner rim, applied amber
handle, New England Glass Co.,
6½" h. (ILLUS.) 400.00

Cruet w/original amber stopper,
bulbous melon-ribbed body, applied
amber handle, 6¾" h. (ILLUS. top
next column) 200.00

Decanter w/original amber bubble
stopper, ovoid body tapering to a
cylindrical neck w/pinched spout,
applied amber handle, 4" d.,
9" h..245.00

Amberina Melon-ribbed Cruet

Decanter w/original amber facet-cut
stopper, Inverted Thumbprint patt.,
10½" h...395.00

Tall Amberina Ewer

Ewer, bulbous ovoid Inverted
Thumbprint patt. body tapering to a
cylindrical neck w/small pinched
spout, applied amber angled handle,
5⅛" d., 10⅛" h. (ILLUS.) 200.00

Finger bowl, deep upright ten-crimp
sides, faint optic ribbing, New
England Glass Co., 5½" d., 2½" h. ..172.50

Finger bowls, Hobnail patt., 4⅞" d.,
pr..180.00

Ice bucket, slightly flaring sides w/tab
handles, decorated overall w/deli-
cate blue & yellow flowers & green
foliage, 7¼" d., 5½" h. 200.00

Ice cream set: master bowl & six
plates; pressed Daisy & Button patt.,
7 pcs. 925.00

Liqueur bottle w/original stopper,
Ripple patt., 9½" h. 125.00

Model of a canoe, hanging-type, pressed Daisy & Button patt. 350.00

Pitcher, 4¾" h., flaring base below long angled sides to the flaring squared rim, applied reeded amber handle, Inverted Thumbprint patt., New England Glass Co....................345.00

Pitcher, milk, 5" h., bulbous, melon-ribbed body w/applied amber handle, Herringbone patt. 195.00

Pitcher, tankard, 6¾" h., Diamond Quilted patt., New England Glass Co. 770.00

Pitcher, 8" h., pleated rim, applied reeded clear handle 225.00

Pitcher, 10" h., fluted form, applied handle 220.00

Pitcher, water, Inverted Thumbprint patt..250.00

Plate, 6⅞" d., New England Glass Co. 110.00

Punch cup w/applied reeded amber handle, Diamond Quilted patt. 155.00

Punch cup w/applied amber handle, Inverted Thumbprint patt., Mt. Washington Glass Co. 135.00

Punch cup, Reverse Amberina, Inverted Thumbprint patt....................50.00

Punch cups w/applied handles, Diamond Quilted patt., pr. 121.00

Rose bowl, round melon-ribbed body w/applied amber threading, 3½" h. 70.00

Rose bowl, squatty bulbous body w/five-crimp top, applied amber petal feet, blown Hobnail patt., 4½" d., 4" h. 125.00

Rose bowl, triangular pinched-in rim, applied amber ribbed feet & berry prunt, Inverted Thumbprint patt., 3¾" d., 6" h. 250.00

Salt dips, elongated oval w/pointed ends, pressed Daisy & Button patt., 4½" l., pr..247.50

Spooner, Inverted Thumbprint patt., 4¾" h...95.00

Syrup pitcher w/original silver plate top, ball-shaped, Inverted Thumb-print patt., New England Glass Co...450.00

Toothpick holder, cylindrical body w/tricornered rim 300.00

Toothpick holder, footed, cylindrical w/scalloped rim, pressed Daisy & Button patt., Hobbs, Brockunier & Co. 150.00

Amberina Toothpick Holder

Toothpick holder, square rim, Diamond Quilted patt. (ILLUS.)........235.00

Toothpick holder, fig mold, Mt. Washington Glass Co. 195.00

Toothpick holder, Inverted Thumbprint patt..125.00

Toothpick holder, square rim, Vene-tian Diamond patt............................275.00

Tumbler, juice, Diamond Quilted patt., 2⅝" h......................................125.00

Tumbler, Plated Amberina, embossed ribs, New England Glass Co., ca. 1880, 3¾" h...............................1,320.00

Tumbler, footed, Inverted Thumbprint patt., applied amber foot, 2⅝" d., 4" h..70.00

Tumbler, Inverted Thumbprint patt., 2¾" d., 4" h...96.00

Tumbler, Diamond Quilted patt., decorated w/blue & white flowers 90.00

Tumbler, Optic Rib patt.......................115.00

Tumbler, Reverse Amberina, Inverted Thumbprint patt. 75.00

Tumbler, Reverse Swirl patt. 65.00

Tumbler, Swirled Rib patt., decorated w/small flowers & leaves.................125.00

Tumbler, Tiny Inverted Thumbprint patt...70.00

Tumblers, cylindrical, Diamond Quilted patt., 3⅝" h., pr. 148.50

Vase, 5⅜" h., 3¼" d., squatty ovoid body tapering to flaring trumpet-form neck, Inverted Thumbprint patt. 110.00

Vase, 6" h., cylindrical w/quadrilateral top, Inverted Thumbprint patt...........220.00

Vase, 6" h., lily-form, Mt. Washington Glass Co. 195.00

Vase, 6" h., tapering cylindrical body, fluted swirling pattern.......................192.50

Vase, 7" h., lily-form w/tricorner rim, New England Glass Co....................345.00

Vase, 8" h., lily-form, set in a silver plate holder w/decorative handles, four raised medallions of a classic warrior & scrolling, holder marked "Meriden" 265.00

Vase, bud, 8" h., 2¼" d., bottle-shaped tapering to flaring rim, disc foot, applied clear spiral trim 195.00

Vase, 10¾" h., bulbous base, flared neck & applied ruffled rim, Swirled Rib patt. 330.00

Vase, 12" h., cylindrical w/three applied triangular ribbed feet, Swirled Rib patt., polished pontil......250.00

Vase, 12" h., 5" d., gladiolus-type, rim decorated w/a wide gold tracery band & the center enameled w/florals...485.00

Vase, 13" h., bulbous w/circular foot & folded ruffled rim, Inverted Thumb-print patt. 330.00

Vase, 14" h., 6" d., cylindrical form w/fluted rim 425.00

Water set: pitcher & four tumblers; New England Glass Co., 5 pcs. 1,195.00

APPLIQUED

Ewer with Applique Trim

In glass terms, 'appliqued' refers to any type of Art glass decorated with applied glass decoration. Usually free-blown or mold-blown vases or ewers had three-dimensional leafy branches of fruit or flowers applied to their sides using vivid colors. Sometimes buttons of molten glass were daubed on the object or ribbons of molten glass were trailed around the piece. This decorative technique required a great deal of skill from the glassmaker and the best examples in perfect condition are much sought-after today. Appliqued

decoration was used on both cased (two-layer) and single layer glass. Various glassworks in this country and Europe produced appliqued wares, but the English firm of Stevens and Williams (which see), is especially noted for their examples.

Basket, rose bowl-shaped w/six-crimp top, creamy opaque w/amber applied twisted handle, applied amber branch & leaves, pink & white spatter applied flowers w/amber centers, 4½" d., 7" h......................$195.00

Bowl, 4⅞" d., 5" h., bulbous sapphire blue body w/applied crystal scroll feet, six applied clear berry prunts around top w/three crystal fan-like applied designs, applied clear berry prunt on base, probably Webb.........195.00

Cornucopia-vase, shaded pink opalescent Diamond Quilted patt. body on clear scalloped foot, applied w/lavender spatter flowers & clear opalescent branch w/leaves & flowers, 3½"d., 8½" h. 88.00

Decanter w/original blue faceted stopper, footed ovoid body tapering to tall slender neck w/applied blue handle, golden amber w/applied blue trim & applied blue salamander, 3¾" d., 12½" h. 175.00

Ewer, ovoid body w/flaring crimped rim, applied amber handle, creamy white opaque body applied w/a fine cranberry edging & an applied blue flower w/amber branch & green leaves, 2¾" d., 5¾" h. (ILLUS.).........88.00

Rose bowl, bulbous w/eight-crimp top, cased rose body applied w/large white flower & clear leaf & branch, white shading to opalescent lining, 3⅞" d., 2⅞" h. 85.00

Appliqued Rose Bowl

Rose bowl, squatty bulbous cased shaded deep rose-colored bowl w/an eight-crimp rim, applied clear leaves, branch & large blossom, white opalescent interior, 3⅞" d., 2⅞" h. (ILLUS.) 85.00

Appliqued Rose Bowl with Cherries

Rose bowl, spherical body w/a four-lobe rim pulled into points, creamy white exterior & pink interior, applied w/clear leafy branch & two red cherries, 3½" d., 4¼" h. (ILLUS.) 145.00

Urn, cov., bulbous base w/domed lid, cranberry w/applied large clear flowers & leaves on sides, applied clear handle, feet & leaf top edge, applied clear finial on lid & clear flower prunt, 5½" d., 8¾" h...............495.00

Vase, 2⅝" h., 5½" l., log-shaped, cased orange w/crystal applied leaves & looped branch feet, creamy lining 100.00

Vase, 4¼" h., 4⅛" d., bulbous body w/folded heavenly blue four-petal rim w/applied clear edging, creamy overlay exterior w/applied crystal ruffled leaf band 135.00

Vase, 4⅝" h., 3⅛" d., bulbous thorny body, four-lobe top w/applied clear edging, pink ground w/applied flower & leaves decoration, applied clear wishbone feet...................................125.00

Vase, 4⅝" h., 3⅝" d., bulbous melon-ribbed body tapering to a narrow neck w/widely flaring ruffled rim, peach opalescent swirl w/iridized exterior, applied opalescent flower & leaves on front................................88.00

Vase, 4⅝" h., 4¼" d., bulbous body tapering to an eight-scallop flaring neck, shaded green opalescent striped exterior w/applied pink & white spatter flower on front, applied vaseline leaf & branch 105.00

Vase, 4¾" h., 3" d., cased pink ovoid body w/four-petal rim, applied clear feet & edging on the rim, body applied w/clear flower, leaves & thorny nubs, white lining 118.00

Vase, 5" h., ovoid, butterscotch shading to pale yellow mother-of-pearl Diamond Quilted patt., applied branch & blossoms 75.00

Vase, 5" h. 3" d., cased heavenly blue ovoid body w/flared & ruffled three-petal rim w/crystal edging, overall blue nubs on body, white lining........100.00

Vase, 6" h., 2½" d., baluster-shaped, creamy opaque w/amber applied ruffled leaf, applied cranberry ruffled rim 85.00

Vase, 6" h., 4⅜" d., opaque white ovoid body tapering to a flaring neck w/crimped rim applied w/amber edging, body applied w/pink & white flowers w/green & amber leaves & amber branches...............................110.00

Vase, 6" h., 4½" d., footed trumpet-shape w/pinched together rim, lime green opalescent w/clear shell trim applied on sides 65.00

Vase, 6⅝" h., 3½" d., cased pink tall cylindrical melon-sectioned body applied w/a pink & white spatter flower w/amber branch & leaves, applied amber petal feet 100.00

Victorian Appliqued Vase

Vase, 6¾" h., 4¼" d., white opalescent ovoid body tapering to a flaring ruffled rim cased in deep rose, three large applied dark amber leaves swirling around the sides & forming feet, probably England, 19th c. (ILLUS.) 165.00

Vase, 6¾" h., 4½" d., opaque white ovoid body tapering to a flaring & crimped rolled rim, center applied w/amber acorns & large ruffled cranberry leaf, applied amber wishbone feet & rim edging 135.00

Vase, 6¾" h., 5⅜" d., bulbous cased coral body w/applied ruffled clear opalescent rim, applied opalescent flower prunt on base, applied clear opalescent ruffled leaves & loop feet, creamy lining, Thomas Webb & Sons 295.00

Vase, 8¾" h., 4⅜" d., cased pink slender ribbed stick body w/applied clear wide ruffle around base, body applied w/large clear flowers & branch, white lining 125.00

Vase, 9½" h., footed ovoid body tapering to a three-lobed crimped & ruffled rim, cased shaded blue to pale blue exterior applied w/red cherries, white flowers & green leaves & vines, white lining, late 19th c. 450.00

Vase, 12½" h., 5½" d., ovoid amethyst body w/a flaring six-petal-shaped rim w/applied sapphire blue edging, applied w/large green branches, leaves & small amber flowers, applied amber petal-shaped feet..295.00

ART GLASS BASKETS

Amber & Blue Basket

Popular novelties in the late Victorian era, these ornate baskets of glass were usually hand-crafted of free-blown or mold-blown glass. They were made in a wide spectrum of colors and shapes. Pieces were highlighted with tall applied handles and often applied feet but fancier ones might also carry additional appliqued trim. Also see STEVENS & WILLIAMS.

Amber, squatty bulbous lightly ribbed body w/applied scalloped & crimped blue edging & applied blue rope-twist handle, polished pontil, 6½" d., 6¾" h. (ILLUS.) $145.00

Cased, creamy white exterior,

yellowish green interior, melon-sectioned w/scissor cut rim, applied clear handle, 6½" d., 6½" h. 150.00

Cased, crystal, oxblood red & opaline swirled stripes, splotches of gold Aventurine, gold enamel decoration, applied crystal handle, 7½" h. 285.00

Cased, lemon yellow exterior, rectangular-shaped form w/applied clear twisted handle, ruffled edge, 4 x 4¾", 6½" h....................................85.00

Cased, pink & white candy stripe swirl exterior, white interior, bulbous w/ruffled rim, applied clear twisted thorn handle, 5½" d., 8" h. 175.00

Cased, pink swirl exterior, clear interior, rose bowl form w/closely crimped top, applied clear twist handle, 5" d., 8½" h.........................165.00

Cased, shaded pink satin exterior, white interior, bulbous base w/eight-crimp rim, applied frosted handle, 3½" d., 5⅜" h. 125.00

Cased, white exterior, heavenly blue shaded satin interior, ruffled rim w/applied clear frosted edging, applied clear frosted braided handle, 5¼" d., 6" h. 145.00

Cased, white exterior, pink interior, deeply ruffled rim, applied clear braided handle, 5½" d., 5½" h.............85.00

Cased, yellow exterior, clear interior, footed, rectangular w/applied clear twist handle, 4¾" w., 6⅜" h. 85.00

Creamy opaque, cylindrical body tapering to a ruffled fan-shaped rim, applied amber handle & edge trim, exterior decorated overall w/small blue, yellow & maroon flowers & green leaves, 4½ x 6", 6" h. 175.00

Crystal w/cranberry threading pulled up to form a drape design, applied crystal feet & applied crystal & cranberry handle & large crystal flowers & leaves applied on either side where handle attaches, 11½" h...640.00

Electric blue, pressed w/scalloped edge & basketweave exterior w/applied floral sprays & applied blue reeded handle, France, 4 x 6½" oval, 5½" h. 100.00

Green opalescent, eight-crimp rim, applied clear twist handle & pink & white spatter flower w/clear leaf & branch, 4" d., 6½" h. 135.00

Lemon yellow opaque w/embossed

Hobnail exterior, ruffled edge &
applied clear handle, 4¾" d.,
5¾" h..88.00

Lemon yellow opaque w/embossed
Swirl patt., beaded band & swirls
embossed around exterior, ruffled
edge & applied clear handle, 5" d.,
5½" h..89.00

Lime green, ovoid body w/applied
clear ruffled rim, shell feet & reeded
handle, overall thorny nubs, 4½" d.,
7¾" h..135.00

Lime green shaded to white
opalescent, exterior embossed
w/florals & rope design, scalloped
rim, applied clear braided handle,
5½" d., 7¾" h. 115.00

Spangled & Opalescent Baskets

Lime green opalescent, deeply fluted
& crimped rim, swirled white
opalescent stripes, clear applied
rope handle, 5⅞" d., 6½" h. (ILLUS.
right)...145.00

Medium blue center w/band of clear
vaseline, white rim, decorated
w/orange enamel, applied crystal
thorn handle, 7½" w., 7½" h............350.00

Orchid Swirl patt., flared ruffled rim,
applied clear twisted thorn handle,
5" d., 6" h. 95.00

Pink opalescent Diamond Quilted
patt., lightly ruffled rim, applied
vaseline leaves & applied vaseline
twist handle, 5" d., 6½" h. 145.00

Pink opalescent, rectangular ruffled &
crimped rim, applied vaseline thorn
handle & applied vaseline leaves on
the front, 5 x 6½", 6¾" h. 265.00

Ruby & crystal, iris-form, bulbous
ovoid deep ruby body tapering to
clear applied rim petals, the back
two pulled up to form a handle, the
front two rolled down, 3⅝" d., 7" h.
(ILLUS. top next column) 118.00

Shaded lime green Diamond Quilted

Iris-Form Glass Basket

patt., ruffled edge, applied clear
handle, 5½" d., 5½" h.........................95.00

Spangled, baby blue exterior, white
interior w/silver mica flecks, tightly
ruffled rim, applied clear feet & clear
twisted thorn handle, 8¼" h. 275.00

Spangled, cased shaded deep rose
exterior w/profuse mica flecks,
spherical body w/eight-crimp rim,
clear applied thorn handle, white
lining, 4½" d., 7¼" h. (ILLUS. left)....195.00

Spangled, green w/mica flecks,
molded Swirl & Swirl Rosette patt.,
rounded sides w/ruffled rim, applied
clear twist handle, 5" d., 6½" h.........110.00

Spangled, maroon, green, yellow &
white w/green mica flecks exterior,
white interior, rounded sides
w/ruffled rim & applied clear thorn
handle, 4¼" d., 5½" h......................105.00

Spangled, white & amber w/gold mica
flecks, ruffled rim, applied clear twist
handle, 9" d. 65.00

Spatter, cased maroon, pink & yellow
exterior, white interior, bulbous body
w/ruffled rim, applied clear handle,
5" d., 6½" h. 145.00

Spatter, cased maroon, blue, white,
yellow & green spatter exterior,
white lining, bulbous melon ribbed
body w/fluted top & applied clear
twisted handle, 4¼" d., 7¼" h. 95.00

Spatter, cased pink, tan & white
spatter exterior, white lining, clear
applied thorn handle, upright
crimped rim, 6¼" d., 5⅝" h.
(ILLUS. top next column) 165.00

Spatter, cased pink, maroon, yellow &
blue spatter exterior, white interior,
rectangular-shaped body w/ruffled
edge & applied clear thorn handle,
5 x 6¼", 6" h.....................................165.00

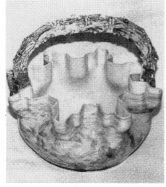

Spatter Art Glass Basket

Shaded lime green Diamond Quilted
Spatter, cased pink, green, white,
yellow & maroon spatter exterior,
white interior, bulbous body w/ruffled
rim & applied clear twisted thorn
handle, 4¾" d., 7⅛" h.........................165.00

Ruffled Art Glass Basket

Spatter, cased pink, white & yellow
exterior, yellow interior, melon-
ribbed body w/flaring ruffled rim,
applied angular thorn handle,
5½" d., 7½" h. (ILLUS.) 175.00

Spatter, cased yellow & white spatter
exterior w/embossed swirl &
rosettes design trimmed in gold,
yellow interior, star-shaped rim,
applied clear twisted thorn handle,
4⅜" d., 5¾" h. 95.00

Spatter, green & white spatter, green
applied thorn handle, upright
crimped rim, 4¾ x 7", 6" h. (ILLUS.
left, top next column) 165.00

Spatter, lemon yellow & white spatter
exterior w/six-point star-shaped top,
bulbous body w/embossed
Medallion & Swirl patt. exterior,
applied clear twisted handle, 4¼" d.,
6¼" h..88.00

Spatter & Yellow Opaque Baskets

Spatter, pastel pink, yellow & blue
spatter encased in crystal opalescent Coin Spot patt., applied crystal
rim & loop handle, 7½" h..................415.00

Yellow opaque, embossed Diamond
Quilted & Paneled patt., upright
crimped star-form rim, clear applied
handle, 4¼" d., 5¼" h. (ILLUS.
right)...88.00

BACCARAT

Baccarat Rose Teinte Sunburst Bowl

*One of the most famous French glass-
makers, the Cristalleries de Baccarat has been
in operation since 1765. Over the centuries
Baccarat has produced a wide range of fine
glass objects but today their mold-blown and
pressed wares are most often encountered,
especially dresser accessories. In the mid-19th
century they were a major producer of fine glass
paperweights. Baccarat also developed a rose to
amber shade of glass they called Rose Teinte
which is often referred to as Baccarat's
Amberina.*

Bowl, 15½" d., Rose Teinte Sunburst
patt., deep rounded sides on a small
footring, rolled rim w/scalloped
edge, Amberina-like coloring
(ILLUS.) $935.00

Box, cov., Rose Teinte Sunburst patt.,
square w/fitted square cover,
Amberina-like coloring w/molded
swirled design, signed, 3¼" w., 3" h.
(ILLUS. right, with candlesticks) 110.00

Box, cov., Rose Teinte Swirl patt.,
8" d., 2" h. 325.00

Cameo box, cov., shaped circular
form, clear overlaid w/pink & carved
w/delicate flowers, scrolls & a
lattice design, acid-stamped mark,
5¼" d...440.00

Cameo vase, 12" h., tapering form
w/bulbous mouth, opalescent
overlaid w/raspberry & carved
w/pendant roses heightened w/gilt,
acid-stamped mark 632.50

Baccarat Candlesticks & Box

Candlesticks, Rose Teinte Swirl patt.,
baluster-form standard above a
flaring base & tapering to a tulip-
form socket, Amberina-like coloring,
marked, 4" d., 7⅛" h., pr. (ILLUS.
left) 295.00

Baccarat Rose Teinte Pieces

Cologne bottle w/original stopper,
Rose Teinte Sunburst patt., cylindrical shouldered body w/a short,
flaring neck w/original bulbous
patterned stopper, Amberina-like
coloring, 2⅜" d., 6" h. (ILLUS. right) ..70.00

Cologne bottle w/original bulbous
stopper, bulbous body, Swirl patt.,
shaded blue to clear, 7" h. 70.00

Cologne bottle w/original bulbous

Baccarat Cologne Bottle

stopper, cylindrical shouldered body
tapering to a cylindrical neck w/a
ringed neck, Rose Teinte Swirl
patt., 3" d., 7¼" h. (ILLUS.) 75.00

Compote, open, Rose Teinte Swirl
patt., 4¾" d., 3¼" h. 70.00

Decanter w/original stopper, Rose
Teinte Swirl patt., spherical base
below a tall, slender ribbed neck
w/arched spout, clear applied
handle, original bulbous swirled
stopper, Amberina-like coloring,
4⅝" d., 10" h. (ILLUS. center) 225.00

Baccarat Dresser Set

Dresser set: a pair of 7" h. cologne
bottles w/stoppers, a 3" d., 2" h.
cov. box, a 3" h. ring tree & a
8⅜ x 10½" oval tray; Rose Teinte
Swirl patt., Amberina-like coloring,
marked, the set (ILLUS.).................395.00

Dresser set: covered powder jar &
perfume bottle w/atomizer; clear
w/intaglio cutting, signed Baccarat
w/Marcel Franck fittings, 2 pcs. 295.00

Fairy lamp, Rose Teinte, the cylindrical shade w/ribbed bands flanking
a swirled comet-like pattern band,

flattened underplate w/matching comet design & upturned scalloped rim, Amberina-like coloring, marked, 5¼" d., 4¾" h. (ILLUS. left) 265.00

Flower holder, bridge-shaped, five divisions for flowers, Swirl patt., sapphire blue, marked, 2 x 12", center 5" h.......................................195.00

Goblet, Diamond Point Swirl patt..........55.00

Hurricane lamps, Rose Teinte Swirl patt. base, clear shade etched w/an inscription within a wreath, bobeche w/4½" l. prisms & screw-on candle-holders, base 8" h., overall 21½" h., pr..1,125.00

Models of elephants, w/trunk down, clear, 3" h., pr....................................160.00

Perfume bottle & stopper, grey molded to resemble gears, designed for Celoron, mid-20th c., acid-stamped "BACCARAT - FRANCE," 6⅜" h..633.00

Perfume bottle w/original stopper, "Le Roy Soleil," by Schiaparelli, clear sharply tapering conical bottle w/an overall molded wavy design & traces of gilt & blue enamel, the gilt flat-tened stopper molded w/long sun rays w/black birds in black enamel, designed by Salvador Dali, the original gilt-metal box w/satin lining, the pedestal edged in purple velvet, original blue satin ribbons & gilt paper label, acid-stamped "BACCARAT - FRANCE" & "BOITE - MADE IN FRANCE," bottle 6⅜" h., 2 pcs. 8,625.00

Tumbler, encased w/an enamel on gold leaf medal of the Royal and Military Order of St. Louis of France in the form of a four-point white star w/a gold figure against a red ground suspended from a gold ring & a red ribbon facing a medal of the Order of the Legion of Honor (used between 1814-30) in the form of a five-point white star w/a central gold portrait of King Henry IV framed in a blue border against a green laurel wreath suspended from a gold crown & red ribbon, both pendant from a gold floret & scroll frieze within a series of three graduating oval panels encompassed by a continuous strawberry-cut body, set on a semicircular ribbed foot, twenty-four point star-cut base, 3¾" h. (minor chips) 1,840.00

Tumbler, the chamfered central panel encased w/an enamel on gold leaf medallion depicting a figure of a

young man in a relaxed stance, wearing gold-flecked yellow knickers, a blue sash, a red vest & a straw hat, leaning against a spade beside a gold basket filled w/pink roses on a grassy mound encompassed by diamond-shaped panels w/alternating strawberry-cut motifs, reverse panel engraved in script "P. Soukes" terminating to a triple-ring foot, sixteen-point star-cut base, 3¹³⁄₁₆" h. (minor chips)..........2,645.00

Tumbler, cylindrical, Rose Teinte, Sunburst patt., 2⅞" d., 4" h. 55.00

Vase, 3½" h., goblet-shaped, decorated w/cut & enameled busts of Cleopatra, Mark Antony & Julius Caesar, satin finish 495.00

Vase, 4¼" h., paneled, green clover in base reflecting into the panels 50.00

Vase, 5⅞" h., the shouldered clear body set w/scattered millefiori canes in shades of blue, pink, red, green, coral & white interspersed between gold leafy vines & throughout terminating to a strawberry-cut rim (slight imperfection to rim) 2,760.00

Vases, 10⅝" h., square, grey sides cut w/poppy blossoms & leafage & raspberries & foliage, enameled in yellow, crimson, green & orange, heightened in gilt against a frost-patterned ground, fitting into subtle whiplash cast feet in gilt-metal, unsigned, one retains original manufacturer's label, ca. 1900, pr..4,025.00

Baccarat Glass & Gilt-Bronze Vase

Vases, 16" h., crystal trumpet-form paneled bowl w/a scalloped rim, fitted into a gilt-bronze base w/leaf-tips supporting the vase above a downturned leaf band above a

swirled rib pedestal on a domed foot
w/a band of leaftips, stamped
"Baccarat," pr. (ILLUS. of one)......4,025.00

BOHEMIAN

Ornate Cut & Enameled Pokal

*For centuries the region of Bohemia
(later part of Czechoslovakia) has been a
famous glassmaking center. Many types of
glass have been produced there including
fine colored, cut and engraved glasswares.
The most famous and abundant type was
flashed and stained, commonly amber-
and ruby-shaded glass which featured
etched and engraved scrolls and animal
scenes. Widely exported to the United
States since the 19th century, two popular
ruby-etched-to-clear designs are known as
Deer and Castle and Deer and Pine Tree.*

Beaker, cylindrical, the paneled sides
w/gilt foliate decoration, late 19th c.,
6¼" h...$258.00

Center bowl, yellow flashed cut to
clear w/a floral design, 8" d................77.00

Compote, cov., 13" h., ruby-flashed
cut to clear, the tapered bowl on a
slender standard w/a circular foot,
shaped cover & knopped finial,
engraved w/running stags, castles &
scrolls...137.50

Compotes, open, 8" d., oval bowls,
ruby-flashed & etched to clear w/a
stag & ferns, on a hexagonal foot,
pr..330.00

Decanter, ruby-flashed cut to clear
Deer & Castle patt., 15" h. 215.00

Goblet, ruby-flashed, the deep rounded bowl facet-cut ruby to clear &
raised on a paneled stem & round
notched foot, the bowl w/a central
ruby oval reserve etched w/a building titled "The President's House,
Washington," ca. 1850, 6" h............825.00

Pokals, cov., bulbous form on a
tapered pedestal & circular foot, tall
pointed finial on cover, cobalt blue
cut to clear & enameled w/floral
designs, one finial repaired, pr.
(ILLUS. of one) 715.00

Tumbler, round tapering bowl facet-
cut above the hexagonal ringed foot,
the sides cut w/thirteen oval panels
each featuring a different German
building including "Schlofs,"
"Wilhelmshof," & "Marlafibein," each
scene highlighted w/amber &
cranberry stain, mid-19th c.,
4¾" h..302.50

Tumble-up set (water carafe
w/tumbler lid), red cut to clear floral
pattern, overall 8" h., the set..............85.00

BRIDE'S BASKETS & BOWLS

Decorated Blue Cased Bride's Basket

*Large bowls of colorful blown glass
were popular late Victorian wedding gifts,
hence the name. Used as berry or fruit
bowls, or just for show, many originally
were displayed in fancy silver plate frames.*

Amethyst shaded to lavender bowl
w/pie crust rim, wide border of
orange & white enameled
flowers, no frame, 11" d. $240.00

Cased bowl, blue shaded interior,
embossed leaf pattern around bowl
trimmed in gold, white exterior,
pointed & crimped rim, resilvered
frame w/ornate handle, 10" d. 295.00

Cased bowl, blue shaded textured
interior, "seaweed" Coralene
beading on white exterior, ornate
footed silver plate frame w/wide
fluted base & lavishly trimmed feet
w/raised lady's faces marked
"Meriden" 550.00

Cased bowl, heavenly blue interior decorated w/enameled lavender pink flowers & brown & gold foliage, crimped & ruffled sides w/clear applied edging, white exterior, ornate silver plate footed frame, 11¼" d., 11" h. (ILLUS.) 275.00

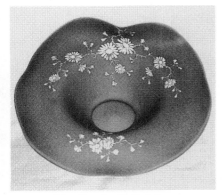

Blue Bowl with Daisies

Cased bowl, heavenly blue interior decorated w/enameled white daisies w/yellow centers, frosted binding at edge, frosted clear rim binding, white exterior, front edge turned-down, back edge turned-up, no frame, 13½" d., 6½" h. (ILLUS.) 325.00

Cased Shaded Blue Basket

Cased bowl, shaded heavenly blue interior, deeply scalloped sides pulled into crimped points, white exterior, ornate silver plate footed replated frame, 13" d., 13" h. (ILLUS.) 325.00

Cased bowl, shaded heavenly blue satin interior enameled w/white flowers & heavy gold foliage decoration, white exterior, closely ruffled rim, no frame, 9¾" d., 3¼" h..325.00

Cased bowl, shaded pale blue satin interior decorated w/dainty gold flowers, leaves & branches, ruffled brown shading on edge w/heavy raised enameled dots in lines all around edge, white exterior, no frame, 11" d., 5" h. 165.00

Cased bowl, miniature, cranberry, ruffled edge folded to center, silver plate footed frame, marked "Acme Silver Co." 395.00

Cased bowl, chartreuse interior, shaded pink exterior decorated w/gold leaves & branches & dainty white enameled flowers, ruffled rim w/applied clear edging & gold trim, ornately engraved silver plate frame w/tall decorative handle & ball feet, 12" d., 8¼" h. 595.00

Decorated Bride's Basket

Cased glass, greenish cream interior enameled w/sprays of colored flowers & leaves & one small butterfly, flattened crimped rim w/one side turned-up, white exterior, silver plate frame w/double-bar handle, 11⅞" d., 8" h. (ILLUS.) 265.00

Cased bowl, pink satin interior enameled w/lacy coral-colored flowers, foliage & dotting on rim, white exterior, bowl center melon-sectioned w/flaring ruffled rim, no frame, 10½" d., 2¾" h. 350.00

Cased bowl, pink shaded dimpled & hobnail pattern interior, white exterior decorated w/enameled floral decoration, ruffled rim w/applied clear edging, ornate ball-footed silver plate frame w/cut-out daisies, beading & fancy etching, 10" d., 13½" h..295.00

Cased bowl, pink shaded interior decorated w/dainty pink & white daisies, blue forget-me-nots & green leaves, white exterior, ruffled rim applied w/clear ribbon candy edging, no frame, 10¼" d., 3" h. 225.00

Mother-of-Pearl Satin Basket

Cased bowl, shaded pink mother-of-pearl Diamond Quilted satin bowl, squared form w/crimped & ruffled rim, ornate silver plate frame marked "Manhattan," 7 x 11½", 10½" h. (ILLUS.) 795.00

Cased bowl, pink satin interior w/chartreuse green satin exterior, upright sides w/fluted & crimped rim, no frame, 10½" d., 4½" h. 325.00

Cased bowl, pink shaded interior decorated w/dainty enameled creamy white garland leaves & dainty clusters of white flowers, white exterior, scalloped rim, re-silvered ornate footed base w/top fastener, 12" d., 10" h. 325.00

Cased bowl, pink shaded interior w/opaque white & vaseline glass ruffled ribbon edge, white exterior, no frame, 11¼" d., 3⅜" d. base, 3⅜" h..195.00

Cased bowl, pink shaded interior decorated w/gold leaves & scrolls, white exterior, pleated, ruffled rim, no frame, 10¾" d., 3¾" h. 175.00

Cased bowl, pink shaded to green interior w/enameled yellow scrolls & flowers, white exterior, scalloped sides, silver plate stand w/pedestal base, 11½" d., overall 9½" h. 325.00

Cased bowl, rose bloom interior, white exterior, ruffled basketweave rim, restored ornate footed silver plate frame, bowl signed "Webb," 10¼" d., bowl 4" h. 705.00

Cased bowl, shaded deep rose interior, white exterior, deeply ruffled sides w/crimped rim, ornate footed silver plate frame marked "Rogers & Bros.," 9¾" d., 11" h. (ILLUS. top next column) 275.00

Cased bowl, white interior, Peach

Blow exterior, squared shape w/closely crimped sides & widely crimped corners, clear rim, polished pontil, no frame, 11" d., 3" h............125.00

Cased Rose & White Basket

Satin Glass Bride's Basket

Cased bowl, white interior, yellow satin exterior w/blue ruffled rim, in ornate footed Pairpoint silver plate frame, bowl 9" d., overall 12" h. (ILLUS.) 450.00

Cranberry opalescent bowl, double crimped rim, vertical opalescent stripes radiating from center, no frame, 10⅝" d., 3¾" h. 150.00

Cranberry opalescent bowl, embossed rib design, fluted rim, ornate silver plate footed holder, bowl 10½" d. 450.00

Cranberry opalescent bowl, Spanish Lace patt. w/ruffled rim, original silver plate frame, 10¾" d. 295.00

Cranberry bowl /enameled decoration, ruffled top, no frame, 12" d. ..250.00

Golden amber bowl, pressed Daisy & Button patt., ornate silver plate frame decorated w/cherubs picking fruit & flowers, 10½" d., 10" h...........195.00

Heavenly blue overshot bowl, deeply ruffled & crimped rim, ornate brass stand w/hanging brass rings, 7¾" d., overall 12" h. 188.00

New Martinsville Peach Blow Basket

New Martinsville Peach Blow bowl, deep pink shaded to creamy white, deeply fluted ribbed sides w/crimped rim, ornate silver plate frame, 11¼" d., 12½" h. (ILLUS.) 295.00

Peach Blow bowl, eight-crimp top, polished pontil, silver plate frame w/grape & vine cluster at top, bowl 11½" d., 3¾" h., overall 14" h. (frame needs replating)....................225.00

Spangled bowl, cased white interior, shaded blue exterior w/mica flecks, clear double-crimped edge, polished pontil, no frame, 8" d., 2½" h. 65.00

White bowl, high tightly pleated back flaring down to a wide pleated front w/scrolls, decorated w/delicate pink roses & two little birds, in original silver plate frame decorated w/flowers & beading, 10½" d., overall 13" h. 350.00

BRISTOL

A number of glasshouses operated in Bristol, England over the years and they produced a variety of wares. Today, however, the generic name Bristol refers to a type of semi-opaque glass, often accented with ornate enameling. Such wares were produced in England, Europe and America in the 19th and early 20th centuries.

Bowl, 3¾" d., 1¾" h., footed, decorated w/gold bands & small yellow flowers & leaves overall on a turquoise blue ground, three applied clear snail feet..................................$60.00

Box w/hinged lid, opaque white ground w/pink highlights, decorated w/black & white enameled bird on the lid, 1⅝" d., 1⅛" h. 95.00

Box, cov., lacy gold scrolls & heavy gold decoration on the lid & gold scrolls on the sides, turquoise blue ground, 3" d., 2¼" h., ...45.00

Candlestick, long candle socket on a cylindrical shaft & round foot, turquoise blue decorated w/dainty pink, white & peach flowers & dainty green leaves, gold trim, 3⅜" d., 6½" h...88.00

Cologne bottle w/original decorated turquoise blue opaque tulip-form stopper, turquoise blue opaque bulbous footed body tapering to a tall slender neck w/flared rim, decorated w/dainty pink & white flowers, white leaves & lacy green foliage, matching stopper, 2¼" d., 5¼" h. 100.00

Cologne bottle w/original ball-shaped stopper, tapering cylindrical body w/a long cylindrical neck, decorated w/an orange-breasted bird in flight, green holly leaves & red berries on a grey ground, 2¾" d., 7⅛" h. 125.00

Bristol Cologne Bottle

Cologne bottle w/original blue pointed stopper, bottle-shaped, deep glossy blue w/off-white Bristol ring around neck & center of stopper, 3⅛" d., 7¾" h. (ILLUS.) 100.00

Cologne bottle w/original bulbous stopper, footed bulbous body tapering to a slender neck w/flat flaring rim, turquoise blue decorated w/sanded gold scalloped designs & dainty white dot flowers around the middle, 3⅛" d., 8⅞" h. 110.00

Cologne bottle w/original green scalloped-top stopper, soft green satin tapering cylindrical body w/applied green reed handles w/gold trim, 3¼" d., 9½" h. 88.00

Cologne bottles w/original blue teardrop-shaped stoppers, bottle-shaped, blue decorated w/oval medallions of colorfully painted Grecian busts, 2¾" d., 7¼" h., pr. ...175.00

Cracker jar, cov., barrel-shaped, turquoise blue enameled overall w/pink, gold & white daisies & green leaves, silver plate cover, rim & bail handle, 4⅝" d., 6½" h. (resilvered)...225.00

Cracker jar, cov., ovoid, delicate pink, blue, peach & yellow flowers & green leaves on an opaque blue ground, silver plate rim, flat lid & bail handle, 4⅞" d., 6⅞" h......................195.00

Cracker jar, cov., opaque tan cylindrical body decorated w/grey & white herons w/orange beaks & feet on front & green trees & foliage reverse, resilvered silver plate rim, flat cover & strawberry finial & bail handle, 4¾" d., 7¼" h.......................250.00

Bristol Glass Cracker Jar

Cracker jar, cov., barrel-shaped, glossy turquoise blue w/grey & white enameled herons, trees & pink flowers, resilvered rim, cover & bail handle, 5½" d., 7½" h. (ILLUS.) 235.00

Ewer, conical body tapering to a cylindrical neck w/angled rim, opaque turquoise blue decorated w/pink roses & green leaves w/gold scrolls, applied blue handle, 2¾" d., 5⅜" h..48.00

Ewers, conical base w/cylindrical neck ending in a diagonal rim, enameled overall w/pink roses, white leaves &

yellow scrollwork against a turquoise blue ground, applied angular turquoise blue handle, 2¾" d., 4¾" h., pr..135.00

Perfume bottle w/original green ball stopper, apple green glossy cylindrical body w/short small neck, gold band lip & gold flowers & scrolls around body, 2⅜" d., 4" h. 85.00

Perfume bottle w/original blue mushroom-shaped pointed stopper, deep blue glossy cylindrical body tapering to a tall ringed neck w/flared rim, decorated w/creamy dots, coral flowers, lavender scrolls & gold trim, 1¾" d., 6⅝" h. 98.00

Perfume cruet w/original stopper, turquoise blue bulbous body tapering to a cylindrical neck w/pinched lip, applied blue handle, blue stopper w/gold trim, body decorated w/white flowers & scrolls & gold foliage & small red jewels, 2⅜" d., 5¼" h. 165.00

Rose bowl, egg-shaped w/crimped rim, opaque turquoise blue decorated w/gold ropes & tassels w/gold around the top, all trimmed w/enameled white outlining & dots, 3¼" d., 4⅛" h. 75.00

Rose bowl, footed, six-crimp top, spherical body, decorated overall w/gold leaves & flowers & gold trim on a turquoise blue ground, applied gold ball-shaped feet, 4⅛" d., 4¾" h..125.00

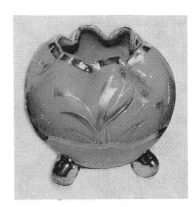

Bristol Rose Bowl

Rose bowl, glossy blue opaque spherical body on three applied feet, six-crimp rim, gold flowers & leaves w/gold ground & grass decoration, gold trim on feet & rim, 4⅝" d., 4¾" h. (ILLUS.) 125.00

Rose bowl, footed spherical body
w/six-crimp top, turquoise blue
w/gold panels highlighted w/pink
flowers on the upper portion, gold
leaves & yellow enameled leaves &
dotting on the lower half, three
applied ball-shaped feet, 4⅝" d.,
5¼" h..125.00

Salt dip w/original stand, hod-shaped,
enameled orange & white flower
buds & white flowers w/orange
centers on an opaque green ground,
1¾ x 3", 3" h.....................................75.00

Sweetmeat jar, cov., tapering cylindrical form, enameled w/large pink
leaves & small tan flowers & leaves
on a milk white ground, silver plate
rim, cover & bail handle, 4" d.,
5¼" h..125.00

Tumbler, cylindrical, enameled rose &
yellow flowers w/green & brown
foliage decoration on a grey ground,
rose lining, 2¾" d., 3¾" h. 60.00

Vase, 6¾" h., 3" d., compressed
globular body w/expanding
cylindrical neck, gold-trimmed loop
handles at the shoulder, body
decorated w/small pink & white
flowers, gold leaves & a gold band
w/blue, white & yellow flowers
against a turquoise blue ground 95.00

Vase, 16½" h., opaque white w/h.p.
enameled floral decoration & a
butterfly 72.50

Vases, miniature, 2¾" h., 1¼" d.,
squatty bulbous opaque turquoise
blue body w/slender cylindrical neck,
decorated w/dainty pink & white
flowers & green leaves & lacy gold
decoration, pr.....................................79.00

Vases, 3⅛" h., 2½" d., glossy
turquoise blue squatty bulbous body
tapering to a bulbous cylindrical
neck & slightly flaring rim w/gold
trim, decorated overall w/yellow
flowers, leaves & dotting, pr...............69.00

Vases, 5" h., 2½" d., baluster-form
w/short cylindrical neck, turquoise
blue w/bright gold scrolls & swags
w/pink enameled flowers w/yellow
centers around the shoulder, yellow
leaf & dot trim, pr. (ILLUS. top next
column) 145.00

Vases, 6¾" h., 3⅝" d., turquoise blue
squatty bulbous body w/slightly
flaring cylindrical neck, gold bands
highlighted w/pink & white flowers &
green leaves decorate the rim, base
of neck & center of body, pr.............145.00

Blue Bristol Vases

Vases, 7" h., 2¾" d., glossy turquoise
blue tall trumpet-form w/flaring rim &
flat, circular foot, decorated w/heavy
gold bands & gold rope garland
highlighted w/white enamel trim,
pr...145.00

Vases, 13" h., 4¼" d., turquoise blue
cylindrical body raised on a squatty
bulbous cushion foot, overall heavy
gold leaves & scrolls decoration,
pr...265.00

Vases, 13¼" h., 5¾" d., tall ovoid
body w/small neck, rich pink cased
body decorated overall w/large blue
& lavender flowers & brown leaves,
white lining, pr. 295.00

Vases, 13½" h., 4⅝" d., footed
baluster-form tapering to a slightly
flared cylindrical neck, h.p. snowy
wooded landscape, a small brown
cottage w/snow-covered roof & blue
sky on a white ground, cream
colored foot w/gold trim, pr. 225.00

Vases, 16¾" h., tall baluster-form
body w/a ring centering the tall,
flaring neck, clear frosted w/blue
enamel trim & a large center oval
wreath framing a gold-encrusted
floral bouquet, late 19th c., pr. 253.00

BURMESE

*Burmese is another of the famous late
Victorian heat-reactive Art glass lines.
This single-layer ware shading from pale
pink to pale yellow, was patented in 1885
by Frederick S. Shirley and made by the
Mt. Washington Glass Company. The
English firm of Thomas Webb & Sons was
licensed to produce the glass, which they
called Queen's Burmese. The Gundersen-
Pairpoint Glass Co. briefly revived*

Burmese in the 1950s and the Pairpoint Crystal Company is making limited quantities today.

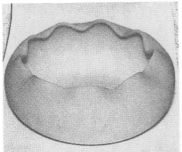

Small Burmese Bowl

Bell, high body w/flaring base, applied amber handle, glossy finish, 6¾" h. $400.00

Bell, high domed bell w/flaring base, tall applied clear handle w/beehive-form finial, glossy finish, 11½" h. 450.00

Bowl, 4" d., 3¼" h., spherical body w/hexagonal-shaped rim, enameled red berries & green leaves, satin finish, unsigned Webb 325.00

Bowl, 4⅜" d., 2⅛" h., squatty bulbous form w/incurved scalloped rim, satin finish, Mt. Washington Glass Co. (ILLUS.) 225.00

Bowl, 6½" widest d., 2½" h., cylindrical base w/a flaring & folded over elongated oval rim, applied yellow rigaree trim on rim, Mt. Washington Glass Co. 750.00

Bowl, 8" d., 4¼" h., squatty bulbous body tapering to a widely flaring four-lobed rolled & crimped rim, attributed to the Mt. Washington Glass Co. 220.00

Bowl-vase, small rounded bowl w/a widely flaring tri-lobed rim, raised on three small applied feet, 4" w., 2½" h..80.00

Butter dish, cov., fluted dish w/domed cover w/applied clear handle, satin finish, Mt. Washington Glass Co., 9" d...780.00

Celery vase, footed, fluted rim, Mt. Washington Glass Co., 10" h..........425.00

Cologne bottle w/original stopper, Mt. Washington Glass Co., 4" d., 5" h....975.00

Creamer & sugar bowl, pitcher-shaped creamer w/applied yellow handle, globular open sugar bowl, creamer 3¾" h., sugar bowl 3½" d., 2" h., pr. 665.00

Creamer & open sugar bowl, individual, satin finish, Mt. Washington Glass Co., pr. 550.00

Rare Burmese Cruet

Cruet w/original bulbous ribbed & pointed stopper, squatty bulbous ribbed body tapering to a slender neck w/arched spout, applied yellow handle, glossy finish, Mt. Washington Glass Co., 7¼" h. (ILLUS.) 1,250.00

Cup & saucer, conical cup w/applied angled handle, satin finish, saucer 4¾" d..345.00

Cup & saucer, cylindrical cup w/applied yellow angled handle, wide & deep saucer, glossy finish 325.00

Dish, ruffled rim, satin finish, 4¾" d., 1½" h..120.00

Dish, tricornered, satin finish, 5" w. 150.00

Finger bowl, nine-crimp top, satin finish, Mt. Washington Glass Co., 4⅜" d., 2¼" h. 225.00

Pitcher, 5½" h., slightly tapering cylindrical body in the Hobnail patt., applied yellow handle, Mt. Washington Glass Co. 605.00

Plate, 9" d., satin finish, Mt. Washington Glass Co. 225.00

Rose bowl, miniature, spherical w/eight-crimp top, satin finish, unsigned Webb, 2⅜" d., 2⅛" h. 175.00

Rose bowl, spherical w/eight-crimp top, decorated w/pink, green & blue maidenhair fern & outlined in gold, satin finish, unsigned Webb, 2⅜" d., 2¼" h..295.00

Rose bowl, wide squatty bulbous form w/flat rim, decorated w/h.p. blue butterfly, bittersweet blossoms & gold foliage, Thomas Webb, 4" d., 2½" h..585.00

Rose bowl, ruffled rim, applied
molded leaf, 4" d., 2¾" h. 700.00

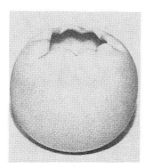

Webb Burmese Rose Bowl

Rose bowl, spherical w/eight-crimp
top, satin finish, Thomas Webb &
Sons, 3" d., 3" h. (ILLUS.) 200.00

Rose bowl, bulbous base tapering to
a hexagonal rim, decorated
w/lavender five-petal flowers &
green & brown leaves, satin finish,
unsigned Webb, 3" d., 3¼" h. 295.00

Rose bowl, spherical, six-crimp top,
decorated w/bronze & gold-tinted
chrysanthemums & leaves all
outlined in gold, unsigned Webb,
3⅜" d., 3⅜" h. 650.00

Salt shaker w/original top, tomato-
shaped, Mt. Washington Glass
Co. 150.00

Sweetmeat jar, cov., compressed
globular body, decorated w/enam-
eled flowers & foliage, silver plate
rim, cover & overhead handle 300.00

Toothpick holder, bulbous base
w/square top, h.p. pine cone
decoration, satin finish, Mt.
Washington Glass Co. 295.00

Toothpick holder, cylindrical w/tri-
cornered top, Mt. Washington Glass
Co. 245.00

Toothpick holder, Diamond Quilted
patt., satin finish 285.00

Tumbler, decorated w/yellow roses,
Mt. Washington Glass Co., 3¾" h. 565.00

Tumbler, cylindrical, satin finish, Mt.
Washington Glass Co., 3⅞" h.
(ILLUS. top next column) 285.00

Vase, miniature, 2½" h., squatty
bulbous body w/a diamond quilted
design 80.00

Vase, 2½" h., 2" d., bulbous body
w/collared hexagonal top, decorated
w/flowers, leaves & branches 295.00

Mt. Washington Burmese Tumbler

Vase, 2½" h., 3½" d., squatty body
below a hexagonal rim, decorated
w/flowers & leaves, satin finish 225.00

Vase, 3⅛" h., 3⅛" d., ovoid body
tapering to a flattened ruffled rim,
satin finish, unsigned Webb 200.00

Vase, 3¼" h., ruffled top, decorated
w/wild roses, glossy finish, signed
"Webb" 300.00

Vase, 3¼" h., 3¼" d., bulbous body
w/pinched-in sides, satin finish 150.00

Vase, 3¼" h., 3½" d., a footed,
squatty bulbous body tapering to a
narrow neck below a widely flaring
fluted rim w/pointed fluting, decorated w/enameled oak leaves &
acorns, satin finish 325.00

Decorated Burmese Small Vase

Vase, 3½" h., 3" d., bulbous ovoid
body tapering to a short cylindrical
neck, decorated w/narrow black
bands flanking a band of small blue
flowers w/red centers & green
leaves, glossy finish, Thomas Webb
& Sons, unsigned (ILLUS.) 275.00

Vase, 3¾" h., 2⅝" d., bulbous base
tapering to a cylindrical neck
w/flaring & crimped rim, enameled
w/lavender five-petal flowers &
green & brown leaves, satin finish,
unsigned Webb 300.00

Small Webb Burmese Vase

Vase, 3⅞" h., 2⅞" d., squatty bulbous
  base below a cylindrical neck
  w/widely flaring ruffled & crimped
  rim, satin finish, Thomas Webb &
  Sons, unsigned (ILLUS.).................225.00

Vase, 4" h., 2¾" d., bulbous body
  tapering to a flaring neck w/crimped
  rim, decorated w/blue & white
  flowers & brown leaves, satin finish,
  unsigned Webb...............................295.00

Vase, 4" h., 2⅞" d., conical body
  w/flaring ruffled rim, satin finish
  w/peach striped effect in glass,
  unsigned Webb...............................225.00

Vase, 4" h., 2⅞" d., waisted cylindrical
  body w/folded-over star-shaped rim,
  satin finish, unsigned Webb.............225.00

Vase, 4¼" h., 2½" d., ovoid body w/a
  four petal-shaped rim, enameled
  w/coral flower buds & green leaves,
  satin finish, unsigned Webb.............365.00

Vase, 4½" h., footed baluster form
  w/deeply ruffled rim, decorated
  w/flowers & foliage..........................275.00

Burmese Vase by Webb

Vase, 7" h., tapering egg-shaped
  body w/three-lobed rim, raised on
  three ribbed & pointed legs,

enameled around the sides w/large
  ivy leaves & vines, signed by
  Thomas Webb & Sons (ILLUS.) 950.00

Burmese Urn-Form Vase

Vase, 7¼" h., classic baluster-shaped
  urn-form, the bulbous ovoid body
  raised on a short pedestal foot, wide
  cylindrical neck w/flaring rim flanked
  by slender angled handles down to
  the shoulder, Mt. Washington Glass
  Co. (ILLUS.) 750.00

Burmese Jack-in-the-Pulpit Vase

Vase, 7¼" h., 3½" d., jack-in-the-pulpit
  style, crimped & upturned rim on a
  slender trumpet-form body on a disc
  foot, satin finish, Mt. Washington
  Glass Co. (ILLUS.)...........................345.00

Vase, 8" h., lily-type, tall slender body
  w/flaring tri-lobed rim, round disc
  foot, the sides enameled w/delicate
  forget-me-nots, satin finish, Mt.
  Washington Glass Co. (ILLUS. top
  next column) 975.00

Vase, 8" h., spherical body below a
  tall slender stick neck swelled at

Burmese Lily Vase

the base, decorated w/enameled blue & white forget-me-nots, Mt. Washington Glass Co. 495.00

Vase, 8⅛" h., 3⅞" d., ovoid body tapering to a cylindrical neck, decorated w/coral flower buds w/green & tan foliage, satin finish, unsigned Webb................................750.00

Vase, 10" h., cushion foot, expanding cylinder w/short narrow flaring cylindrical neck, decorated w/florals filled w/intricate lines in red, green, blue & gold, heavy gold outlining, Mt. Washington Glass Co. 1,250.00

Vase, 10½" h., trumpet-form w/jack-in-the-pulpit tightly ruffled rim, satin finish 467.50

Vase, 12½" h., bulbous base w/long stick neck, clear applied handles at the base of the neck, decorated overall w/dainty blossoms, shadow foliage & fragile gold branches 1,950.00

Vase, 12½" h., slender trumpet-form w/jack-in-the-pulpit rim, satin finish..250.00

Vase, 14½" h., trumpet-form w/jack-in-the-pulpit tightly crimped rim, glossy finish, Mt. Washington Glass Co......785.00

Vase, 23½" h., trumpet-form, footed slender body w/a tricorner rim 800.00

CHOCOLATE

Originally produced at The Indiana Tumbler and Goblet Company, Greentown, Indiana around the turn of the century, it was later produced by other glasshouses. A variety of patterns of pressed glass were made using the Chocolate formula and two of the most popular were Cactus and Leaf Bracket. Sometimes called Caramel Slag,

some pieces have been reproduced in recent years so some caution is needed when buying this desirable ware.

Smooth-Edged Dolphin Dish

Animal covered dish, Dolphin, beaded top rim, Greentown $220.00

Animal covered dish, Dolphin, smooth rim, Greentown, 9" l., 4" h.(ILLUS.)..375.00

Berry set: master bowl & five sauce dishes; Leaf Bracket patt., Greentown, 6 pcs......................................250.00

Butter dish, cov., small, Dewey patt., Greentown, 4" d. 105.00

Butter dish, cov., large, Dewey patt., Greentown, 5" d. 165.00

Chocolate Cactus Compote

Compote, 8¼" d., Cactus patt., Greentown (ILLUS.) 240.00

Austrian Pattern Child's Creamer

Creamer, child's, Austrian patt.,
Greentown (ILLUS.) 190.00

Creamer, cov., Cactus patt.,
Greentown 85.00

Creamer, tankard-shaped, Shuttle
patt., Greentown 95.00

Creamer & open sugar bowl, Dewey
patt., Greentown, pr. 125.00

Mug, Herringbone patt., Greentown 85.00

Chocolate Serenade Mug

Mug, Serenade (or Troubador) patt.,
McKee, 3½" d., 5" h. (ILLUS.) 95.00

Salt & pepper shakers w/original tops,
Leaf Bracket patt., Greentown,
pr......................................150.00 to 200.00

Sauce dish, Leaf Bracket patt.,
Greentown 55.00

Spooner, Cactus patt., Greentown 95.00

Chocolate Cactus Sugar Bowl

Sugar bowl, cov., Cactus patt.,
Greentown (ILLUS.) 145.00

Sugar bowl, cov., Dewey patt.,
Greentown ....100.00 to 125.00

Tumbler, iced tea or lemonade,
Cactus patt., Greentown,
5" h. (ILLUS.) ....50.00 to 75.00

Chocolate Cactus Tumbler

Tumbler, Fleur-de-lis patt.,
Greentown 110.00

CHRYSANTHEMUM SPRIG,
BLUE

Blue Chrysanthemum Sprig Compote

The Chrysanthemum Sprig pattern, originally called "Pagoda," was one of several patterns produced by the Northwood Glass Company at the turn of the century in their creamy white Custard glass (which see). A limited amount of this pattern was also produced in a blue opaque color, sometimes erroneously called 'blue custard.'

Berry set, master berry bowl & two
sauce dishes, 3 pcs. $450.00

Bowl, berry, individual, w/gold
trim 225.00

Celery vase, w/gold trim 1,295.00

Compote, jelly (ILLUS.) 475.00

Creamer.............................375.00 to 400.00

Blue Chrysanthemum Sprig Cruet

Cruet w/original facet-cut stopper,
   blue & gilt trim, 6½" h. (ILLUS.) 1,000.00

Salt & pepper shakers, pr. 475.00

Sugar bowl, cov. 465.00

Toothpick holder ....250.00 to 300.00

Tumbler ....175.00 to 225.00

CORALENE

Creamer with Coralene Fruit

Coralene refers to a decorating technique sometimes used on Victorian satin glass where a design composed of tiny glass beading is applied to the surface with the use of molten enamels. Coralene decoration has been faked with the use of glue to apply the beading.

Cracker jar, cov., Amberina body
   decorated w/coralene beaded fruit,
   branches & leaves, silver-plate rim,
   cover & bail handle $500.00

Creamer, ovoid body tapering to a
   slightly flaring cylindrical neck,
   applied pale amber handle, orange
   body decorated w/colored "fruit"
   coralene beading, enameled
   "Patent" mark, 2½" d., 3½" h.
   (ILLUS.) 265.00

Lamp, oil-type, square, white shaded
   to yellow dimpled satin glass base
   w/pink "seaweed" coralene beading,
   applied frosted leaf feet, clear
   chimney & frosted shade, marked
   "Patent" 600.00

Perfume bottle w/sterling silver neck &
   cap, spherical body in blue mother-
   of-pearl satin Raindrop patt., decorated w/a green, white, pink & other
   colors floral coralene decorative
   band, silver neck & cap w/London,
   England hallmarks, 4⅛" h. 385.00

Sugar shaker w/original top, shaded
   rose mother-of-pearl satin Diamond
   Quilted patt. exterior w/yellow
   "seaweed" coralene beading, white
   interior, 8" h.....................................325.00

Vase, 4" h., blue mother-of-pearl satin
   exterior w/yellow "wheat" coralene
   beading, white lining 475.00

Small Coralene Vase

Vase, 4½" h., 3⅞" d., footed bulbous
   ovoid body tapering to a short flaring
   neck, shaded heavenly blue cased
   satin decorated w/yellow "seaweed"
   coralene beading (ILLUS.) 395.00

Vase, 5" h., jack-in-the-pulpit-form,
   white satin ground covered
   w/aquamarine beading, aquamarine
   interior, signed "Webb" 450.00

Vase, 6" h., apricot mother-of-pearl
   satin exterior w/yellow "wheat"
   coralene beading, white lining 425.00

Vase, 6" h., 4" d., ruffled & crimped
   rim, blue shaded to white satin body
   decorated w/overall yellow
   "seaweed" coralene beading 525.00

Vase with Seaweed Coralene

Vase, 6¼" h., slender ovoid body
  tapering to a short cylindrical neck,
  shaded blue cased satin glass
  decorated w/yellow "seaweed"
  coralene beading (ILLUS.) 350.00

Vase, 7½" h., deep rose shading to
  pale pink satin ground w/yellow
  "seaweed" coralene beading, white
  lining 725.00

Vase, 7½" h., satin Peach Blow
  ground w/yellow "seaweed" coralene
  beading, gold trim, signed "Mt.
  Washington".....................................650.00

Vase, 8" h., ribbed body, soft yellow
  satin finish w/"drape" design yellow
  coralene beading, Mt. Washington
  Glass Co. 290.00

Vase, 12" h., blue satin ground decorated w/yellow "wheat" coralene
  beading 1,250.00

Vases, 8¾" h., ovoid body tapering to
  a short narrow swelled neck
  tapering to a flat rim, shaded pink to
  white satin ground w/overall yellow
  "seaweed" coralene beading, pr. 495.00

COSMOS

*Cosmos was one of the most popular
patterns produced by The Consolidated
Lamp and Glass Company of Coraopolis,
Pennsylvania. The pieces were mold-blown
in milk white glass and the design features
relief-molded clusters of Cosmos blossoms.
These blosssoms and edge bands were then
stained with various pastel hues including
pink, blue and yellow.*

*For further listings of Consolidated
patterns see* Antique Trader Books American
Pressed Glass & Bottles Price Guide.

Cosmos Butter Dish

Butter dish, cov., blue band
  decoration (ILLUS.).......................$195.00

Condiment set: salt & pepper shakers
  & mustard jar w/original tops, in
  handled glass stand; pink band
  decoration, the set ....325.00 to 375.00

Cosmos Miniature Lamp

Lamp, miniature, pink band
  decoration (ILLUS.)..........................250.00

Pitcher, milk, 5" h., pink band
  decoration......................................170.00

Salt shaker w/original top, pink band
  decoration, short 75.00

Salt & pepper shakers w/original tops,
  blue band decoration, pr. 125.00

Spooner, pink band decora-
  tion ....125.00 to 150.00

Water set: pitcher & two tumblers;
  pink band decoration, 3 pcs.............275.00

CRANBERRY

*The cranberry red hue of this popular
glass was obtained by the use of gold*

added to the glass batch. Since the late 19th century numerous glassworks in Europe, England and America have made Cranberry and it is currently being reproduced. Pieces were both free-blown and molded in a wide range of forms. A less expensive version was produced by substituting copper for gold in the batch..

Cranberry Box with Strawberries

Basket, Optic Rib patt., applied clear "snake" handle, applied clear rigaree around the rim, twelve applied clear feet & applied clear berry prunt, 7½" h..$265.00

Bowl, cov., 7" d., 7½" h., deep gently tapering sides to the flat bottom raised on applied amber feet, the low domed cover w/applied fruit in two shades of amber & green, brass fittings 302.50

Bowl, 4" d., 5¼" h., rose bowl-shaped, applied clear reeded fans, six applied clear berry prunts around the rim, three applied clear scroll reeded feet & clear berry prunt 275.00

Box w/lift-off lid, round, gold strawberries & leaves decorate the lid, 4⅛" d., 2¼" h. (ILLUS.) 165.00

Box w/hinged lid, enameled white, yellow & blue flowers decorate the lid, gold scrolls around the sides, 4½" d., 3¼" h. 175.00

Box w/hinged lid, white enameled scene of a European village nestled in the mountains on the lid & white enameled flowers around the base, 4½" d., 3¾" h. 275.00

Box w/lift-off lid, cylindrical, cranberry cover w/applied clear finial, sides w/sanded gold designs outlined in white, white & gold flowers, 2¾" d., 4½" h..135.00

Cologne bottle w/original cranberry bubble stopper, tapered cylindrical body w/slender ringed neck w/flared rim, decorated w/white enameled flowers & leaves, 3" d., 3¾" h. 195.00

Cologne bottle w/atomizer, spherical body decorated w/white enameled designs, 3" d., 4¾" h. 95.00

Cologne bottle w/original facet-cut clear stopper, squatty bulbous body w/short slender neck & flared rim, decorated w/gold flowers, leaves & vines, 3⅜" d., 5½" h. 175.00

Cologne bottle w/original cylindrical cranberry stopper, tapered cylindrical body w/deep shoulder, a cylindrical neck w/a flat flaring rim, decorated w/gold scrolls & small gold flowers, 2⅜" d., 8⅝" h. 165.00

Condiment set: mustard pot w/silver plate cover, pepper shaker w/silver plate top & open salt dip in a silver plate wire frame w/center loop handle, 5" w., 5½" h., the set 175.00

Cranberry Glass Cracker Jar

Cracker jar, cov., square body, decorated overall w/gold florals & leaves, silver plate cover, rim & ornate bail handle, 4" w., 7¼" h. (ILLUS.)..........275.00

Cracker jar, cov., Inverted Thumbprint patt., heavy enameled apple blossoms, blueberries & green & brown shaded leaves, ornate silver plate "crown-type" rim, cover w/finial & bail handle, overall 8" h. 550.00

Cracker jar, cov., decorated w/yellow iris & blue, white & pink flowers, silver plate rim, cover & bail handle 475.00

Creamer, opalescent, squatty w/heart-shaped rim, clear reeded applied handle & clear petal applied feet, 4" l., 3⅝" h..75.00

Creamer, Inverted Thumbprint patt., bulbous body tapering to a squared mouth, applied clear handle, 4"d., 4¾" h..135.00

Creamer, Optic patt., footed bulbous body tapering to a flaring, fluted rim, clear applied handle, 3⅛" d., 4⅞" h. ..65.00

Cranberry Creamer & Sugar Bowl

Creamer & open sugar bowl, tankard-shaped creamer w/applied clear handle & petal-shaped feet & squatty bulbous open sugar bowl w/applied clear petal feet, creamer 2½" d., 4" h., sugar bowl 5⅜" d., 2¾" h., pr. (ILLUS.) 135.00

Cruet w/original clear bubble stopper, cushion-footed ovoid body tapering to a cylindrical neck w/petal-shaped rim, decorated w/lavender thistle blossoms, green leaves & gold trim, applied clear handle, 3⅜" d., 8¼" h...195.00

Cruet w/original clear bubble stopper, Optic patt., cushion-footed ovoid body w/deep shoulder, a short cylindrical neck w/petal-shaped lip, applied clear handle, decorated w/white enameled daisies & gold foliage, 3⅛" d., 8¾" h. 195.00

Cruet w/original clear bubble stopper, dimpled bulbous base tapering to a cylindrical neck w/lipped rim, applied clear handle, enameled w/blue, white & yellow flowers & green leaves decoration, 4" d., 9" h. 195.00

Decanter w/original clear facet-cut stopper, bulbous body w/cylindrical neck & flared lip, decorated w/gold flowers, buds & leaves, 3⅜" d., 7½" h...145.00

Decanter w/clear bubble stopper, footed, cylindrical body w/deep shoulder, a short cylindrical neck w/a flat flaring rim, pink, blue, yellow & white enameled flowers, green & gold leaves decoration, 2¾" d., 8¼" h...165.00

Decanter w/original clear double-ring bulbous stopper with gold trim, baluster-form body tapering to a

cylindrical neck w/flared rim, overall decoration of blue, gold, green & white flowers & green leaves, 2¾" d., 8¼" h. 165.00

Decanter w/clear ball stopper, footed tapering cylinder w/slender ringed neck, enameled dainty blue & pale pink flowers & creamy yellow leaves decoration, applied clear pedestal foot, 3" d., 8½" h. 175.00

Decanter w/original embossed pewter stopper, footed baluster-form body w/tall slender neck, applied clear rigaree around base, embossed pewter neck ring & handle, 3⅛" d., 8½" h...195.00

Decanter w/original clear facet-cut stopper, flaring cylindrical body w/deep shoulder, a cylindrical neck w/ringed rim, upper body decorated w/a tiny gold dot band & small gold daisy-like flowers & gold bands on top & bottom, 3" d., 8¾" h. 100.00

Decanter w/original clear bulbous stopper, spherical body tapering to a cylindrical neck w/pinched spout, applied clear handle, lacy white enameled decoration of fans, dots & arches, 4¾" d., 9" h. 235.00

Decanter w/original clear bubble stopper, footed bulbous body tapering to a tall slender neck w/applied clear handle, 4⅛" d., 9½" h...125.00

Cranberry Double-Gourd Decanter

Decanter w/original squatty bulbous stopper, double gourd-form body tapering to a cylindrical neck w/flaring rim, decorated w/overall silver flowers, gold leaves & gold bands on the body & stopper, 4½" d., 10½" h. (ILLUS.) 175.00

Decanter w/original clear flattened
   stopper, ovoid body w/deep
   shoulder, a cylindrical neck w/three-
   petal rim, applied angular handle &
   wafer foot, engraved w/branches &
   leaves, 3¾" d.,11¼" h. 145.00

Decanter w/original clear bubble
   stopper, pedestal foot, bulbous body
   tapering to a cylindrical neck
   w/flaring rim, overall lacy white
   enamel decoration, 5" d.,11½" h. 225.00

Decanter w/original clear teardrop-
   shaped stopper, squatty bulbous
   body tapering to a cylindrical neck
   w/flaring flat rim, decorated overall
   w/small gold stars & gold trim, 5" d.,
   11¾" h..225.00

Cranberry Glass Epergne

Finger bowl, cylindrical w/flaring
   crimped rim, air trap zipper pattern,
   inscribed "Rd. 55693" on base,
   England, 4⅞" d., 2⅝" h. 125.00

Liqueur set: 8¼" h. decanter
   w/original clear bubble stopper, a
   flaring cylindrical body w/deep
   shoulder to the cylindrical neck
   w/petal shaped rim, six 1⅝" h. mugs
   w/clear applied handles & an 8½" d.
   tray; each piece decorated w/blue
   flowers & dainty green & gold
   leaves, 8 pcs. 395.00

Liqueur set: cylindrical 8½" h., 3¼" d.
   decanter w/applied clear handle &
   clear ball stopper, six 1½" h., 1⅜" d.
   liqueur mugs w/clear applied
   handles & a 9¼" d. tray; all
   decorated w/enameled white
   daisies, pale green leaves & gold
   trim, 8 pcs. 425.00

Ornate Cranberry Decanter

Decanter w/original clear ringed
   bubble stopper, spherical optic
   ribbed body tapering to a tall stick
   neck w/pinched spout, applied clear
   notched handle & ribbed wafer foot,
   decorated w/heavy gold scrolls &
   baskets of flowers, 4¾" d., 12¼" h.
   (ILLUS.) 175.00

Decanter w/original clear facet-cut
   stopper, footed ovoid body below a
   bulbous ring tapering to a cylindrical
   neck w/petal-shaped lip, applied
   clear handle & applied clear wafer
   foot, body etched w/sprays of
   flowers, 4½" d. 12¾" h. 210.00

Epergne, single-lily, the shaded
   trumpet-form lily applied around the
   top w/white threading & w/an
   applied snake in blue & white
   spatter down the sides, clear
   connector to the wide dished lower
   bowl w/applied white edge
   threading, on an applied clear
   pedestal foot, 11½" d., 15¼" h.
   (ILLUS.) 295.00

Cranberry Glass Pitchers

Pitcher, 4¾" h., 4" d., ovoid body
   tapering to a cylindrical neck
   w/pinched spout, applied clear
   angled handle (ILLUS. left) 88.00

Pitcher, 5" h., 2⅝" d., footed bulbous
   base tapering to a short cylindrical
   neck w/flaring ruffled rim, applied
   clear handle 65.00

Optic Rib Pitcher

Pitcher, 5" h., 2⅝" d., Optic Rib patt.,
footed ovoid body tapering to a short
cylindrical neck w/pinched spout,
applied clear reeded handle
(ILLUS.) 80.00

Pitcher, 6" h., ovoid w/short neck,
applied clear handle, melon-ribbed
body decorated w/white floral &
swag design......................................60.00

Inverted Thumbprint Pitcher

Pitcher, 6¼" h., 3⅞" d., Inverted
Thumbprint patt., ovoid body
tapering to a short cylindrical neck
w/flaring rolled & fluted rim, applied
clear reeded handle (ILLUS.)...........118.00

Pitcher, 6½" h., 3⅝" d., Optic Rib
patt., bulbous ovoid body w/squared
neck & applied clear handle.............100.00

Pitcher, tankard, 6½" h., 4⅛" d.,
applied clear reeded handle (ILLUS.
right, above) 135.00

Pitcher, 6⅝" h., 3¾" d., squared
bulbous shouldered body tapering to
short cylindrical neck, w/pinched
spout, applied clear angular handle
(ILLUS.) 95.00

Pitcher with Angular Handle

Pitcher, 7" h., 6" d., Inverted
Thumbprint patt., squatty bulbous
body tapering to a widely flaring
squared rim.....................................195.00

Pitcher, milk, 7½" h., 4½" d., mold-
blown optic design, footed bulbous
body w/short flared neck w/a pinched spout, applied clear handle.........105.00

Rose bowl, squatty bulbous body
w/six-crimp rim, decorated w/applied
vaseline mat-su-no-ke flowers &
branches & applied vaseline rigaree
edge trim, 4¾" d., 2½" h. 550.00

Salt dip, master size, cylindrical, in
footed silver plate frame, 2¾" d.,
2" h...95.00

Salt dip, master size, footed squatty
bulbous body w/applied crystal
rigaree around sides, applied crystal
scalloped feet, 3¾" d., 2½" h 85.00

Salt dip, master size, squatty bulbous
body w/applied clear ruffled rigaree
rim, in silver plate scroll-footed
holder w/ornate fixed bail handle,
overall 4" d., 4" h..............................165.00

Salt dip, master size, boat-shaped,
decorated overall w/h.p. gold enameled foliage & colored flowers............95.00

Salt shaker w/original top, Honey-
comb patt. 60.00

Salt shaker w/original top, tapering
pillar shape, enameled floral
decoration 125.00

Salt & pepper shakers w/original two-
piece pewter tops, cylindrical,
enameled w/h.p. blue & white forget-
me-nots & green & blue leaves,
pr...195.00

Sugar shaker w/original top, Argus
Swirl patt. 369.00

Sugar shaker w/original top, Aurora
patt...230.00

Sugar shaker w/original top, bulbous,
Optic patt. 285.00

Sugar shaker w/original top, Venecia
patt...265.00

Sugar shaker w/original top, Venetian
Diamond patt. 195.00

Toothpick holder, Inverted Thumbprint
patt., bulging base tapering to a
cylindrical neck 145.00

Tumbler, decorated w/acid cut-back
roses around the rim & sprays of
roses around the body, 2¾" d.,
4¼" h...30.00

Tumbler, Inverted Thumbprint patt.,
decorated w/floral enameling.............50.00

Ornate Cranberry Tumblers

Tumblers, cylindrical, decorated
w/dainty white & blue enameled
flowers, gold-framed panels & gold
trim, 2½" d., 4" h., set of 6
(ILLUS.) 440.00

Ornate Cranberry Urn

Urn, cov., footed bulbous base
w/domed cover w/clear applied
flower-shaped handle, clear applied
flowers & leaves around the center
of the base & clear applied handles
& leaf shapes around the rim,
applied leaf-shaped feet, 5½" d.,
8¾" h. (ILLUS.) 595.00

Vase, 4¼" h., 4¼" d., wide ovoid
body tapering to a short flaring neck
trimmed w/applied clear rigaree.........60.00

Vase, 4½" h., 3¾" d., Diamond
Quilted patt., bulbous base tapering
to a short cylindrical neck, applied
clear rigaree trim forming points
around the rim.................................135.00

Vase, 4½" h., 4½" d., bulbous spherical body w/short cylindrical neck
applied w/clear ruffled rigaree..........145.00

Drape Pattern Cranberry Vase

Vase, 4¾" h., 4¾" d., Drape patt.,
bulbous body tapering to a flaring
ruffled rim w/vaseline applied
rigaree trim (ILLUS.) 95.00

Vase, 4⅝" h., 3⅜" d., squatty bulbous
base below the flaring trumpet-form
body, decorated w/panels of small
white & blue flowers separated by
gold trim 69.00

Vase, 5¼" h., 4" d., ovoid body
tapering to a flat rim cut w/a band of
half-round panels, clear applied
shell rigaree at center continues
down to form four legs 145.00

Vase, 7¾" h., 2½" d., Hobnail patt.,
narrow ovoid body tapering to a
slender neck below a widely flaring
crimped & ruffled rim, applied clear
feet..85.00

Vase, 8¾" h., 4½" d., applied clear
pedestal base supports an ovoid
body, applied clear upright leaves
around top edge w/clear rigaree
applied below the leaves & near
the base 165.00

Vase, 9¼" h., 3½" d., spherical base
below a tall slightly flaring cylindrical
neck w/angle-cut rim, applied clear
bell-shaped flowers & leaves around
the body, applied clear wishbone
feet...125.00

Vase, 9½" h., 4½" d., bulbous base
tapering to a tall cylindrical neck,

Decorated Cranberry Vase

decorated w/dainty blue & white
flowers, green leaves & green,
gold & blue paisley-like designs
(ILLUS.) 275.00

Vase, 9½" h., 6" d., footed spherical
body tapering to a cylindrical neck
flanked by clear applied rigaree
handles, applied clear wafer foot,
enameled white, green & blue
flowers & gold fan & leaves 475.00

Vase, 9⅝" h., 4⅛" d., footed funnel-
shaped body tapering to cupped rim,
mold-blown optic design w/applied
clear spiraling rigaree around body ...75.00

Vase, 10½" h., 3⅜" d., swelled
cylindrical shouldered body tapering
to a cylindrical neck w/flared rim,
raised on a pedestal base, decorated w/white enameled flowers &
leaves 95.00

Vase, 14" h., 3⅝" d., pedestal foot
supporting an elongated ovoid body
w/flaring trumpet-shaped neck, front
decorated w/white enameled
scrolling & white dotting 165.00

Vases, 2¼" h., 1½" d., footed
baluster-form tapering to a short

Small Decorated Vases

cylindrical neck, enameled w/blue &
yellow flowers & gold band
decoration, pr. 95.00

Vases, 3⅛" h., 1⅞" d., footed ovoid
body w/ruffled rim, decorated
w/enameled white flowers & leaves,
gold trim, pr. (ILLUS. bottom pre-
vious column)....................................118.00

Floral-Embossed Vases

Vases, 4¾" h., 3¾" d., spherical
body w/flaring fluted neck, deeply
embossed floral pattern, pr.
(ILLUS.) 165.00

Vases, 5¾" h., 3" d., baluster-form,
sanded white enamel Roman Key
design around the middle & sanded
white scallops above & below the
Greek Key design, fitted in ornate
ormulo footed base, pr. 248.00

Vases with Enameled Flowers

Vases, 6⅜" h., 4½" d., squatty
bulbous body tapering to a
cylindrical neck w/a wide ringed rim,
enameled w/blue forget-me-nots,
white daisies & green leaves
decoration on a frosted ground, pr.
(ILLUS.) 210.00

Vases, 9¼" h., 3½" d., footed
baluster-form body tapering to a
small trumpet-form neck, decorated
w/white enameled daisies & leaves,
pr...235.00

Water set: tankard pitcher & six
tumblers; Inverted Thumbprint patt.,
7 pcs. 325.00

(End of Cranberry Section)

CROWN MILANO

Crown Milano Cracker Jar

*Another lovely glass produced by the
Mt. Washington Glass Company in the late
19th century, Crown Milano is an opal
glass decorated with fine hand-painting
and enameling. It is apparently identical
to another Mt. Washington line they called
Albertine. Some examples of Crown Milano
carry a monogram mark on their base.*

Printed Crown Milano Mark

Bowl, 9½" w., 3¼" h., tricorner-form
w/rolled-under sides, yellowish
green ground decorated w/pansies,
roses & forget-me-nots, purple
"CM" & crown mark (some interior
stain) $460.00

Box, cov., w/tiny applied feet, melon-
ribbed, decorated overall w/enam-
eled pansies & gold accents,
3½" d., 2½" h. 275.00

Cracker jar, cov., cylindrical,
decorated w/pastel pansies outlined
w/gold & round panels of swirled
spiderwebbing in gold on a creamy
white ground, low domed silver plate
cover molded in relief w/embossed
florals & a figural butterfly finial,
marked w/Crown Milano logo &
"534," 4¼" d., 5" h. (ILLUS.).............785.00

Cracker jar, cov., squatty melon-
ribbed body decorated w/dainty
multicolored flowers & ornate gold
scrolling, original ornate silver plate
cover, rim & bail handle, 5¼" d.,
5¾" h. to top of handle.....................860.00

Cracker jar, cov., barrel-shaped,
creamy Burmese-colored decorated
w/a cluster of large exotic blossoms
on a branch, all trimmed in gilt, silver
cover, rim & swing bail handle, silver
impressed "MW," "CM" crown mark
on base, 7¼" h.................................575.00

Cracker jar, cov., squatty bulbous
body in creamy white satin
decorated w/gold-outlined exotic
blossoms & leaves, silver plate
ruffled rim, cover & bail handle,
silver marked "MW 4419/C," base
w/purple "CM" crown mark, 7¼" d....862.50

Cracker jar, cov., barrel-shaped,
creamy satin ground decorated
w/stylized scrolling florals trimmed
w/find dotting, silver plate cover
w/figural turtle, rim & swing bail
handle, silver marked "MW 524,"
paper label on base w/"Mt. W.G. Co.
Crown Milano," 7½" h. 690.00

Cracker jar, cov., peach shaded to
cream body decorated w/gold
flowers & leaves overall, ornate
silver plate rim, bail handle & cover
marked "Pairpoint" 750.00

Creamer & cov. sugar bowl, creamy
satin ground decorated w/h.p.
lavender violets framed by pink
blush edging & gold trim, paper
label, creamer 3½" h., sugar bowl
4¼" h., pr. 920.00

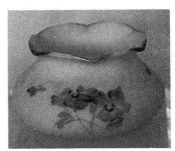

Crown Milano Sugar Bowl

Creamer & open sugar bowl, squatty
bulbous body tapering to a high
arched spout on the creamer & a
flared ruffled rim on the sugar,
applied handle on creamer, each
decorated w/purple & blue pansies
& stems on a yellow shaded to white

ground, gilt trim on rims, signed,
sugar 4" d., creamer 3½" h., pr.
(ILLUS. of sugar) 985.00

Creamer & open sugar bowl, white
satin ground decorated w/blush pink
around the edge, lavender violets &
gold trim, w/paper label, sugar bowl
4¼" d., creamer 3½" h., pr. 915.00

Dresser box, cov., round swirled
mold, the center top decorated w/a
graduated line of dancing white
herons, colored florals & scrolls
around edge of top & on base,
silver plate fittings, unsigned,
7" d., 4" h. 1,610.00

Jar, cov., wide low squatty footed
body tapering to a tiny cover w/knob
finial, the sides applied w/two small
reeded scrolled gold handles, decorated w/four open roses, blossoms
& colorful tulips & overall heavy
gilt trim, marked "1013," 9" d.,
5¾" h...1,850.00

Jardiniere, squatty bulbous body w/a
wide flat bottom, short & wide
cylindrical neck, gold-outlined large
autumn leaf decoration, purple
"CM" crown & "598" mark, 8¼" d.,
6" h..1,092.00

Jardiniere, bulbous body decorated
w/ten pansies w/ten medallions in
violet, yellow & tan, heavy gold trim
around the neck, signed on the
bottom, 9¼" d., 7" h. 795.00

Rose bowl, spherical, eight-crimp rim
yellow beige satin ground decorated
w/blue & lavender pansies, purple
"CM" & crown mark, 5" h.................690.00

Rose bowl, spherical, decorated w/ten
pansies h.p. in pastel shades of
purple, blue, brown & white &
highlighted w/delicate gold foliage,
three gold blossoms & randomly
placed gold embellishments,
5⅛" d...585.00

Salt dip, master size, enameled
w/pink & mauve floral decoration.....130.00

Spooner, embossed diamond quilted
body decorated w/chrysanthemums
& gold trim.......................................750.00

Sweetmeat jar, cov., melon-ribbed,
decorated w/h.p. pastel flowers &
gold foliage, signed.........................650.00

Syrup pitcher w/original top, white
ground shaded to deep orange,
decorated w/a blue daisy, green
leaves & foliage & a large gold
butterfly above the flower, dated
"1884," 7½" h. 495.00

Crown Milano Syrup Pitcher

Syrup pitcher w/original silver plate
top, melon-ribbed body, decorated
w/enameled gold flowers & leaves
& hundreds of blue, white, black,
coral & turquoise enamel dottings
on a soft butter cream ground
(ILLUS.) 1,245.00

Table set: creamer, open sugar bowl
& cov. jam jar; slightly globular lobed
form, shaded pink decorated w/gold
chrysanthemums, ormolu mounts,
signed, 3 pcs................................1,100.00

Tumbler, cylindrical, decorated
w/heavy gold garlands, flowers,
ribbons & bows on a semi-glossy
white ground, marked w/red crown &
wreath, 2⅞" d., 3⅞" h......................550.00

Crown Milano Vase

Vase, 6" h., 5¾" d., footed bulbous
body lightly molded w/narrow
swirled ribs tapering to a short small
neck w/four-crimp rim, decorated
w/clusters of tiny white & blue
flowers on the yellow shaded to
creamy white ground, logo signature
(ILLUS.) 965.00

Vase, 7¼" h., spherical body tapering to a swelled cylindrical neck w/a flaring rim w/the back edge pulled up into a pointed petal, slender arched handles from the neck to the shoulder, the body in creamy opal decorated w/a central reserve w/two costumed children framed by gilt scrolls, scenic medallion on the reverse, both on a delicate gold latticework ground, purple "CM" crown mark 1,380.00

Vase, 8" h., four-sided body w/two applied handles outlined in gold, body enameled w/heavy gold acorns & leaves decoration, signed.............625.00

Vase, 9¾" h., bulbous ovoid body tapering to a waisted narrow neck w/a tall cupped rim, small applied loop handles flank the neck, creamy sides decorated on the obverse w/three flamingoes in shallow waters within a leafy framework, the reverse w/two flamingoes in flight, in shades of rose, pink, white, salmon, olive green & rust trimmed w/gold, unsigned, ca. 1890 ....1,380.00

Vase, 10¼" h., large ovoid body tapering to a slender stick neck w/a bulbous ovoid tip, the neck flanked by tiny double loop handles, the creamy satin body decorated w/light scrolled ground decorated w/delicate dark gold florals & vines, unsigned 1,610.00

Vase, cov., 10½" h., decorated w/heavily enameled ivy leaves & vines in green & brown outlined in gold, lighter swirl designs on the cover, the background of the body & around the base 2,295.00

Vase, 12¼" h., ribbed base forming three-paneled sides & flaring to a gently rolled rim, beige ground w/russet & gold decoration & gold beading, signed 1,050.00

CUSTARD GLASS

This popular pressed glassware derives its name from its creamy white to creamy yellow color, said to resemble custard pudding. Developed by Harry Northwood, Custard was most popular from the late 1890s until about 1915 and was produced largely by the Northwood Glass Co., but also by the Heisey Glass Co., Fenton Art Glass Co., Jefferson Glass Co. and a few others. There were over 20 patterns produced in Custard with the most

collectible considered to be Argonaut Shell, Chrysanthemum Sprig, Inverted Fan and Feather, Louis XV and Winged Scroll. Most pieces were trimmed with gold or colored enamels and some carried a brown stain called "nutmeg." Unless otherwise noted our listings feature colored decoration. A limited amount of Custard has been reproduced but the color is not a good match to the original pieces. Some Northwood Custard was marked with a raised script mark under the base.

Northwood Script Mark

ARGONAUT SHELL (Northwood)

Argonaut Shell Cruet

Berry set, master bowl & 6 sauce dishes, 7 pcs. $575.00

Bowl, master berry or fruit, 10½" l., 5" h...................................185.00 to 225.00

Butter dish, cov....................................282.00

Compote, jelly, 5" d., 5" h. 136.00

Creamer..145.00

Cruet w/original stopper (ILLUS.) 850.00

Pitcher, water......................................433.00

Salt & pepper shakers w/original tops, pr......................................325.00 to 350.00

Sauce dish..60.00

Spooner ....125.00 to 150.00

Sugar bowl, cov. 205.00

Toothpick holder ....300.00 to 325.00

Tumbler 110.00

BEADED CIRCLE (Northwood)

Butter dish, cov....................................485.00

Creamer............................150.00 to 175.00

Beaded Circle Pitcher

Pitcher, water (ILLUS.) ....600.00 to 650.00

Spooner..154.00

Sugar bowl, cov. 175.00

Tumbler 130.00

BEADED SWAG (Heisey)

Beaded Swag Sauce Dish

Goblet....................................55.00 to 65.00

Goblet, souvenir 62.50

Sauce dish..25.00

Sauce dish, souvenir (ILLUS.)..............45.00

Sugar bowl, open.................................45.00

Wine 48.50

Wine, souvenir......................................58.00

CARNELIAN - See Everglades Pattern

CHERRY & SCALE or FENTONIA (Fenton)

Berry set, master bowl & 6 sauce
  dishes, 7 pcs. 395.00

Bowl, master berry or fruit 115.00

Butter dish, cov................................235.00

Creamer..95.00

Cherry & Scale Spooner

Spooner (ILLUS.)................................110.00

Tumbler 75.00

CHRYSANTHEMUM SPRIG (Northwood's Pagoda)

Chrysanthemum Sprig Tumbler

Berry set, master bowl & 10 sauce
  dishes, 11 pcs. 975.00

Bowl, master berry or fruit, 10½" oval,
  decorated 165.00

Bowl, master berry or fruit, 10½" oval,
  undecorated ....150.00 to 175.00

Butter dish, cov..................250.00 to 275.00

Celery vase.......................................715.00

Compote, jelly, decorated...................115.00

Compote, jelly, undecorated.................65.00

Condiment tray ....575.00 to 600.00

Creamer.............................100.00 to 125.00

Cruet w/original stopper.....................334.00

Pitcher, water, decorated....400.00 to 475.00

Pitcher, water, undeco-
  rated................................200.00 to 250.00

Salt & pepper shakers w/original tops,
  pr. 210.00

Sauce dish..62.00

Sauce dish, blue trim 140.00

Sauce dish..62.00

Sauce dish, blue trim 140.00

Spooner..110.00

Sugar bowl, cov., decorated 210.00

Sugar bowl, cov., undecorated 145.00

Table set, cov., sugar bowl, creamer,
cov. butter dish & spooner,
4 pcs. 725.00

Toothpick holder w/gold trim & paint,
signed 245.00

Toothpick holder, undecorated 175.00

Tumbler (ILLUS.) 60.00

Water set, pitcher & 6 tumblers,
7 pcs. 800.00

DIAMOND MAPLE LEAF (Dugan)
Bowl, master berry..............................145.00

Butter dish, cov...................................350.00

DIAMOND WITH PEG (Jefferson)

Diamond with Peg Butter Dish

Butter dish, cov. (ILLUS.) ...250.00 to 275.00

Creamer, individual size 30.00

Creamer, individual size, souvenir........85.00

Creamer...60.00

Mug, souvenir ....35.00 to 45.00

Napkin ring 145.00

Pitcher, 5½" h. 140.00

Pitcher, tankard, 7½" h. 250.00

Pitcher, tankard, 7½" h., souvenir.......230.00

Pitcher, water, tankard, decorated......395.00

Salt shaker w/original top 60.00

Spooner...95.00

Sugar bowl, cov. ....125.00 to 150.00

Toothpick holder 75.00

Tumbler 75.00

Tumbler, souvenir................................39.00

Whiskey shot glass..............................45.00

Wine 37.50

Wine, souvenir.....................................55.00

EVERGLADES or CARNELIAN (Northwood)

Everglades Sugar Bowl

Bowl, master berry or fruit, footed
compote ....165.00 to 185.00

Compote, jelly.....................250.00 to 275.00

Creamer...120.00

Sauce dish...60.00

Spooner...130.00

Sugar bowl, cov. (ILLUS.)...................175.00

Table set, 4 pcs. 850.00

Tumbler 105.00

FAN (Dugan)

Fan Creamer

Bowl, master berry or fruit ..175.00 to 200.00

Creamer (ILLUS.) 90.00

Ice cream dish 50.00

Pitcher, water......................................290.00

Sauce dish...60.00

Spooner...65.00

Tumbler 72.50

FENTONIA - See Cherry & Scale Pattern

FLUTED SCROLLS or KLONDYKE (Northwood)
Bowl, master berry or fruit, footed 145.00

Creamer..65.00

Spooner..48.00

FLUTED SCROLLS WITH FLOWER BAND -
See Jackson Pattern

GENEVA (Northwood)

Geneva Creamer

Banana boat, four-footed,
11" oval ....95.00 to 125.00

Banana boat, four-footed, green stain,
11" oval 145.00

Berry set, oval master bowl & 6 sauce
dishes, 7 pcs. 318.00

Bowl, master berry or fruit, 8½" oval,
four-footed 90.00

Bowl, master berry or fruit, 8½" oval,
four-footed, green stain.....................85.00

Bowl, master berry or fruit, 8½" d.,
three-footed 135.00

Butter dish, cov.................................171.00

Compote, jelly.....................................75.00

Creamer (ILLUS.) ....80.00 to 100.00

Cruet w/original stopper .....350.00 to 450.00

Pitcher, water.....................225.00 to 250.00

Salt & pepper shakers w/original tops,
pr.....................................225.00 to 275.00

Sauce dish, round.................................40.00

Spooner.............................75.00 to 100.00

Sugar bowl, cov. ....125.00 to 150.00

Syrup pitcher w/original top 275.00

Table set, 4 pcs. ....450.00 to 500.00

Toothpick holder, decorated...............125.00

Toothpick holder, undecorated.............60.00

Tumbler 55.00

GEORGIA GEM or LITTLE GEM (Tarentum)

Bowl, master berry or fruit, deco-
rated................................100.00 to 125.00

Butter dish, cov., deco-
rated.................................175.00 to 200.00

Butter dish, cov., undecorated............100.00

Celery vase..132.00

Creamer, decorated..............................95.00

Creamer, breakfast size 30.00

Creamer & cov. sugar bowl, souvenir,
pr.......................................75.00 to 125.00

Creamer & open sugar bowl, break-
fast size, decorated, pr. 95.00

Creamer & open sugar bowl, break-
fast size, souvenir, pr........................90.00

Cruet w/original stopper......................295.00

Hair receiver, souvenir..........................45.00

Pitcher, water, undeco-
rated.................................150.00 to 200.00

Powder jar, cov., souvenir 52.00

Salt shaker w/original top 50.00

Sauce dish, decorated..........................35.00

Spooner...70.00

Georgia Gem Sugar Bowl

Sugar bowl, cov., decorated
(ILLUS.) 105.00

Sugar bowl, cov., undecorated 45.00

Table set, decorated, 4 pcs. 495.00

Toothpick holder ....75.00 to 100.00

Toothpick holder, souvenir 32.00

Tumbler 50.00

Tumbler, souvenir.................................35.00

GRAPE & CABLE - See Northwood
Grape Pattern

GRAPE & GOTHIC ARCHES (Northwood)

Berry set, master bowl & 3 sauce
dishes, 4 pcs. 215.00

Grape & Gothic Arches Berry Bowl

Bowl, master berry or fruit (ILLUS.) 125.00

Goblet 60.00

Spooner ....50.00 to 75.00

Sugar bowl, cov. 195.00

Sugar bowl, cov., blue stain 195.00

Tumbler 55.00

Vase, 10" h. ("favor" vase made from
   goblet mold) 75.00

Vase, ruffled hat shape.........................55.00

GRAPE & THUMBPRINT - See Northwood Grape Pattern

INTAGLIO (Northwood)

Intaglio Butter Dish

Berry set, 9" d. footed compote &
   6 sauce dishes, 7 pcs. 438.00

Bowl, fruit, 7½" d. footed compote 146.00

Bowl, fruit, 9" d. footed
   compote ....300.00 to 350.00

Butter dish, cov. (ILLUS.) 250.00

Compote, jelly.....................................100.00

Creamer...100.00

Creamer & cov. sugar bowl, pr. 275.00

Cruet w/original stopper 315.00

Pitcher, water......................350.00 to 375.00

Salt shaker w/original top 85.00

Sauce dish...43.00

Spooner 130.00

Sugar bowl, cov. ....125.00 to 150.00

Table set, green stain, 4 pcs. 540.00

Tumbler 83.00

INVERTED FAN & FEATHER (Northwood)

Inverted Fan & Feather Berry Bowl

Berry set, master bowl & 6 sauce
   dishes, 7 pcs. ....575.00 to 600.00

Bowl, master berry or fruit,
   10" d., 5½" h., four-footed,
   (ILLUS.) ....200.00 to 250.00

Butter dish, cov. 282.00

Compote, jelly.....................350.00 to 425.00

Creamer...125.00

Pitcher, water......................................650.00

Punch cup..265.00

Salt & pepper shakers w/original tops,
   pr...495.00

Sauce dish...59.00

Spooner 140.00

Sugar bowl, cov. 215.00

Table set, 4 pcs. 800.00

Toothpick holder ....600.00 to 650.00

Tumbler ....75.00 to 100.00

IVORINA VERDE - See Winged Scroll Pattern

JACKSON or FLUTED SCROLLS WITH FLOWER BAND (Northwood)

Bowl, master berry or fruit 85.00

Creamer...85.00

Cruet, no stopper...............100.00 to 125.00

Pitcher, water, undecorated................275.00

Salt shaker w/original top, undeco-
rated...58.00

Salt & pepper shakers w/original tops,
pr...135.00

Tumbler 37.00

Water set, pitcher & 4 tumblers,
5 pcs. ....365.00 to 385.00

KLONDYKE - See Fluted Scrolls Pattern

LITTLE GEM - See Georgia Gem Pattern

LOUIS XV (Northwood)

Louis XV Tumbler

Berry set, master bowl & 4 sauce
dishes, 5 pcs. 425.00

Bowl, berry or fruit, 7¾ x 10" oval 142.00

Butter dish, cov...................175.00 to 200.00

Creamer...................................75.00 to 85.00

Creamer & cov. sugar bowl, pr. 250.00

Cruet w/original stopper 450.00

Pitcher, water.....................................237.00

Salt shaker w/original top 80.00

Sauce dish, footed, 5" oval 40.00

Spooner ....60.00 to 75.00

Sugar bowl, cov. 120.00

Table set, 4 pcs. ....500.00 to 550.00

Tumbler (ILLUS.) 70.00

Water set, pitcher & 6 tumblers,
7 pcs. 800.00

MAPLE LEAF (Northwood)

Banana bowl.......................................175.00

Maple Leaf Butter Dish

Butter dish, cov. (ILLUS.) 290.00

Compote, jelly.....................425.00 to 450.00

Creamer...160.00

Pitcher, water......................................395.00

Salt & pepper shakers w/original tops,
pr...500.00

Sauce dish...80.00

Spooner 128.00

Sugar bowl, cov. ....200.00 to 225.00

Toothpick holder 650.00

Tumbler 90.00

**NORTHWOOD GRAPE, GRAPE & CABLE
or GRAPE & THUMBPRINT**

Northwood Grape Cologne Bottle

Banana boat 325.00

Bowl, 7½" d., ruffled rim........................42.50

Bowl, master berry or fruit, 11" d.,
ruffled, footed...................................445.00

Butter dish, cov...................................250.00

Cologne bottle w/original stopper
(ILLUS.) 550.00

Cracker jar, cov., two-
  handled ....575.00 to 600.00

Creamer.............................125.00 to 150.00

Creamer & open sugar bowl,
  breakfast size, pr. ....100.00 to 125.00

Dresser tray ....275.00 to 325.00

Humidor, cov. 650.00

Pin dish...165.00

Plate, 7" d. 55.00

Plate, 8" w., six-sided 65.00

Plate, 8" d. 55.00

Punch cup...75.00

Sauce dish, flat 30.00

Sauce dish, footed................................40.00

Spooner...135.00

Sugar bowl, cov. 150.00

Sugar bowl, open, breakfast size 62.00

Tumbler 50.00

Water set, pitcher & 6 tumblers,
  7 pcs. 1,250.00

PRAYER RUG (Imperial)
Plate, 7½" d. 60.00

PUNTY BAND (Heisey)

Punty Band Tumbler

Creamer, individual size, souvenir........35.00

Cuspidor, lady's 75.00

Mug, souvenir 55.00

Mug, 4½" h. 29.00

Toothpick holder, souvenir 45.00

Tumbler, floral decoration, souvenir
  (ILLUS.) 45.00

RIBBED DRAPE (Jefferson)
Compote, jelly......................................150.00

Creamer...125.00

Pitcher, water.......................................255.00

Sauce dish..35.00

Spooner..115.00

Sugar bowl, cov. 185.00

Toothpick holder w/rose decoration... 195.00

Tumbler 82.00

RING BAND (Heisey)

Ring Band Jelly Compote

Berry set, master bowl & 6 sauce
  dishes, 7 pcs. ....450.00 to 500.00

Bowl, master berry or fruit, deco-
  rated...295.00

Butter dish, cov.....................................200.00

Compote, jelly (ILLUS.) ....145.00 TO 175.00

Condiment tray 150.00

Cruet w/original stopper 300.00

Pitcher, water.......................................250.00

Salt shaker w/original top,
  undecorated......................................50.00

Sauce dish..37.50

Spooner..120.00

Sugar bowl, cov. ....150.00 to 175.00

Syrup pitcher w/original top 365.00

Toothpick holder, deco-
  rated.................................100.00 to 120.00

Toothpick holder, undecorated 85.00

Toothpick holder, souvenir 75.00

Tumbler, decorated 75.00

Tumbler, undecorated 70.00

VICTORIA (Tarentum)
Berry set, master bowl & 6 sauce
  dishes, undecorated, 7 pcs. 275.00

Butter dish, cov...................275.00 to 325.00

Celery vase..........................150.00 to 200.00

Pitcher, water.......................................275.00

Spooner, decorated.............................130.00

Spooner, undecorated..........................70.00

Vase, bud ....300.00 to 350.00

WINGED SCROLL or IVORINA VERDE (Heisey)

Winged Scroll Sugar Bowl

Berry set, master bowl & 5 sauce
dishes, 6 pcs. 445.00

Bowl, fruit, 8½" d................................165.00

Butter dish, cov.....................................176.00

Celery vase...350.00

Cigarette jar ....145.00 to 175.00

Creamer, decorated...............................94.00

Cruet w/original stopper, deco-
rated ....175.00 to 200.00

Cruet w/original stopper, undeco-
rated 100.00

Match holder.......................190.00 to 225.00

Pin tray, small 195.00

Pitcher, water, 9" h., bulbous...............230.00

Pitcher, water, tankard, deco-
rated..................................300.00 to 375.00

Pitcher, water, tankard, undecorated..230.00

Powder jar, cov.......................................99.00

Salt & pepper shakers w/original tops,
pr...150.00

Sauce dish, 4½" d.................................36.00

Spooner 89.00

Sugar bowl, cov., decorated
(ILLUS.) 135.00

Sugar bowl, cov., undecorated.............95.00

Syrup pitcher w/original top 365.00

Toothpick holder...................................137.00

Tumbler 77.50

Water set, bulbous pitcher &
4 tumblers, 5 pcs. 550.00

MISCELLANEOUS PATTERNS

Delaware

Berry set, master bowl & 5 sauce
dishes, 6 pcs. 190.00

Creamer, individual size 36.00

Creamer w/rose decoration 67.00

Pin tray w/blue decoration 75.00

Pin tray w/green decoration, 7"............70.00

Pin tray w/rose stain, 4½" 68.00

Punch cup..40.00

Ring tree, 4" h.......................80.00 to 100.00

Spooner..65.00

Sugar bowl, breakfast size 45.00

Tumbler w/blue decoration 70.00

Tumbler w/green decoration.................45.00

Peacock and Urn

Bowl, master berry..............................200.00

Ice cream bowl, master, w/nutmeg
stain, 9¾" d. ....300.00 to 375.00

Ice cream dish, individual, w/nutmeg
stain 65.00

Vermont

Bowl, master berry..............100.00 to 125.00

Butter dish, cov....................................104.00

Candlestick, finger ....50.00 to 70.00

Celery vase..225.00

Creamer w/blue decoration 97.00

Creamer w/green & pink florals 95.00

Salt shaker w/original top, enameled
decoration 77.50

Salt & pepper shakers w/original tops,
blue decoration, pr. 135.00

Spooner..95.00

Spooner w/green decoration 75.00

Toothpick holder w/blue trim &
enameled decoration 90.00

Toothpick holder w/green deco-
ration..135.00

Tumbler 75.00

Tumbler w/blue decoration 60.00

Vase w/enameled decoration 135.00

Wild Bouquet

Wild Bouquet Cruet

Butter dish, cov.....................................565.00

Creamer ....100.00 to 125.00

Cruet w/original stopper, w/enameling
& gold trim (ILLUS.) 1,000.00

Sauce dish, undecorated......................42.00

Spooner w/gold trim & colored
decoration 165.00

Spooner, undecorated..........................70.00

Toothpick holder, decorated 475.00

Tumbler, undecorated 86.00

OTHER MISCELLANEOUS PIECES:

Alba, sugar shaker w/original lid.........125.00

Basket (Northwood) w/nutmeg stain.....85.00

Beaded Cable, rose bowl, w/nutmeg
stain 87.50

Beaded Scroll, butter dish, enameled
floral top 175.00

Blackberry Spray, hat, ribbon candy
edge..35.00

Butterfly & Berry, vase, 7" h..................25.00

Canadian, compote 30.00

Chrysanthemum, Heacock No. 463,
tray, 8½ x 4½" 38.00

Circled Scroll, sauce dish, round,
green opalescent 25.00

Creased Bale, condiment set
w/original tops 125.00

Cut Block, sugar bowl, individual size ..35.00

Dandelion, mug w/nutmeg stain 135.00

Drapery, vase, swung-type...................48.00

Drapery, vase, 10" h., w/nutmeg stain..47.50

Drapery, vase, 12" h., w/nutmeg stain..45.00

Finecut & Roses, rose bowl w/nutmeg
stain 63.00

Footed Wreath, bowl 85.00

Fruits & Flowers, (N), bowl, 7¼" d.,
flared...65.00

Gothic Arches, goblet 35.00

Grape Arbor, hat-shape w/nutmeg
stain 42.00

Grape Arbor, vase, 3¾" h. 85.00

Grape Arbor, vase, No. 200..................40.00

Heart, salt 45.00

Honeycomb, cordial..............................70.00

Honeycomb, wine 60.00

Horse Medallions, bowl, grapes
exterior, 6½" d....................................50.00

Horse Medallions, bowl, green stain,
7" d..60.00

Iris, cruet w/original stopper,
undecorated......................................285.00

Jefferson, salt shaker, roses
decoration, souvenir 35.00

Jefferson Optic, butter dish, cov...........50.00

Jefferson Optic, pitcher, tankard,
souvenir 275.00

Jefferson Optic, salt dip w/rose
decoration 65.00

Jefferson Optic, sugar bowl, cov. 90.00

Jefferson Optic, table set, vases
w/gold, 4 pcs. 350.00

Jefferson Optic, toothpick holder,
souvenir. 40.00

Jefferson Optic, tumbler 30.00

Lacy Medallion, tumbler........................38.00

Ladder w/Diamond, butter dish, cov. 85.00

Ladder w/Diamond, creamer 60.00

Ladder w/Diamond, spooner 60.00

Ladder w/Diamond, sugar bowl, cov. ...70.00

Lion, plate, 7" d., w/green
stain ....100.00 to 200.00

Lion, plate, 8" d., w/green stain 95.00

Lotus, nappy, handled, 6½" 35.00

Lotus & Grape, bonbon, green stain.....65.00

Lotus & Grape, bonbon, nutmeg
stain 110.00

Lotus & Grape, bonbon, handled, red
  stain 45.00

Lotus & Grape, nappy, handled............65.00

Many Lobes, sugar shaker w/original
  top...95.00

Mug, "Court House, Alexandria, S.D."
  scene, miniature 45.00

Nine Panels, lamp, miniature................65.00

Peacock & Dahlia, plate, 7¾" d., flat,
  w/green stain 75.00

Peacock & Urn, ice cream bowl,
  9¾" d., w/nutmeg stain ....250.00 to 275.00

Pineapple & Fan, pitcher, 5½" h.,
  souvenir 65.00

Pods & Posies, butter dish, cov.,
  w/gold trim 125.00

Poppy, relish tray, nutmeg stain 60.00

Ribbed Thumbprint, toothpick holder,
  w/floral decoration.............................75.00

Rings & Beads, pitcher, 2¾" h.,
  souvenir 25.00

Rings & Beads, toothpick holder,
  souvenir 45.00

Royal Oak tumbler, w/green stain 45.00

Shell & Scroll, spooner, 3½ x 4¼" h. ..150.00

Singing Birds, mug 85.00

Smocking, bell w/original clapper 45.00

Spool, spooner 32.00

Strawberry, compote 75.00

Three Fruits, bowl, 6¾" d., flared rim,
  nutmeg stain 95.00

Tiny Thumbprint, goblet, souvenir 60.00

Tiny Thumbprint, table set, 4 pcs. 65.00

Tiny Thumbprint, toothpick holder,
  souvenir 85.00

Trailing Vine, sauce dish, footed 30.00

Trailing Vine, spooner, blue..................65.00

Twigs, plate 70.00

Water Lily, cracker jar, cov. 185.00

Woven Cane, salt shaker 30.00

(End of Custard Glass)

CUT GLASS

From the 1880s until World War I, the so-called "Brilliant Period," fine cut glass was among the most expensive and pop- *ular types of glass, often used as wedding and anniversary gifts. Numerous glass companies produced cut glass and the best examples are eagerly sought today. Some companies used acid-etched markings on some of their wares, but these markings can be reproduced. Quality of the piece rather than a mark should guide the buyer. We list pieces alphabetically by the type of article.*

Hawkes, Hoare, Libbey and Straus Marks

BASKETS

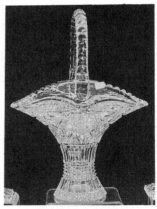

Brilliant Period Basket

Hawkes signed, Pattern No. 1298,
  hobstars & flashed stars, cut handle,
  6½ x 8½".......................................$475.00

Hobnail & crosshatching, circular
  base tapering in & flaring out to a
  wide rim, thumbprint edge & applied
  handle, 19" h. 2,530.00

Hobstars, pinwheel & crosshatching,
  twisted handle, 7" d., basket 1¾" h.,
  overall 5¼" h. 310.00

Hobstars, cane & diamond point,
  6" h..300.00

Hobstars, strawberry diamond & fan,
  St. Louis diamond handle, 4½ x 9"
  oval, overall 8" h. 825.00

Panel-cut waisted lower portion w/step-cutting at waist, the flaring upper section cut w/hobstars, cross-cut vesicas & other cutting, serrated rim, cut handle, 11" w., overall 16" h. (ILLUS.) 975.00

BOTTLES

Tall Whiskey Bottle

Bitters, vertical notched prism & elon-gated bull's-eye, sterling silver pourer, 8" h. 190.00

Boudoir, notched prism, star-cut base, sterling silver top w/cherub decoration, 7½" h. 70.00

Ketchup, notched prism bands w/alternating panels of hobstar diamonds & strawberry diamond, fans at top, cylindrical w/incurving neck, triple notched handle at shoulder, rayed base, octagonal flattened stopper, overall 9½" h. 675.00

Whiskey, hobstars, cane, hobnail, strawberry diamond & fan, rayed base, matching stopper, overall 11½" h...425.00

Whiskey, hobstars, separated by notched prism, bow ties of strawberry diamond between each hobstar, triple notched handle, hobstar base, matching hobstar stopper, overall 12½" h. (ILLUS.)..1,000.00

Worcestershire sauce, strawberry diamond & fan, faceted ball-shaped stopper...275.00

BOWLS

Banana, fan-shaped curving sides cut w/large hobstar each side, further cut w/St. Louis diamond at each end flanked by fans & triple notching, paneled stem, 16-point hobstar base, 3½" w., 6" l., 5" h. 325.00

Banana, Hunt's Royal patt., Russian motif w/hobstar button, five-sided strawberry diamond lozenge & large hobstars, 8 x 11"..............................500.00

Unusual Two-part Banana Bowl

Banana, two-part, bowl cut w/four 32-point hobstars separated by a flaring design of strawberry diamond, fan, notched prism & beading beneath a scalloped & serrated rim, fitting into a base w/alternating fields of hobnail & strawberry diamond above a notched prism standard, 14-point serrated foot, bowl 8¾ x 12", 3¼" h., overall 9" h. (ILLUS.) 3,000.00

Berry, Libbey signed, hobstars & deeply cut stars, 8¼" d., 3½" h. 250.00

Cetus Pattern Bowl

Cetus patt., panels of cane alternating w/panels of hobstars, large hobstar in base, 10½" d. (ILLUS.)..............2,600.00

Clark signed, central pinwheel w/rows of hobstars & hobnail beneath a cross-hatched border, 8¼" d............275.00

Clark signed, Quatrefoil Rosette patt., 9½" d...1,200.00

Egginton signed, Arabian patt., cluster of hobstars around hexagon center, 10" d., 5" h. 2,300.00

Egginton's Cambria patt., beading,
fan, cane & hobstar, 7" d. 70.00

Egginton's Trellis patt., checkerboard-
type motif, shallow, 7" d. 1,000.00

Elite Cut Glass Company's Expanding
Star patt., fan, hobstar, star &
strawberry diamond, 9" d. 175.00

Empire's Albemarle patt., beading,
hobstar & strawberry diamond, low,
8" d..50.00

Fruit, Harvard patt., 10" d. 225.00

Fruit, Harvard patt. variant of small
hobstars, cross-hatched hobnail &
crosshatching, large hobstar base,
irregular scalloped & serrated rim,
12½" l..440.00

Fruit, hobstar & strawberry diamond
vesicas alternating w/cane vesicas,
on standard & domed base cut
w/strawberry diamond & four-sided
figures w/fans below, 8¾ x 10½",
8½" h...700.00

Fruit, pinwheel & fan cutting divided
by vesicas centering a hobstar at
the base, scalloped & serrated rim,
8" d..165.00

Fry signed, Chicago patt., crossed
bars, low, 7¾" d. 500.00

Hawkes signed, Panel & Kohinoor
patt., deep cut panels & diamonds of
Harvard patt., 8" d., 3½" h................575.00

Hawkes' Brazilian patt., fan, star
& strawberry diamond, low,
8¾" d..300.00

Hoare signed, Trellis patt., checker-
board motif, low, 7 ¾" d. 700.00

Hobstars & strawberry diamond,
bulbous, silver mount w/a
gadrooned border, mono-
gramed, 7" d. 357.50

Hobstars, six 48-point hobstars within
fields of nailhead diamond w/single
stars, 60-point hobstar base, 10" d.,
4½" h..2,600.00

Hobstars, strawberry diamond &
curving splits w/notched prism, six-
pointed star shape, 10" w. 500.00

Hobstars & crosshatching, shallow,
Gorham silver mount chased
w/scrolling, monogramed, 10½" d....495.00

Hunt signed, Limoges (Rosettes &
Stars) patt., overall hobstars,
8" d..250.00

Hunt's Royal patt., Russian motif
w/hobstar button, five-sided
strawberry diamond lozenge & large
hobstars, 7¾" d...............................300.00

Ice, Libbey, middle section cut in a triangle of cross-cut diamond flanked
w/strawberry diamond, a section of
fans & another triangle of large
hobnail, St. Louis diamond handles,
24-point hobstar footed base 400.00

Libbey signed, Delphos patt., vesicas
of hobnail w/clear borders,
surrounded by further hobnail,
10" d., 4¼" h. 600.00

Libbey's Kimberly patt., cross-cut
diamond, fan & hobstar, 9" sq..........400.00

Libbey's Neola patt., feather (or fern)
motif, flared sides, 9" d. 225.00

Orange, chain of hobstars separated
by fans, further cut w/hobstars,
5" w., 7½" l., 3" h. at center, 4¼" h.
at ends 275.00

Orange, large hobstar on each side &
at each end in a circle of clear
surrounded by cane, wavy ridged
edge, low stem, star-cut foot,
6½ x 9", 6½" h.............................2,300.00

Orange, Libbey signed, Delphos patt.,
vesicas of hobnail w/clear borders,
surrounded by further hobnail,
8¼ x 11¾", 4" h...............................500.00

Orange, Llbbey's Marcella patt.,
clusters of six hobstars separated
by hobnail vesicas, 8 x 11¾",
4½" h..1,800.00

Pitkin & Brooks' Heart patt., notched
prism flares, 8" d. 230.00

Pitkin & Brooks' Rajah patt., flashed
hobstar w/strawberry diamond
points, 9" d. 100.00

Rosette patt. variant, hobstars set in
the center of notched prism,
terminating in small fans, cane
& vesica, 8" d. 175.00

Salad, Hawkes' Chrysanthemum
patt., 9½" sq. 900.00

Salad, Russian patt., 9¾" d. 250.00

Strawberry diamond & fan, low,
9½" d..125.00

BOXES

Dresser, pinwheel & cross-cut diamond on lid & sides, 3¾" d., 2½" h. ...75.00

Dresser, sides cut in bull's eye, fan &
star, star-cut base, sterling silver lid,
3½" d., 3" h. 55.00

Dresser, red cut to clear, hinged lid &
sides cut in flashed fan w/a
diagonally cut band of cane, rayed
base, gold fittings, 4¼ x 6"............1,550.00

Dresser, Harvard patt. on hinged lid & sides, gold fittings, 7" d................475.00

Jewelry, hinged lid cut w/chain of hobstars, hobstars & fan, sides similarly cut, star-cut base, silver fittings, 6½ x 7" oval, 3½" h.............190.00

Powder, pinwheel & fan, 4½" w., 3¾" h...175.00

Powder, Hawkes signed, Rock Crystal patt., sterling silver lid, 5½" d., 4½" h...350.00

BUTTER DISHES & TUBS

Cut Glass Covered Butter Dish

Covered dish, chain of hobstars w/notched prism, dome lid & matching underplate (ILLUS.)..........700.00

Small Cut Glass Butter Dish

Covered dish, hobstars, cane, cross-cut diamond & vesicas, dome lid w/knob finial, the underplate cut in hobstars & small vesicas w/24-point hobstar in center, quarter pound size (ILLUS.)....................................500.00

Tub, Hawkes signed, intaglio-cut florals & foliage, 3" d. base, 5" d. top, 4" h. 50.00

Tub, hobstars & crosshatching, hobstar base, raised handles, 5" d., overall at top of handles 3" h. 300.00

Tub, hobstar & nailhead cutting, 3½" d. base, 6½ d. top, 3" h...............40.00

Tub, cov., strawberry diamond & fan, w/matching underplate, the set........250.00

BUTTER PATS

Emerald green cut to clear, fans, triangles of cane w/center star, 3" d., set of 6...................................450.00

Hobstar Cluster patt., set of 6............300.00

Persian (Russian patt. w/hobstar button) patt...70.00

CANDLESTICKS & CANDLEHOLDERS

Honeycomb cutting overall, teardrop in stem, 6" h. (single) 350.00

Pairpoint, St. Louis diamond, fine cross-cut diamond, cosmos, floral leaf & thistle cutting on bulbous stem, star-cut base, 12" h., pr. 625.00

Russian & Pillar patt., square Russian patt. foot & swirl cylindrical pillar stem, 8" h., pr................................1,400.00

Other

Candelabrum, five-light, four-arm, base cut in hobstars, cane & fan, flared in w/notched prism, continuing to six hobstars, arms cut in St. Louis diamond, silver holder for section w/hobstars in a swirl design, center extends up to swirl & flute cutting to fifth bobeche to candle holder, each holder w/silver insert, each bobeche w/nine prisms, base 7" w., overall 18½" d., 19½" h.................4,100.00

Exceptional Cut Glass Chamberstick

Chamberstick, flared skirted base cut

in fans, deep oblong splits, notched
prism, hobstar & strawberry
diamond, conformingly cut bobeche,
screw-in candle nozzle, applied
handle, 6" d., 12½" h. (ILLUS.) 1,100.00

CARAFES

Dorflinger's Marlboro patt., chain of
hobstars w/fan & strawberry
diamond, hobstar base, waisted
form...220.00

Hawkes signed, Brunswick patt.,
chain of hobstars, zipper-type
beading & flute, rayed base,
6" d., 7½" h. 325.00

Hobstars & pinwheel, step-cut neck,
6½" d., 8" h. 100.00

Peerless patt., fan, hobnail, hobstar &
strawberry diamond, 9" h. 40.00

Strawberry diamond, fan & other
cutting, star-cut base, notched prism
neck, 6" d., 8" h. 95.00

CHAMPAGNES, CORDIALS & WINES

Grecian Pattern Wine Glass

Champagne, Hawkes signed,
Middlesex patt., hollow stem............120.00

Champagne, Hoare signed, Hindoo
patt., hobstar & notched prism...........60.00

Champagne, Libbey signed, Imperial
patt., cane (variation of hobnail &
star), fan, hobstar & star, elongated
teardrop extending up stem from
foot, rayed base, 3¾" bowl,
overall 4¾" h. 210.00

Champagnes, Hawkes signed,
Queens patt., chain of hobstars &
bull's-eye, set of 6 ....1,440.00

Cordial, hobstars & split vesica, bell-
shaped bowl w/flared rim, teardrop
stem w/knop, 16-point hobstar base,
2¼" d., 4½" h. 60.00

Cordials, Hoare's Richelieu patt., swirl
motif, knopped stem w/teardrop,
set of 4 ....1,100.00

Cordials, hobnail cutting, hob in
teardrop stem, flashed star base,
3¾" h., set of 6................................180.00

Wine, cranberry cut to clear, Grecian
patt., vesicas, fan & Russian patt.,
4¾" h. (ILLUS.) 825.00

Wine, cranberry cut to clear, Russian
patt. w/cut buttons, teardrop stem,
rayed base, 4½" h. 350.00

Wine, green cut to clear, cross-cut
diamond, strawberry diamond & fan,
six-sided ring beneath bowl, stem
flares out w/teardrop in lower
portion, rayed base, 2½ h. bowl,
overall 5" h. 675.00

Wine, Hawkes signed, Middlesex
patt...55.00

Wine, hobstars separated by cross-
cut diamond & strawberry diamond,
faceted ball under bowl, double
teardrop hollow stem, rayed base,
bowl 2" h., overall 4¼" h. 30.00

Wine, Honeycomb patt., panel-cut
knopped stem, rayed base, 4¼" h. 35.00

Wine, Rhine-type, emerald green cut
to clear, tulip-shaped bowl cut
w/modified hobstars & fans,
strawberry diamond fields at base of
bowl, clear stem, 20-point hobstar
base, 7" h. 225.00

Wine, Rhine-type, hobstar & flashed
fan, stem w/faceted knob, rayed
base 100.00

Wine, ruby cut to clear, cut overall in
triple miter on the bowl, paneled
lapidary-cut teardrop stem & foot,
5" h..1,100.00

Wine, Russian patt., honeycomb
stem, rayed base 40.00

Wine, strawberry diamond & fan 27.50

Russian Pattern Wine Glass

Wine, turquoise cut to clear, Russian patt. w/cut buttons, teardrop stem, rayed base, 4½" h. (ILLUS.) 525.00

CHEESE DISHES

Cheese Dish with Silver Finial

Hawkes signed, hobstar & fan, dome lid w/faceted knob, matching underplate 600.00

Hawkes' Gladys patt., chain of hobstars, fan & strawberry diamond, dome lid w/knob finial, matching underplate.......................................625.00

Hobstars, hobnail, crosshatching & vesicas, 7½" dome lid & 9" d. underplate w/scalloped rim 495.00

Prism & fine crosshatching, dome lid w/faceted knob, matching 9" d. underplate w/central hobstar 450.00

Sunburst motif, fan & other cutting, dome lid w/ornate sterling silver finial, matching 12" d. underplate (ILLUS.) 1,200.00

COMPOTES

Covered Cut Glass Compote
Clark signed, pinwheel & nailhead diamond, cut stem, pinwheel base, 7½" d., 7" h. 160.00

Elmira Glass Company's Pattern #100, chain of hobstars, cane, fan & strawberry diamond, teardrop stem, hobstar base, 10" d., 13½" h.........1,500.00

Hobstars, cane & crosshatching, faceted stem, large hobstar base, 8¼" d., 7¾" h. 200.00

Hobstars, crosshatching, curved split, notched prism stem w/teardrop, serrated hobstar base, 7½" d., 9" h..325.00

Hobstars, cross-cut diamond & vesicas on shallow bowl, narrow, notch-cut tall stem w/a teardrop, circular foot w/hobstar, 9½" h., pr. ...660.00

Hobstars, single stars, hobnail & cross-hatching, elongated stem w/controlled air bubble, scalloped hobstar base, 11¾" h. 550.00

Hobstars, notching, crosshatching & fan cutting on deep dish w/two applied thumbprint handles, low standard, 5½" d. hobstar base, bowl 13" d. 715.00

Hobstars & fan, cover conformingly cut w/a 16-point hobstar on finial, thumbprint around top of bowl & bottom of cover, notched teardrop stem, 24-point hobstar base, 8" d., 15" h. (ILLUS.) 3,100.00

Brilliant Period Compote

Hobstar panels (3) alternating w/panels of two hobstars & strawberry diamond, separated by tracks of notching, notch-cut stem, 32-point hobstar base, 9" d., 9½" h. (ILLUS.) 1,300.00

Hunt's Royal patt., three-part, bowl & lower part of the flared base cut in the pattern, the upper portion of the base in notched prism, the bowl screws into a silver fitting at top of base, notched prism ball fits over

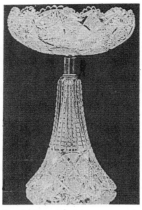

Hunt's Royal Pattern Three-part Compote

silver collar on standard, bowl
w/scalloped & serrated rim, 10" d.
bowl, overall 15" h. (ILLUS.) 3,500.00

Libbey signed, hobstars, pinwheel,
hobnail & fan, step-cut stem,
6" d., 6" h. 160.00

Sterling Glass Company's Arcadia
patt., pentagonal strawberry
diamond figure w/hobstar & single
star, prism-cut standard, 28-point
hobstar base, 12" d., 12" h..............625.00

CREAMERS & SUGAR BOWLS

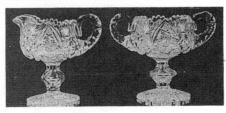

Cut Glass Creamer & Sugar Bowl

Clark signed, hobstars & crosshatching, strawberry diamond
handle, pr. 130.00

Clark signed, 24-point hobstar each
side & nailhead diamond, cut
handles, pr. 190.00

Cross-cut diamond & fan, wafer
bases, sugar bowl w/cover, pr. 300.00

Hoare's Hindoo patt., chain of
hobstars, beading & fan, pr..............320.00

Hobstars, fan & prism, pedestal base,
notched handles, 4¼" h., pr. 425.00

Hobstars w/beaded vesicas beneath
flashed fans, faceted knobbed stem,
notched handles, notched foot
w/16-point hobstar, 6" h., pr.
(ILLUS.) 2,100.00

Hobstars, fan & stars, pedestal base
cut w/a hobstar, 6½" h., pr. 850.00

Hobstar (24-point) each side, fan &
cross-hatching, star-cut base, pr. 50.00

Hunt's Royal patt., Russian motif
w/hobstar button, five-sided strawberry diamond lozenge & large
hobstars, pr. 220.00

Strauss' Ulysses patt., round cov.
sugar 5" d., 5½" h., milk-type
creamer 4½" d., 5" h., pr. 850.00

DECANTERS

Large Footed Decanter

Bullseye & Diamond patt., w/original
stopper, overall 10¾" h....................175.00

Chain of hobstars alternating w/fan,
triple-notched handle, 20-point
hobstar base, original lapidary-cut
stopper 1,050.00

Clark's Jewel patt., chain of hobstars,
cross-cut diamond, fan & strawberry
diamond 75.00

Eleanor patt., clear tusks w/hob-
star, cane & crosshatching, honeycomb neck, original faceted stopper, 6" d. bulbous base, overall
13" h. 1,000.00

Harvard patt. overall, step-cut neck,
bell-shaped body, cordial size,
8" h...275.00

Harvard patt., bowling pin-form,
matching stopper w/hobstar on top,
overall 15" h. 1,300.00

Hawkes' Middlesex patt., chain of
hobstars & fan, notched handle,
w/original stopper.............................350.00

Hoare's Pluto patt., chain of hobstars,

beading, fan & strawberry diamond, neck cut w/three rings, w/original stopper 500.00

Hobstars (3) separated by bands of cane & topped w/strawberry diamond & fan, fluted notched prism neck, double-notched applied handle, 16-point hobstar foot, conformingly cut steeple stopper, overall 17" h. (ILLUS.)...................1,000.00

Meriden's Plymouth patt., flashed hobstar w/strawberry diamond points 200.00

Russian Pattern Decanter

Russian patt., bulbous body, three ringed faceted neck, star-cut base, conforming teardrop stopper, 11½" h. (ILLUS.) 935.00

St. Louis Diamond patt. overall, applied handle, 24-point hobstar base, matching cut teardrop stopper, 13" h................................1,200.00

DISHES, MISCELLANEOUS

Bonbon, Tuthill signed, notch-cut & intaglio-cut flowers & leaves centering a star, octagonal, 6½" w.....99.00

Celery, pinwheel, hobstars & strawberry diamond, on a notched stem, rayed foot, 5" w., 11½" l., 7" h..400.00

Ice cream, Hunt signed, stars & fan cutting, 5" d., set of 5 ....220.00

Mint, hobstars & crosshatching & deeply cut vesicas around a central hobstar, scalloped & serrated rim, 6" d...110.00

Relish, hobstar, bands of cane & crosshatching, four-part, handles, 11¼" l., 2" h. 275.00

Relish, Sinclaire signed, oval, two-part, engraved w/ivy leaves & vines, 14" l..132.00

Roll, Sterling Glass Company's Regal patt., flowers, hobnail, hobstar, star & strawberry diamond, 12¾" l.........121.00

Straus signed, star & miter cutting, 8" d..99.00

FERNERS

Chain of hobstars & double fans, footed, 9" d..100.00

Harvard border centering floral center, footed, 8" d..125.00

Hoare signed, hobstars & fan, three-footed, 7½" d....................................143.00

Hobstars, fan & crosshatching, star-cut base, three-footed, 7½" d...........110.00

ICE TUBS

Meriden's Alhambra Pattern Ice Tub

Comet-type design w/a large shooting star in the base, the sides cut w/flashed fans, crosshatching, miters & further shooting stars, scalloped rim w/two rectangular handles, 5½" h. 187.00

Elite Cut Glass Company's Expanding Star patt., fan, hobstar & strawberry diamond, two handled, across handles 9" d. 300.00

Hoare's Carolyn patt., hobstars, cane, fan & beading, 5½" h. 725.00

Meriden's Alhambra patt., Wilcox signed sterling silver rim & handle (ILLUS.) 2,250.00

Straus' Corinthian patt., cane, hobstar, fan & strawberry diamond, 6" d., 5½" h. 160.00

JARS

Candy, hobstars, strawberry diamond & fan cutting on swelled

Deeply Cut Cracker Jar

cylindrical base, matching cover
w/faceted finial, 8¾" h. 660.00

Caviar, cov., hobstars, cane, hobnail
& strawberry diamond, rayed base,
matching cut lid w/faceted finial,
w/inner glass liner, 4¾" d.,
7½" h. 1,300.00

Cracker, hobstar, cane, strawberry
diamond, notched prism & fan,
matching lid w/faceted finial,
6" d., overall 9" h. (ILLUS.) 2,100.00

Tobacco, Alhambra (Greek Key) patt.,
hobstars, cane & wide band of
Greek key design, matching
stopper, 24-point hobstar base,
6" d., 9½" h. 2,600.00

Tobacco, Hoare's Carolyn patt.,
beading, cane, fan & hobstar, 24-
point hobstar mushroom stopper,
5" d., 8" h. 1,100.00

Tobacco, hobstars & notched prism,
24-point hobstar base, conformingly
cut mushroom-shaped stopper,
6" d., 10" h. 900.00

Tobacco, the three-section body
separated by two outer bands of
miters & stepped notching, the
middle band composed of hobstars,
the lid cut w/single hobstar within a
circle of thumbprints, 8½" h. 605.00

MISCELLANEOUS ITEMS

Banana boat, Libbey signed, hobstar,
cane & cross-hatching w/dished
center, on a 24-point serrated
hobstar base, 6⅞ x 13", 6¾" h. 3,400.00

Banana boat, Maple City Glass Co.
signed, large hobstars, miters &
strawberry diamond, ovoid, 10" l......330.00

Berry set: 8" d. master bowl & six
individual dishes; Clark signed,
pinwheel & hobstars, 7 pcs. 1,100.00

Cake plate, Tuthill signed, hobstars
alternating w/hobnail patches, low
standard, foot w/24-point hobstar
w/fans between points, 12" d.,
2" h. 400.00

Cake Stand with Cut Gallery

Cake stand, 1½" gallery cut
w/hobstars & cross-cut diamond
hobstars alternating w/fans &
strawberry diamond, paneled
baluster standard, notched twenty-
four point hobstar base, 10½" d.,
9½" h. (ILLUS.) 2,500.00

Celery vase, four half-moon cuts at
rim, hobstars, strawberry diamond &
chain of diamonds up side, rayed
base, 4" d., 4" h. 225.00

Celery vase, Drape patt. variant,
hobstars separated by deep curving
splits, knobbed stem, 24-point
hobstar base, 3¾" d., 7¼" h. 550.00

Center bowl, flashed hobstars within a
circle of vesicas, the whole
surrounded by hobnail, crosshatching & flashed fan, scalloped
rim, 9" d. 110.00

Center bowl, ovoid, hobstars, hobnail
& notching, large hobstar in base,
irregular scalloped rim, 12¾" l. 632.50

Champagne cooler, hobstars &
Harvard patt. w/notched prism splits,
24-point hobstar base, w/original
silver plate liner, top 7½" d., 7" h. 850.00

Charger, six-pointed star design
w/hobstars between the points,
crosshatched tusks on the points of
the stars, hobnail, cane & strawberry diamond patches toward the
center, 14" d.................................1,000.00

Cuspidor, bishop's hat form, rim cut
w/21 hobstars on top separated by
notched prism, bottom cut w/six-
pointed large star w/hobstar in each
point & in between, strawberry
diamond points on hobstars,
12½" d., 3½" h. 1,500.00

Finger bowl, hobstar center extending
out in cane points & strawberry
diamond figures w/three splits each,
hobstars on sides w/vesicas of
strawberry diamond & fan, 5" d.,
2½" h...75.00

Flower center, compressed form cut
w/daisies, hobstars & crosshatching, notched neck, scalloped rim,
12" d..1,017.50

Libbey's Diana Pattern Flower Holder

Flower holder, Libbey signed, Diana
patt., hobstars, flashed fan & cross-
cut diamond, raised ends forming a
crescent-shaped bowl, low standard,
notched foot w/24-point hobstar,
5¼ x 9" bowl, 6" h. at middle, the
ends 10½" h. (ILLUS.) 11,000.00

Flowerpot, Florence patt., cross-cut
diamond, fan, star & strawberry
diamond, 6" d., 6" h...........................40.00

Ice cream set: 17½" l. tray & six 7" d.
dishes; star pattern in center,
scalloped edges, 7 pcs. 715.00

Ice cream set: 10 x 18" serving tray
& six 7" d. plates; Straus' Drape
patt., 7 pcs 2,900.00

Jam jar, cov., Egginton signed, chain
of hobstars, rayed base, fluted &
notched top, 4" d., overall 6" h. 385.00

Loving cup, three-handled, cane,
strawberry diamond, hobnail & fan,
sterling silver rim stamped "WSW,"
rayed base, 5" d., 6¼" h..................425.00

Ornate Cut Glass Loving Cup

Loving cup, three-handled, hobstars,
strawberry diamond & notched
prism, notched handles, twenty-four
point notched hobstar foot, 5¼" d.,
8½" h. (ILLUS.) 1,500.00

Mayonnaise bowl & underplate,
Libbey's Wedgemere patt., hobstars,
strawberry diamond & vesicas, plate
7" d., bowl 5" d., 2⅝" h., the set 1,300.00

Napkin ring, Cane patt.........................75.00

Paperweight, book-shaped, hobnail &
crosshatching, 1 x 1½ x 2"...............175.00

Pickle castor, St. Louis diamond
cutting on lower half, the top half
w/etched florals & foliage, in an
ornate silver plate frame w/cover 250.00

Ramekin & underplate, turquoise cut
to clear, Russian patt., cup 3" d.,
plate 5" d., the set 1,800.00

Salad serving fork & spoon, Cane
patt. handles w/teardrop, silver plate
tines & bowl, pr. 525.00

Salad serving set, Russian patt.
handles, Gorham silver plate spoon
bowl & fork tines, 11" l., pr. 302.50

Stick dish w/center stem & faceted
knob top, Florence hobstar
alternating w/hobnail vesicas, 5" d.,
4" h..300.00

Sugar shaker, Russian patt. alternating w/clear panels, original silver
top 375.00

Whiskey jug, Dorflinger's Marlboro
patt., chain of hobstars, fan &
strawberry diamond 175.00

NAPPIES
Empire Cut Glass Company's Orinoco
patt., 6" d...30.00

Fry's Carnation patt., fan, hobstar & strawberry diamond, handled 60.00

Hawkes' Jupiter patt., 6" d. 170.00

Hoare's Elfin patt., 7" d. 121.00

Hobstars, 6" d. 40.00

Hobstars, hobnail & deep miters around a central flat star, scalloped & serrated rim accented w/fan cutting, two-handled, 7" d. 132.00

Libbey's Melrose patt., 5" d. 30.00

Libbey's Princess patt., cross-cut diamond, fan & strawberry diamond, 6" d...25.00

Libbey's Venetian patt., 5" d. 45.00

Pinwheel cutting overall, two-handled ..80.00

Strawberry diamond & fan, hobstar base, strawberry shape, handled, 5 x 6½" 80.00

PITCHERS

Cranberry Cut to Clear Tankard Pitcher

Cider, Hawkes' Gladys patt., chain of hobstars, fan & strawberry diamond, 7½" h...400.00

Milk, vertical & horizontal jeweled miters separating sections composed of hobstars, hobnail, crosshatching & fan, large hobstar in base, applied thumbprint handle, 6¾" h. 275.00

Milk, chain of hobstars, cane & cross-cut diamond, star-cut base, triple-notched handle, 8" d., 7½" h. 475.00

Milk, Libbey's Florence patt., chain of hobstars, fan, star & strawberry diamond, 7½" h. 250.00

Milk, Maple City Glass Co. signed,

pinwheel & crosshatching, low bulbous body w/everted spout, 7½" h...297.00

Tankard, cranberry cut to clear, vertical panels of hobstars alternating w/clusters of cane, strawberry diamond & other cutting, scalloped & serrated rim (ILLUS.) 6,500.00

Tankard, hobstars w/cane centers, pinwheel, strawberry diamond, curved splits, triangles of Russian patt., 24-point hobstar base, triple-notched handle, 5½" d., 7" h. 450.00

Tankard Pitcher with Silver Top

Tankard, hobstar, strawberry diamond & fan, hobnail cut handle, fourteen-point hobstar base, ornate sterling silver top w/relief floral decoration, stamped "Dorflinger Sterling," 5" base d., 13" h. (ILLUS.) 450.00

Tankard, Unger Brothers' Hobart patt., 11" h.......................................275.00

Water, Alhambra (Greek Key) patt., hobstars, cane & wide Greek key border, pedestal base, dentil edge at rim & base, 12¼" h. 5,750.00

Water, Hawkes signed, hobstars, hobnail, notch-cutting & vertical miters, thumbprint & fan handle, 8¾" h. 253.00

Water, hobstars, single stars, fan, crosshatching & miters, star-cut base, applied thumbprint handle, undulating serrated rim, 7½" h. 247.50

Water, hobstars, crosshatching & notching, applied thumbprint handle, scalloped lip w/geometric notch cutting, 8½" h. 247.50

Water, hobstars, crosshatching,

notched miters & fan, star-cut base, double thumbprint handle, serrated rim, 8¾" h...165.00

Water, hobstar, cane & strawberry diamond fans, 32-point hobstar base, cut handle, fluted spout, 6" d., 9" h..475.00

Water, Libbey's Imperial patt., cane, fan, hobstar & star, hobstar bottom, cut handle, 10½" h. 4,750.00

Libbey's Marcella Pattern Pitcher

Water, Libbey's Marcella patt., cluster of hobstars around a hexagon center, cane. strawberry diamond & fans, 11" h. (ILLUS.) 6,000.00

Water, Libbey's Prism patt., beading, cane & strawberry diamond, 10" h...357.50

Water, Libbey's Wedgemere patt., 11" h...4,500.00

Water, Pitkin & Brooks' Beverly patt., hobnail, hobstar, star & strawberry diamond, 6" d., 9" h.........................700.00

PLATES
6" d., Hawkes' Brazilian patt., chain of hobstars, fan, star & strawberry diamond 160.00

6" d., Hoare's Florence patt. 45.00

6" d., Libbey signed, Colonna patt., chain of hobstars, crosshatched triangle, star & strawberry diamond 100.00

7" d., Blackmere's Zephyr patt., crossed bars & other cutting 110.00

7" d., Libbey signed, Wedgemere patt., beading, flute, hobstar & strawberry diamond, set of 6 ....2,700.00

7" d., Triple Miter Trellis patt., hobstars & cane w/triple miter cutting....900.00

7" d., Tuthill's Rex patt., chain of hobstars, cane vesicas, fan & strawberry diamond 1,025.00

8½" d., Dorflinger's Parisian patt., cranberry cut to clear, beading, fan, hobstar & strawberry diamond......2,100.00

12" d., hobstar, diamond & vesicas 350.00

12" d., Libbey signed, Colonna patt., chain of hobstars, crosshatched triangle, star & strawberry diamond 900.00

PUNCH BOWLS & SETS
Alford signed, Triest patt., notched prism w/large triangle from side to base to side, further cut w/hobstars alternating w/crosshatching, 12" d., 5½" h..750.00

Elite Cut Glass Company's Expanding Star patt., fan, hobstar, star & strawberry diamond, 14" d. 300.00

Hobstars, cane, fan, deep miter cutting & other cutting, scalloped & serrated rim, on conforming base, 12" d., 12½" h., 2 pcs. 440.00

Hunt's Royal patt., Russian motif w/hobstar button, five-sided strawberry diamond lozenge & large hobstars, matching base, 12" d., 2 pcs. 1,500.00

Libbey signed, Colonna patt., chain of hobstars, crosshatched triangle, fan, star & strawberry diamond, 14" d., together w/matching ladle, the set 2,100.00

Punch set: 14" d. bowl, eight cups & 15" l. ladle; Hawkes' Holland patt., 10 pcs. 700.00

SALT & PEPPER SHAKERS
Hobstar & drape cutting, brass tops, pr...95.00

Libbey signed, intaglio-cut flowers & swags, baroque Wilson sterling silver tops, pr. 250.00

Notched prism, sterling silver tops, 1¾" h., pr. 50.00

SALT DIPS
Cranberry cut to clear, overall strawberry diamond, serrated rim...............95.00

Green cut to clear, finecut & button around sides, 1¾" d., ⅞" h.................65.00

Hobstars & fan, pedestal base, rayed foot, master size 125.00

SPOONERS

Egginton signed, stars, hobnail &
    miters, 8" l. 88.00

Elite's Expanding Star patt., fan,
    hobstar, star & strawberry diamond,
    5 x 7"...40.00

Hawkes signed, hobstars &
    strawberry diamond, 7½" l. 88.00

TOOTHPICK HOLDERS

Crosscut diamond & fan, 2" h. 20.00

Crosshatching & fan, 2½" h. 55.00

Hobstars & other cutting 75.00

TRAYS

Hawkes Signed Three-section Tray

American Cut Glass Company's
    Lansing patt., hobstars, flashed
    cross-cut hobstar vesicas &
    strawberry diamond, 14" d. 400.00

Bread, Clark signed, cane, hobstars &
    fan, further engraved w/leaf designs,
    rectangular w/rounded corners,
    12½" l. 302.50

Bread, Colonna patt., chain of hob-
    stars, crosshatched triangle, fan,
    star & strawberry diamond, 8 x 11"..450.00

Celery, Empire Cut Glass Company's
    Plaza patt., 13" l. 75.00

Celery, Festoon patt., hobstars &
    other cutting 275.00

Celery, strawberry diamond & fan,
    scalloped & serrated rim, 13" l. 120.00

Celery, Tuthill signed, stars, cross-
    hatching & fans, 12" l. 165.00

Cranberry cut to clear, Russian patt.,
    cranberry buttons & edges,
    remainder clear, 5¼ x 10½",
    1½" h..350.00

Eleanor patt., hobstars, cane,
    clear tusks & strawberry diamond,
    12" d...225.00

Hawkes' Grecian patt., vesicas, fan &
    Russian patt., butterfly-shaped,
    9" w. 1,000.00

Hawkes signed, divided into three
    free-form sections w/feathering in
    between & strap handle on one
    division, cut in Kohinoor w/185
    pyramidal stars in each section,
    11½" d. (ILLUS.) 4,250.00

Hoare, scalloped sides centered by a
    large star surrounded by miters &
    stars, 15" d. 1,760.00

Ice cream, American Cut Glass
    Company's Mary patt., hobstars,
    strawberry diamond & feathered
    vesicas, 10¼ x 17½".....................2,200.00

Ice cream, Empire Cut Glass
    Company's Atlantic patt., crossed
    bars, hobstars & other cutting,
    10 x 17½"..250.00

Hawkes Ice Cream Tray

Ice cream, Hawkes' Gladys patt.,
    chain of hobstars, fan & strawberry
    diamond, 16" l. (ILLUS.)..................935.00

Ice cream, Hoare signed, Marquis
    patt., feather, hobnail, star &
    strawberry diamond, oval w/closed
    end handles, 10½ x 18" 1,175.00

Ice cream, Hoare's St. Louis patt.,
    fan, hobstar, notched prism flairs &
    strawberry diamond, 9 x 13" 150.00

Ice cream, Libbey signed, Star patt.,
    chains of hobstars, fan & other
    cutting, 10½ x 18" 1,500.00

Ice cream, Libbey's Gloria patt.,
    chain of hobstars, beading,
    hobstar & strawberry diamond,
    10¼ x 17½"...................................2,200.00

Ice cream, single stars, fan, cross-
    hatching, notched vesicas & other
    cutting within a border of hobstars,
    serrated rim, 15" l............................550.00

Libbey signed, fan, stars & miters,
    shaped oval form, 13½" l. 330.00

Libbey signed, Snowflake patt.,
12" d..2,250.00

Hawkes' Chrysanthemum Pattern Tray

Sandwich, Hawkes' Chrysanthemum
patt., split vesicas, hobstars, cane &
fan, slightly dished center, 11½" sq.
(ILLUS.) 2,200.00

Sinclaire's Assyrian (Bird-in-a-Cage)
patt., checkerboard-type design,
hobstar w/cane center, hobnail &
crosshatching, 8 x 10½", 2" h. 500.00

Taylor Bros. signed, chains of
hobstars, strawberry diamond bow
ties, 32-point hobstar base w/straw-
berry diamond points & fans between points, strawberry diamond
rim, 9 x 14½" oval, 2¾" h. 1,700.00

TUMBLERS

Butterfly & deeply cut floral decora-
tion 75.00

Hobstars, cross-cut diamond & fan,
12-point hobstar in base, 3½" h. 110.00

Libbey's Harvard patt............................55.00

Libbey's Imperial patt., cane, fan,
hobstar & star, 3¾" h. 90.00

VASES

Egginton's Victoria patt., beading,
bull's eye, hobstar & split oval,
cylindrical form, 12" h.......................209.00

Fry Glass Company's Vardin patt.,
trumpet-form, 9" h. 132.00

Harvard patt. & hobstars, three feet
cut w/bull's-eye, waisted form,
4½" d., 12" h. 550.00

Hawkes signed, Brunswick patt.,
chain of hobstars, beading, fan &
flute, 12" h., pr..................................495.00

Hawkes signed, hobstars &
diamonds, baluster-form w/lobed
mouth, 9" h......................................330.00

Hawkes' Brazilian patt., chain of
hobstars, fan, star & strawberry
diamond, trumpet-form, 5" h. 325.00

Hawkes' Queens patt., trumpet-
shaped, 12" h. 625.00

Hoare signed, stars, crosshatching &
miters, waisted form, 6¼" h. 88.00

Hobstars around middle & at bottom,
bands of hobnail & cane, St. Louis
diamond, stars & horizontal step-
cutting, hobstar base, bulbous at
bottom, narrowing w/a slight bulge in
middle & flaring out at serrated rim,
7" d., 13½" h. 1,100.00

Brilliant Period Vase

Hobstars, zipper, strawberry diamond
& other cutting, corset-shaped,
14" h. (ILLUS.) 400.00

Intaglio-Cut Vase

Hobstars, cross-cut diamond, crosshatching & notch-cutting interspersed w/daisies, fans & miters, scalloped & serrated rim, hobstar base, 25½" h. 2,530.00

Intaglio-cut florals overall, horizontal step-cutting at neck, conformingly cut everted rim, facet-cut knob above serrated pattern-cut foot, 18" h. (ILLUS. bottom previous column) 1,900.00

Libbey signed, cobalt blue cut to clear frosted, stylized geometric & bud design, baluster form, 9" h. 687.50

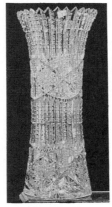

Libbey's Elsmere Pattern Vase

Libbey signed, Elsmere patt., beading, triple miter cane, hobstar & straw-berry diamond, serrated rim, 16" h. (ILLUS.) 1,600.00

Pairpoint's Savoy patt., bull's-eye & cross-cut diamond, 10" h. 395.00

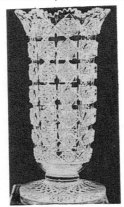

Sinclaire's Bird-in-a-Cage Pattern

Sinclaire's Bird-in-a-Cage patt., urn-form w/scalloped & serrated rim, twenty-four point hobstar foot, 6" top d., 12" h. (ILLUS.) 5,000.00

WATER SETS

Pitcher & six tumblers, Libbey signed, stars, fan, strawberry diamond & miters, pitcher 9" h., 7 pcs. 1,320.00

Pitcher & six tumblers, Plymouth patt., flashed hobstar w/strawberry diamond points, 7 pcs. 130.00

Pitcher & six tumblers, Madeline patt., flashed hobstar, large leaves of cane & intaglio-cut cattails, hobstar base, pitcher 8½" h., 7 pcs. 250.00

(End of Cut Glass Section)

CUT VELVET

Cut Velvet Rose Bowl

This mold-blown, two-layer glassware is usually lined in white with a colored exterior with a molded pattern. Pieces have a satiny, acid finish, giving them a 'velvety' appearance. The Mt. Washington Glass Company was one of several firms which produced this glass.

Rose bowl, spherical w/four-crimp top, light heavenly blue satin Diamond Quilted patt., white lining, 3⅜" d., 3¼" h. $145.00

Rose bowl, spherical w/six-crimp top, rose red satin Diamond Quilted patt., white lining, 3¾" d., 3½" h.......225.00

Rose bowl, spherical, six-crimp top, blue satin Diamond Quilted patt., white lining, 3½" d., 3¾" h.......165.00

Rose bowl, ovoid w/four-crimp top, apple green satin Diamond Quilted patt., white lining, 3" d., 4" h. (ILLUS.) 165.00

Rose bowl, egg-shaped, six-crimp top, rose pink satin Diamond Quilted patt., white lining, 3⅜" d., 4" h.........155.00

Rose bowl, egg-shaped, four-crimp top, lavender pink satin Diamond Quilted patt., white lining, 3¼" d., 4¼" h..165.00

Rose bowl, egg-shaped, three-crimp
top, heavenly blue satin Diamond
Quilted patt., white lining, 3⅝" d.,
4⅜" h. 150.00

Cut Velvet Egg-Shaped Rose Bowl

Rose bowl, egg-form, tri-lobed rim,
deep rose Diamond Quilted patt.,
satin finish, 3½" d., 4½" h.
(ILLUS.) 165.00

Vase, 5" h., 3" d., ovoid body tapering
to short cylindrical neck, heavenly
blue satin Diamond Quilted patt.,
white lining 145.00

Vase, 5½" h., 3¼" d., baluster-form
w/ringed neck & flaring mouth,
heavenly blue satin Rib patt.,
decorated w/applied clear frosted
bell-shaped flower & stem, white
lining 165.00

Vase, 6" h., 3⅛" d., ovoid body
tapering to a squared flaring rim,
shaded heavenly blue satin
Diamond Quilted patt., white lining ..175.00

Vase, 6" h., 3⅛" d., ovoid body
tapering to a short cylindrical neck,
apple green satin Rib patt., white
lining 125.00

Vase, 6¼" h., 3½" d., bulbous body
tapering to cylindrical neck,
heavenly blue satin Diamond
Quilted patt., white lining..................125.00

Vase, 6¾" h., 3¼" d., ovoid w/short
cylindrical swelled tapering neck,
glossy rose Rib patt. exterior, white
lining 95.00

Vase, 8¾" h., ovoid body tapering to a
tall slightly flaring cylindrical neck,
robin's-egg blue satin Diamond
Quilted patt., Mt. Washington Glass
Co. (ILLUS. top next column) 385.00

Vases, 8½" h., tapering cylinder
w/angled shoulder, ruffled rim, green
satin Diamond Quilted patt., white
lining, pr. 275.00

Cut Velvet Vase

Ribbed Cut Velvet Vases

Vases, 9" h., 4⅛" d., ovoid body
tapering to a tall cylindrical neck,
deep rose ribbed pattern, white
lining, pr. (ILLUS.) 175.00

Cut Velvet Vases with Ruffled Rims

Vases, 9⅞" h., 4" d., ovoid body
tapering to a cylindrical neck w/a
widely flaring tricorner rim w/crimped

edge, pink deep ribbed pattern,
white lining, clear edging around
rim, glossy finish, pr. (ILLUS.)..........210.00

CZECHOSLOVAKIAN

*The country of Czechoslovakia, includ-
ing the glassmaking region of Bohemia,
was not founded as an independent
republic until after the close of World War
I in 1918. The new country soon developed
a large export industry, including a wide
range of brightly colored and hand-painted
glasswares such as vases, tablewares and
perfume bottles. Fine quality cut crystal or
Bohemian-type etched wares were also
produced for the American market. Some
Bohemian glass carries faint acid-etched
markings on the base.*

*With the recent break-up of Czecho-
slovakia into two republics, the wares
produced between World War I and II
should gain added collector appeal.*

Basket, orange w/applied black trim &
handle, 7½" h. $135.00

Basket, applied jet black handle & rim,
red w/clear overlay, debossed floral
decoration, signed 65.00

Basket w/applied pink spiral handle,
red, yellow & white spatter body 180.00

Candlestick, free-blown w/a cylindrical
socket w/a wide slightly dished drip
pan upon a tapering columnar
standard & wide thin disc foot,
yellow w/applied black thin ribs
ending in teardrops, components
assembled in the Powlnoy manner,
9½" h..316.00

Compote, 10" d., orange & black, oval
mark 125.00

Figure of a black musician w/a guitar,
6½" h..350.00

Figure of a doctor w/stethoscope,
wearing jacket, tan pants,
multicolored base, 8¾" h. 295.00

Rose bowl, Amberina w/controlled
bubble design, original label, 5½" h. ..35.00

Vase, 4½" h., yellowish orange
w/brown mottled exterior, signed 20.00

Vase, 6" h., tapering hexagonal form
in bright green shading to pale
green, engraved w/a floral design....165.00

Vase, 7¾" h., fluted rim, jet black
w/red & iridescent green spattered
exterior, red lining, signed..................45.00

Vase, 8" h., 6½" d., bulbous base

w/large petal rim, black ground,
orange lining, signed........................40.00

Vase, 8¼" h., blue opaque ground
w/applied jet black rim, signed 35.00

Vase, 9" h., clear w/black, red &
orange overlay, inverted sides 225.00

Vase, 10" h., purple iridescent ground
w/yellow pulled feather decoration,
1920s 175.00

Vase, 12" h., overlay, white cut to
emerald green w/h.p. florals & gold
trim, scalloped rim............................250.00

Vase, 12" h., ruffled rim, green
w/black trim 150.00

Wines, clear ground w/etched birds &
swirl decoration, set of 12 ....275.00

D'ARGENTAL

D'Argental Cameo Lamp

*This is a marking used on a range of
cameo glass produced at the St-Louis
Glass Factory from the late 19th century to
1918. The factory, located in the Alsace-
Lorraine region, was part of Germany
during that period but carried the French-
sounding marking or was sometimes
marked "Arsale," "Arsal" or "St-Louis-
Munzthal."*

D'Argental Mark

Cameo chandelier, domical central
shade in grey mottled w/yellow,
overlaid w/cranberry red & cut

w/orchid blossoms & leafage, fitting into a wrought-iron frame cast w/alternating leaves, w/three scrolling arms to support the small shades, suspended from three wrought-iron chain links cast w/a leafy branch, floraform ceiling cap, large shade & two small shades signed in cameo "D'Argental" w/cross of Lorraine, one small shade unsigned, ca. 1920, 22" d., 26" h...$4,025.00

Cameo lamp, table model, 8⅞" d., domical triple layered shade in yellowish amber cased in orange & dark brown & cut w/blossoms on leafy stems w/three butterflies in flight, matching swelled slender cylindrical base w/domed foot, signed "D'Argental" w/cross of Lorraine in cameo, 19" h. (ILLUS.) 5,175.00

Cameo vase, 4⅜" h., sharply compressed globular body w/everted rim, grey infused w/deep yellow, overlaid in crimson & deep cranberry & cut w/stylized orchid blossoms & delicate foliage, signed in cameo "D'Argental" w/cross of Lorraine, ca. 1920........................1,840.00

Cameo vase, 5" h., slightly swelled cylindrical body, yellow frosted overlaid in blue & etched w/thistles, signed "D'Argental" & the cross of Lorraine...546.00

Cameo vase, 7¾" h., simple ovoid body tapering to a small, flared neck, grey mottled w/ochre yellow, overlaid in deep cranberry & cut w/a Venetian scene w/sailboats in the harbor, signed in cameo, ca. 1920...1,265.00

Cameo vase, 11½" h., baluster-form, yellow overlaid w/cranberry & cut w/large roses on pendent stems, signed in cameo..............................935.00

Cameo vase, 13⅝" h., shouldered ovoid body, grey infused w/pale ochre & amber, overlaid in deep amber & cut w/a pattern of undulating underwater vegetation, signed in cameo "D'Argental" w/cross of Lorraine, ca. 1920........1,150.00

Cameo vase, 14" h., tall ovoid body in grey shaded to pale yellow, overlaid w/caramel & brown & cut w/a tranquil forest & lake landscape, signed in cameo, ca. 1920 (ILLUS. top next column) 1,380.00

Cameo vase, 14" h., wide trumpet-

D'Argental Cameo Vase

form body tapering to a small cushion foot, frosted grey overlaid in medium blue & chocolate brown & cut w/two oval panels enclosing tranquil mountainous landscapes w/a stream & fir trees in the foreground, reserved against a ground cut w/stylized linear flowerheads, signed in cameo "d'Argental" w/cross of Lorraine, base w/original retailer's paper label, ca. 1920 ....2,070.00

DAUM NANCY

Daum Nancy Marks

The brothers Auguste and Antonin Daum founded a glass factory in Nancy, France in 1875 and proceeded to produce fine wares, including much quality cameo glass. Their best cameo and enameled glass dates from the 1890s into the early 20th century

Bottle w/stopper, the cylindrical shouldered body w/a short neck & inset stopper w/flat, fan-shaped handle, mottled powder blue ground finely etched to depict swans on a lake w/grasses & trees in the foreground, enameled in white, green & black, the stopper trimmed w/gilding, enameled "DAUM NANCY" 3" h. $2,760.00

Bowl, 5" d., 2½" h., low sides w/a four-lobed indented rim, grey mottled w/white & purple, cut w/wildflowers & leafage & enameled in shades of green, yellow & brick red, signed in cameo 1,840.00

Bowl, 5⅛" h., wide squatty ovoid body tapering to a wide flat rim, mottled yellow & purple etched, enameled & gilded w/ cornflowers & wasps, gilt signature "Daum Nancy" w/cross of Lorraine.......................................5,175.00

Bowl, 7½" d., low spherical body w/quatrefoil lip, grey mottled w/white, golden yellow, purple & orange, cut w/orange pips pendent from leafy branches, enameled in green, orange, brown & black, signed in enameled cameo "DAUM NANCY - FRANCE" w/cross of Lorraine, ca. 1915.........................2,415.00

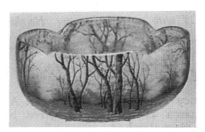

Daum Nancy Enameled Bowl

Bowl, 8" d., 3¾" h., low hemispherical vessel w/four lobes at the rim in grey mottled w/lemon yellow & tangerine, cut w/a winter landscape & enameled *en grisaille* w/charcoal black & frosty white, signed in enamel "Daum - Nancy" w/cross of Lorraine, ca. 1915 (ILLUS.) 2,875.00

Bowl, 8¼" d., a narrow footring supporting a wide squatty bulbous body below a short, wide flaring neck, mottled tangerine opalescent streaked in green, etched & enameled to depict burgundy blossoms on olive-colored vines, trimmed w/gilding, incised "DAUM NANCY" 1,380.00

Bowl, 8¾" d., 4¾" h., clear shading to emerald green, cut w/clusters of blossoms & leafage, heightened in gilt, signed in gilt "DAUM - NANCY" w/cross of Lorraine, ca. 1900........2,185.00

Bowl, 11½" d., the acid-etched opalescent sides overlaid & enameled w/sprays of wildflowers & leafage in shades of rose, crimson & charcoal heightened w/gilding, signed in gilt enamel "DAUM - NANCY" w/cross of Lorraine, ca. 1910..2,013.00

Bowl, 13½" d., the acid-etched pale champagne walls spirally streaked in pale rose & lemon yellow, overlaid & enameled w/sprays of sunflowers, buds & leafage in shades of rose, maroon & charcoal, the whole heightened w/gilding, signed in gilt "DAUM - NANCY" w/cross of Lorraine, ca. 1900.........................4,025.00

Daum Nancy Scenic Bowl-vase

Bowl-vase, the low ovoid body w/squared sides & incurvate lip, grey internally decorated w/pale pink & lime green, cut w/a spring forest scene w/young trees bending in the wind in driving rain storm, the trees & ground enameled *en grisaille*, signed in intaglio "DAUM - NANCY" w/cross of Lorraine, ca. 1900, 4¼" h. (ILLUS.) 10,925.00

Bowl-vase, low bulbous body w/cylindrical rim, green mottled w/rose, cut w/a pattern of storks in flight above a tranquil pond w/various types of blossoming plants including arrowroot & lotus interspersed w/cattails all beneath an intaglio floral border, enameled in charcoal & rust, the whole heightened in gilt, worn signature, ca. 1900, 5¼" h.................................4,025.00

Cameo bowl, 4" h., hemispherical w/three loop supports, the clear body splashed w/creamy white shading to deepest violet, overlaid & enameled in shades of violet, grass green & cherry red w/violet blossoms, buds & leafage, the lower section w/foliate strapwork height-ened w/gilding, the loop supports in grey striated w/violet, signed in gilt "DAUM - NANCY" w/cross of Lorraine, ca. 1910 ....4,313.00

Cameo bowl, 5⅜" d., clear sides mottled w/white shading to deepest violet, overlaid in violet, green & red & cut w/African violets & leafage, signed in cameo 2,300.00

Cameo bowl, 11⅛" d., 5½" h., low stepped foot, grey mottled w/pale orange & purple, overlaid in charcoal grey & cut w/chestnut leaves & branches, signed in cameo "DAUM - NANCY" w/cross of Lorraine, ca. 1910 ....3,163.00

Cameo ewer, bulbous w/elongated pulled rim, applied angled side handle, grey streaked w/brilliant lemon yellow & mottled purple, overlaid w/mottled green, silvery-white & rose & cut w/geranium blossoms & leafage, signed in intaglio "Daum Nancy" w/cross of Lorraine, ca. 1900, 15¼" h. 5,750.00

Cameo inkwell, the squatty bulbous body w/a flattened top centered by a domed cap cover, grey mottled w/pale blue, overlaid in mottled lime green, yellow & purple & cut w/water lily blossoms & leafage & a dragon-fly, the body applied & finely wheel-carved, inscribed "DAUM NANCY" w/cross of Lorraine, ca. 1900, 4⅛" h. (cover replaced) 2,760.00

Cameo lamp, boudoir model, the shade & base in grey mottled w/crimson & lemon yellow, over-laid in charcoal brown & cut w/a tranquil river landscape, w/three-arm foliate wrought iron mount, signed in cameo "DAUM - NANCY - FRANCE" w/cross of Lorraine, ca. 1915, 4¼" d., 11⅛" h. 6,900.00

Cameo lamp, table-type, the shouldered open conical shade & baluster-form base in grey mottled w/pale blue & violet, overlaid w/mot-tled shades of green, brown & yellow & cut w/lotus blossoms & leafage, the shade w/two applied & finely wheel-carved dragonflies, the base w/one, w/simple three-arm wrought-iron mount, shade & base signed in intaglio "DAUM NANCY" w/cross of Lorraine, ca. 1910, 9½" d., 19½" h. 50,600.00

Cameo vase, 3" h., pillow-type, acid-etched clear walls mottled w/lemon yellow & orange, cut w/a winter

landscape & enameled *en grisaille*, signed in enamel DAUM - NANCY" w/cross of Lorraine, ca. 1915........2,300.00

Cameo vase, 4" h., tapering four-sided body w/short neck raised on a low foot, pale opalescent overlaid in lime green & cut w/stalks of lily of the valley against a finely *martelé* ground, inscribed "Daum - Nancy" w/cross of Lorraine, ca. 1900........1,380.00

Cameo vase, 6⅜" h., shouldered ovoid body in grey overlaid in mottled orange, amber & purple, cut w/a design of pendent grape clus-ters & leafage, signed in cameo ...2,013.00

Daum Nancy Art Deco Style Cameo Vase

Cameo vase, 6¾" h., flaring cylindrical body w/incurvate rim, raised on a cushion-form base, grey mottled w/white, overlaid in brilliant red & cut w/an Art Deco-style design of stylized clusters of ripe cherries pendent from leafy branches, inscribed "Daum Nancy" w/cross of Lorraine, ca. 1925 (ILLUS.) 1,495.00

Cameo Vase with Woodbine

Cameo vase, 7½" h., ovoid body

tapering to a cushion foot & a small, flat-rimmed mouth, grey infused w/bubblegum pink, overlaid in emerald green & cut w/woodbine berries & trailing leafage against a finely *martelé* ground, the whole selectively fire-polished, signed "DAUM - NANCY" w/cross of Lorraine, ca. 1900 (ILLUS.) 2,875.00

Cameo vase, 8½" h., shouldered baluster-form, grey streaked w/raspberry shading to lemon yellow & lime green, mottled w/maroon at the foot, overlaid at the shoulder in emerald green & cut w/pendent pine boughs, the sides applied w/finely wheel-carved pine cones, traces of slightly iridescent brown & cinnamon enamel, signed in intaglio "DAUM - NANCY" w/cross of Lorraine, ca. 1910..13,225.00

Daum Nancy Art Deco Vase

Cameo vase, 9" h., 9¾" d., Art Deco style, spherical body on a small footring, tapering to a short rolled neck, crystal overlaid in amethyst & acid-etched w/a repeating stylized blossom & zigzag band design, impressed mark "Daum Nancy France" w/cross of Lorraine (ILLUS.) 2,875.00

Cameo vase, 10¾" h., slightly swelled cylindrical body in grey internally mottled w/lemon yellow, crimson & purple & overlaid in mottled crimson, green, white & purple & cut w/a design of clusters of grapes & leafage, some of the grapes padded, two applied grey snails on either side, each wheel-carved, signed in cameo, minor rim chip, antenna chip to one snail, internal inclusion at one side, ca. 1915 (ILLUS. top next column) 12,650.00

Cameo vase, 12¼" h., squatty bulbous base below a tall slightly

Cameo Vase with Applied Snails

flaring neck, clear overlaid w/orange & heavily etched to depict laburnum branches, etched "Daum Nancy" w/cross of Lorraine 1,840.00

Graceful Daum Nancy Cameo Vase

Cameo vase, 13¾" h., gently waisted flaring cylindrical body raised on a low knopped base, grey mottled w/tangerine, crimson & green, overlaid in mottled crimson, tangerine & green & cut w/clusters of blossoms & leafy branches, enameled in soft peach, green, yellow, violet & brown, signed in cameo "DAUM - NANCY" w/cross of Lorraine, ca. 1915 (ILLUS.) 5,175.00

Cameo vase, 15½" h., footed bulbous ovoid body tapering to a short rolled neck, grey mottled w/frosty white, overlaid in brilliant orange & cut w/berried leafy branches, signed in intaglio "DAUM - NANCY - FRANCE" w/cross of Lorraine, ca. 1920 (ILLUS. top next column) 4,025.00

Large Daum Cameo Vase

Cameo vase, 18¼" h., baluster-form, grey mottled w/tangerine, pale rose & purple, overlaid w/mottled yellow & green & cut w/clusters of berries amid leafy branches, enameled in ochre, green, rust & brown, signed in cameo DAUM - NANCY - FRANCE" w/cross of Lorraine, ca. 1915 ....4,140.00

Cameo vase, 24" h., elongated baluster-form, mottled white ground overlaid in green & orange, etched w/banana leaves, cameo signature w/cross of Lorraine 1,150.00

Center bowl, deep wide rounded sides w/the rim pulled into four small points, raised on a small domed foot, heavy walled pink & cream-colored mottling throughout the frosted body, engraved on sides "Daum Nancy" w/the cross of Lorraine, 11½" d., 6" h. 330.00

Compote, open, 11" d., circular w/everted rim, green mottled body w/metal inclusions, raised on a circular foot, wheel-cut signature w/cross of Lorraine 230.00

Decanter, bottle-form, emerald green cut w/strawberries & leafage, enameled in crimson & heightened in gilt, w/silver stopper & pierced coaster base, signed in gilt "Daum - Nancy" w/cross of Lorraine, ca. 1900, 9⅝" h. (ILLUS. top next column) 1,495.00

Ewer, a pedestal foot supporting a tall, slender tapering cylindrical body w/a high, pointed spout, a long, arched applied handle, mottled pink ground shading to mottled green & brown w/a rough texture below, applied w/clear, brightly colored

Daum Nancy Silver-Mounted Decanter

carved cabochon insects, their legs shallowly carved on the body, engraved "DAUM NANCY," 8¾" h...6,325.00

Enameled Daum Nancy Ewer

Ewer, souvenir-type, wide ovoid body w/sharply angled upper half to the arched rim spout & applied strap handle, opalescent finely enameled *en grisaille* on the obverse w/a wine cask between berried leafy grapevines & ring-turned borders, further decorated w/the inscription "Souvenir de l'Exposition 1900 - Le plus grand foudré du monde - AEd. Fruhinsholz. Nancy," the whole trimmed w/gilding & raspberry enamel, signature effaced, ca. 1900, 12¼" h. (ILLUS.) 2,588.00

Inkwell, cov., squared body w/a wide shoulder to the short neck fitted w/a mushroom cover, orange & green mottled ground etched, enameled & gilded to depict dandelions in the wind, matching cover, glass insert, gilt signature "Daum Nancy" w/cross of Lorraine, 4¾" h. (hairline in cover) 1,495.00

Lamp, table-model, a 9¼" d. stepped domed shade raised on a ovoid base upon a wide, round disc foot, each in frosted white etched w/a vertical rib design w/a wide band of dots, shade & base w/etched signature, overall 14½" h. 4,025.00

Tumbler, swelled cylindrical body of polished mottled orangish amber, engraved "Daum Nancy," 4⅞" h. 230.00

Vase, miniature, 2¾" h., small ovoid body tapering to a small, short neck, opalescent etched to depict dandelions, etched "Daum Nancy" w/cross of Lorraine 345.00

Vase, 5" h., swollen cylindrical body, opalescent, etched w/bands at the top & bottom & strawberry vines, all flanking a central medallion enameled *en grisaille*, further enameled in red & blue, also enameled "Souvenir de L'Exposition 1900 Le Plus grand foudre du monde Ad. Fruhinsholz Nancy," applied w/a circular pad on reverse enameled "Daum Nancy".............2,760.00

Vase, 5⅝" h., the bulbous cylindrical neck above a bulbous base, applied scrolling side handles, in grey opalescent internally streaked w/orange & tangerine, cut w/a spray of blossoms & a dragonfly, the dragonfly enameled in pink, lavender, blue & amber & heightened in gilt, signed in gilt "Daum - Nancy" w/cross of Lorraine, ca. 1900......................28,750.00

Vase, 6⅞" h., shouldered cylindrical body in orangish amber, acid-etched w/geometric designs, inscribed "DAUM NANCY FRANCE" w/cross of Lorraine.......................................920.00

Vase, 11½" h., swelled flattened conical body tapering to a wide flared rim, frosted peach ground etched w/butterflies, bees, grasshoppers & stylized flowers, enameled in soft pastels & trimmed w/gold, enameled signature (ILLUS. top next column) 51,750.00

Vase, 13" h., slightly waisted cylindrical shouldered body tapering to a short flaring neck, acid-etched clear shading to soft pink then grass green at the base, overlaid & enameled *en grisaille* w/a spring landscape w/newly leafed trees

Daum Nancy Etched & Enameled Vase

Daum Enameled Vase

bending in a rain storm, signed in enamel "DAUM - NANCY" w/cross of Lorraine, ca. 1910 (ILLUS.) 21,850.00

Vase, 15" h., flaring cylindrical body w/an opened mouth, pale blue ground w/turquoise inclusions cased w/clear, raised on a circular foot, etched "Daum Nancy France".......1,725.00

Vase, 18¾" h., elongated ovoid body tapering to a thick folded rim, smoky topaz heavily etched to depict stylized scrolls & lozenges, etched signature.......................................2,875.00

Vide poche (figural dish), *pate de verre*, irregular circular form molded in low relief w/leafy branches, inscribed "DAUM NANCY" w/cross of Lorraine, ca. 1925, 5⅞" d..........1,035.00

(End of Daum Nancy Section)

DE LATTE

DeLatte Cameo Boudoir Lamp

Andre de Latte of Nancy, France, produced a range of opaque and cameo glass after 1921. His company also produced light fixtures but his cameo wares are most collectible today.

DeLatte Marks

Cameo boudoir lamp, the bullet-form shade & baluster-form base in orange overlaid in purple & cut w/flowering leafy vines, simple wrought-iron mounts, shade signed in intaglio "A - Delatte - Nancy," base signed in cameo "ADelatte - NANCY," shade 3¼" d., overall 15¼" h. (ILLUS.) $1,980.00

Cameo box, cov., squatty bulbous body w/fitted domed cover, grey mottled w/pale yellow & overlaid in raspberry red, cut w/bleeding hearts & leafage around the base & butterflies on the cover, signed in cameo "A DELATTE - NANCY," ca. 1920, 3¾" h. 920.00

Cameo box, cov., squatty bulbous round body w/domed, fitted cover, opaque pink overlaid in deep purple & cut w/morning glories, signed in cameo "DELATTE - NANCY," ca. 1900, 5¾" d. (ILLUS. top next column) 518.00

Cameo lamp, table model, baluster-form standard on a spreading foot,

DeLatte Cameo Box

domical closed shade, pea green overlaid in cobalt blue, the shade cut w/birds in flight above a standard cut w/sailing ships, the foot cut w/a pattern of kelp, w/leaf-form wrought-iron mount, shade & base signed in cameo "A. Delatte - Nancy," ca. 1925, 7" d., 17½" h. 2,875.00

Cameo vase, 5" h., baluster-form, yellow overlaid in orange & dark burgundy, carved w/an orchid blossom & a bud, engraved "A DELATTE NANCY" 1,100.00

Cameo vase, 6¼" h., flattened bulbous spherical body tapering to a short cylindrical neck w/flat rim, applied tooled frosted white loop handles on the shoulder, pink & frosted white overlaid in raspberry pink & cut w/a waterfront Venetian-style cityscape, selectively polished, signed at the side "A. DeLatte - Nancy" 1,210.00

Cameo vase, 7⅜" h., teardrop-form body on a small footring, the sides tapering to a short swelled neck w/flat rim, clear splashed w/lime green & overlaid in amber, finely wheel-carved w/an iris blossom & leafage, signed in intaglio "A DeLatte - Nancy," ca. 1920 ....575.00

Cameo vase, 13½" h., flaring cylindrical body, yellow overlaid in black & cut w/an Art Deco-style border of stylized flowers & a diaper pattern of square dots, raised on a textured wrought-iron base of circular rings decorated w/bosses & fan designs, signed in enamel "DE LATTE - NANCY," ca. 1925......575.00

Vase, 15½" h., elongated ovoid, grey acid-etched w/bands & chevron patterns, w/a medial band of highly stylized flowers in orange,cobalt blue, grey, black & green, the upper & lower sections enameled in transparent blue, signed in cameo

Enameled & Etched DeLatte Vase

"ADELATTE - NANCY," ca. 1925
(ILLUS.) 3,450.00

DE VEZ & DEGUE

Degué Cameo Lamp

The Saint-Hilaire, Touvier, de Varreaux and Company of Pantin, France used the name De Vez on their cameo glass earlier this century. Some of their examples were marked "Degué," after one of their master glassmakers. Officially the company was named "Cristallerie de Pantin."

DeVez and Degué Marks

Cameo lamp, table model, 10½" d. domical shade raised on a baluster-

form base w/round foot, mottled white & yellow overlaid in deep red & etched to depicting morning glories, w/wrought-iron mount, shade & base w/cameo signature "Degué," overall 17¼" h. $2,300.00

Cameo lamp, table model, 19" d. stepped domical shade raised upon a slender ovoid base w/a cushion foot, each in pale blue shaded w/red & overlaid w/mottled blue shading to amethyst, cut w/a leafy forest scene, simple three-arm mount, shade & base each signed in cameo "Degué," ca. 1925, 26" h. (ILLUS.) 7,475.00

Cameo vase, 6¾" h., ovoid body w/everted rim, grey cased over white, overlaid in orange & emerald green & cut w/a tranquil Dutch river landscape, signed in cameo, ca. 1920..660.00

Cameo vase, 6¾" h., large squat form, mottled dark orange overlaid in white & purple, etched to depict flowering anemonies, etched "Degué"...345.00

Cameo vase, 7" h., expanding cylindrical body, bubble gum pink overlaid in navy blue & cut w/the scene of an Alsatian village on the banks of a mountainous lake, leafy trees & sailboats in the foreground, signed in cameo "DeVez," ca. 1920..825.00

De Vez Cameo Vase

Cameo vase, 10" h., cylindrical body w/bulging neck, lemon yellow splashed w/cherry red, overlaid in cherry red & navy blue & cut w/a mountainous landscape w/boating in

the near distance, the neck further
cut w/butterflies within flowerhead
surrounds, signed in cameo
"deVez," ca. 1920 (ILLUS.) 880.00

Cameo vase, 15¾" h., inverted pear
form w/wide mouth & bulbous base,
mottled greyish pink & yellow, cut
w/a continuous row of red flowers
on blue stems continuing to the
base, signed in intaglio "Degué,"
ca. 1925 ....748.00

Cameo vase, 16½" h., large inverted
pear-shaped body tapering to a
cushion foot & to a short, flared wide
neck, yellow cased in shaded
orange to brown & etched w/a band
of upright stylized blossoms above
broad serrated upright leaves,
etched "Degué" on the foot 1,430.00

Cameo vase, 18½" h., baluster-form,
mottled blue ground overlaid in
orange & brown, etched to depict
trees, etched "Degué" 1,265.00

Cameo vase, 18¾" h., ovoid body
w/swollen neck, raised on a flat
circular base, grey mottled w/orange
& red, overlaid in deep teal blue &
cut w/stylized bamboo leaves,
signed in cameo "Degué," inscribed
"Made in France" 920.00

Vase, 15" h., ovoid body applied at
the flat mouth w/three amethyst
handles looping down the sides &
joining a notched band, the body in
clear internally decorated w/mottled
shades of green, brown, yellow &
blue, inscribed "Degué - Made in
France," ca. 1928.........................1,495.00

Degué Acid-Etched Vase

Vase, 17" h., large baluster-form body
w/flaring rim, deep amethyst acid-
etched w/row of deep intersecting
arches, signed "Degué - Made in
France," ca. 1925 (ILLUS.) 1,380.00

DURAND

Durand Vase with Leaf Decoration

*The Vineland Flint Glass Works
Company of Vineland, New Jersey,
produced a range of decorative glass
similar to that of Louis Tiffany. Founded
by Victor Durand, Sr., the firm was taken
over by his son, Victor Durand, Jr. After
the younger Durand died in 1931 the
factory was merged into the Kimble Glass
Company and art glass production ceased.*

Bowl, 6" d., shallow cased bowl w/a
wide flattened & gently ruffled rim,
overall gold iridescence, signed
"V. Durand" $431.00

Center bowl, ruffled rim, red crackle
iridescent exterior, stretch iridescent
interior, 11" d..................................385.00

Center bowl, blue iridescence, signed,
14" w. 850.00

Jar, cov., wide tapering ovoid body
w/a domed cover centered on the
shouldered top, overall green & opal
white swirled & 'crackled' surface,
berry finial on the cover, overall
iridescent finish, unsigned, 10" h. 990.00

Vase, 4½" h., gold iridescence,
signed 395.00

Vase, 6³⁄₁₆" h., ovoid, amber
iridescence decorated w/heart-
shaped leaves & random trailing in
pale green, inscribed "Durand -
1968-6," ca. 1920............................575.00

Vase, 6⅞" h., ovoid body w/everted
rim, amber iridescence decorated
w/heart-shaped leafage & trailings
in green, inscribed "DURAND -
1710-9," ca. 1920 (ILLUS.) 748.00

Vase, 7" h., King Tut patt., the
shouldered ovoid body in brilliant
amber iridescence decorated
w/blue-green iridescent scrolls &
trailings, inscribed "Durand," ca.
1925..575.00

Iridescent Durand Vase

Vase, 7¾" h., squatty bulbous base
tapering to a trumpet-form neck,
brilliant silvery blue iridescence,
signed "Durand - 1986 - 8," ca. 1925
(ILLUS.) 518.00

Gold Durand Vase

Vase, 8" h., simple baluster-form
body w/flaring rim, overall smooth
orangish gold iridescence, inscribed
on base "V. Durand 1812-8"
(ILLUS.) 575.00

Vase, 8¼" h., King Tut patt., wide
footed baluster-form body w/a wide
short cylindrical neck w/flaring
flattened rim, cased amber to opal
w/gold iridescent interior, swirling
green hooked & coiled decoration
on the exterior, unsigned 1,210.00

Vase, 9¼" h., footed ovoid body
tapering to a short neck w/wide
flattened flaring rim, bright cobalt
blue w/iridescent gold heart-leaf &
vine decoration, gold iridized interior, base inscribed "Durand" 1,265.00

Vase, 9⅝" h., shouldered ovoid body,
brilliant amber iridescence decorated w/opalescent striated feathering edged in blue-green iridescence,
the whole w/applied amber

iridescent stringing, inscribed
"Durand - 1812-10," ca. 1925
(losses) 518.00

Vase, 11⅞" h., cylindrical w/squared
lip, brilliant amber iridescence
decorated w/opalescent heart-
shaped leafage & trailings, inscribed
"Durand," ca. 1925..........................518.00

Vase, 12" h., "Moorish" type crackle
glass, cushion foot tapering to a
trumpet-form body w/ten molded
ribs & overall crackled finish, ambergris w/gold iridescence, silver
mark "V. Durand" on base 1,035.00

Tall Decorated Durand Vase

Vase, 12⅛" h., tall ovoid body
w/waisted neck & flaring lip, brilliant
amber-orange iridescence
decorated w/green heart-shaped
leafage & trailings, inscribed
"Durand - 2011-12," ca. 1925
(ILLUS.) 805.00

Vase, 12⅜" h., shouldered ovoid
body, brilliant amber iridescence
decorated w/opalescent striated
feathering edged in blue iridescence, inscribed "Durand," ca.
1925..920.00

Vase, 16¼" h., globular body tapering
to a tall trumpet neck, brilliant blue
shading to purple iridescence,
signed "Durand - 1716.16," ca.
1900...1,380.00

FINDLAY ONYX & FLORADINE

*In January, 1889, the glass firm of
Dalzell, Gilmore & Leighton Co. of
Findlay, Ohio began production of these
scarce glass lines. Onyx ware was a white-
lined glass produced mainly in onyx*

(creamy yellowish-white) but also in bronze and ruby shades sometimes called cinnamon, rose or raspberry. Pieces featured raised flowers and leaves that are silver-colored or, less often, bronze. By contrast the Floradine line was produced in ruby and autumn leaf (gold) with opalescent flowers and leaves. It is not lined.

Findlay Onyx Celery Vase
Celery vase, creamy white w/silver
flowers & leaves, 6½" h. (ILLUS.) ..$495.00

Findlay Onyx Sugar Bowl
Creamer & cov. sugar bowl, creamy
white w/silver flowers & leaves,
pr. ((ILLUS. of sugar bowl)...........1,050.00

Findlay Onyx Spooner

Spooner, creamy white w/silver
flowers & leaves, 4½" h. (ILLUS.) 425.00

Findlay Onyx Sugar Shaker
Sugar shaker w/original top, creamy
white w/silver flowers & leaves,
5½" h. (ILLUS.) ....450.00 to 475.00

Sugar shaker w/original top, unlined
ruby w/white opalescent flowers &
leaves 495.00

Findlay Onyx Tumbler
Tumbler, barrel-shaped, creamy white
w/silver flowers & leaves, 2⅞" d.,
3¾" h. (ILLUS.) 325.00

Tumbler, cylindrical, creamy white
w/silver flowers & leaves,
3⅝" h...............................350.00 to 375.00

FIREGLOW

This glass, which somewhat resembles so-called Bristol glass, usually transmits a reddish-brown glow when held to strong light. Popular in the late Victorian era, a number of American and foreign firms produced pieces.

Pitcher, 8½" h., decorated w/h.p.
flowers & leaves............................$265.00

Vase, 8½" h., h.p. castle scene
decoration, England..........................45.00

Vase, 10" h., white shaded to green

ground decorated w/pink & purple enameled flowers, in gold-tone metal frame 175.00

Decorated Fireglow Vase

Vase, 11¾" h., 5" d., tall ovoid body tapering to a short gently flaring cylindrical neck, opaque peach pink satin ground decorated w/fine tan & maroon enameled birds & branches w/blossoms below a shoulder & neck design of stylized leaf bands (ILLUS.) 225.00

FRANCES WARE

Frances Ware Creamer

The name "Frances Ware" refers to a decorative treatment used on certain patterns of glass produced by Hobbs, Brockunier & Co., Wheeling, West Virginia, in the 1880s. Pieces were decorated with an amber-stained band at the rim while the lower body was left clear or frosted clear. Three patterns carried this treatment: Hobb's Hobnail pattern, their pattern No. 300 (Hobb's Block) and their swirled rib pattern, No. 326.

Butter dish, cov., frosted swirl
w/amber rim $65.00

Creamer, frosted hobnail w/amber rim
(ILLUS.) 60.00

Creamer & cov. sugar bowl, frosted hobnail w/amber rim, pr. 150.00

Cruet w/original stopper, frosted hobnail w/amber rim 695.00

Finger bowl, frosted hobnail w/amber rim 25.00

Frances Ware Hobnail Pitcher

Pitcher, 8½" h., square top, frosted hobnail w/amber rim
(ILLUS.) ....150.00 to 175.00

Salt shaker w/original top, frosted hobnail w/amber rim 150.00

Sauce dish, frosted hobnail w/amber rim 25.00

Spooner, frosted hobnail w/amber rim..70.00

Syrup pitcher w/original top, frosted hobnail w/amber rim 350.00

Table set: cov. butter dish, cov. sugar bowl, creamer & spooner; frosted swirl w/amber rim, 4 pcs. 275.00

Toothpick holder, frosted hobnail w/amber rim 62.00

Tumbler, frosted hobnail w/amber rim ..45.00

Water set: pitcher & six tumblers; frosted swirl w/amber rim, 7 pcs. 300.00

GALLÉ

Emile Gallé, the master glass artisan, founded the Nancy School in Nancy, France in the late 19th century and eventually became a leader in the Art Nouveau movement in France. His diverse glasswares, both enameled and cameo, were decorated with various naturalistic designs with major production in the 1890s and early 1900s. After Gallé's death in 1904, glasswares from his firm carried a star preceeding the mark on pieces. The factory closed in 1931.

Various Gallé Marks

Bottle w/original stopper, the wide flattened rectangular body w/a cylindrical neck at the top center fitted w/a flattened mushroom stopper, the body finely etched w/a cartouche reserve of a warrior on horseback against a gilt ground, the reverse w/a reserve of seated figures against a gilt ground, the ground elaborately etched w/Islamic-inspired foliate designs & further enameled in black, white & red, 4½" h. $12,650.00

Bottle w/stopper, bulbous cylindrical body w/the rounded shoulder tapering to a tiny neck w/flared rim & fitted w/a small domed stopper, clear 'crackle' design, finely enameled w/branches in black trimmed w/gilding & a grasshopper & fly in medium-relief in gold & burgundy, enameled "E.Gallé a Nancy," 6½" h. 4,140.00

Bottle w/stopper, cylindrical body w/rounded base & shoulder tapering to a small, short neck w/flattened rim & low domed stopper, the ice blue ground w/crackled pattern finely enameled w/branches in black trimmed w/gold & a grasshopper & fly in medium-relief in gold & burgundy, enameled "E. Gallé a Nancy," 6½" h. 3,450.00

Bottle w/original stopper, wide flattened oblong body w/wide, rounded shoulders to the short, flaring neck, smoky topaz etched w/heraldic shields on both sides, one side w/a medieval princess enameled in red, grey & gold, the verso w/a coat-of-arms, surmounted by a lozenge-shaped stopper w/gold foil inclusions, enameled mark "E. Gallé 1884," 9" h. 9,350.00

Bottle w/original stopper, flattened bulbous form w/bifurcated rim, the

Gallé Enameled Bottle

swirled celadon green body enameled *en grisaille* to depict an isolated lake scene w/architectural remains, framed by a curving branch in sienna & umber interspersed w/finely enameled shells in high relief, fitted w/a large tapered stopper decorated w/seaweed & a shell, all heightened w/gilding, enameled "CRISTALLERIE D'EMILE MODELE ET DECOR DEPOSES NANCY" & w/the maker's monogram, 9¼" h. (ILLUS.) 23,000.00

Bowl, 4¾" h., clear deep rounded sides of shield-form outline, composed of scalloped panels decorated w/hunting vignettes in gilt, carved w/scrolling vines & stylized floral designs, the border w/a shield diaper pattern trimmed w/burgundy & black enamel, enameled "Emile Gallé a Nancy" 2,875.00

Bowl, 7½" l. oval, deep slightly flaring ruffled sides, clear enameled w/large wildflowers in the foreground & a pond scene in the background *en grisaille*, gilt signature "Emile Gallé" 1,430.00

Cameo bowl, 8¾" d., footed squatty body, the upper half angled upward to a wide, flat mouth, pale frosted yellow overlaid in crimson & etched to depict flowering bleeding hearts, cameo signature 1,430.00

Cameo bowl, 10" d., the bulbous opalescent body internally decorated w/olive green splashes, overlaid in rose & cut w/magnolia blossoms & leafage, the ground w/martelé, signed in cameo "Cristallerie - de Gallé - Nancy," ca. 1900 ....3,300.00

Cameo bowl-vase, wide bulbous body tapering slightly toward the base, a rounded shoulder tapering to a wide short neck w/flat rim, bright yellow overlaid in burgundy & etched w/an intricate overall network of Persian-inspired flower & leaves w/a central cartouche on either side, one enclosing a mounted soldier w/bow & arrow, the other w/Persian-style letters, cameo signature, 4¾" h. 5,280.00

Cameo box, cov., wide & slightly tapering cylindrical sides, fitted w/a low, domed cover, frosted clear overlaid w/amethyst, the cover cut w/a dragonfly, the sides of the base cut w/a continuous leaf & berry design, cameo signature on base & cover, 2½" h. 1,045.00

Cameo box, cov., squatty bulbous body raised on a small foot, fitted low domed cover, grey mottled w/pink & overlaid in white, lavender & moss green, cut w/hydrangea blossoms & leafage, signed in cameo after a star, ca. 1904-10, 3⅜" h............1,380.00

Cameo box w/fitted lid, grey mottled w/lemon yellow, overlaid w/crimson & deep red & cut w/hibiscus blossoms & leafage, base & lid signed in cameo "Gallé," ca. 1900, 7¼" d., 3⅞" h. 4,830.00

Cameo compote, open, 6" h., conical w/flaring rim, the walls shading from pale yellow to lemon yellow, overlaid w/red & cut w/thorny rose stems, blossoms & foliage, signed in cameo "Gallé," ca. 1900 ....3,335.00

Cameo compote, open, 8" h., conical w/incurvate rim, raised on a slender standard & circular foot, grey mottled w/pale tangerine, overlaid in lime green & dark amber & cut w/a pattern of vining hops & foliage, signed in cameo "Gallé," ca. 1900 ....2,645.00

Cameo jar w/silver cover, the squared cylindrical body of frosted yellow overlaid in ruby red, each side etched w/an oval panel depicting flowering branches & foliage, the short neck mounted w/silver & fitted w/a domed round silver cover finely tooled w/a fierce fire-breathing dragon, jar etched "Gallé," cover w/hallmarks of Lefebvre, 7" h........2,875.00

Cameo lamp, table-type, the semi-spherical shade & bulbous ovoid base each w/a yellow & white frosted ground overlaid w/purplish blue & cut to represent flowering chrysanthemums, cameo signature on shade & base, shade 8¾" d., overall 12⅝" h. 20,700.00

Cameo lamp, table-type, the tapering elongated floriform shade in grey mottled w/pale orange, overlaid w/lime green & olive green & cut w/multiple blossoms & leafage, suspended from a curved gilt-bronze stem cast w/leafage above a circular base, shade signed in cameo "Gallé," ca. 1900, 18⅝" h. 3,565.00

Cameo perfume bottle w/teardrop stopper, slightly tapering cylindrical shouldered body w/a short neck w/flared rim, pale salmon overlaid in periwinkle blue & cut w/undulating convolvulus blossoms & leafage, signed in cameo, ca. 1910, 7⅝" h.................................1,093.00

Cameo vase, 4⅞" h., the double conical vessel w/short rolled lip w/grey sides shading to rich lemon yellow, internally decorated w/sea green & turquoise trailings suggesting algae, overlaid in amber, ochre & rich deep pumpkin & finely wheel-carved w/a Portuguese man-o-war, a starfish, sea grasses & other underwater vegetation, the sides partially martelé, signed in intaglio "Gallé," ca. 1900.............10,350.00

Cameo vase, 5⅝" h., ovoid shouldered body w/a short rolled neck, pale grey overlaid in purple & etched w/stems & blossoms, the whole polished, signed "Cristallerie d'E Gallé, Nancy Modele et decor deposes," early 20th c. 1,380.00

Cameo vase, 6" h., bulbous w/a tall cylindrical neck, grey mottling to pink & green in parts, overlaid in reddish brown & green & cut w/fruiting acorn branches, signed in cameo "Gallé," ca. 1900...............978.00

Cameo vase, 6" h., spherical body tapering to a short, flared neck, clear frosted ground overlaid in lime green & umber, cut to depict a serene wooded lake scene, cameo signature 1,725.00

Cameo vase, 8" h., *marquetrie-sur-verre*, bulbous base & long slender neck, grey internally mottled w/amber & finely textured bubbles, inlaid in pale lavender, amber, white, yellow & teal blue w/a daffodil blossom & leafage, the leaves partially wheel-carved, the whole fire-polished, signed in intaglio "Gallé," ca. 1900 ....34,500.00

Gallé Cameo Vases

Cameo vase, 8½" h., footed ovoid body tapering to a short flaring neck, grey shaded w/lavender & overlaid in olive green & cut w/chestnut branches & leafage, signed in cameo, ca. 1900 (ILLUS. left) 1,495.00

Cameo vase, 8½" h., slightly flattened teardrop form, clear mottled to pale blue & deeper blue at bottom, overlaid in pale amber, pink & green & cut w/apple blossoms, signed in cameo "Gallé," ca. 1900 ....1,610.00

Cameo vase, 9½" h., slender ovoid body raised on a pedestal foot, lemon yellow overlaid in cobalt blue & purple & cut w/sprays of wildflowers & leafage, signed in cameo, ca. 1900 (ILLUS. right).................1,610.00

Cameo vase, 10½" h., cylindrical body w/a narrow shoulder to the short flared neck, grey mottled w/turquoise blue & overlaid in deep amber & cut in an aquatic landscape w/arrowroot blossoms & leafage & water lilies, signed in cameo "Gallé" after a star, 1904-10 ....2,875.00

Cameo vase, 13¼" h., elongated oval on a flaring foot, frosted white, pink & blue layered in pink & green, etched, wheel-cut & polished w/wild geranium blossoms & leafy stems, "Gallé" in design...........................1,320.00

Cameo vase, 13½" h., internally decorated *marquetrie-sur-verre,* tall ovoid body on a thick cushion foot, grey internally decorated w/streaks of purple & amber, the bulbous base w/teal blue opalescence, inlaid

Gallé 'Marquetrie-sur-Verre' Vase

w/large crocus blossoms in purple & amber, each finely wheel-carved, signed in intaglio, ca. 1900 (ILLUS.) 20,700.00

Cameo vase, 14" h., ovoid body, the green walls overlaid w/amber & brown & cut w/leafy branches pendent w/ berries, signed in cameo "Gallé," ca. 1900 ....4,600.00

Cameo vase, 14½" h., conical body w/a rounded base & tapering to a flaring rim, yellow overlaid in crimson, mold-blown & etched to depict a design of flowering calla lilies & foliage, signed 79,500.00

Gallé Cameo Polar Bears Vase

Cameo vase, 14½" h., bulbous ovoid body tapering to a small flaring mouth, pale turquoise blue overlaid in frosty white & cut w/a scene of three polar bears striding on ice floes in choppy waters w/icebergs in the distance, signed in cameo, ca. 1900 (ILLUS.) 48,875.00

Cameo vase, 15½" h., a tapering cylindrical body w/a wide shoulder to the short, rolled neck, cream ground overlaid in caramel, etched to depict fruiting branches & leaves, the entire piece wheel-polished, cameo signature 2,875.00

Cameo vase, 17⅜" h., swollen cylindrical form, grey mottled w/ochre & lime green, overlaid in lime green & olive, cut w/a pattern of unfurling fern fronds, signed in cameo "Gallé," ca. 1900 ....2,875.00

Cameo vase, 17⅝" h., expanding cylinder w/shaped rim, pale amber cut w/chrysanthemum blossoms & leafage, enameled in shades of pink, rose red, ochre yellow, peach & brown, heightened in gilt, signed in gilt cameo "Gallé," ca. 1900 ......5,175.00

Cameo vase, 23½" h., tall conical body w/flaring rim, grey mottled w/ochre yellow & overlaid in cobalt blue & purple & cut w/tall stalks of delphinium blossoms & leafage, signed in cameo, ca. 1900 ....28,750.00

Tall Gallé Cameo Vase

Cameo vase, 25½" h., wide cushion foot on a tall, slender gently tapering body w/a flared rim, grey mottled w/mustard yellow, overlaid in caramel & cut w/a river & forest landscape, signed in cameo, ca. 1900 (ILLUS.) 5,750.00

Decanter w/original stopper, ruffled foot, ovoid body w/long slender neck, the paneled body decorated in enamel w/a spray of apple blossoms & a dragonfly in green, pink & blue, heightened in gilt, signed in enamel "E. Gallé - 5," ca. 1890, 11¼" h. ...1,380.00

Ewer, tankard-form, olive green w/applied band of glass from top of handle curving across the front & continuing to the base, further decorated w/wildflowers enameled in shades of purple, lavender, green & yellow, heightened in gilt, signed in gilt intaglio "Cristallerie - d'Emile Gallé," ca. 1900, 11¼" h. 3,450.00

Enameled Gallé Perfume Bottle

Perfume bottle w/stopper, squatty bulbous body below a cushion-form neck tapering to a flat rim, acorn-form stopper, pale transparent celadon green enameled w/sea grasses & shells in shades of chocolate brown, Chinese red, rose, cream & white, the sides further enameled *en grisaille* w/a landscape w/a turreted castle in the distance, the stopper further enameled w/a shell, signed in enamel "Cristallerie d'Emile Gallé - Nancy - Model et décor déposés - EG," ca. 1890, 5½" h. (ILLUS.) ...13,800.00

Scent bottle w/stopper, short wide cylindrical body w/the wide flat shoulder centered by a tiny short neck w/flared rim supporting pale amber floriform stopper, the body in opalescent grey overlaid in teal blue & cut w/berries & leafage, signed in cameo, 3¾" h. 3,163.00

Vase, 4½" h., bulbous squared sides w/a closed rim, on applied ruffled foot, pale topaz enameled w/a dragonfly & lilies-of-the-valley in shades of burnt orange, light blue & chartreuse, all trimmed w/gilding, signed in enamel...........................2,013.00

Vase, 5¾" h., footed wide ovoid body w/a wide incurved mouth, rich mottled amber w/a honeycomb pattern, enameled w/flowering branches & hovering bees in naturalistic colors trimmed w/gold, etched stylized honeycomb signature "EMILE GALLE FECIT" & enameled "Modele et decor déposés" 4,830.00

Vase, 7⅛" h., squatty bulbous body tapering to a wide pinched, pulled & everted rim, marine blue acid-etched on the interior w/a veiny leaf design, the exterior enameled w/blossoms, leafage, a cicada & a grasshopper, in various shades of enamel & trimmed in gold, inscribed & gilded "Emile Gallé - Serie B déposée," ca. 1890...2,875.00

Etched & Enameled Gallé Vase

Vase, 8½" h., swelled cylindrical body, etched & enameled w/decorative Islamic designs, featuring three cartouches within the design, one depicting a man flanked by birds, another of a horseman, the third of a standing figure, engraved "Emile Gallé" (ILLUS.) 17,250.00

Very Tall Enameled Gallé Vase

Vase, 23¼" h., squatty cushion base tapering to a very tall cylindrical neck, translucent ambergris etched w/floral blossoms & long leafy stems & embellished w/multicolored enamel & gilt trim, signed in cameo (ILLUS.) 3,737.00

Water set: 9⅝" h. pitcher & four tumblers; the footed ovoid pitcher tapering to a cylindrical neck over slightly paneled sides enameled on the obverse w/figures clothed in 19th c. costume at various pursuits including a maiden pouring a glass of wine for a young man seated at a table in red, blue, yellow & black, within foliate borders, the reverse enameled w/various phrases including "Quanrd le vin - a tiré - foi le boir" in white, the cylindrical tumblers w/matching figures, signed in enamel "E. Gallé - déposé," ca. 1890, the set................................2,300.00

HOBBS, BROCKUNIER & CO.

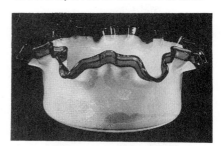

Decorative Hobbs, Brockunier Bowl

The Hobbs Company originated about 1845 in Wheeling, West Virginia with the founding of Hobbs, Barnes & Co. by John L. Hobbs and James B. Barnes, both former employees of the New England Glass Company. Their sons eventually joined the firm and in 1863 the company became Hobbs, Brockunier & Co. when John L. and John H. Hobbs and Charles Brockunier took over. That year they hired William Leighton, Sr., former superintendent of the New England Glass Company. Leighton took charge of production and in 1864 he revolutionized the American glass industry by devising a formula for soda lime glass, a cheaper method of producing clear glass which didn't require lead oxide. By the 1880s Hobbs was producing a number of decorative glassware lines including Peach

Blow, Spangled, pressed Amberina and various opalescent patterns. The plant closed in the 1890s. Also see OPALESCENT GLASS.

Bowl, 10" d., 3½" h., blown, pale lemon yellow w/wide band of applied ruffled cranberry at rim (ILLUS.) ....$200.00 to 225.00

Celery vase, square, pressed Daisy & Button patt., No. 101, tab-handled rim, vaseline......................................85.00

Cheese dish, cov., mold-blown, Inverted Thumbprint patt. cover, pressed Daisy & Button patt. base, blue 75.00

Creamer, Satina Swirl patt., yellow satin 95.00

Cruet w/original stopper, Hobnail patt., vaseline opalescent 215.00

Cruet w/original stopper, Inverted Thumbprint patt., cranberry 195.00

Toothpick holder, bulbous Ring Neck mold, Optic patt., Rubina 110.00

Butter dish, cov..............................$1,500.00

Spooner, base 2⅝" d., top 3½" d., 4" h..625.00

Toothpick holder (ILLUS.)...600.00 to 650.00

Holly Amber Tumbler

Tumbler (ILLUS.) ....350.00 to 375.00

Vase, 6" h., footed ....600.00 to 650.00

HOLLY AMBER

Holly Amber Toothpick Holder.

A rare pressed line of glass, Holly Amber was originally advertised under the name "Golden Agate" when it was introduced in 1903 by The Indiana Tumbler and Goblet Company, Greentown, Indiana. Only a few months after its introduction the Greentown factory burned to the ground and all production there ceased. The pressed "Holly" pattern was also produced in clear glass but it is the scarce milky opalescent shaded to amber version that commands very high prices today. The St. Clair Glass Company reproduced some Holly Amber pieces a number of years ago but careful study should help avoid any confusion between them and the original pieces.

HONESDALE

Honesdale Cameo Vase

The Honesdale Decorating Company, Honesdale, Pennsylvania, was originally founded to decorate glass for the C. Dorflinger & Sons firm. Purchased in 1918 by C.F. Prosch, the firm then bought other glass blanks which they etched and decorated. The factory closed in 1932.

Cameo vase, 14" h., tall baluster-form body w/widely flaring mouth, clear acid-textured sides overlaid in tangerine orange & cut w/chrysanthemums on leafy stems, trimmed w/gilt, signed (ILLUS.) ....$1,200.00 to 1,500.00

Tumblers, sherry, clear w/enameled
rooster decoration, 4½" h., set of 6..275.00

Vase, 12" h., tubular-shaped, iridescent ground w/gold enameling.........450.00

Vase, 12½" h., iridescent ground
decorated w/Greek Key design
w/medallions of horses & florals 295.00

Vase, 14½" h., clear etched w/geo-
metric designs w/yellow & gilt
details, signed, ca. 1900 ....412.00

JACK-IN-THE-PULPIT VASES

Jack-in-the-Pulpit Vases

*A wide range of free-blown and mold-
blown vases have been produced since the
late 19th century in this style. The name is
based on the form of the vases, which
resemble the jack-in-the-pulpit wildflower.
All sorts of solid color and shaded glasswares were produced in this unique shape.*

Cased, white opaque exterior, rose
interior, ovoid body w/applied
opaque white wishbone-shaped
feet, 3¼" d., 5" h. $75.00

Cased, white exterior, shaded green
interior, bulbous body w/applied
clear petal-shaped feet, 5½" d.,
6¼" h...110.00

Cased, white exterior, shaded pink
interior, swirling ruffled rim, 6½" d.,
6½" h...110.00

Chartreuse green opalescent,
trumpet-form w/crimped rim, 4½" d.,
7¼" h. (ILLUS. right) 65.00

Deep orange opalescent shading to
green, a spherical ribbed body
below a widely flaring rim, applied
vaseline leaf feet, 3" d., 5½" h.
(ILLUS. left).....................................125.00

Maroon Opalescent Vase

Maroon opalescent shaded to
vaseline, trumpet-form w/ruffled rim
4¼" d., 7¼" h. (ILLUS.) 75.00

Sapphire Blue Decorated Vase

Sapphire blue, squatty bulbous base
below a wide cylindrical body w/a
crimped & ruffled rim, Diamond
Quilted patt., enameled w/dainty
pink flowers w/green & gold foliage,
gold rim band, 4⅝" d., 9⅜" h.
(ILLUS.) 245.00

Spatter, tapering cylindrical body,
green, white & pink spatter interior,
green exterior w/diamond quilted
design, 4¼" d., 6¾" h. 95.00

White opalescent w/applied ruffled
green edging, 4½" h............................45.00

KELVA

This ware is another decorative line of

glass produced by the C.F. Monroe Co., Meriden, Connecticut, early in this century. It is also an opal glass with molded designs and hand-painted decorations, closely related to Wave Crest and Nakara, the Monroe firm's other notable lines. Production ceased by World War I. Also see NAKARA and WAVE CREST.

Kelva Hexagonal Box

Box w/hinged lid, Hexagonal mold, lid decorated w/a molded yellow rose on a mottled green ground, 3¾" d., 2½" h. (ILLUS.) $590.00

Box w/hinged lid, Octagonal mold, lid enameled w/pink & white flowers on a mottled green ground, 4" w., 3¾" h..325.00

Kelva Rose Ground Box

Box w/hinged lid, lid decorated w/white flowers & green leaves on a mottled rose ground, 4½" d., 2½" h. (ILLUS.) 425.00

Box w/hinged lid, lid decorated w/pink flowers on a mottled bluish grey ground, mirror inside the lid, 4½" d..515.00

Box w/hinged lid, heavy gold floral decoration on a dark green ground, 5½" d., 5" h. 350.00

Box w/hinged lid, bluish-grey flowers on red ground, 6" d., 3½" h. 695.00

Box w/hinged lid, pink flowers on blue ground, 6" d., 3½" h. 695.00

Humidor w/hinged cover, mottled blue ground, "Cigars" in gold across the front, 5" d. 795.00

Jewelry dish, dainty pink flowers on a mottled green ground, ornate ormolu handles & rim, signed, overall 4½" w...185.00

Watch box, cov., green mottled ground w/dusty rose floral & beige ribbon, heavy beading on cover, ornate ormolu fittings (one bead missing) 550.00

KEW BLAS

Kew Blas Candlestick

In the 1890s the Union Glass Works, Somerville, Massachusetts, produced a line of iridescent glasswares closely resembling Louis Tiffany's wares. The name was derived from an anagram of the name of the factory's manager, William S. Blake.

Candlestick, cylindrical socket w/flattened wide rim raised on a swirled baluster-form shaft on a round foot, overall gold iridescence, inscribed mark, 8¼" h. (ILLUS.) $247.50

Vase, 7" h., elongated ovoid w/flaring rim, gold iridescent & green diagonally striped large fishscale design, engraved "Kew Blas"..........605.00

Vase, 9" h., waisted cylindrical body w/scalloped rim, overall gold iridescence w/carved bees 715.00

Vase, 10" h., cylindrical w/flared base, rim w/alternating peaks & lower scallops, iridescent gold body w/repeating green pulled leaf decoration, inscribed "Kew Blas" 302.50

LALIQUE

Lalique "Longchamps" Book End

Lalique is synonymous with the finest quality glass produced in France this century. Founded around 1910 by noted designer René Lalique, the factory has produced a wide range of colored and clear molded glass, especially in the Art Deco style of the 1920s and 1930s. The company was led by René's son, Marc, until his death in 1977 and today the firm is lead by Marc's daughter, Marie-Claude. All pieces of Lalique are clearly marked, usually on or near the bottom and either an engraved or molded signature was used. Pieces were marked "R. Lalique" until René Lalique's death in 1945 and thereafter, just "Lalique." Most pieces listed here will date before 1945.

R LALIQUE
FRANCE

R.LALIQUE
FRANCE

R. Lalique France N°3152

Stamped & Engraved Lalique Marks

Ashtray, "Feuilles," oval w/circular recessed cavetto in brilliant cobalt blue molded in low-relief w/leaves, inscribed "R. Lalique," introduced in 1928, 6⅞" l. $1,870.00

Ashtray, "Medicis," oval reserve w/a wide oval rim in opalescent, the rim molded in low-relief w/pairs of languishing nude maidens within a garland of flowers, original navy blue patina, molded "R. LALIQUE" & inscribed "France," 5⅞" l. 920.00

Bar pin, "Barrette Aubepines," a narrow rectangle of frosted clear molded in low-relief w/flowering stems, backed w/pale teal foil, brass backing w/a pin, stamped "LALIQUE" & w/artist's monogram, 2¾" l. 1,725.00

Beakers, "Coq Et Plumes," tapering cylindrical vessel molded in medium- & low-relief w/a band of strutting roosters, their feathery tails encircling the acid-etched sides, traces of blue patina, inscribed "R. LALIQUE, FRANCE," introduced in 1928, 6¼" h., pr. 1,430.00

Bonbonniere, cov., "Cigales," the cover molded w/twelve cicada flies, opalescent, impressed "R. Lalique," w/original satin-lined composition box, 10" d., 2" h. 1,100.00

Book ends, "Longchamps," the greyish crystal figural horse head hood ornament w/a threaded chrome radiator cap base mounted on a rectangular black glass base, molded "R. Lalique France," 3¾ x 6½", 6½" h., pr. (ILLUS. of one) 7,475.00

Bottle w/tiara stopper, "Trois Hirondelles," the clear plain slightly tapering cylindrical body wheel-carved w/"VOEUX DE D'ANCONA," the wide flat long fanned stopper molded w/three large birds in flight in frosted on clear, stopper engraved "R. Lalique France," 5" h. 14,950.00

Bowl, 8" d., "Volutes," gently rounded sides, molded w/swirling bubbles, stamped "R. LALIQUE - FRANCE," introduced in 1934 ....633.00

Bowl, 8½" d., "Ondines," shallow rounded sides w/a molded band of swirled female nudes around the bottom, opalescent, signed "R. LALIQUE FRANCE".........................977.00

Bowl, 8½" d., wide shallow sides, the underside molded in low-relief w/three large morning glory blossoms, their centers extending to form feet, clear & frosted, introduced in 1921, molded "R. LALIQUE," inscribed "FRANCE" 1,265.00

Bowl, 11¾" d., "Coquilles," shallow body molded on the underside in low- & medium-relief w/overlapping scallop shells, shading to pale amber in the center, inscribed "R. LALIQUE - FRANCE," introduced in 1924 ....1,093.00

Bowl, 12½" d., "Muguet," flared sides molded w/lily-of-the-valley blossoms radiating from the center, stamped mark "R. LALIQUE FRANCE," opalescent w/blue patina 1,265.00

Lalique "Madagascar" Bowl

Bowl, 13" d., 4¾" h., "Madagascar," deep rounded sides molded around the rim w/twelve monkey faces, opalescent, molded mark on rim "R. Lalique France" (ILLUS.).........6,875.00

Bowl, 13⅞" d., "Calypso," wide shallow grey body molded w/five mermaids on the exterior, inscribed "Lalique France"...........................2,415.00

Bowl, 15¼" d., "Flora-Bella," circular w/flaring rim, molded on the exterior in medium-relief w/a flower blossom, the center surrounded by overlapping petals, cobalt blue, inscribed "R. LALIQUE FRANCE - no. 407," introduced in 1930 ....3,630.00

Box, cov., "Veronique," the cover molded in low-relief w/two ribbon-tied bouquets, black, molded "R. LALIQUE," inscribed "France," introduced in 1919, 3⅛" d. 1,760.00

Box, cov., "Genevieve,"' circular, the cover molded w/two doves sitting on a branch & surrounded by stylized pine branches, blue patina, engraved "R. Lalique France No. 65," 4" d. 528.00

Box, cov., "Hirondelles," rectangular, the base molded w/chevrons, the cover w/swallows, frosted clear, molded mark "R. LALIQUE" & etched "Lalique," 4" l. 605.00

Brooch, "Mouches," circular frosted disc molded in high-relief w/entwined wasps, gilt-metal mount, impressed "LALIQUE FRANCE," introduced 1911, 1¾" d. 1,035.00

Candlesticks, "Mesanges," the standard cast as a flowery wreath w/a plump bird perched in the center, frosted clear, introduced in 1943, inscribed "Lalique," 6½" h., pr. 978.00

Center bowl, "Nemours," deep rounded sides w/a flat rim, molded

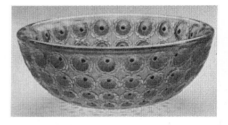

Lalique "Nemours" Center Bowl

w/graduated rows of daisies decorated w/black enamel centers & overall dark sepia patina on clear, molded mark at center "R. Lalique France," 10" d., 4" h. (ILLUS.).......1,035.00

Center bowl, "Sirenes," flattened flared rim molded w/eight full-length nude women in different poses, frosted clear, 14¼" d., 2½" h.........1,300.00

Clock, "Deux Colombes," the arched case molded in relief w/a pair of birds & flowers, opalescent, 9½" h..3,960.00

Clock, "Inseparables," square flattened case molded w/a pair of lovebirds facing each other on either side of the round enameled dial w/Arabic numerals, center of dial also enameled in colors w/a pair of lovebirds, clear opalescent, molded R. LALIQUE" & engraved "France No. 760," 4½" h. 4,025.00

Clock, "Naiades," the square frosted opalescent body molded in low-relief w/six swimming mermaids centered by a circular clock face, molded "R. LALIQUE," introduced 1926, 4⅜" w., 4½" h. 3,450.00

Clock, "Quatre Moineaux Du Japon," the square frosted face molded in low- and medium-relief on the front w/four fat sparrows perched in flowering branches, enclosing a circular clock face in grey metal, inscribed "R. LALIQUE FRANCE," clock face embossed "ATO," impressed "MADE IN FRANCE," printed retailer's label "HONEGGER - LYON," introduced 1928, 7¼" h..3,163.00

Cordial set: a conical decanter w/a tall, slender neck & four-petal stopper & two slender cylindrical cordial tumblers; "Six Figurines," each piece in clear molded in relief w/narrow panels enclosing diaphanously-draped maidens w/brown patina in the recessed areas, decanter molded "R. LALIQUE," cordials engraved "R. Lalique - France," decanter 14" h., the set 3,850.00

Cups, "Ormeaux," wide rounded low sides w/angled tab leaf handle, molded overall w/elm leaves, clear w/blue patina, etched signature "R. LALIQUE," 4⅞" d., set of 4 ....275.00

Decanter w/original pointed spire stopper, "Sirenes et Grenouilles," bulbous body tapering to a slender tapering neck w/a flared rim, molded w/elongated panels of sinuous nudes amid surf w/frogs alternating w/wider ribbed panels, figural panels w/dark staining, engraved "R. Lalique France," 15½" h...............6,600.00

"Faucon" Hood Ornament

Hood ornament, "Faucon," modeled as a full-figure perched falcon, clear & frosted, molded "R. LALIQUE," inscribed "No. 1124," 5⅞" h. (ILLUS.) 1,265.00

Hood ornament, "Grande Libellule," modeled as a dragonfly perched w/wings aloft, grey, faint mold mark & script engraved "R. Lalique France," 8¼" h. 4,400.00

Hood ornament, "Tete d'Aigle," molded as an eagle's head on a circular base, clear, molded "R. LALIQUE," 4" h. 805.00

Hood ornament, "Tete de Belier," molded as the head of a ram, grey, molded "R. LALIQUE FRANCE," introduced in 1928, 3¾" h. (chip on left ear, minor flecks) 1,093.00

Lamp, table model, "Saint-Vincent," the wide domical shade molded w/bands of large stylized grape clusters & leaves separated by plain bands, raised on a straight octag-

onal base w/flaring foot, clear frosted, shade molded "R. LALIQUE FRANCE," 16½" h. 9,775.00

Lalique Table Lamp

Lamp, table model, the standard molded w/five horizontal panels of peonies & leafage, mounted on a black marble base, frosted clear, w/a modern black silk shade, minor chips to base, acid signature "R. LALIQUE - FRANCE," ca. 1925, 28½" h. (ILLUS.) 5,750.00

Lamp base, "Papillons," the flat tapering standard molded w/overlapping butterflies, fitting into a rectangular pyramidal base also molded w/butterflies, conjoined by a silver-colored metal mount, frosted, inscribed "Lalique," introduced 1919, 14⅜" h. (minor chips to base, top mount loose from base) 4,600.00

Luminiere, "Thais," modeled as a nude female dancer w/outstretched arms draped w/fabric, opalescent, signed "R. Lalique - France," introduced in 1925, 10¾" h. 10,350.00

Pendant, "Fioret," rondel w/molded seated nude woman among flowers, rose patina, mold pierced for silk cord, signed in mold.........................385.00

Perfume bottle, "Amphitrite," molded in full-relief w/a crouching maiden stopper above a coiled snail shell bottle, turquoise, molded "R. LALIQUE," introduced in 1920, 4" h...6,038.00

Perfume bottle, "Bouchon Cassis," cylindrical, molded in a low- and medium-relief paneled effect, the top molded as stems of black currants, clear & black, molded "R. LALIQUE," inscribed "France," introduced in 1920, 4½" h. 7,475.00

Lalique Perfume Bottle

Perfume bottle w/figural stopper, "L'Air du Temps," clear ovoid bottle w/molded, swirled ribs, figural stopper molded as two lovebirds, introduced in 1947, w/original contents, inscribed "Lalique," 12½" h. (ILLUS.) 1,955.00

Plaque, "Hirondelles," molded as two birds in flight, frosted grey, fitting into a rectangular bronze base cast w/random flowerheads, plaque molded "R. LALIQUE," introduced in 1922, 12" l., 14½" h. (chip to lower edge) 4,888.00

Plate, salad, 8" l. crescent-shaped, clear molded w/six frosted thistle blossoms encircled by thorny branches, signed "Lalique France" ..345.00

Plate, 13¾" d., "Ormeaux No. 2," molded on the underside in low-relief w/bands of leafage, original green patina, introduced in 1931, acid-stamped R. LALIQUE - FRANCE" 920.00

Statuette, "Grande Nue Bas Leves," clear frosted figure of a nude female w/arms up & standing on a rectangular base, wheel-cut signature "R. LALIQUE FRANCE," 23" h. (base cracked) 5,980.00

Statuette, "Source de la Fountaine Telphuse," cast as a standing maiden w/arms folded across her torso, mounted on a stepped chromed-metal base, frosted grey, unsigned, introduced in 1924, 21¼" h. (ILLUS. top next column) 8,338.00

Stemware: ten sherry & eight water glasses; "Blois," clear w/the stems molded w/leaves below a plain swelled cylindrical bowl, introduced in 1930, marked "R. Lalique - France," 3⅛" & 4⅛" h., 18 pcs. 460.00

Tall Lalique Statuette

Lalique Stemware Service

Stemware service: conical decanter w/short flaring neck & flat blossom-form stopper, twelve water goblets, ten wine glasses & nine champagnes; all clear, each goblet w/a figural blossom stem, all inscribed "R. Lalique - France," introduced in 1924, decanter 10¾" h., 32 pcs. (ILLUS. of part) 3,738.00

Vase, 4¾" h., "Grenade," spherical body on a small footring, the top tapering to a short neck w/rolled rim, molded in shallow relief w/bands of graduated arches, medium bluish grey w/traces of original frosted white patina, inscribed "R. Lalique - France," introduced in 1930..........1,725.00

Vase, 4⅞" h., "Rennes," flaring ovoid body in frosted clear molded w/a frieze of stylized antelope, w/a frosted background of leafy foliage, acid-stamped "LALIQUE FRANCE" 403.00

Vase, 5⅛" h., "Moissac," the clear opalescent tapering conical body molded in high-relief w/vertical band

of ribbed leaves, inscribed "R.
LALIQUE FRANCE"......................1,725.00

Vase, 5⅝" h., "Avallon," flaring
cylindrical body molded in high-relief
w/birds perched in intertwining
berried branches, original green
patina on frosted opalescent,
inscribed "R. LALIQUE FRANCE
No. 986".......................................1,955.00

Vase, 6⅛" h., "Pierrefonds," grey
cylindrical body w/a flaring rim, the
sides flanked by large wide scrolling
pierced handles cast as stylized fern
fronds, inscribed "R. LALIQUE -
FRANCE," model introduced in 1926
(small chips on handles) 5,175.00

Vase, 6⅜" h., "Eucalyptus," bell-form
body molded in low-relief w/upright
leafage, raised on molded berry
feet, frosted opalescent w/original
pale blue patina, molded "R.
LALIQUE" 2,070.00

Vase, 6⅝" h., "Orly," swollen conical
body cast w/four demilune side
handles decorated w/ranges of
small graduated oval bubbles, clear,
introduced 1935 ....2,185.00

Lalique "Farandole" Vase

Vase, 7" h., 10¼" d., "Farandole,"
bright blue flaring sides above a
cylindrical base molded w/a
continuous band of naked cherubic
children dancing against a floral
ground, inscribed on base "R.
Lalique France" (ILLUS.) 15,400.00

Vase, 7⅜" h., "Oursin," spherical body
w/short flaring neck, molded as a
large sea urchin w/a knobbed &
striped surface, original blue patina
w/selectively polished areas, acid-
stamped "R. Lalique France"
(ILLUS. top next column) 935.00

Vase, 7½" h., "Graines," Alexandrite
(reactive: appears blue-green in
shadow; bright pink in light), lower
portion of body molded w/graduated

Lalique "Oursin" Vase

rows of marble-like devices, etched
"R. Lalique" on base (worn base
edge)..2,860.00

Vase, 8¼" h., "Domremy," ovoid,
sides molded in low- and high-relief
w/thistles & spiky leafage, frosted,
inscribed "R. Lalique France,"
molded "R. LALIQUE," introduced
1926..1,035.00

Vase, 9" h., "Marguerite," ovoid body
tapering to a small flared neck,
molded w/a profusion of daisies, the
white ground decorated in the
recesses w/black enamel high-
lighting the blossoms, molded
"R. LALIQUE"...............................2,990.00

Lalique "Borromée" Vase

Vase, 9⅛" h., "Borromée," bulbous
ovoid body tapering to a flared rim,
fiery blue opal molded w/a repeating
band of peacock heads, accented
w/grey wash, block signature "R.
Lalique France" (ILLUS.) 4,312.50

Vase, 9⅛" h., "Ronces," elongated
ovoid body w/narrow cylindrical
neck, molded in low- and medium-
relief w/intertwining thorny branches,
brilliant aquamarine, molded "R.
LALIQUE," inscribed "France,"
introduced 1921 ....3,450.00

Vase, 9¼" h., "Martin-Pecheurs," ovoid body tapering to a short flaring neck, molded in low-relief w/birds in various poses perched in leafy branches, molded "R. LALIQUE," introduced in 1923 (rim slightly ground) 9,775.00

Vase, 9⅝" h., "Bacchantes," tapering cylinder molded in high-relief w/nude maidens in various dance poses, frosted & opalescent clear, inscribed "R. LALIQUE - FRANCE," introduced in 1927 ....14,950.00

Lalique "Alicante" Vase

Vase, 10" h., "Alicante," large ovoid body molded in medium-relief w/three pairs of parakeets, emerald green cased over opalescent white, inscribed at a later date "R. Lalique France," introduced in 1927 (ILLUS.) 32,200.00

Vase, 10" h., "Perruches," wide ovoid body tapering to a short cylindrical neck, deep ruby red molded in low-relief w/paired lovebirds perched in flowering branches, retains amber patina, inscribed "R. Lalique," model introduced in 1919 (minor rim chips) 20,700.00

Lalique Wall Sconce

Vase, 10½" h., "Oran," slightly flaring wide cylindrical thick-walled body molded w/giant round peony blossoms amid stylized foliage, yellow, wheel-carved "R. LALIQUE FRANCE" 17,250.00

Wall sconce, upright flattened rectangular cylinder in grey molded w/rows of graduated dahlia blossoms, fits into a chrome framework, acid-stamped "R. LALIQUE - FRANCE," 4¾ x 6½", 13⅜" h. (ILLUS. bottom previous column) 1,840.00

(End of Lalique Section)

LEGRAS

Decorative Legras Pieces

The Legras glassworks of Saint Denis, France, produced cameo and enameled glass similar to that made by Gallé, Daum Nancy and other French works in the late 19th and early 20th century.

Typical Legras Mark

Basket, amber w/cream & brown spatter & gold Aventurine cased over deep cranberry "Mosaic" edge pulled up at four corners & rolled down inbetween, amber handle, 6½" h...$350.00

Bowl, 8½" d., 4¼" h., wide bottom w/angled sides to a wide short neck, clear frosted etched w/stylized Art Deco blossoms & enameled in bright red & black, signed in cameo

"Legras," "Made in France" on the base (ILLUS. right front) 632.50

Cameo compote, open, 7½" w., 5¼" h., wide tricorner bowl tapering to a wide pedestal, beige layered in carnelian & carved w/a large leaf design, signed "Legras St. D." 575.00

Cameo vase, 5⅞" h., tapering ovoid body w/a bulbous rim, mottled caramel cased in beige-opal & acid-etched & carved w/a riverscape w/trees & distant mountains, signed 632.50

Cameo vase, 6¼" h., ovoid body tapering to a flaring short neck, beige carnelian overlaid & etched & enameled w/sea grasses & shells, signed in cameo..............................402.50

Cameo vase, 7" h., baluster-shaped, opaque yellow overlaid & cameo-carved & enameled w/a coral & shell design, signed in cameo..................165.00

Cameo vase, 14¾" h., 5¼" d., tall ovoid body tapering to a short flared neck, amethyst stylized fountain on mottled, stippled lavender, signed "Legras" 995.00

Cameo vase, 16¼" h., tapering ovoid body on a cushion foot, clear cased to mottled white & brown & etched & engraved w/life-sized birds against an angular Art Deco border, in-scribed "Legras" on the side & "made in France" on the base..........935.00

Cameo vase, 18⅜" h., tall slightly swelled cylindrical body on a cushion foot, tapering up to a short flared neck, white layered in lavender & olive brown & acid-etched w/long draping wisteria blossoms & leaves down the sides, signed in cameo............................1,035.00

Cameo vase, 25½" h., tall slender waisted cylindrical form, carnelian cased to opaque pinkish beige & deeply etched w/flowerheads on slender leafy stems, enameled in naturalistic colors of green, amber & brown, signed in cameo "Legras" w/the Saint Denis mark (ILLUS. left)..3,450.00

Vase, 8⅜" h., ovoid body tapering to a short, narrow flaring neck, grey internally mottled w/white & yellow, acid-etched w/a stylized geometric band about the shoulder & enameled in deep burgundy, acid-etched & enameled "Legras," ca. 1930..460.00

Vase, 9½" h., tapering ovoid body w/a deep cupped mouth, clear & white speckled etched w/stylized grape-vines highlighted by green & purple enamel decoration, signed in cameo (ILLUS. right back) 575.00

Vase, 12½" h., ovoid body tapering to a short flaring neck, clear etched surface cut w/blossom sprays accented w/maroon enameling, signed on the side..........................825.00

Vase, 16" h., expanding cylinder w/tricorn mouth, h.p. & enamel decorated w/a winter scene w/houses & peasant woman in foreground, unsigned.......................275.00

Etched & Enameled Legras Vase

Vase, 25½" h., bottle-form, bulbous base below a tall stick neck, grey cut w/raspberries & leafy vines & enameled in shades of raspberry, engraved & enameled signature "Legras," & impressed "OVING-TONS - NEW YORK - PARIS," ca. 1920 (ILLUS.)..............................690.00

LE VERRE FRANCAIS

Various LeVerre Francais Marks

Glassware carrying this marking was produced at the French glass factory founded by Charles Schneider in 1908. A great deal of cameo glass was exported to the United States early in this century and much of it was marketed through Ovingtons in New York City.

Cameo bowl, 10" d., 4" h., tapering rounded sides in orange cased to mottled tortoiseshell, acid-etched w/five stylized scarab beetles, engraved mark "Le Verre Francais, France - Ovington, New York" $747.50

Cameo compote, 5⅜" d., 4¼" h., inverted dome-shaped bowl on a low foot, mottled yellowish pink overlaid in polished brown & acid-etched w/stylized Art Deco foliate design, signed.................................357.50

Le Verre Francais Boudoir Lamp

Cameo lamp, boudoir-type, domical shade w/angled sides raised on metal leaftip supports above a standard w/a bulbous top over tapering cylindrical sides ending on a lightly ruffled round foot, mottled white layered in polished bluish amethyst & etched w/an Art Deco design of stripes & overlapping ribbed fan devices, stylized oval blossoms & leafy stems on the lighted base, signed "Charder" at the side & "Le Verre Francais" on the foot, shade 6½" d., overall 14" h. (ILLUS.) 1,650.00

Cameo vase, 8¾" h., conical shouldered body w/tapering sides & flaring lip, grey mottled w/pale yellow shading to turquoise blue, overlaid in mottled reddish orange & royal blue & cut w/a design of pendent fuchsia blossoms, buds & leafage, signed in intaglio, ca. 1925..1,265.00

Cameo vase, 11½" h., shouldered ovoid body w/everted rim, grey mottled w/turquoise blue, overlaid in reddish orange shading to cobalt blue & cut w/a design of fuchsia blossoms, buds & leafage, inscribed "Le Verre Francais," & acid-stamped "FRANCE," ca. 1925 ......1,495.00

Cameo vase, 15½" h., elongated ovoid body raised on a low foot, mottled yellow overlaid in polished blue above & orange below w/a cameo design of exotic seed pods on stylized leafy stems, signed 825.00

Cameo vase, 15¾" h., bulbous ovoid body w/flaring neck & applied side handles, grey mottled w/pale amber, overlaid in deep mottled purple & cut w/a design of stylized pendent grape clusters, signed in intaglio, ca. 1925 ....1,265.00

Tall Le Verre Francais Cameo Vase

Cameo vase, 16" h., tall ovoid body w/flaring rim, mottled amber layered in brown, yellow, green & cut w/the Art Deco style Ming Tree design, etched "Charder - Le Verre Francais" at the lower side (ILLUS.).....1,870.00

Cameo vase, 16½" h., swollen cylindrical body w/flaring lip & applied side handles, grey mottled in pale yellow shading to turquoise blue, overlaid in royal blue, tomato red & orange & cut w/a design of fuchsia blossoms & buds, signed in intaglio, ca. 1920.........................2,185.00

Cameo vase, 17¾" h., double-gourd form body in 'Tango' orange overlaid w/mottled amethyst brown & cameo etched w/stylized berries, leaves & a panel border design, two applied loop handles at the center of the

Isides, etched signature "Le Verre Francais - France" 1,485.00

Cameo vase, 18½" h., slender ovoid body tapering to a flaring neck, grey shaded w/lemon yellow & mottled orange, overlaid w/brown & cut w/stylized architectural designs below a band of cats in various poses, inscribed "Le Verre Francais," ca. 1925 ....4,312.00

Cameo vase, 18½" h., tall slender slightly swelled cylindrical body w/a flat mouth flanked by small applied loop handles, raised on a short pedestal & cushion foot, mottled yellowish orange overlaid w/amethyst shaded to bright red, cameo-cut w/four Art Deco stylized floral panels, engraved "Le Verre Francais" on foot, "Charder" in cameo in the design.....................1,320.00

Le Verre Francais Cameo Vase

Cameo vase, 23" h., footed trumpet-form shouldered body w/a short rolled neck, grey mottled w/lemon yellow & orange, overlaid in mottled orange & red & cut w/stylized blos-soms & leafage, signed in cameo "Charder" & inscribed "Le Verre Francais," ca. 1925 (ILLUS.).........1,610.00

Cameo *veilleuse* (night light), conical, mottled white & yellow frosted ground overlaid in purple & red, etched w/stylized leaves, etched signature, "Le Verre francais," on a wrought-iron footed mount, 11" h..1,035.00

LIBBEY

In 1878 the New England Glass Company of Cambridge, Massachusetts

was leased to William L. Libbey who changed the company name to the New England Glass Works, W.L. Libbey and Son, Proprietors. William Libbey died in 1883 and his son, Edward D. Libbey, continued to operate the plant in Cambridge until 1888. That year the factory was closed and Libbey moved the company to Toledo, Ohio where he set up the firm again as the Libbey Glass Company. The Libbey firm continued to make some of the Art glass wares they had been famous for in New England but also became known for their fine Brilliant Period cut glass. In the early 20th century other fine quality wares were produced and today they continue to operate as a division of Owens-Illinois, Inc.

Libbey Silhouette Compote

Bowl, 2½" w., 5½" l., Amberina, rectangular, embossed vertical ribbing $285.00

Bowl, 5½" d., 2½" h., Amberina, bulbous base w/rectangular rim, ribbed pattern...................................285.00

Bowl, 6" d., 4" h., Amberina, paneled optic design w/ruffled rim, signed 595.00

Bowl, 6" d., Peking patt., pink, scalloped edge, Libbey-Nash series 100.00

Bowl, 7" d., clear shallow sides etched w/satin holly leaves & berries forming a large snowflake, flared rim cut w/satin icicles, signed 225.00

Candlesticks, pedestal foot supporting a bulbous base tapering to a tall cylindrical neck, intaglio-cut floral design, 12" h., pr.............................400.00

Chalice, overlay, green paneled bowl cut to clear w/overall design of deer & foliage, applied clear stem deco-rated w/cut teardrops & applied oc-tagonal cut base, signed, 5½" h.......295.00

Cocktail, Silhouette patt., clear bowl, frosted figural bear stem 75.00

Cocktail, Silhouette patt., clear bowl, opalescent figural kangaroo stem, signed, 6" h. ....100.00 to 125.00

Cocktail, Silhouette patt., clear bowl, opalescent figural squirrel stem, signed, 6" h. 90.00

Compote, open, 7½" d., 3¼" h., Amberina, a flattened & widely flaring rim on a rounded bowl raised on a short knop stem w/a round foot, marked "Amberina" & "Libbey" in a circle, ca. 1917.................................440.00

Compote, open, 11" d., 7½" h., Silhouette patt., wide crystal bowl on an opalescent figural elephant stem, signed (ILLUS.)...............................385.00

Console set: bowl & 12" h. candle-sticks; cobalt blue over clear, polished pontils, 3 pcs. 595.00

Cordial, Silhouette patt., clear bowl, opalescent figural greyhound stem 175.00

Maize Pattern Tumbler

Maize tumbler, creamy opaque w/blue husks (ILLUS.) 195.00

Maize tumbler, creamy opaque w/green husks trimmed in gold 135.00

Model of a shoe, embossed florals on the toe, peach shoe w/black heel 145.00

Sherbet, Silhouette patt., clear bowl, black figural squirrel stem, signed, 4" h...145.00

Engraved Libbey Decanter

Decanter w/pointed teardrop stopper, the clear footed inverted pear-shaped body tapering to a slender panel-cut neck w/flared rim, the body engraved w/a design of long-stemmed wheat & grain grasses w/an elaborate monogram, the stopper also engraved, signed, 13" h. (ILLUS.) 575.00

Goblet, Silhouette patt., clear bowl, opalescent figural monkey stem, Libbey-Nash series 145.00

Maize salt shaker w/original top, condiment size, creamy opaque 95.00

Maize sugar shaker w/original top, creamy opaque w/blue husks 170.00

Maize sugar shaker w/original top, creamy opaque w/green husks ....275.00 to 300.00

Libbey Silhouette Sherry

Sherry, Silhouette patt., clear bowl, opalescent figural monkey stem (ILLUS.) ....75.00 to 100.00

Vase, 8½" h., Diamond Quilted patt., cranberry, unsigned 185.00

Vase, 9" h., two applied handles, fuchsia flower etching on a clear ground, signed 120.00

Vases, 8" h., clear pedestal base, white opal ground w/pink pulled feather design, signed in pontil, pr...595.00

LOETZ

In the late 19th and early 20th century a range of decorative glasswares, much of it somewhat resembling Louis Tiffany's famous iridescent wares, was produced by the Bohemian company, J. Loetz Witwe of Klostermule. Today these wares are referred to as 'Loetz.' Some pieces carry an engraved mark.

Loetz, Austria

Engraved Loetz Mark

Basket, applied clear handle, iridescent green, signed, 9½" d., 17½" h...$385.00

Unusual Loetz Bowl

Bowl, 5½" h., the orange body w/rumpled rim set within an applied leaf-shaped iridescent blue base (ILLUS.) 1,150.00

Bowl, 10" d., 5½" h., yellow iridescent top portion w/flat flaring rim above a low-footed black base w/heavy blue mottled overlay forming a wavy border at midsection, design attributed to Dagobert Peche........3,500.00

Cameo vase, 9⅞" h., tall slender waisted cylindrical sides above a flaring base & flaring to a squatty bulbous wide top w/flaring rim, bottle green overlaid in greenish iridescence, acid-etched overall w/scrolling arabesques & stylized leafage, unsigned, ca. 1900..........1,725.00

Centerpiece, model of a large conch shell raised on a ruffled foot, gold decorated w/an iridescent oil spot design, 5½" h. 1,265.00

Centerpiece, star-pointed edge, blue 'oil spot' iridescent exterior, blue iridescent interior, signed "Loetz Czechoslovakia," 12" d. 550.00

Cracker jar, cov., random threading on iridescent green ground, silver plate rim, cover & bail handle 335.00

Ewer, the tall slender, curved neck pulled into a long peaked spout opposite a pulled strap handle, the wide squatty body w/a compressed shoulder, deep cobalt blue textured as elephant skin on the lower body & decorated w/silver iridescent spots, engraved "Loetz Austria," 10½" h..4,830.00

Garniture set: cov. box & pair of vases; footed vases w/black lower half & pink top, the compressed globular box w/black bottom section & pink top w/black ball finial, decorated w/black & white enameled designs, designed by Dagobert Peche, ca. 1916, box 5" h., vases 8⅛" h., 3 pcs. 1,725.00

Loetz Cuspidor-Form Vase

Vase, 3¾" h., 5¾" d., cuspidor-form w/a squatty bulbous body tapering sharply to a narrow neck below the widely flaring, flattened rim, brilliant ruby red w/blue iridescent 'oil spot' exterior, base pontil signed "Austria" w/double arrow & star mark (ILLUS.) 2,300.00

Vase, 4" h., rounded shoulder, low wide neck, amber w/vertically arranged threading, applied rim & applied gold iridescent full-form fruits, leaves & stems.......................467.50

Vase, 4⅞" h., ovoid body tapering to a tiny short flaring neck, cobalt blue decorated overall w/a fine bluish gold iridescent 'oil spot' finish 770.00

Vase, 5" h., pinched teardrop form, greenish amber iridescent decorated w/random blue & purple iridescent trailings, overlaid w/swirling engraved silver arabesques, signed "Loetz - Austria," numbered "68 - 1056," ca. 1900 ....5,175.00

Vase, 5" h., wide ovoid body tapering slightly to the pinched & flaring four-lobed rim, amber w/pulled iridescent gold feather decoration, engraved circular arrow mark & "Austria" 1,210.00

Vase, 6" h., iridescent amethyst decorated w/a silver overlay thistle design 225.00

Vase, 6" h., ovoid body tapering toward the everted & ruffled rim, the shoulder & neck deeply pinched, the gold iridescent ground decorated w/small circles interspersed w/large ruby red spots containing concentric rings, decoration attributed to Koloman Moser, ca. 1902.............7,700.00

Vase, 6¼" h., a squatty bulbous base below a widely flaring trumpet-form neck, deep violet blue at the base shading to apricot on the neck, decorated overall w/ silver iridescent 'oil spots' 2,760.00

Vase, 6½" h., wide ovoid body deeply pinched-in around the lower half & w/a tricorner pinched rim, cased yellow w/overall iridescent gold spotted surface 1,430.00

Loetz Vase with Columnar Handles

Vase, 7⅜" h., wide flattened rim above a cylindrical body flaring widely at the base, nearly straight columnar applied handles from underside of rim to the base, lemon yellow decorated w/silvery blue iridescent dashes & pulled trailings in salmon & lime green, designed by Josef Hoffman, ca. 1900, unsigned (ILLUS.) 11,500.00

Vase, 7½" h., a wide slightly tapering & undulating cylindrical body w/a tri-lobed rim, applied around the flat base w/three long teardrop-form feet, grey decorated w/iridescent amber & silvery blue waves & trail-ings, three large gold undulating bands w/navy lines, oil-spotting on the feet, attributed to Marie Kirschner, signed "Loetz - Austria," ca. 1900 ....20,700.00

Vase, 8" h., double-gourd form body tapering to a short cylindrical neck, dimpled grey shading from orange to amber, decorated w/silvery blue iridescent waves & trailings, shaded w/cobalt blue swirls at the base, signed "Loetz - Austria," ca. 1900...8,050.00

Vase, 8¾" h., bulbous base tapering to a widely flaring scalloped rim, the sides applied w/four full-length slender ribs which form raised feet at the base, amber iridescent deco-rated w/silvery blue swirls, signed "Loetz - Austria," ca. 1900 ....4,312.00

Vase, 8⅞" h., ovoid body tapering to a bulbous neck w/flaring rim, the lower body decorated w/raised upward-pulled "fork" devices in a row, the upper body & neck w/lime green iridescence, the lower raised designs in blue iridescence...........2,090.00

Loetz Vase with Pulled Feather Decor

Vase, 10" h., undulating conical body w/cylindrical neck & flared rim, brilliant iridescent yellow decorated w/salmon pink & silvery blue pulled feathering about the sides, the lower section overlaid in deepest purple w/silvery pulled trailings, inscribed "Loetz - Austria," ca. 1900 (ILLUS.)........................13,800.00

Vase, 10⅞" h., waisted ovoid w/slender undulating 'gooseneck' w/pulled rim, amber decorated w/pulled feathering in brilliant bluish green iridescence, unsigned, ca. 1900 ....5,175.00

Vase, 11¼" h., applied double reeded amber handles rising from shoulder to above the applied amber rim, ovoid cobalt blue body w/lustrous textured surface, polished pontil 522.50

Vase, 11¾" h., deeply waisted cylindrical body w/tripartite folded lip, clear streaked w/pale amber, decorated w/silvery blue & pale pink iridescent trailings, inscribed "Loetz - Austria," ca. 1900..........................2,588.00

Silver Overlay Loetz Vase

Vase, 12¾" h., squatty bulbous base tapering to a slightly swelled cylindrical body tapering to a flaring rim, deep cobalt blue decorated w/thin red trailings in a random design & overlaid w/a band of silver stylized bellflowers on thin stems above feathery fronds around the base, in the manner of Koloman Moser, ca. 1900, inscribed "Loetz - Austria," & enameled "1/174" & "579" (ILLUS.) 20,700.00

Vase, 13½" h., jack-in-the-pulpit type, free-blown floriform decorated w/striated gold amber pulled feather decoration w/gold & blue iridescent surface 1,430.00

Vase, 14⅝" h., tall slender waisted cylindrical shape w/a widely flaring base, pale lemon yellow opalescent body decorated around the lower half w/salmon pink trailing w/deep cinnamon wavy lines & randomly splashed silvery blue oil spots, unsigned, ca. 1900 ....3,163.00

Vase, 15¼" h., gently waisted cylindrical body, dark red shaded w/gun metal grey, decorated w/an iridescent silver & blue pulled feather design, unsigned, ca. 1900..........1,380.00

Vase, 16" h., cylindrical, grey decorated w/pulled trailings in silvery-blue iridescence & upright grasses in emerald green, the rim & base w/silver overlay, the grass design delineated by incising, signed "Loetz - Austria," ca. 1900 ....21,850.00

Vase, 19¾" h., tall trumpet-form body on a cushion foot & w/a widely flaring ruffled rim, rose iridescent body decorated w/silvery blue oil spotting & encased within angular silver overlay bands, unsigned, ca. 1900...3,768.00

LUSTRES

Decorated Cranberry Lustres

Lustres were Victorian glass vase-like decorative objects often hung around the rim with prisms. They were generally sold as matched pairs to be displayed on fireplace mantels. A wide range of colored glasswares were used in producing lustres and pieces were often highlighted with colored enameled decoration.

Bristol, scalloped bowl-form top supported on a cylindrical standard & domed round foot, pink satin ground decorated w/gold trim on cylindrical standard & foot, hung w/ten spear-point prisms, 5⅛" d., 12¼" h., pr. $595.00

Cranberry, wide dished & flaring bowl above a ringed knop over the baluster-form pedestal above a domed cushion foot, decorated w/gold sprigs & fanned leaves, facet-cut prisms from the bowl, 19th c., 11½" h., pr. (ILLUS.) 550.00

Opaque white cut to emerald green, a
tapered bowl w/a scalloped rim hung
w/facet-cut prisms above a pedestal
base, the white ground decorated
w/colored florals, Bohemia, late
19th c., pr..687.50

Pink overlay w/enameled floral
decoration & 23k gold trim, hung w/a
double row of long cut glass prisms,
15" h., pr. 550.00

MARY GREGORY

Mary Gregory Dresser Box

*Today any colored glass decorated with
white enameled silhouette-type figures,
generally children, is referred to as "Mary
Gregory." Early collectors of this Victorian
glass believed that it was produced at the
Boston and Sandwich Glass Company in
Sandwich, Massachusetts where a
decorator named Mary Gregory was
employed. Current research has proven,
however, that this type of glassware was
never produced at the Sandwich factory.
Miss Gregory, according to old records,
was assigned the painting of naturalistic
landscape scenes on larger items such as
lamps and shades, but she never painted
the charming children so long associated
with her name.*

*Today it is known that all Mary
Gregory-type wares were produced in
Bohemia beginning in the late 19th
century. It was extensively exported to
England and the U.S. well into this
century.*

*Further information is available by
consulting* The Glass Industry in
Sandwich, Volume 4, *by Raymond E.
Barlow and Joan E. Kaiser, and the new
book,* Mary Gregory Glassware, 1880-
1990, *by R. & D. Truitt.*

Apothecary jar, cov., cranberry, white
enameled girl gathering flowers w/a
basket of flowers at her feet, ornate
cover w/pointed finial, 16" h. $395.00

Box w/hinged lid, blue opaque, white
enameled young girl wearing a hat
& carrying a book on lid, 3⅛" d.,
1⅝" h..195.00

Box w/hinged lid, black amethyst,
white enameled young girls making
rose wreaths on lid, the detail
includes a basket & trees, white
enameled floral band on base, 7" d.,
3¼" h..225.00

Box w/hinged lid, cranberry, white
enameled girl nicely detailed on lid &
white enameled floral sprays around
base, brass feet & side ring handles,
2¾" d., 3½" h. 300.00

Box w/hinged lid, golden amber, white
enameled young girl holding a bird
on lid, brass feet & side ring hand-
les, 4" d., 4" h. 295.00

Box w/hinged lid, blue, white
enameled young boy on lid, metal
feet & side ring handles, 3¾" d.,
4¼" h..270.00

Box w/hinged lid, amber, white enameled young boy wearing a hat &
sitting on a fence on lid, brass feet &
side ring handles, 4¼" d., 4½" h. 375.00

Box w/hinged lid, cobalt blue, white
enameled young girl in a fancy
dress & bonnet & holding an
umbrella while watching birds in the
sky, background of florals & foliage
on lid, sides decorated w/florals,
brass frame w/ball feet, 5¼" d.,
5½" h..550.00

Box, cov., footed base, domed cover
w/tall teardrop-shaped finial, emerald green, white enameled young
boy lying in grass & watching a
butterfly on base, 3⅝" d., 6½" h.
(ILLUS.) 225.00

Creamer, cranberry, white enameled
young boy w/flowers 125.00

Creamer & open sugar bowl: tankard-
shaped creamer w/clear applied
handle, tapering cylindrical body
w/flaring rim, sugar bowl w/flaring
sides, sapphire blue, white enameled standing boy on creamer &
white enameled boy lying on ground
smelling the flowers on sugar,
4⅜" d., 2" h. sugar bowl, 2⅛" d.,
3¾" h. creamer, pr. 235.00

Cruet w/original clear stopper, applied
clear handle, sapphire blue, white
enameled girl holding a bird............125.00

Mary Gregory Decanter

Decanter w/original stopper, footed
amber spherical internally ribbed
body tapering to a cylindrical neck,
applied amber handle, bulbous
amber stopper, white enameled girl
in garden, 3½" d., 8¾" h. (ILLUS.) ...245.00

Decanter w/original clear blown
teardrop stopper, spherical base
tapering to a cylindrical neck
w/three-petal rim, lime green, white
enameled young boy holding a
flower & sitting on a chair, 5¼" d.,
10½" h...245.00

Decanter w/stopper, clear, white
enameled young boy w/a telescope,
13½" h..60.00

Mary Gregory Ewer

Ewer, turquoise blue opaque, footed
bulbous body tapering to a slender
cylindrical neck w/cupped rim,
applied blue handle, white enameled
girl holding flowers, 3" d., 5" h.
(ILLUS.) 175.00

Liqueur mug, cylindrical w/applied
sapphire blue handle, sapphire blue,
white enameled girl rolling a hoop,
1½" d., 2" h. 65.00

Lustres, cylindrical bowl w/ruffled rim,
cranberry, white enameled facing
pair of girls, one holding a flower &
the other holding up her apron,
colorful flowers surround both girls,
six 4½" l. prisms, overall 10¼" h.,
pr...2,025.00

Mug, electric blue, white enameled
girl, 4" h. 85.00

Rose bowl, cranberry, white enam-
eled young boy w/a bird..................145.00

Toothpick holder, citron, white
enameled girl standing in foliage
watching a bird................................250.00

Mary Gregory Dresser Tray

Tray, dresser, oval, orangish amber,
low rib-molded sides, white
enameled young boy & girl walking
in a landscape, 7¾ x 10½", 1" h.
(ILLUS.) 325.00

Mary Gregory Footed Tumbler

Tumbler, footed, tapering cylindrical
internally ribbed form, amber
w/white enameled girl in landscape,
2⅞" d., 4" h. (ILLUS.) 70.00

Vase, 3" h., spherical footed body w/a

Small Mary Gregory Vase

flaring cylindrical neck, mold-blown
optic ribbing, cranberry, white enameled young boy (ILLUS.) 225.00

Mary Gregory Vase with Girl

Vase, 3⅞" h., 2" d., footed bulbous
body tapering to a trumpet neck,
cranberry w/white enameled little girl
(ILLUS.) 125.00

Mary Gregory Vase with Boy

Vase, 7¾" h., 3" d., baluster-form
w/trumpet neck, medium green
w/white enameled boy in landscape
(ILLUS.) 135.00

Vase, 8" h., 3¼" d., bottle-form, a

Mary Gregory Bottle-Form Vase

cushion foot below the spherical
body tapering to a slender cylindrical
neck w/a cupped rim, cobalt blue
w/white enameled young lady in a
landscape (ILLUS.) 165.00

Vase, 8" h., 3" d., footed ovoid body,
royal blue, white enameled young
girl sitting on a bench.......................195.00

Vase, 8½" h., 3¾" d., bottle-shaped,
ovoid body tapering to a narrow
cylindrical neck w/slender ringed
rim, sapphire blue, white enameled
young girl holding flowers 195.00

Vase, 9⅝" h., 4¼" d., footed ovoid
body tapering to a short cylindrical
neck w/flared rim, opaque turquoise
blue, white enameled young girl 225.00

Vase, 9¾" h., pedestal foot, baluster-
form w/flat, flaring rim, black amethyst, white enameled young girl
wearing a hat 225.00

Vase, 11" h., cranberry, white enameled young girl w/basket 225.00

Vase, 12½" h., medium green, white
enameled figure of woman holding a
hoop around her w/birds perched on
it 330.00

Vase, 16¼" h., 5" d., footed baluster-
form w/deep shoulder, a short
cylindrical neck & a ringed wide
cylindrical rim, amethyst, white
enameled young girl tying her
bonnet while a young boy kneels
w/large mirror in front of her, ornate
ormolu footed base 995.00

Vases, 3¾" h., 2" d., spherical body
tapering to a tall flaring cylindrical
neck, cranberry, white enameled
boy on one & girl on the other,
facing pr. 225.00

Fine Mary Gregory Vases

Vases, 10⅜" h., 4½" d., baluster-form
w/ringed pedestal & cushion foot,
opaque turquoise blue, one w/white
enameled young boy on a tan
enameled ground, the other w/a
white enameled young girl standing
on a tan enameled ground, facing
pr. (ILLUS.) 550.00

Water set: 10" h. pitcher & four
tumblers; sapphire blue, white
enameled girl holding a staff on the
pitcher & white enameled boy or girl
on the tumblers, 5 pcs. 475.00

Water set: cov. tankard pitcher & six
tumblers; clear, white enameled
figures of children at play, hinged
pewter lid on pitcher, 7 pcs. 680.00

MERCURY or SILVERED

Mercury Glass Candlestick

Developed in the mid-19th century, this

*glassware featured clear double-walled
objects which are coated on the interior
with silver nitrate to give them a silvery
appearance. Amber glass pieces were used
to obtain a gold effect. A hole in the base of
the piece, through which the silver nitrate
solution was injected, was then sealed.
Silvered wares were made in the U.S. and
England through the turn of the century.*

Candlestick, cylindrical candle socket
w/flared rim above a waisted shaft
on a domed cushion foot, 10½" h.
(ILLUS.) $110.00

Curtain tie-back, starflower design,
pewter fittings, 4½" d. 60.50

Dresser jars, cov., w/knob finial, 8" h.,
pr..195.00

Rose bowl, gold, w/plug, Czecho-
slovakia, 10" d.................................200.00

Mercury Glass Decorated Vase

Vase, 12½" h., low pedestal foot
supporting a ringed & slightly
tapering cylindrical body below a
flaring wide neck, h.p. flowers
around the center (ILLUS.) 65.00

Vase, cuspidor-shaped w/plug, teal
blue, Germany 225.00

MILLEFIORI

*The term Millefiori (Italian for
"thousand flowers") refers to a glass
decorated or patterned with tiny slices of
thin multicolored glass canes. Most often
used in glass paperweights, other objects
such as lamps, vases and tablewares have
also been produced using this technique
which was, in fact, developed by the
ancient Romans. Today Millefiori continues to be made in Murano, Italy, and
elsewhere*

Millefiori Table Lamp

Boudoir lamp, the bulbous teardrop-shaped closed shade set upon a metal ring & neck fitting above the slender cylindrical base w/a flaring, thick cushion foot, various red, blue, turquoise & white canes, Bryant socket, early 20th c., overall 11½" h. (one socket screw missing) $275.00

Lamp, table model, kerosene-type, pear-shaped font base w/metal fittings supporting a bulbous shade tapering to a wide flat top, multi-colored canes in base & shade, satin finish, electrified, 4¾" d., 11½" h. (ILLUS.) 595.00

Lamp, table model, pointed mush-room-shaped shade on a baluster-form body, blue, green, yellow & white canes, Venice, Italy, 20" h. 325.00

MONOT & STUMPF

Monot & Stumpf Boudoir Lamp

E.S. Monot established a glass factory in LaVillette, near Paris, France, in 1850. In 1858 the plant moved to Pantin and became Monot & Stumpf when Mr. F. Stumpf joined the company in 1868. Mr Monot's son joined the firm which became Monot, Pere et Fils, et Stumpf, in 1873. An iridescent ware they produced was called "Chine Metallique," and was patented in 1878. By the beginning of the 20th century the company had become known as Cristallerie de Pantin and was operated by Saint-Hilaire, Touvier, de Varreux & Company.

Bowl, 2⅞" d., 2⅝" h., ruffled rim, opalescent rose pink striped effect exterior, lustred gold interior $85.00

Lamp, banquet, kerosene-type, shade w/cylindrical sides & deeply crimped & ruffled rim in shaded & swirled pink opalescent Stripe patt., match-ing onion-form font supported on a brass ribbed columnar standard on round foot, w/original brass burner & clear chimney, 7¾" d., 22" h. 698.00

Lamp, boudoir, kerosene-type, shade w/squared sides in swirled pink opalescent Stripe patt., matching waisted cylindrical base, original burner, complete w/chimney, 4" d., 10" h. (ILLUS.) 850.00

Punch cup w/clear applied spun rope handle & scalloped wafer base, opalescent pink exterior w/craquelle finish, lustred gold interior, 3⅝" d., 2⅞" h...75.00

Salt dip, squatty bulbous body w/four-petal flared rim, striped pink opales-cent exterior, lustred gold interior, 2⅛" d., 1½" h. 65.00

Salt dip, squatty bulbous body w/fluted rolled rim, pink opalescent striped exterior, lustred gold interior, 2⅛" d., 1⅞" h. 65.00

MOSER

The Moser Company has a long history as a producer of fine decorative glasswares in Karlsbad, Bohemia (now Karlovy Vary, in the former Czechoslovakia). In 1857 Ludwig Moser opened his first glass shop in Karlsbad where it specialized in engraved and decorated glasswares meant

to appeal to rich visitors to the local health
spas. Glass shops were later opened in
other cities and today the richly enameled
and colorful wares they produced are
highly collectible. Ludwig died in 1916
and his sons continued the operation but
were forced to merge with the Meyer's
Nephews glass factory after World War I.
The factory was sold out of the Moser
family in 1933. Today any pieces attributed to Moser, especially signed examples,
bring strong prices.

Moser Intaglio-cut Cologne Bottle

Box, cov., green, decorated w/a large
yellow daisy on the cover, paper
label "Glasfabrik, Karlsbad," 6" d.,
4" h...$140.00

Center bowl, green, decorated w/in-
taglio-cut flowers, 9" d., 5" h. 425.00

Cologne bottle w/original ball stopper,
cylindrical w/rounded shoulder to a
small cylindrical neck, amethyst
shaded to clear decorated w/gold
garlands, scrolls, dots & bands,
stopper w/matching decoration,
2" d., 5" h. 225.00

Cologne bottle w/original bubble
stopper, cut paneled sides
decorated w/intaglio-cut flowers,
stopper conformingly decorated,
deep amethyst shading to clear,
marked "Moser Karlsbad," 3½" d.,
7¾" h. (ILLUS.) 795.00

Compote, open, 6¾" h., 7" d., dark
amethyst, the exterior of the deep
rounded bowl engraved w/a band of
Amazon warriors highlighted in gold,
the slender facet-cut pedestal flaring
to a facet-cut round foot...................357.50

Cordial, deep cranberry ground
w/heavy gold decoration, 1¼" d.,
2¾" h..45.00

Cordial set: decanter w/original
stopper & four cordial glasses;
smoky topaz decanter molded w/a
frieze of nude women around the
lower half, the glasses similarly
decorated, decanter 10¼" h., 5 pcs.
(stopper shortened) 247.50

Moser Decorated Cordial Set

Cordial set: spherical decanter
w/original stopper & applied handle,
tray & four pedestaled glasses;
decorated w/applied acorns, colorful
enameled foliate designs & gold
tracery, decanter 8" h., the set
(ILLUS.) 1,320.00

Cordial set: decanter w/clear bubble
stopper, six small cups w/applied
clear handles & a round tray; each
in cranberry, the spherical footed
decanter tapering to a tall slender
neck w/a pinched spout, decorated
w/arched panels, filled w/colorful
flowers below beaded bands on
the shoulder & neck, similar decoration on the cylindrical cups, the
set..650.00

Cruet w/original teardrop-shaped
stopper, applied clear handle,
cushion foot supporting an ovoid
body tapering to a cylindrical neck
w/petal-shaped rim, cobalt blue
decorated w/white & gold florals,
9" h..590.00

Cup & saucer, amber decorated
w/heavy gold scrolls & multicolored
flowers 295.00

Decanters w/stoppers, footed
cylindrical ovoid body tapering to a
tall neck molded w/thin swirled
ribbing below the arched spout,
hollow bulbous stopper & applied
strap handle, moss green enameled

Moser Decanters

overall w/ornate & delicate flower blossoms & leaves in orange, green, blue & gilt, 8½" h., pr. (ILLUS.) 1,265.00

Finger bowl & underplate, cranberry decorated w/multicolored enameled flowers & swags, 3½" d. bowl, scalloped rim 5½" d. underplate, 2 pcs. 260.00

Decorated Moser Jardiniere

Jardiniere, footed squatty bulbous body w/short collared neck, pink opalescent decorated w/gold bands at neck w/gold scrolls & small colored jewels set-in, scallops & fan decoration w/small jewels below neck, gold band w/jewels around base, signed "Moser," 9½" d., 7½" h. (ILLUS.) 975.00

Pitcher, 4¾" h., squatty bulbous body raised on a flaring foot & tapering to a ringed shoulder & a wide neck w/a wide arched spout, deep ruby red h.p. overall w/gilt lappet bands on the neck, upper body & base, a colorful enameled band of scrolling flowers around the center, applied ruby handle 700.00

Pitcher, 6¾" h., Inverted Thumbprint patt., Amberina decorated w/four bunches of grapes highlighted w/applied yellow, red, blue & green glass beads, colorful three-dimensional bird below spout & overall decorative enamel & gold leaves, vines & tendrils, signed "Moser" 3,025.00

Pitcher, 7½" h., spherical body w/a cylindrical neck w/tricorner rim, sapphire blue Coin Spot patt., enameled overall w/long multi-colored scrolls & stylized foliage, clear applied reeded handle 747.50

Pitcher, 8½" h., 6½" d., rubina, clear reeded applied handle, decorated w/elaborate florals & leafy enameling, artist-signed within design in script................................950.00

Pitcher, tankard. 12½" h., applied clear handle, apple green shaded to clear w/intaglio-cut poppy design on front..765.00

Ring holder, amethyst decorated w/heavily enameled blue, white, orange & yellow flowers, overall lacy gold & green leaves, 2¾" d., 4" h...110.00

Rose bowl, pedestal base, turned-out rim, cranberry decorated w/delicate gold tracery branches & leaves, blue & white flowers & tiny blue & green buds, signed, 3¾" d., 3½" h. 175.00

Sherbet & underplate, each in green heavily gilded & decorated w/small flowers, underplate 4½" d., sherbet 3¼" h., 2 pcs. 475.00

Syllabub set: 9" h. cov. bowl, six 3¼" h. footed mugs & 12¾" d. tray; handles & finial w/ribbed design, green ground decorated w/tiny flowers & flying insects, 8 pcs. 975.00

Toothpick holder, "Malachite," decorated w/enameled cherubs 225.00

Tumbler, rubina verde, decorated w/h.p. florals, signed "Moser," 4" h...95.00

Tumbler, juice, slightly flaring cylindrical-form, overall decoration of lacy gold enameled grape leaves & foliage & applied bunches of blue, red & green grapes all around, 2⅜" d., 4" h. (ILLUS.) 225.00

Ornate Moser Tumbler

Tumbler, juice, pink shaded to clear
decorated w/four applied acorns &
enameled w/green, pink yellow &
blue leaves & gold trim 320.00

Vase, miniature, 2¼" h., cranberry
w/heavy gold & colored floral
enameling 225.00

Vase, miniature, 2¾" h., ovoid body,
carved w/pendent leaves, signed
w/monogram in cameo & w/in-
scribed signature on the base..........165.00

Vase, 3½" h., 3¾" d., clear to
amethyst w/wide continuous gold
band of Amazon warriors, signed
"Moser" 312.00

Vase, 4" h., cranberry body raised on
four gilded feet, enamel decorated
w/a bird, acorns & leaves.................760.00

Vase, 5" h., "Malachite," the deep
green ovoid body tapering to a flat
mouth & to a paneled foot, the sides
deeply molded w/six nude women
dancing below fruit-laden grape-
vines, polished highlights.................522.50

Vase, 6" h., paneled, cranberry
decorated w/blue & gold enameling,
unsigned 195.00

Vase, 6½" h., cognac decorated
w/applied blue glass fish &
enameled flowers, signed................500.00

Vase, 6½" h., 2⅞" d., slightly swelled
cylindrical body, emerald green, cut
paneled sides w/wide heavy gold
cut-back band w/repeating design of
women warriors, signed "Moser" on
base (ILLUS. top next column) 225.00

Vase, 7" h., "Alexandrite," footed
flaring ovoid body w/a wide flaring
mouth, the sides & foot cut w/long
facets, star-cut base 287.50

Vase, 7" h., amber ground facet-cut
above & below wide bands of

Paneled Green Moser Vase

intricate gold decoration, center
w/scene of Victorian lovers in a
garden..695.00

Vase, 7" h., tapering ovoid body w/a
short neck below a flattened rim cut
w/five squared petals, aquamarine
applied down the sides w/four
S-form snakes decorated w/colorful
enamel spots & interspersed
w/enameled color blossoms 412.50

Vase, 8" h., octagonal alternating
panels decorated w/pink flowers &
buds on gold branches or blue
flowers & buds on gold branches,
each panel divided by columns of
white dotting....................................225.00

Vase, 8¼" h., cobalt blue panel-cut
body w/elephants & palm trees,
signed, "Moser" 3,995.00

Vase, 8¼" h., footed ovoid body
tapering to a short, wide cylindrical
neck, applied heart-shaped handles,
smoky ground enameled w/a scene
of a large standing crane wading
through tall reeds, plants, lotus
flowers, bluebells & w/a dragonfly,
acid stamp mark 247.50

Vase, 8½" h., footed urn-form, dark
amber w/the widely flaring rim cut
w/plain panels above a wide central
panel engraved w/a continuous
scene of Amazon warriors w/wea-
pons on horseback, the bulbous
base & flared pedestal foot further
cut w/plain panels, the base signed
in script "Made in Czechoslovakia
Moser Carlsbad" 467.50

Vase, 9" h., cranberry decorated
w/gold medallions & raised colorful
enameled beading 450.00

Vase, 11¼" h., slender conical body

tapering to a disc foot, cobalt blue w/overall gold outlining & heavy enameled pink & white flowers, unsigned 395.00

Moser Vase with Elephants

Vase, 11½" h., amethyst ovoid bottle-form w/a flattened, flaring rim, the bottom half cut w/graduated rings & w/further rings near the rim, the main body cameo-cut w/a continuous scene of elephants under palm trees, all enameled in white, gold & green, engraved signature (ILLUS.)............................935.00

Vase, 11¾" h., four-sided, green shading to clear, deeply cut w/a design of tulips 302.50

Vase, 12" h., footed trumpet-form, green w/faceted sides, etched & gilt-decorated w/a frieze of classical warriors at the rim, inscribed "made in czechoslovakia - moser karlsbad" 690.00

Vase, 12" h., tall slightly swelled cylindrical body w/optic ribbing, green shaded to clear & decorated w/large enameled chrysanthe-mums 395.00

Vase, 12¼" h., 4" d. base, corset-shaped w/a wide gold border on the six-scallop rim, clear satin w/an applied 'icy lace curtain' design & decorated w/branches, leaves & cherries in life-like enameled colors of brown, red & green outlined in gold, signed "Moser - Karlsbad".......495.00

Vase, 13" h., overlay, pedestal foot supporting a trumpet-form body, white cut to cobalt blue w/a floral design & accented w/multicolored enameled flowers & gold trim, signed 275.00

Vase, 13½" h., baluster-form, rasp-berry acid-cut to frosted clear in the form of raindrops, enameled w/two cranes striding through a swamp among lotus, iris & lily pads, trimmed w/gilt...................................660.00

Scenic Moser Vase

Vase, 16" h., dark cobalt blue tall ovoid body tapering to a flared rim, the upper section w/plain cut panels above a deep cut band over a wide center band etched & engraved w/a gold-trimmed scene of whim-sical costumed characters in an outdoor setting under Japanese lanterns & trees w/a monkey, cat, dog, turtle & rabbit looking on, the lower section w/another cut band over cut panels, the center scene signed "Moser," the base stamped "made in Czechoslovakia Moser Carlsbad" (ILLUS.) 1,980.00

Water set: 9" h. baluster-form pitcher w/flaring ruffled rim & applied reeded cobalt blue handle & two 4" h. tumblers; cobalt blue ground decorated w/white, yellow, gold & black enameled flowers, signed, 3 pcs. 750.00

Water set: 9½" h. tankard pitcher & six 4" h. matching tumblers; rim decorated w/white enameled chain w/heavy gold bands, body high-lighted w/overall gold leaves speckled w/blue "jewels" & delicate branches w/coralene flowers on a clear ground, 7 pcs. 950.00

Water set: 10¼" h. baluster-form pitcher & two 4" h. tumblers; cranberry decorated w/white, yellow, orange & blue floral & diamond design, 3 pcs....................................575.00

(End of Moser Section)

MT. WASHINGTON

Rare Mt. Washington Punch Bowl

Originally founded in 1837 by noted glass entrepreneur Deming Jarves, the Mt. Washington Glass Company was eventually sold to William L. Libbey who moved the plant to New Bedford, Massachusetts in 1869. Between that date and 1900 the Mt. Washington factory became famous for a diverse range of beautiful Art glass. In 1900 the company was succeeded by the Pairpoint Corporation. Below we list a variety of glasswares produced during Mt. Washington's heyday. Also see BUR-MESE, AMBERINA and PEACH BLOW.

Bowl, 4½ x 4½", pillow-shaped, satin Diamond Quilted patt., creamy white ground decorated w/pink enameled florals & a yellow rim.....................$275.00

Bowl, 8½" d., 3½" h., "Napoli," clear ground, interior decorated w/h.p. flowers & exterior decorated w/gold outlining of the flowers, signed 500.00

Bride's basket, cased bowl w/pointed & ruffled rim, shaded rose interior, white exterior, ornate footed silver plate frame w/scrolling handle, 10¼" d. bowl, frame 12" w., 12¼" h..400.00

Bride's basket, pink shaded to white satin Hobnail patt., w/applied blue rim, on a tall footed Barbour silver plate frame w/large parrots on the handles, bowl 9" d., 4¾" h., overall 13½" d.,...875.00

Condiment set: salt & pepper shakers, cov. mustard pot & holder; robin's egg blue ground decorated w/daisies, silver plate holder w/swan-shaped feet & center ring

handle signed "Wilcox," 4 pcs..........225.00

Creamer & cov. sugar bowl, "Albertine," deeply ribbed milk white body w/gold trim, silver plate cover marked "MW," creamer & sugar bowl signed w/Wreath & Crown, pr...750.00

Dresser tray, free-form shape w/three turned-in scallops, h.p. purple irises & green leaves decoration on a white satin ground, 8 x 8".................145.00

Flower bowl, raised satin Diamond Quilted patt., decorated w/a soft pink rim & enameled bouquets of yellow & white forget-me-nots, 4 x 4½", 3¼" h..295.00

Flower holder, footed mushroom shape, pale blue shading to white, decorated w/small white & yellow flowers & green leaves, 5" d., 3½" h..200.00

Mustard pot, cov., bulbous ribbed body, decorated w/florals, silver plate rim & cover.............................300.00

Perfume bottle w/original steeple-shaped stopper, bell-shaped body, applied opalescent ring around neck, decorated w/birds & florals, 6" h...295.00

Punch bowl on stand, decorated in the Royal Flemish manner, deep rounded bowl w/a flaring & notched rim, domed base, the bowl decorated w/three reserves of Palmer Cox Brownies in comic scenes involving a keg of ale, gilt scrolling trim, some gold loss, chip on base insert edge, 16" d., 13½" h. (ILLUS.) 18,400.00

Ring holder, saucer base supports a beaded ring-stick, satin white ground enameled w/blue forget-me-nots 85.00

Rose bowl, bulbous base w/rim flaring to twelve protruding "fingers," white satin ground decorated w/lavender pansies & yellow rim, 4" d., 3" h.......285.00

Rose bowl, "Verona," clear ground w/heavy gold pond lilies decoration, 6½" d...295.00

Salt shaker w/original top, egg-shaped, decorated w/a band of red berries & green leaves....................110.00

Salt shaker w/original top, egg-shaped, decorated w/enameled Shasta daisies & leaves, shaded pink ground 85.00

Salt shaker w/original top, egg-shaped, embossed "Egg in Blossom" & trimmed in gold.............110.00

Salt shaker w/original top, egg-shaped, h.p. orchid decoration 350.00

Salt shaker w/original top, egg-shaped, reclining-type w/a flat base, decorated w/pink apple blossoms on a white satin ground....................125.00

Salt & pepper shakers w/original tops, bulbous melon-ribbed body, h.p. florals on a white ground, pr 145.00

Salt & pepper shakers w/original tops, egg-shaped, decorated w/heavy gold florals, pr. 180.00

Salt & pepper shakers w/original tops, tapering five-lobed pear shape, delicate floral decoration on a white satin ground, pr. 95.00

Salt & pepper shakers w/original two-piece metal tops, five-lobed apple-shaped body, matching decoration of pink & blue florals, pr. 150.00

Sugar shaker w/original metal top, egg-shaped, satin white ground decorated w/delicate pale pink & blue flowers....................................250.00

Sugar shaker w/original metal top, egg-shaped, satiny white ground decorated w/purple violets 450.00

Sugar shaker w/original top, tomato-shaped, yellow ground w/enameled floral decoration 275.00

Syrup pitcher w/original top, cannon ball-shaped, h.p. roses & foliage on a white opal ground, 5¾" h. 245.00

Toothpick holder, bulbous melon-lobed body, decorated w/h.p. blue florals on a shaded yellow to white ground...110.00

Mt. Washington Napoli Vase

Vase, 5" h., 6" d., "Napoli," globular w/widely flaring rim, colorless crystal

dimpled bowl w/molded swirl decorated w/gold floral tracery, green blossoms on rim, marked "Napoli 837" (ILLUS.)....................1,380.00

Vase, 6" h., 5¾" d., footed squatty bulbous body tapering to a short cylindrical neck flaring to a four-fold rim, twenty-four swirling molded ribs in body, decorated w/blue & white forget-me-nots, signed.....................965.00

Vase, 10⅝" h., slender cylindrical base flaring to a fluted rim, rim applied w/wide clear edging, pale water green satin ground decorated w/floral designs in heavy raised enamels 475.00

Vase, 11½" h., decorated w/enameled spider mums & leaves & heavy gold branches, signed 895.00

Vase, 14" h., ruffled rim, Delft blue h.p. windmill scene on white ground..295.00

MULLER FRERES

Muller Freres Cameo Ewer & Vase

Luneville, France was the location of the glassworks founded by the brothers, Henri and Désiré Muller in 1910. Their firm produced a range of acid-etched cameo and other fine glass until the outbreak of World War II in Europe.

Muller Freres Mark

Box, cov., oval, mottled orange & purple body etched & enameled w/red currants in naturalistic tones, enameled signature "Muller Fres Luneville," 7" l. $1,610.00

Cameo bowl, 10" l., deep oblong form w/the tips of the ends pulled & turned down into small loop handles, raised on a cushion foot, grey streaked w/sea green & raspberry, overlaid in purple & cut w/a river landscape w/boating in the foreground, mountains in the distance, signed in cameo "Muller Fres - Luneville," ca. 1920.......................2,875.00

Cameo ewer, tapering cylindrical body w/flat flared rim & pointed spout, the cased clear vessel w/a continuous carved & enameled frieze in *fluogravure* of a shepherdess & her flock in a windy landscape in shades of ochre, umber, chocolate brown, sapphire blue & opalescent crimson, her cloak finely wheel-carved, signed in cameo "Muller Croismare," ca. 1900, 8" h. (ILLUS. right) 7,475.00

Cameo vase, 6⅛" h., slender ovoid body w/flat rim, grey splashed w/rose & emerald green, overlaid in emerald green & finely wheel-carved w/crocus blossoms, buds & leafage, signed in intaglio "Muller - Croismare pres Nancy" within a butterfly, ca. 1915 ....1,725.00

Muller Freres Cameo Vase

Cameo vase, 6¼" h., Art Deco style, squat ovoid body w/thick rolled rim, pale amber opalescent internally decorated w/gold & silver foil inclusions, overlaid in clear & deeply cut in an Art Deco type design of stylized butterflies, inscribed "MULLER FRES LUNEVILLE," ca. 1925 (ILLUS.) 2,013.00

Cameo vase, 6⅜" h., footed baluster form w/short neck & flaring rim, clear splashed w/olive green, overlaid in

olive green & wheel-carved w/marguerite blossoms, buds & leafage, signed in intaglio "Muller - Croismare - pres Nancy" within a butterfly, ca. 1910 (ILLUS. left) 1,438.00

Cameo vase, 7⅞" h., slender trumpet-form body on cushion foot, the shoulder tapering to a bulbous short incurved neck, frosted grey streaked w/bubblegum pink & overlaid in bubblegum pink, amber & chocolate brown, cut w/pendent bleeding heart blossoms, buds & leafage, signed in cameo, ca. 1910 ....633.00

Cameo vase, 8" h., ovoid body, mottled yellow overlaid in deep red & cut to depict a wooded river scene, cameo signature................1,012.00

Muller Freres Scenic Cameo Vase

Cameo vase, 9" h., flattened upright quatreform, yellow overlaid w/orange & brown & etched w/a lowland Dutch scene w/a windmill, cottages & sailboats beyond, "Muller Fres Luneville" in cameo (ILLUS.) 1,760.00

Cameo vase, 10¼" h., ovoid body tapering to a short, flaring neck, luminous orange overlaid in dark burgundy & black & acid-etched w/a riverside scene w/grasses & leafy trees, signed on the side "Muller Fres Luneville" 1,210.00

Cameo vase, 11¾" h., bottle-form, footed tapering cylindrical body below a tall slender stick neck w/flared mouth, grey infused w/lemon yellow, overlaid in deep teal blue & cut w/a wild windswept landscape w/rugged trees, signed in cameo, ca. 1925 ....575.00

Cameo vase, 14½" h., flaring cylindrical body raised on a cushion-

form base, grey internally mottled
w/lemon yellow & lavender, overlaid
in blue, rose & purple & cut w/jack-
in-the-pulpit blossoms & anemones,
signed in cameo "MULLER FRES -
LUNEVILLE," ca. 1925 ....1,840.00

Cameo vase, 19½" h., tall ovoid body
tapering up to a wide rolled rim &
tapering down to a cushion foot,
grey mottled w/soft peach, overlaid
w/yellow & red & cut w/thorny rose
blossoms & leaves, signed in cameo
"MULLER FRERES - LUNEVILLE,"
ca. 1920 ....4,025.00

Vase, 8½" h., baluster-form, opalescent yellow etched & enameled
w/berries, cameo signature "MUL-
LER Fres LUNEVILLE" 978.00

Internally Decorated Muller Vase

Vase, 9" h., cylindrical footed body
deeply etched w/wide vertical flutes
below a thick rim, deep eggplant
cased in clear & internally decorated
w/silver foil, engraved mark
"MULLER FRES LUNEVILLE"
(ILLUS.) 1,725.00

Vase, 14" h., blue & grey w/silver foil,
signed "Muller Fres - Luneville" 1,500.00

NAILSEA

*Nailsea was another glassmaking
center in England where a variety of wares
similar to those from Bristol, England
were produced between 1788 and 1873.
Today most collectors think of Nailsea
primarily as a glass featuring swirls and
loopings, usually white, on a clear or
colored ground. This style of glass
decoration, however, was not restricted to
Nailsea and was produced in many other
glasshouses, including some in America.*

Nailsea Bellows-Shaped Bottle

Bottle, bellows-shaped, applied clear
rigaree down sides & on front &
back, applied clear threading around
slender base portion, opaque white
w/cranberry looping cased in clear,
some roughness at ends of rigaree,
8½" l. (ILLUS.) $192.50

Flask, flattened ovoid body w/short
neck, clear casing w/red & white
loopings, 1½ x 4", 7" l. 165.00

Flask, flattened tapering ovoid form
w/short cylindrical neck, cranberry
loopings on opaque white, 7" l. 121.00

Flask, cobalt blue w/white loopings,
7¼" l..244.00

Flask, white opaque w/red & blue
loopings, 7½" l. 260.00

Flask, white opaque w/pink loopings,
8" l..208.00

Flask, pocket-type, flattened ovoid
form, clear w/white loopings, applied
blue lip, rough pontil, 8" l.................115.50

Gemel bottle, double flask-form, aqua
w/white crosshatched loopings, 7" h.
(a few bubbles & some wear) 110.00

Gemel bottle, double flask-form in
clear w/white loopings, short
cylindrical necks w/applied blue
threading, applied clear rigaree
down the sides, 8½" h. (minor
sickness)...60.50

Gemel bottle, double flask-form in
clear w/red & white loopings, white
threading around short necks,
metal-tipped cork for one neck,
10½" h...121.00

Vase, 8½" h., tall trumpet-form bowl
w/a flaring ruffled rim in clear w/red,
white & blue loopings, applied to

a short clear pedestal & clear
disc foot, American-made,
mid-19th c. 2,475.00

NAKARA

Nakara Box with Portrait Decoration

*Nakara, like Kelva (which see), was a
decorative line of opal glass produced early
in this century by the C.F. Monroe
Company. For further details see WAVE
CREST.*

Box w/hinged cover, decorated w/h.p.
cupids on a blue ground, 3" d. $395.00

Box w/hinged cover, Hexagonal mold,
green ground w/pink roses top &
bottom, 4" d.....................................385.00

Box w/hinged cover, h.p. pink daisies
decoration on a blue ground, 4" d.,
2¾" h..310.00

Box w/hinged cover, green satin
ground w/portrait of woman on
cover, raised beading at border,
original lining, 4½" d........................650.00

Box w/hinged cover, footed,
Octagonal mold, green ground
decorated w/large pink rose,
4½" d...450.00

Box w/hinged cover, Octagonal mold,
plum ground w/Kate Greenaway tea
party scene, 4½" d. 685.00

Box w/hinged cover, oval, light green
w/pink roses & crown in center of lid,
5½" l...475.00

Box w/hinged cover, Burmese
coloring w/18th century courting
couple on cover, 6" d. (ILLUS.).....1,085.00

Box w/hinged cover, yellow shaded to
green ground decorated w/pink &
white flowers outlined in gold, white
beading on cover, 6" d. 795.00

Box w/hinged cover, Octagonal mold,
lemon yellow shaded to deep peach
ground decorated w/h.p. orchid-like
blossoms in shades of orchid
w/green foliage & white beading
trim, 6" w. 485.00

Box w/hinged cover, Octagonal mold,
shaded pale peach to brown ground
decorated w/h.p. yellow flowers
w/pink centers, 6¼" d., 4½" h. 960.00

Box w/hinged cover, Rococo mold,
decorated overall w/dainty beaded
flowers, 8" d. 1,150.00

Box w/hinged cover, Crown mold,
cover decorated w/five h.p. roses on
an olive green ground, sides
w/similar decoration, 8" d.,5" h......1,350.00

Cigar humidor, cov., blue mottled
ground decorated w/h.p. pink
flowers, "Cigars" in gold on side 795.00

Humidor, cov., base decorated w/h.p.
enameled florals & "Tobacco" in
gold, 7" w., 7" h. 595.00

Humidor, cov., decorated w/an owl
sitting in a tree, metal lid 1,220.00

Pin tray, Bishop's Hat mold, pink &
white flowers on green ground,
5½" w. 275.00

Salt shaker w/original metal top,
concave bulb shape, decorated w/a
transfer scene of Niagara Falls
applied over a tan painted
background, 2⅝" h. 145.00

Vase, 8" h., squatty bulbous base
tapering to a tall cylindrical neck,
h.p. florals & white beading
decoration on a blue shaded to
yellow ground, w/decorative footed
ormolu base 360.00

Vase, 13½" h., footed, burnt orange
ground decorated w/purple
irises 1,050.00

NASH

*A. Douglas Nash, a former employee of
Louis Comfort Tiffany, purchased Tiffany's
Corona Works in December 1928 and
began his own operation there. For a brief
period Nash produced some outstanding
glasswares but the factory closed in March*

of 1931 and Nash then became associated with Libbey Glass of Toledo, Ohio. This quality glass is quite scarce.

Small Nash Vases

Bowl, 4½" d., 4½" h., blue ground w/silver mottling decorated w/red pulled-up stripes $145.00

Bowl, small, raised Maize patt. in gold iridescent w/blue highlights, signed 175.00

Compote, open, 3¼ x 6¼", low, footed, scalloped top & ribbed body, overall gold iridescence, signed.......475.00

Cordials, Chintz patt., red w/overall silver decoration, signed, set of 6 ....950.00

Nut bowl, ruffled rim, iridescent gold w/blue highlights, 3" d., 2⅜" h. 95.00

Vase, 5½" h., Chintz patt., bulbous body tapering to cylindrical neck, red w/overall silver decoration, signed & numbered..975.00

Vase, 7" h., 4" d., flared square shape, overall gold iridescence, signed 290.00

Vase, 8½" h., Chintz patt., dark blue w/silvery iridescence 575.00

Vases, 4¼" h., tapering ovoid body w/indented panels around the base & interior ribbing on the short, flaring rim, applied to a disc foot, overall gold iridescence, signed "Nash 544," pr. (ILLUS.) 747.50

OPALESCENT

Opalescent glass is one of the most popular areas of glass collecting today. This unique glass was developed and first became popular in the 1880s with production continuing right through the turn of the century. The opalescent effect is obtained by adding bone ash chemicals to areas of an object while it is still hot and refiring the piece at tremendous heat. A wide range of pressed and mold-blown patterns were produced and our listings

distinguish between these two types. A standard reference is Opalescent Glass from A to Z *by the late William Heacock.*

MOLD-BLOWN OPALESCENT PATTERNS

ARABIAN NIGHTS
Pitcher, water, blue...........................$450.00

Tumbler, blue........................75.00 to 100.00

Tumbler, white 60.00

Water set: pitcher & four tumblers; white, 5 pcs. ....800.00 to 1,100.00

BUBBLE LATTICE
Bowl, master berry, blue.......................65.00

Cruet w/original stopper, blue.............400.00

Salt shaker w/original top, blue.............95.00

Sauce dish, blue 28.00

Spooner, blue 95.00

Sugar shaker w/original top, bulbous Ring Neck mold, blue......................450.00

Sugar shaker w/original top, canary ..295.00

Sugar shaker w/original top, white......175.00

Tumbler, blue..85.00

Tumbler, cranberry 145.00

BUTTONS & BRAIDS
Pitcher, water, blue.............................215.00

Tumbler, cranberry 135.00

Water set: pitcher & six tumblers; blue, 7 pcs. 785.00

Water set: pitcher & six tumblers; green, 7 pcs. 675.00

CHRISTMAS SNOWFLAKE
Lamp, cranberry, variant, 4" sq., 8" h...475.00

Lamp, cranberry shade & white base, variant 395.00

Lamp, finger-type w/applied handle, white, variant...................................250.00

Lamp, table model, kerosene-type, cranberry...950.00

Pitcher, water, 8½" h., blue................175.00

Pitcher, water, cranberry 1,200.00

Pitcher, water, white 395.00

Tumbler, blue.......................................85.00

CHRYSANTHEMUM SWIRL
Bowl, master berry, cranberry, satin finish 250.00

Butter dish, cov., blue 350.00

Celery vase, blue 195.00

Celery vase, white 115.00

Creamer, blue 139.00

Creamer, cranberry 395.00

Chrysanthemum Swirl Cruet

Cruet w/original stopper, cranberry
(ILLUS.) 395.00

Pitcher, water, blue 495.00

Pitcher, water, cranberry 300.00

Pitcher, water, white 195.00

Sauce dish, blue 35.00

Sauce dish, cranberry 42.50

Spooner, cranberry 295.00

Sugar bowl, cov., white.........75.00 to 100.00

Chrysanthemum Swirl Sugar Shaker

Sugar shaker w/original top, blue
(ILLUS.) 245.00

Sugar shaker w/original top,
cranberry...495.00

Sugar shaker w/original top, white......245.00

Syrup pitcher w/original top, blue 285.00

Syrup pitcher w/original top,
cranberry...825.00

Tumbler, blue......................................92.50

Tumbler, cranberry ....100.00 to 115.00

COIN SPOT

Coin Spot Sugar Shaker

Bowl, 7" d., green 95.00

Celery vase, ribbed mold, cranberry...210.00

Compote, pleated edge, canary 30.00

Cruet w/original stopper, blue.............225.00

Cruet w/original facet-cut stopper,
canary, Hobbs, Brockunier 175.00

Cruet w/original stopper, tapered
mold, cranberry 235.00

Cruet w/original stopper, white 65.00

Mug, cranberry 95.00

Pitcher, 8" h., crimped rim,
cranberry..150.00

Pitcher, water, blue 119.00

Pitcher, water, Jefferson variant,
blue ....150.00 to 175.00

Pitcher, water, Jefferson variant,
cranberry..250.00

Pitcher, water, Jefferson variant,
white 95.00

Pitcher, water, nine-panel mold,
white 149.00

Sugar shaker w/original top, blue 138.00

Sugar shaker w/original top, green.......85.00

Sugar shaker w/original top, bulbous
body, white.......................................110.00

Sugar shaker w/original top, nine-
panel mold, blue 195.00

Sugar shaker w/original top, nine-
panel mold, cranberry ......225.00 to 250.00

Sugar shaker w/original top, nine-
panel mold, green 195.00

Sugar shaker w/original top, ring
neck mold, blue.................................168.00

Sugar shaker w/original top, ring
neck mold, cranberry (ILLUS.) 215.00

Sugar shaker w/original top, ring
neck mold, Rubina 275.00

Sugar shaker w/original top, wide-
waisted mold, blue 165.00

Sugar shaker w/original top, wide-
waisted mold, cobalt blue 220.00

Sugar shaker w/original top, wide-
waisted mold, white 110.00

Syrup pitcher w/original top, bulbous-
based mold, blue ....145.00 to 155.00

Syrup pitcher w/original metal top,
bulbous-based mold, cranberry 395.00

Syrup pitcher w/original top, nine-
panel mold, blue 175.00

Coin Spot Syrup Pitcher

Syrup pitcher w/original top, nine-
panel mold, green (ILLUS.)..............260.00

Syrup pitcher w/original top, ring
neck mold, blue.................................169.00

Syrup pitcher w/original top, ring
neck mold, Rubina 345.00

Syrup pitcher w/original top, ring
neck mold, white 110.00

Syrup pitcher w/original top, Rubina...245.00

Toothpick holder, hat-shaped, white,
2½ x 5½" 50.00

Tumbler, Northwood mold, cran-
berry..85.00

Vase, 4¼" h., 5¼" w., square-top
mold, canary 125.00

Water set: pitcher & two tumblers;
square-top mold, cranberry, 3 pcs. ..635.00

Water set: pitcher & four tumblers;
Northwood mold, cranberry, 5 pcs...650.00

Water set: pitcher & four tumblers;
white, 5 pcs. ....135.00 to 165.00

COIN SPOT & SWIRL
Pitcher, water, white 195.00

Syrup pitcher w/original metal top,
applied blue handle, blue................170.00

Syrup pitcher w/original metal top,
applied clear handle, white 150.00

DAISY & FERN

Daisy & Fern Sugar Shaker

Barber bottle, rolled lip, blue...............185.00

Creamer, white 110.00

Cruet w/original stopper,
blue ....125.00 to 150.00

Cruet w/original stopper, cranberry ...225.00

Cruet w/original stopper,
white ....75.00 to 95.00

Pitcher, 6" h., ball-shaped, cran-
berry..................................475.00 to 500.00

Pitcher, 6" h., applied clear reeded
handle, cranberry 225.00

Pitcher, water, ball-shaped, cran-
berry..................................300.00 to 350.00

Sugar shaker w/original top, blue 250.00

Sugar shaker w/original top, canary 90.00

Sugar shaker w/original top, cran-
berry..................................350.00 to 400.00

Sugar shaker w/original top, white
(ILLUS.) 159.00

Syrup pitcher w/original metal top,
applied clear reeded handle,
blue ....225.00 to 250.00

Syrup pitcher w/original top, cran-
berry...275.00

Syrup pitcher w/original top, Parian
   Swirl mold, cranberry 600.00

Toothpick holder, cranberry...............115.00

Toothpick holder, Parian Swirl mold,
   cranberry..225.00

Tumbler, blue..........................50.00 to 60.00

Tumbler, cranberry 55.00

Daisy & Fern Water Set

Water set: pitcher & four tumblers;
   cranberry, 5 pcs. (ILLUS. of part) 285.00

Water set: pitcher & six tumblers;
   blue, 7 pcs. 425.00

FERN
Barber bottle w/original stopper,
   cranberry...285.00

Cruet w/original stopper, blue.............225.00

Cruet w/original stopper, white 45.00

Spooner w/ruffled rim, blue.................140.00

Sugar shaker w/original top, cran-
   berry...525.00

Toothpick holder, white.......................225.00

Tumbler, blue...30.00

Tumbler, cranberry 125.00

HOBNAIL, HOBBS
Barber bottle w/original stopper,
   blue 175.00

Bowl, 8" d., cranberry 145.00

Bowl, berry, 9" sq., 3" h., ruffled rim,
   cranberry..295.00

Celery vase, cranberry, 4" d., 6" h. 175.00

Celery vase, vaseline 90.00

Creamer, square top, cranberry,
   4¾" h..95.00

Cruet w/original stopper, cranberry 340.00

Hobnail Pitcher

Pitcher, 5" h., w/square mouth,
   applied clear handle, cranberry
   (ILLUS.) 195.00

Spooner, blue 55.00

Spooner, vaseline.................................40.00

Syrup pitcher w/original top,
   cranberry...435.00

Toothpick holder, vaseline....................30.00

Tumbler, blue...65.00

Tumbler, cranberry, 4" h. 110.00

Tumbler, Rubina Verde, 4" h. 210.00

Tumbler, vaseline 75.00

Tumbler, white 20.00

Vase, 5" h., triangular form, blue 65.00

Vase, 5½" h., 5½" d., ruffled rim,
   cranberry...55.00

Water set: pitcher & five tumblers;
   cranberry, 6 pcs. 340.00

HONEYCOMB
Lamp base, miniature, cranberry
   opalescent w/Mercury glass lining,
   nutmeg burner, 3½" d., overall
   w/chimney 8½" h..............................750.00

Tumblers, cranberry, set of 4.............200.00

POINSETTIA
Lemonade set: tankard pitcher & four
   tumblers; cranberry, w/enameled
   trim, 5 pcs. 395.00

Pitcher, lemonade, tankard, blue,
   factory-decorated 200.00

Pitcher, tankard, blue..........275.00 to 325.00

Sugar shaker w/original top, blue 375.00

Syrup pitcher w/original top, blue 700.00

Tumbler, blue..........................50.00 to 75.00

POLKA DOT

Barber bottle w/original stopper,
cranberry...125.00

Bowl, 6" d., cranberry 135.00

Pitcher, 6½" h., cranberry 500.00

Pitcher, water, blue.............................375.00

Pitcher, water, cranberry 995.00

Tumbler, cranberry ....75.00 to 95.00

Water set: pitcher & one tumbler;
white, 2 pcs. 225.00

REVERSE SWIRL

Reverse Swirl Sugar Shaker

Bowl, master berry, blue........................65.00

Butter dish, cov., blue 225.00

Lamp, finger-type w/applied clear
handle, cranberry 425.00

Pickle castor, white insert, silver plate
frame..225.00

Pitcher, water, canary..........................250.00

Salt & pepper shakers w/original tops,
blue, 3⅜" h., pr.................125.00 to 150.00

Spooner, cranberry..............................125.00

Sugar shaker w/original top, blue
(ILLUS.) 395.00

Sugar shaker w/original top,
canary ....250.00 to 300.00

Sugar shaker w/original top, cran-
berry.................................400.00 to 450.00

Syrup pitcher w/original top,
blue (ILLUS. top next
column) ....250.00 to 275.00

Syrup pitcher w/original top, canary ...350.00

Toothpick holder, blue 100.00

Tumbler, canary.....................................75.00

Reverse Swirl Syrup Pitcher

Tumbler, cranberry 140.00

RIBBED OPAL LATTICE

Pitcher, water, blue.............................500.00

Salt shaker w/original top, cranberry
(ILLUS.) ....300.00 to 350.00

Sugar shaker w/original metal top,
blue 295.00

Sugar shaker w/original top, cran-
berry ....300.00 to 325.00

Toothpick holder, cran-
berry..................................225.00 to 250.00

SEAWEED

Cruet w/original stopper, blue.............395.00

Pitcher, water, tricorner rim, cran-
berry..1,100.00

Tumbler, cranberry ....100.00 to 115.00

SPANISH LACE

Spanish Lace Sugar Shaker

Bride's bowl, cranberry, 10" d., 4" h....250.00

Butter dish, cov., white 150.00

Celery vase, canary...............75.00 to 95.00

Pitcher, water, cranberry ....900.00 to 950.00

Pitcher, tankard, white........225.00 to 275.00

Rose bowl, white 65.00

Salt & pepper shakers w/original tops,
  blue, pr..275.00

Sugar shaker w/original top, blue
  (ILLUS.) ....200.00 to 250.00

Sugar shaker w/original metal top,
  canary ....225.00 to 250.00

Sugar shaker w/original top, white........90.00

Tumbler, blue.......................................82.00

STARS & STRIPES

Stars & Stripes Tumbler

Cruet w/original stopper, cranberry 445.00

Pitcher, 8" h., cranberry 1,100.00

Tumbler, cranberry (ILLUS.).................85.00

STRIPE

Celery vase, footed, canary................110.00

Sugar shaker w/original top, canary ...275.00

Syrup pitcher w/original top, canary ...375.00

Tumbler, whiskey, blue, 2" d., 2⅝" h. ...45.00

Tumbler, water, blue..............................95.00

SWIRL

Barber bottle, square base tapering to
  a cylindrical neck w/rolled lip,
  cranberry...250.00

Cruet w/original stopper, cranberry 495.00

Lamp, finger-type w/applied handle,
  blue 300.00

Pitcher, water, w/square ruffled rim,
  blue ....175.00 to 195.00

Pitcher, water, white 95.00

Pitcher, water, w/square ruffled rim,
  ball-shaped, cranberry .....300.00 to 325.00

Pitcher, w/star crimp rim, cranberry....695.00

Pitcher, water, green 385.00

Tumbler, blue.......................................85.00

Water set: pitcher & five tumblers;
  green, 6 pcs. 300.00

Water set: pitcher & six tumblers;
  cranberry, 7 pcs. 595.00

SWIRLING MAZE

Bowl, 9⅝" d., 4" h., crimped rim,
  green...50.00

Tumbler, green 65.00

TWIST

Sugar shaker w/original top, cran-
  berry...550.00

Sugar shaker w/original top, green.....345.00

Sugar shaker w/original top, white........95.00

Toothpick holder, canary 110.00

Tumblers, blue, set of 4 ....250.00

WINDOWS, BIG

Bowl, master berry, cranberry 235.00

Pitcher, water, cranberry 950.00

Sauce dishes, cranberry, pr................250.00

Syrup pitcher w/original top,
  white ....200.00 to 225.00

Tumbler, cranberry 150.00

WINDOWS, PLAIN

Lamp, kerosene, finger-type w/applied
  clear handle, cranberry 425.00

Lamp, kerosene, finger-type, white 295.00

Pitcher, white 200.00

Salt shaker w/original top, blue.............85.00

Syrup pitcher w/original top, blue 395.00

Toothpick holder, blue 245.00

Tumbler, blue.........................50.00 to 75.00

Tumbler, white 42.50

Water set: pitcher & six tumblers;
  cranberry, 7 pcs. 1,150.00

WINDOWS, SWIRLED

Cruet w/original stopper, cran-
  berry................................600.00 to 650.00

Salt shaker w/original top, white 60.00

Salt & pepper shakers w/original tops, cranberry, pr. 285.00

Sugar shaker w/original metal top, blue 350.00

Sugar shaker w/original top, cranberry..495.00

Sugar shaker w/original top, white......175.00

Tumbler, blue..95.00

PRESSED OPALESCENT PATTERNS

ACORN BURRS
Sugar shaker w/original top, white......115.00

ARGONAUT SHELL
Banana bowl, canary, 7" l. 72.00

Compote, 7½" d., 4" h., blue.................52.00

Cruet w/original stopper, white ....150.00 to 200.00

Spooner, blue 95.00

Sugar bowl, cov., blue 195.00

Tray, blue..90.00

Tray, canary...90.00

BEATTY RIBBED
Celery, blue 84.00

Creamer, individual, blue......................50.00

Mug, blue..48.00

Sauce dish, rectangular, blue 27.50

Sauce dishes, white, set of 6..............125.00

Spooner, blue 36.00

Sugar shaker w/original top, blue ....225.00 to 250.00

Sugar shaker w/original top, cranberry...435.00

Toothpick holder, blue 40.00

Water set: pitcher & five tumblers; blue, 6 pcs. 495.00

BEATTY SWIRL
Celery vase, blue..................................68.00

Pitcher, water, white 365.00

Sauce dish, blue 20.00

Tumbler, blue..55.00

CIRCLED SCROLL
Butter dish, cov., blue 450.00

Bowl, master berry, white 70.00

Creamer, blue.......................................75.00

Cruet w/original stopper, green 450.00

Spooner, blue 110.00

Sugar bowl, cov., green......................100.00

Wine, green 60.00

DIAMOND SPEARHEAD

Diamond Spearhead Butter Dish

Berry set: master bowl & six sauce dishes; canary, 7 pcs. 275.00

Butter dish, cov., green (ILLUS.) 230.00

Celery vase, canary............100.00 to 110.00

Compote, jelly, blue 125.00

Compote, jelly, canary 95.00

Cuspidor, lady's, canary 125.00

Sauce dish, blue 27.00

Spooner, canary 100.00

Spooner, green.....................80.00 to 100.00

Sugar bowl, cov., canary 150.00

Table set: cov. butter dish, cov. sugar bowl, creamer & spooner; canary, 4 pcs. ....700.00 to 800.00

Toothpick holder w/scalloped rim, canary, 2¼" d., 2¾" h.......................90.00

Toothpick holder, green.........................60.00

Toothpick holder, sapphire blue ....100.00 to 110.00

Tumbler, canary....................................60.00

Tumbler, sapphire blue.........................65.00

DOLLY MADISON
Bonbon, tricornered, green...................30.00

Bowl, master berry, green 80.00

Table set, blue, 4 pcs. 850.00

DRAPERY
Bowl, 9" d., white 60.00

Butter dish, cov., blue w/gold trim.......175.00

Pitcher, water, blue w/gold
  trim...................................200.00 to 250.00

Sauce dish, blue...................................36.00

Spooner, blue......................................72.00

Water set: pitcher & six tumblers;
  blue, 7 pcs. 775.00

EVERGLADES

Everglades Creamer & Sugar Bowl

Butter dish, cov., blue.........350.00 to 375.00

Butter dish, cov., white.......................135.00

Compote, jelly, green w/gold trim.......115.00

Creamer, blue (ILLUS. left)...................95.00

Creamer, white w/gold trim...................40.00

Cruet w/original stopper, blue.............450.00

Cruet w/original stopper, canary.........425.00

Sauce dish, blue...................................45.00

Spooner, blue..90.00

Spooner, canary....................................85.00

Sugar bowl, cov., blue (ILLUS. right)..235.00

Sugar bowl, cov., white..........................75.00

Tumbler, blue..........................50.00 to 75.00

FLORA

Bowl, master berry, white.....................65.00

Butter dish, cov., white.......................140.00

Creamer, white......................................45.00

Sugar bowl, cov., blue.......................175.00

FLUTED SCROLLS

Berry set: master bowl & six sauce
  dishes; blue, 7 pcs. 250.00

Bonbon, canary.....................................50.00

Bonbon, green.......................................45.00

Bowl, 7" d., blue.....................................70.00

Creamer, canary w/enameled
  flowers (ILLUS. top next column).......75.00

Fluted Scrolls Creamer

Creamer, white......................................32.00

Cruet w/original stopper, blue.............160.00

Cruet w/original stopper,
  canary..............................200.00 to 225.00

Pitcher, water, blue.............225.00 to 250.00

Puff box, cov., blue...............................45.00

Puff box, cov., canary...........................50.00

Puff box, cov., white..............................45.00

Salt shaker w/original top, canary.........30.00

Sauce dish, canary...............................22.00

Spooner, blue..60.00

Spooner, canary....................................45.00

Sugar bowl, cov., blue........100.00 to 125.00

Table set: creamer, cov. sugar bowl &
  cov. butter dish; blue, 3 pcs. 275.00

Table set, canary w/floral decoration,
  4 pcs. 600.00

Tumbler, blue...70.00

Tumbler, green......................................46.00

HOBNAIL & PANELED THUMBPRINT

Hobnail & Paneled Thumbprint Butter

Butter dish, cov., canary (ILLUS.).......150.00

Spooner, blue 50.00

Spooner, canary 75.00

Spooner, white.....................................60.00

HONEYCOMB & CLOVER
Bonbon, two-handled, white 25.00

Bowl, master berry, 9" d., green 45.00

Bowl, master berry, 9" d., white 35.00

Pitcher, water, green 195.00

Pitcher, water, white 130.00

INTAGLIO
Berry set: master bowl & six sauce
  dishes; white, 7 pcs. ....200.00 to 225.00

Bowl, master berry, blue.....................235.00

Butter dish, cov., blue 295.00

Butter dish, cov., green.......................110.00

Compote, jelly, canary 90.00

Creamer, white 20.00

Cruet w/original stopper,
  blue ....175.00 to 225.00

Cruet w/original stopper, white 75.00

Pitcher, water, blue.............150.00 to 200.00

Pitcher, water, white 85.00

Sauce dish, blue...................................40.00

Sauce dish, crimped rim, white.............20.00

Sugar bowl, cov., green........................90.00

Tumbler, white 45.00

Water set: pitcher & six tumblers;
  white, 7 pcs. 350.00

IRIS WITH MEANDER
Berry set: master bowl & five sauce
  dishes; blue, 6 pcs. 150.00

Berry set: master bowl & six sauce
  dishes; canary, 7 pcs. 250.00

Bowl, master berry, blue.....................125.00

Butter dish, cov., blue ....225.00 to 250.00

Butter dish, cov., canary .....200.00 to 250.00

Butter dish, cov., white 155.00

Compote, jelly, white 35.00

Cruet w/original stopper,
  canary ....450.00 to 500.00

Pitcher, water, canary.........250.00 to 300.00

Plate, 7" d., blue 35.00

Sauce dish, canary 25.00

Sauce dish, white 20.00

Sugar bowl, cov., blue 125.00

Toothpick holder, canary 85.00

Tumbler, blue.......................................85.00

Tumbler, canary...................................70.00

JEWEL & FLOWER

Jewel & Flower Water Set

Butter dish, cov., blue ....375.00 to 400.00

Butter dish, cov., canary 350.00

Creamer, white 75.00

Cruet w/original stopper, canary.........750.00

Pitcher, water, white 345.00

Pitcher, water, white w/gold trim.........375.00

Salt shaker w/original top, white 95.00

Spooner, white.....................................75.00

Sugar bowl, cov., white.......................110.00

Table set, blue, 4 pcs. 650.00

Water set: pitcher & five tumblers;
  blue, 6 pcs. (ILLUS. of part) 725.00

JEWELLED HEART
Berry set: master bowl & four sauce
  dishes; white, 5 pcs. 150.00

Bowl, small, ruffled rim, white 23.00

Creamer, blue.......................................65.00

Cruet w/original stopper, green 395.00

Tumbler, green 69.00

PALM BEACH
Berry set: master bowl & four sauce
  dishes; blue, 5 pcs. 225.00

Bowl, master berry, blue.....................110.00

Butter dish, cov., canary 195.00

Spooner, canary 85.00

Table set, blue, 4 pcs. 650.00

Table set, canary, 4 pcs. ....650.00 to 750.00

Water set: pitcher & five tumblers;
    canary, 6 pcs. ....600.00 to 650.00

REGAL
Butter dish, cov., blue ....325.00 to 350.00

Butter dish, cov., green......................175.00

Celery vase, blue...............................165.00

Celery vase, green 130.00

Creamer, green 75.00

Pitcher, water, green 225.00

Spooner, blue 90.00

Spooner, green......................................55.00

Sugar bowl, cov., blue ....250.00 to 275.00

Sugar bowl, cov., white.........................65.00

RIBBED SPIRAL

Ribbed Spiral Cup & Saucer

Basket, w/clear applied twist handle,
    green, 5¾" d., 6½" h. 138.00

Bowl, master berry, crimped rim, blue ..80.00

Cup & saucer, blue (ILLUS.)................70.00

Sauce dish, crimped rim, blue 30.00

Spooner, white.....................................65.00

Sugar bowl, cov., canary 89.00

SCROLL WITH ACANTHUS
Bowl, master berry, blue......................80.00

Bowl, master berry, canary.................78.00

Compote, jelly, blue 44.00

Compote, jelly, green (ILLUS. top next
    column) 42.00

Compote, jelly, white 38.00

Creamer, blue......................................85.00

Cruet w/original stopper, white 95.00

Nappy, white..22.00

Scroll with Acanthus Jelly Compote

Spooner, blue 85.00

Tumbler, blue.......................................90.00

SHELL
Berry set: master bowl & five sauce
    dishes; green, 6 pcs.........................280.00

Creamer, blue......................................60.00

Sauce dish, footed, green.....................55.00

Sauce dish, green.................................25.00

Spooner, green.....................................55.00

S-REPEAT

S-Repeat Berry Bowl

Bowl, master berry, blue (ILLUS.) 70.00

Tumbler, blue.......................................55.00

SUNBURST-ON-SHIELD
Butter dish, cov., blue 375.00

Butter dish, cov., canary 345.00

Creamer & cov. sugar bowl, white,
    pr..135.00

Sauce dish, canary 35.00

SWAG WITH BRACKETS
Berry set: master bowl & two sauce
    dishes; blue, 3 pcs. 175.00

Butter dish, cov., blue 240.00

Butter dish, cov., canary .....225.00 to 250.00

Butter dish, cov., green.......................140.00

Cruet w/original stopper, blue.............550.00

Spooner, canary 70.00

Tumbler, white 35.00

Water set: pitcher & six tumblers;
blue, 7 pcs. 800.00

TOKYO
Bowl, master berry, blue.......................65.00

Compote, jelly, green............................35.00

Dish, low, white....................................30.00

Pitcher, water, green 195.00

Plate, blue..35.00

Sauce dish, blue 25.00

TWIST
Celery, canary 48.00

Creamer, child-size, blue......................95.00

WATER LILY & CATTAILS
Bonbon, two-handled, blue...................35.00

Bowl, 5 x 7½", green............................45.00

Bowl, 8" d., green 50.00

Bowl, 11" d., white 30.00

Butter dish, cov., white 160.00

Spooner, blue 42.50

Tumbler, blue..50.00

Tumbler, green 22.50

WILD BOUQUET

Wild Bouquet Spooner

Bowl, master berry, blue.....125.00 to 150.00

Creamer, blue.....................100.00 to 125.00

Creamer, green 70.00

Creamer, white 45.00

Spooner, blue (ILLUS.)........................95.00

Spooner, white......................................52.00

Table set: cov. sugar bowl, creamer &
spooner; blue, 3 pcs. 350.00

Table set, white, 4 pcs.........250.00 to 275.00

Tumbler, green 80.00

WREATH & SHELL

Wreath & Shell Cuspidor

Berry set: master bowl & six sauce
dishes: canary, 7 pcs. ....250.00 to 275.00

Bowl, 6½" d., footed, crimped rim,
blue 40.00

Butter dish, cov., blue ....250.00 to 295.00

Cuspidor, lady's, blue (ILLUS.) 60.00

Cuspidor, lady's, canary 95.00

Wreath & Shell Rose Bowl

Rose bowl, blue (ILLUS.)......................60.00

Salt dip, footed, canary.......................120.00

Salt dip, footed, green 75.00

Spooner, canary 85.00

Spooner, canary w/enamel
decoration 135.00

Sugar bowl, cov., canary ....160.00 to 190.00

Table set, white, 4 pcs........................395.00

Tumbler, blue..75.00

Toothpick holder, canary 200.00

Water set: pitcher & five tumblers;
   canary, 6 pcs. 795.00

MISCELLANEOUS PRESSED
NOVELTIES

Abalone bowl, w/handles, 6½" d.,
   blue 40.00

Astro bowl, 8" d., white 20.00

Aurora Borealis vase, white..................25.00

Autumn Leaves dish, turned-up sides,
   green...40.00

Barbells bowl, 8½" d., blue 30.00

Basketweave Base, Open-Edged Bowl

Basketweave Base, Open-Edged
   bowl, 5½" d., green (ILLUS.)..............30.00

Basketweave Base, Open-Edged
   bowl, 6½" d., blue 35.00

Beaded Drapes bowl, 8½" d., footed,
   crimped rim, blue 30.00

Beaded Drapes rose bowl, green 30.00

Beaded Fan bowl, 6½" d., 4½" h.,
   square foot, crimped rim, green 35.00

Beaded Fan bowl, 9" d., crimped rim,
   blue 45.00

Beaded Fan rose bowl, blue.................25.00

Beaded Fleur-de-Lis compote, green,
   8" d...35.00

Berry Patch dish, pedestal base,
   green, 5½" d., 2" h. 27.00

Blooms & Blossoms dish w/applied
   handle, blue, 5⅞" sq., 2½" h. 35.00

Blooms & Blossoms dish w/applied
   handle, white, 5⅞" sq., 2½" h. 30.00

Blossoms & Palms bowl, 8½" d.,
   green...30.00

Blossoms & Web bowl, 8" d., blue........50.00

Boggy Bayou vase, blue.......................50.00

Bushel Basket, blue..............................60.00

Button Panels rose bowl, canary 49.00

Calyx vase, blue 40.00

Cashews Bowl

Cashews bowl, 8" d., crimped rim,
   blue (ILLUS.).....................................40.00

Cashews plate, white............................27.50

Coin Spot, Pressed dish, scalloped
   rim, curved-up sides, blue.................35.00

Concave Columns vase, blue...............35.00

Cornucopia dish, two applied handles,
   white 30.00

Daisy & Plume bowl, three-footed,
   green...35.00

Diamond Point & Fleur-de-Lis Bowl

Diamond Point & Fleur-de-Lis bowl,
   8" d., white (ILLUS.) 40.00

Dolphin compote, blue..........................45.00

Dolphin compote, canary........50.00 to 75.00

Dolphin & Herons compote, blue..........50.00

Dolphin Petticoat candlestick, blue.....100.00

Feathers vase, 9" h., green 45.00

Finecut & Roses dish, white 30.00

Fluted Bars & Beads vase, ruffled rim,
   green (ILLUS. top next column) 45.00

Fluted Scrolls with Vine vase, blue.......30.00

Grape & Cherry bowl, 10" d., ruffled
   rim, blue 80.00

Grapevine Cluster vase, white..............25.00

Hilltop Vines chalice, green 50.00

Jewel & Fan bowl, w/ruffled rim, blue ...30.00

Fluted Bars & Beads Vase

Jewel & Fan bowl, green 27.00

Jewel & Fan celery tray, green, 9" l. 40.00

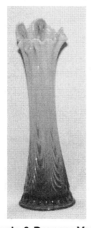

Jewels & Drapery Vase

Jewels & Drapery vase, 12" h., blue
  (ILLUS.) 30.00

Lattice Medallions bowl, 8¾" d.,
  footed, blue 60.00

Laura bowl, w/ruffled rim, white 20.00

Leaf & Beads bowl, 5½" d., three-
  footed, aqua.......................................40.00

Leaf & Beads bowl, blue......................38.00

Leaf & Beads compote, blue 55.00

Maple Leaf Chalice, green....................30.00

Maple Leaf Chalice, white 35.00

Meander bowl, 7" d., crimped rim,
  blue 30.00

Meander bowl, 9½" d., blue 45.00

Northwood's Block celery vase,
  blue w/cranberry rim 50.00

Northwood's Block celery vase,
  green..35.00

Ocean Shell compote, blue 60.00

Old Man Winter basket, footed,
  applied handle, green, small..............45.00

Old Man Winter basket, footed,
  applied handle, canary, large.............75.00

Opal Open rose bowl, blue...................45.00

Opal Open rose bowl, white, 6½" h. 25.00

Pearl Flowers bowl, 9" d., footed,
  green..45.00

Pearl Flowers Bowl

Pearl Flowers bowl, white (ILLUS.) 30.00

Pearls & Scales compote, blue w/cran-
  berry-stained border 30.00

Pearls & Scales compote, canary.........35.00

Pearls & Scales compote, 7" d.,
  green..25.00

Piasa Bird bowl, 8" d., blue..................60.00

Piasa Bird rose bowl, white 65.00

Popsicle Sticks compote, 8" d., 4" h.,
  green..44.00

Pump & Trough, blue, 2 pcs. 160.00

Pump Novelty

Pump & Trough, white, 2 pcs.
  (ILLUS. of pump) ....50.00 to 75.00

Reverse Drapery bowl, 8¼" d., 2¼" h.,
   green..35.00

Roulette bowl, 8" d., crimped rim,
   green..25.00

Roulette bowl, footed, blue 35.00

Ruffles & Rings bowl, 9½" d., green 45.00

Sea Spray nappy, blue 30.00

Sea Spray nappy, green........................27.00

Sea Spray nappy, white.........................20.00

Shell & Wild Rose bowl, 8½" d., blue ...40.00

Sir Lancelot bowl, 8" d., crimped rim,
   blue 50.00

Spokes & Wheels bowl, green..............17.50

Spool compote, green 30.00

Tree Trunk vase, 11" h., blue 42.00

Twig Vase, 4⅝" h., blue........................60.00

Wheel & Block bowl, w/ruffled rim,
   blue 25.00

Windflower bowl, 8" d., blue 50.00

Winter Cabbage bowl, footed,
   crimped rim, blue 60.00

Winterlily vase, blue..............................50.00

(End of Opalescent Glass Section)

traps while their Ravenna is a heavy glass that is usually tinted. All Orrefors glass is desirable but their earlier pieces signed by designers and artists are bringing strongest prices today.

Orrefors

Typical Orrefors Mark

Bowl, 7¾" l., "Ravenna," the narrow curved clear vessel internally decorated w/red & blue overlapping designs, designed by Sven Palmquist, inscribed "ORREFORS - RAVENNA 533 - Sven Palmquist," ca. 1953 ....$2,300.00

Bowl, 5", footed, etched male nudes on a clear background, signed & numbered...285.00

Bowl, 9¼" d., 7" h., exposition-type, clear w/the tall upright sides enameled w/a scene titled "Sailor's Dream" featuring cavorting sailors & naked blonde women & a dance band w/tuba, accordion, bass & violin players, by Gunnar Cyren, signed "Orrefors Expo 682-68 Gunnar Cyren" (ILLUS.)................1,540.00

ORREFORS

Orrefors Enameled Bowl

Orrefors is a well-known Swedish glasshouse founded in 1898 for the production of tablewares. Since 1915 the plant has produced decorative wares and by 1925 the factory was internationally renowned for its unique lines such as Graal glass, an engraved art glass developed by master glassblower Knut Berquist and artist-designers Simon Gate and Edward Hald. Their Ariel glass line is recognized by a design of controlled air

Engraved Bowl & Underplate by Gate

Bowl & underplate, the clear flaring circular bowl engraved w/four scrolling panels depicting nude maidens w/flowing hair, the underplate engraved w/scrolls, designed by Simon Gate, bowl engraved "Orrefors. Gate. 107.28," 7¾" d., 2 pcs. (ILLUS.)..................1,840.00

Center bowl & underplate, the clear bowl w/deep flaring sides engraved w/nude maidens cavorting amid stylized foliage, within fanciful borders, the underplate conform-

ingly engraved, designed by Simon
Gate, inscribed "Gate 128 - Orrefors
1731 E.R.," ca. 1917-21, underplate
9" d., 2 pcs. 2,875.00

Impressive Engraved Bowl & Underplate

Center bowl & underplate, clear
flaring elliptical bowl w/oval
underplate, the bowl engraved w/a
mythological scene of two couples in
a garden, the rim of the underdish
engraved w/a floral band, designed
by Simon Gate in 1920, engraved by
Emil Weidlich in 1927, inscribed
"Orrefors 1927. S. Gate 147.-EW.,"
14¾" l., 4⅝" h. (ILLUS.) 2,875.00

Decanter w/original stopper, the clear
rectangular bottle engraved w/a
cancan dancer balancing martini
glasses on one foot & both hands,
silvered-metal stopper, designed
by Simon Gate, inscribed "S.G.
293.28," ca. 1922, 7⅝" h..................288.00

Orrefors Decanter & Vases

Decanter w/original stopper, flattened
clear shouldered body etched on
each side w/Susanna bathing w/the
Old Men watching her, w/conforming
clear stopper, etched "Orrefors 1230
28 BL," 9½" h. (ILLUS. center).........690.00

Platter, 13 x 16¼" oval, "Ariel," clear
w/symmetrically arranged airtrap
design in concentric bands, signed
"Orrefors Ariel No. 1799E, Edvin
Ohrstrom".......................................230.00

Vase, 4" h., short cylindrical body in
clear shading to blue at the top,
decorated w/an inclusion of a yellow
- blue grid pattern centered by an
air-trap bubble design, designed by
Sven Palmquist, inscribed

"ORREFORS - Kraka No. 428 -
Sven Palmquist"..............................403.00

Vase, 4¾" h., "Graal," thick-walled
ovoid clear body w/internal fish &
seaweed in green & black, engraved
on base "Orrefors Sweden Graal
#2960 Edward Hald".......................546.00

Vase, 5¼" h., "Ariel," cylindrical
colorless body inlaid w/repeating
bubble stripes in cobalt blue, signed
"Ingeborg Lundin Ariel No. 351K" 440.00

Vase, 5½" h., "Graal," heavy green
cylindrical body w/rounded shoulders internally decorated w/a scene
of a deep sea diver meeting a
demure mermaid, inscribed
"Orrefors Graal-301B" (some
staining) 412.50

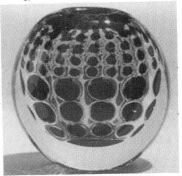

Orrefors Bulbous Ariel Vase

Vase, 5¾" h., "Ariel," bulbous ovoid
body w/thick clear walls internally
decorated w/controlled air bubbles
in cobalt blue, designed by Ingeborg
Lundin, signed "Orrefors - Ariel Nu
334 M - Ingeborg Lundin," ca. 1963
(ILLUS.) 1,150.00

Vase, 6" h., "Graal," bulbous faceted
clear body internally decorated
w/tropical fish among aquatic plants
in shades of green, designed by
Edward Hald, signed "ORREFORS -
SWEDEN - GRAAL - NU 454 - B -
Edward Hald," ca. 1947 ....518.00

Vase, 6" h., "Graal," ovoid body, clear
w/inclusions of green fish & underwater plants, inscribed "Orrefors
Sveden Graal No. 2512".................368.00

Vase, 6¼" h., "Ariel," bulbous body
w/small cylindrical neck & mouth,
internally decorated w/a striped
pattern in pale blue & brown, signed
"Orrefors Sweden Ariel #1863E
Edvin Ohrstrom"............................1,210.00

Vase, 6¾" h., "Ariel," 'Faces,' four-
sided cylindrical body internally

Orrefors Ariel 'Faces' Vase

decorated w/four stylized profiles in deep olive green within the clear sides, the interior in deep ochre, designed by Ingeborg Lundin, inscribed "ORREFORS - Ariel No. 560-F - Ingeborg Lundin," ca. 1982 (ILLUS.) 3,163.00

Orrefors Jellyfish 'Graal' Vase

Vase, 6¾" h., "Graal," the bulbous ovoid body w/thick clear walls internally decorated in shades of green w/jellyfish floating among aquatic plants, designed by Edward Hald, signed "Orrefors - Sweden - Graal Nu. 619 - Edward Hald," ca. 1941 (ILLUS.) 1,380.00

Vase, 7" h., the clear deep vessel w/optically ribbed sides, raised on a black base, inscribed "Of.32 - H. U. 97. H.," 1932 ....460.00

Vase, 7½" h., "Ariel," bulbous tapering form internally decorated w/a female profile & a bird in blue, clear & brown, designed by Edvin Ohrstrom, artist-signed & marked "Orrefors Ariel 559-92" 4,950.00

Orrefors 'Dykaren' Diver Vase

Vase, 9" h., wide flaring cylindrical clear body w/molded 'ocean' ripples & waves as a background for an engraved nude male diver & several fish, inscribed "Orrefors Hald 1399. A.I.G.E.," variation of Lindstrand's 'Dykaren' diver (ILLUS.)...................977.50

Vase, 11" h., clear footed conical body, rippled below to depict turbulent waters beneath an etched sailboat, designed by Vicke Lindstrand, inscribed "Orrefors Lindstrand 1402 C3 R" (ILLUS. right, with decanter) 1,955.00

Vase, 11¼" h., "Dykaren," tapering cylindrical body decorated w/an engraved naked male diver viewed through horizontal ridges forming "waves" w/bubbles, applied black foot, designed by Vicke Lindstrand, inscribed "Orrefors Lindstrand 1343 A3R"...935.00

Vase, 11½" h., clear heavily walled cylinder, slightly rippled for an aquatic effect, etched to depict a muscular nude male diver, designed by Vicke Lindstrand, inscribed "Orrefors Lindstrand 1348 338.RR" (ILLUS. left with decanter) 1,955.00

Vase, 12⅜" h., pale amber w/a trumpet-form neck & foot conjoined to a spherical center section, designed by Edward Hald, model no. 882, ca. 1930 ....345.00

Vase, 12½" h., the flaring clear cylindrical vessel w/optically wavy sides engraved w/two nude male divers, designed by Vicke Lind-strand, inscribed "Orrefors L. 1348 CG?," ca. 1935 ....3,450.00

Vase, 13¾" h., conical body on a

black disc foot, etched to represent
three nude male divers swimming
beneath the sea, designed by Vicke
Lindstrand, signed, ca. 1935........3,680.00

OVERSHOT

*Overshot glass has been popular since
the mid-19th century when original
manufacturers referred to it as "Craquelle."
This ware is produced by having a gather
of molten glass rolled in finely crushed
glass to produce a rough exterior finish.
The object was then blown to the desired
size and shape. The completed piece had a
frosted or iced finish and is sometimes
referred to as "ice glass." Although
Overshot is sometimes lumped together
with the glass collectors now call "crackle,"
that glass was produced using a totally
different technique.*

Overshot Claret Set

Overshot Decanter & Pitcher

Overshot Celery Vase

Basket, opaque lemon yellow
   w/applied opaque lemon yellow
   handle, squatty bulbous body
   w/upright ruffled rim, molded swirling
   ribs, overshot exterior finish, overall
   gilt trim, 3½" d., 3¼" h. $110.00

Celery vase, scalloped top, cranberry,
   3½" d., 6" h. (ILLUS.) 85.00

Claret set: 9½" h. decanter w/ovoid
   glass body fitted w/a pewter pedestal foot, long handle & tall embossed
   neck w/ornate spout & hinged,
   domed cover & four glass-bowled
   clarets fitted on turned pewter stems
   & domed feet; each piece in Rubina
   Crystal w/overshot finish, 5 pcs.
   (ILLUS. top next column) 475.00

Compote, open, 9" d., 7" h., pedestal
   base, clear w/irregular h.p. gold
   design, attributed to the Boston &
   Sandwich Glass Company...............200.00

Decanter w/pointed clear blown
   stopper, bulbous cranberry body
   tapering to a cylindrical neck
   w/rolled rim, 4½" d., 9½" h. (ILLUS.
   left) 125.00

Finger bowl, paneled body w/flared
   rim, pink, 4⅝" h. 65.00

Goblet, clear w/applied cranberry
   snake stem 190.00

Pitcher, 5⅝" h., 3½" d., waisted
   cylindrical body w/flared rim, orange
   shaded to vaseline, vaseline applied
   handle 125.00

Pitcher, tankard, 7¼" h., 3¾" d.,
   slightly tapering cylindrical cranberry
   body, clear applied reeded handle
   (ILLUS. right, with decanter) 145.00

Pitcher, 9¾" h., 4½" d., tapering ovoid
   cranberry body w/indented ice
   bladder at the back, the sides
   tapering to a tricorner rim, clear

Overshot Pitcher with Ice Bladder

applied twisted & braided rope
handle (ILLUS.).................................295.00

Powder jar, cov., clear w/applied
cranberry snake on cover 135.00

Punch bowl, cover & underplate,
clear, large applied green snake
handle on cover, the set 950.00

Vase, 13¼", baluster-form body
w/flaring neck w/flat rim, brilliant
fiery canary yellow w/applied
turquoise blue neck & rim ring,
attributed to the Reading Artistic
Glass Works, Reading,
Pennsylvania, associated
w/Joseph Bornique, late 19th c.....2,415.00

PAIRPOINT

Pairpoint Covered Compote

*The Pairpoint Manufacturing Company
was originally founded in 1880 in New
Bedford, Massachusetts where it was
adjacent to the site of the Mount Washington Glass Company. At first Pairpoint*

*manufactured silver and plated wares but
in 1894 the two famous factories merged to
become the Pairpoint Corporation which
operated successfully for over forty years.
In 1939 a group of local businesssmen
bought the plant but eventually one of the
group bought out the others and then
turned the management over to Robert M.
Gundersen. Gundersen then operated the
Gundersen Glass Works until 1952 when,
after Gundersen's death, the name was
changed to Gundersen-Pairpoint. This
plant closed in 1959, but sometime later
Robert Bryden took charge and began
producing glass abroad for Pairpoint. In
1970 production began again at a plant in
Sagamore, Massachusetts and today the
Pairpoint Crystal Glass Company, now
owned by Robert and June Bancroft,
continues to produce quality blown and
pressed glass.*

Atomizer, bulbous base tapering to a
cylindrical neck, embossed swirl
design, h.p. lily of the valley &
scrolling decoration on white
ground, signed "2341," 6" h. $285.00

Bowl, 6½" d., 2½" h., amber bowl
w/applied cobalt blue feet 150.00

Box w/hinged cover, border of aqua &
white scrolls surrounding vines of
wild roses on cover, aqua base
decorated w/wild roses, raised on a
gilt-metal frame marked "Pairpoint,"
4¼ x 6¾", 4" h.................................675.00

Castor set: two square cruets
w/original square cut stoppers, one
square mustard jar w/original silver
plate top, w/circular handle & a
silver plate holder w/ornate handle
marked "Hartford;" clear w/cut &
etched overall floral designs, the
set 150.00

Compote, cov., 8¾" d., 13" h., clear
deep rounded bowl on a knop
stem & round foot, domed cover
w/knop finial encasing a white
rose & green leaves, the sides
engraved w/a rosebush on trellis
design, leafy floral bands on cover &
foot (ILLUS.) 550.00

Cornucopia-vase, ruby w/clear
"controlled bubble" ball connector,
9" h..125.00

Cracker jar, cov., milk white w/h.p.
blue Delft scenic decoration, silver
plate rim, cover & handle, 5¾" h. 525.00

Cracker jar, cov., barrel-shaped teal
blue Inverted Thumbprint body,
silver plate rim, bail handle & low-
domed cover w/ribbed ball finial,
5" d., 7½" h. 445.00

Pitcher, 12" h., green body & foot
w/clear applied handle & "controlled
bubble" knop stem 155.00

Plates, 8" d., Tavern line, clear w/gal-
leon decoration, set of twelve 2,400.00

Tumbler, barrel-shaped, clear w/h.p.
black enameled galleon under full
sail & rim trim 235.00

Vase, 4½" h., footed spherical body,
clear w/enameled floral decoration,
"controlled bubble" ball connector on
base, numbered in pontil 75.00

Pairpoint 'Tavern' Line Vase

Vase, 6" h., ovoid body tapering to a
short flaring neck, Tavern line (clear
glass w/thousands of bubbles),
decorated in black & colors w/a
sailing galleon on a wavy sea &
enameled rings, signed "D1507"
(ILLUS.) 485.00

Vase, 9½" h., trumpet-form clear bowl
cut in floral decoration w/Aurora
(golden amber) applied rim, knob
stem & an applied base rim 285.00

Vase, 12" h., trumpet-shaped green
body, clear "controlled bubble" ball
connector & green foot 95.00

Vase, 13" h., 6½" d., cobalt blue
trumpet-shaped body & pedestal
foot w/clear "controlled bubble" ball
connector 235.00

Vases, 12" h., ruby body & foot, clear
"controlled bubble" knop connector,
pr..300.00

PAPERWEIGHTS

*Although paperweights have been
produced from many materials, those
made of glass are among the finest and*

*most collectible. A great wave of collecting
began in the mid-19th century when the
French glass factories of St. Louis, Clichy
and Baccarat began producing beautiful
and ornate weights. Similar weights were
later produced in England and other parts
of Europe and even the New England
Glass Company and the Boston &
Sandwich Glass Company in this country
produced some weights. The art of
paperweight making continued on a lesser
scale into the early 20th century, especially
in smaller American factories, but those
examples don't compare in quality to the
early French pieces.*

*Since about the 1960s there has been a
revival in the production of top-quality
paperweights in France and England and
today a number of talented American
artists produce beautiful examples rivaling
the quality of the 19th century French
originals.*

Baccarat Anemone Weight

Baccarat "Anemone" weight, clear set
w/six pointed white petals edged in
monochromatic shades of cobalt
blue about a white stardust stamen
w/a red whorl cane center, growing
from a slightly curved green stem
w/six green leaves & five further
leaves about the flower, star-cut
base, 2¾" d. (ILLUS.) $776.00

Baccarat "Bouquet de Marriage
Mushroom" weight, the tuft
composed entirely of white stardust
canes w/salmon whorl cane centers
about a central grouping of similarly
colored star canes encompassing a
cobalt blue, red & white arrowhead
cane flower w/a star silhouette
stamen, framed w/a white gauze
cable at the periphery within cobalt
blue spiral threads & mercury
bands, star-cut base, 2¹¹/₁₆" d........2,645.00

Baccarat "Close Millefiori" signed &
dated weight, clear set w/assorted
brightly colored millefiori canes
including silhouettes of a rooster, a

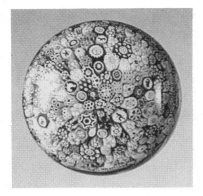

Baccarat Close Millefiori Weight

monkey, an elephant, a dog, a
dancing devil, a horse & a squirrel,
signed & dated "B 1847," wear,
3⅜6" d. (ILLUS.) 2,300.00

Baccarat "Concentric Millefiori
Mushroom" weight, the tuft
composed of three rows of millefiori
canes comprising: coral cogwheel
canes lined w/green trefoils & star
silhouettes; white stardusts w/red
centers & cobalt blue, red & white
arrowhead canes w/red star
silhouette centers about a central
composite cane grouping of green
shamrocks & red whorl canes within
a basket of elongated white staves
lined in yellow w/pink centers
encompassed by a white gauze
cable within cobalt blue spiral
threads & mercury bands, star-cut
base, 3⅜6" d. (minor wear) 1,955.00

Baccarat Faceted Pompon Weight

Baccarat "Faceted Pompon" weight,
the clear glass set w/a flower
composed of white recessed petals
about a yellow stardust stamen,
growing from a curved green stem

w/four leaves & a red bud w/four
further leaves about the flower, cut
w/a window & six side printies,
star-cut base, 3⅛" d. (ILLUS.) 1,725.00

Baccarat Faceted Sulphide Weight

Baccarat "Faceted Sulphide" weight,
the clear glass set w/a sulphide
depicting a hunter & his dog in a
woodland scene, set on a ruby-
flashed ground circular foot, cut w/a
decagonal window & geometric
facets, small chips & surface wear,
3⅜" d. (ILLUS.) 2,070.00

Baccarat "Garlanded Butterfly" weight,
the insect formed w/two shaded
orange, red, purple, yellow & white
millefiori cane wings overlapping two
smaller marbled & brightly colored
wings w/a a purple gauze cable
body, two blue eyes, a black head &
antennae encompassed by a
garland of white, pink & green
cogwheel composite canes
alternating w/ green, red & white
star silhouette canes, star-cut
base, 3⅜6" d. (minor scratches to
surface) 3,450.00

Baccarat Pansy Weight

Baccarat "Pansy" weight, clear set w/a flower composed of two upper purple petals & three lower amber petals edged in white w/purple markings & stripes about a white star honeycomb cane stamen, growing from a curved green stem w/seven leaves, a purple bud & four further leaves about the flower, star-cut base, minor surface wear, 3⅛" d. (ILLUS.) 690.00

Baccarat "Primrose" weight, the clear glass set w/six rounded red petals w/white stripes about a white stardust stamen w/a cobalt blue whorl cane center, growing from a curved green stem w/six leaves & seven further leaves about the flower, 2⁷⁄₁₆" d. 978.00

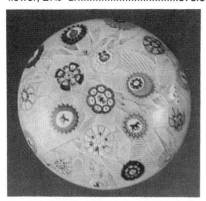

Baccarat Scattered Millefiori Weight

Baccarat "Scattered Millefiori" signed & dated weight, clear set w/assorted brightly colored millefiori canes including silhouettes of a horse, a dog, two pigeons, an elephant, a goat, a rooster & a swan about a central butterfly cane, set on an upset muslin ground w/various cane fragments, signed & dated "B 1838," 3" d. (ILLUS.) 1,840.00

Baccarat "Stylized Flower" weight, clear set w/six rounded yellow petals edged in white & six red ribbed, pointed petals about a white stardust stamen w/a yellow whorl cane center, growing from a curved green stem w/six leaves & five further leaves about the flowers, star-cut base, minor surface wear, 2⁹⁄₁₆" d. (ILLUS.) 3,680.00

Bacchus "Close Millefiori" weight, the clear glass set w/assorted millefiori canes in shades of claret, green, purple, yellow, turquoise, blue &

Baccarat Stylized Flower Weight

white including silhouettes of women, leaves & stars, England, 19th c., 3⁷⁄₁₆" d. (surface wear)......2,300.00

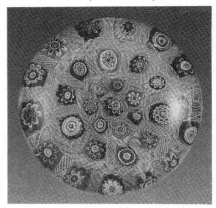

Clichy Chequer Magnum Weight

Clichy "Chequer" magnum weight, the clear glass set w/three concentric rows of assorted brightly colored millefiori canes including a large pink & green rose cane at the periphery & a smaller similarly colored rose cane near the center encompassing a claret, green & white composite pastrymold cane, divided by short lengths of white latticinio tubing, 4⅜" d. (ILLUS.) ...9,488.00

Clichy "Concentric Millefiori Colorground" weight, the clear glass set w/six pink & white stardust canes divided by green pastrymold canes at the periphery above a row of coral pastrymold canes, an inner row of white edelweiss canes & a central pink & green rose cane, set on an opaque cobalt blue ground, 2½" d. 1,725.00

Clichy "Concentric Millefiori Pie-douche" weight, clear set w/seven

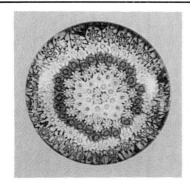

Clichy Concentric Millefiori Piedouche

rows of composite, pastrymold & stardust canes in shades of green, pink, blue, yellow & white about a central grouping of three shaded red pastrymold canes within a basket of alternating fuchsia, green & white elongated stave canes, set on a spreading circular clear foot, chips to foot & minor wear, 2¾" d., 2⁵⁄₁₆" h. (ILLUS.) 690.00

Clichy "Faceted Chequer" magnum weight, the clear glass set w/three rows of assorted brightly colored millefiori canes graduating in size including two pink & green rose canes about a central deep purple, red & white cogwheel composite cane, divided by short lengths of white latticinio tubing above a ground of white horizontal gauze cables, cut w/a window & three rows of printies, 4⁹⁄₁₆" d. 8.,050.00

Clichy "Garlanded Colorground Posy" weight, clear set w/a spray of five bright lime green leaves w/two pink pastrymold canes & a moss cane in the center encompassed by a garland of eighteen white pastry-mold canes w/pink centers divided by six pink & green rose canes, set on an opaque cobalt blue ground w/traces of white areas, surface wear, 2¹¹⁄₁₆" d. 3,680.00

Clichy "Pansy" weight, the clear glass set w/a flower composed of two upper purple shaded petals above three lower yellow petals edged in purple & similarly colored markings about a green stamen center, growing from a curved green stem w/seven shaded green leaves & a purple bud pendant from an elongated green stem, 2¾" d. 1,380.00

Millville-type weight, multicolored segmented mushroom on a pedestal foot, 3½" d., 3¾" h. 115.00

New England Faceted Bouquet Weight

New England "Faceted Upright Bouquet" weight, the clear glass set w/four millefiori canes in shades of yellow, red, and cobalt blue, three flowers in shades of red, white & cobalt blue, each w/similarly colored millefiori cane stamens among six green leaf tips, set on a white latticino ground, cut w/a window & two rows of six side printies divided by vertical ribs, 2¹¹⁄₁₆" d. (ILLUS.) ..2,185.00

New England "Poinsettia" weight, blue blossom w/green & white latticino ground, 19th c., 3" d. 431.00

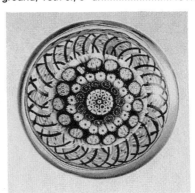

St. Louis Concentric Millefiori Weight

St. Louis "Concentric Millefiori Mushroom " signed & dated weight, clear w/the tuft composed of five rows of assorted millefiori canes in shades of blue, coral, green, red & white about a cobalt blue, red & white floret cane center within a basket of alternating elongated salmon & white composite canes encompassed by a white corkscrew cable within cobalt blue spiral threads & a mercury band, signed & dated "SL 1848," star-cut base, 2¹³⁄₁₆" d. (ILLUS.) 4,600.00

St. Louis Dahlia Weight

St. Louis "Dahlia" weight, clear set
w/a flower composed of numerous
recessed shaded pink, ribbed &
pointed petals about an ochre, pale
blue & white composite cane
stamen encompassed by five green
serrated leaftips, star-cut base,
small bruise to edge of base,
2¹⁵⁄₁₆" d. (ILLUS.) 6,038.00

St. Louis Double Clematis Weight

St. Louis "Double Clematis" weight,
the clear glass set w/two rows of five
overlapping ribbed & pointed petals
in shades of lilac & turquoise about
a yellow stamen center, growing
from a curved green stem w/two
serrated leaves & a further leaf
about the flower, set on a white
latticino ground, 2¹⁵⁄₁₆" d.
(ILLUS.) 1,495.00

St. Louis "Faceted Upright Bouquet"
weight, the clear glass set w/a
central white flower formed w/a
cobalt blue, green & white
composite pastrymold cane stamen
encompassed by four smaller

St. Louis Faceted Bouquet Weight

flowers in shades of amber, coral,
cobalt blue & white, joined by a
cluster of several green leaves
framed in a cobalt blue & white
spiral torsade & mercury bands, cut
w/six side printies & a star-cut base,
2¾" h. (ILLUS.) 1,955.00

St. Louis "Faceted Upright Bouquet"
magnum weight, the clear glass set
w/several flowers in shades of
cobalt blue, orange, red & white
about a central red flower w/a yellow
stamen, the whole joined by
numerous pointed green leaves
forming a full bouquet, cut w/an
octagonal window & geo-metric
facets throughout, 3¹⁵⁄₁₆" d. 4,600.00

St. Louis "Fuchsia" weight, the clear
glass set w/a coral colored flower
w/similarly colored pistils & cobalt
blue inner petals, growing from a
pink stem pendant from a magenta
branch w/four green leaves & three
red buds, set on a white latticino
ground, 2⅞" d. 1,840.00

St. Louis Garland Weight

St. Louis "Garland" weight, clear set
w/ten flowers at the periphery in
shades of amber, coral, cobalt blue
& white w/either yellow or cobalt

blue stamens, each growing from serrated green leaves about a central white flower w/a yellow stamen & four green pointed leaves, the center of the surface w/a convex layer of glass, 2¹³⁄₁₆" d. (ILLUS.) 1,495.00

St. Louis "Pansy" weight, the clear glass set w/a flower composed of two upper purple petals & three lower amber petals edged in cobalt blue w/purple markings about a yellow stamen, growing from a curved green stem w/two leaves & two further leaves about the flower, star-cut base, 2⁷⁄₁₆" (chips) 748.00

St. Louis "Plum" weight, the clear glass set w/two bright cobalt blue plums w/yellow stems pendent from an ochre forked branch w/three serrated green leaves, 2¾" d. 575.00

St. Louis Strawberry Weight

St. Louis "Strawberry" weight, the clear glass set w/a strawberry in different stages of growth as a central flower composed of five white ribbed petals about a shaded blue & green pastrymold cane stamen & two red berries below, growing from a curved green stem w/three green leaves, set on a white latticino ground, 2¹¹⁄₁₆" d. (ILLUS.) ...863.00

Sandwich Weedflower-Pansy Weight

Sandwich "Weedflower-type Pansy" weight, the clear glass set w/a flower composed of two cobalt blue upper petals & two lower pink & white striped petals & one w/pink, blue & white stripes about a red, white & blue composite cane stamen w/gold flecks, growing from a curved green stem w/two leaves & a further leaf about the flower, 2⅝" d. (ILLUS.) 690.00

Stankard (Paul) "Cattleya Orchid Colorground" weight, the clear glass set w/a flower composed of five shaded pink petals about a white stamen, growing from a long curved variegated green stem w/two leaves, set on an opaque green ground w/a white ground below, signed w/a single "S" cane & engraved "26676 66/75," 3" d. 920.00

Stankard (Paul) "Day Lily" weight, the clear glass set w/a flower composed of six bright orange petals about a yellow pistil center edged in black growing from a slightly curved variegated green stem w/three bright orange buds & four long green leaves, signed w/a single "S" cane & numbered "66/95 07676," 2⅞" d...633.00

Stankard (Paul) "Environment" magnum weight, the clear glass set w/four flowers, each stamen center w/red pistils, three pale yellow buds, two variegated green buds & three red berries, growing from creeping vines in shades of green, w/a black & yellow bee w/two translucent brown wings approaching the berries, set on a sandy ground, signed w/a single "S" cane & engraved "A155 1983," 4⅛" d...4,600.00

Stankard Goat's Rue Weight

Stankard (Paul) "Goat's Rue Color-ground" weight, clear set w/seven small bright orange blossoms, each w/yellow pistils, growing from curved & variegated green stems w/curling tendrils, six leaves & two further leaves near the periphery, set on an opaque white ground, signed w/a single "PS" cane, engraved "45/50 1975 A847," extremely small base edge nicks, 2⁹⁄₁₆" d. (ILLUS.) 920.00

Stankard (Paul) "Plantain Color-ground" weight, the clear glass set w/three flowers comprised of numerous tiny red petals, growing from three variegated green stems w/five buds & dark purple roots, set on an opaque white ground, signed w/a single "PS" cane & engraved" 1974 © A566 1/50," 2½" d. (extremely small nicks to edge of base) 805.00

(End of Paperweight Section)

PATE DE VERRE

Pate de Verre Bowl

Pate de Verre, French for "paste of glass," is a unique molded glassware which was produced by only a few artisans, most notably several French firms who worked early this century. The pate de verre technique involves mixing powdered glass with a liquid to make a paste which is then placed in a mold and fired at a high temperature. The resulting pieces have a finely pitted or matte finish quite different from blown or pressed glass. Because of the mold process duplicate pieces can be produced.

A WALTER NANCY   G·ARGY ROUSSEAU

Typical Pate de Verre Marks

Bowl, 3¾" d., circular, molded w/an

abstract lotus pattern in various shades of green, molded signature "A WALTER NANCY" $633.00

Bowl, 4" h., flaring ovoid body in white & green molded w/violet clusters of stephanotis blossoms, signed in the mold "G. ARGY-ROUSSEAU" (ILLUS.) 3,680.00

Bowl, 11¾" d., wide shallow sides molded in low-relief w/flutes radiating from a central stylized swirling star, blue, molded "DECORCHMENT" & inscribed "A 413/1.26," Francois Décorchment, ca. 1925 ....3,162.00

Pate de Verre Bowl-Vase

Bowl-vase, molded decoration of amethyst & purple blossoms w/white accents & articulated black stamen centers, impressed mold mark "G. Argy-Rousseau," 4¾" d., 3" h. (ILLUS.) 6,900.00

Centerbowl, circular w/shallow sloping sides, molded w/a design of seven exotic long-legged birds above a central multi-petalled blossom, design repeated on the exterior & foot, in shades of blue, purple & green, signed "G. Argy-Rousseau," 10⅜" d., 3¾" h. 6,600.00

Coupe, "Sur Pied Aux Anses," grey mottled w/light & dark amber & molded w/central blossoms on the sides flanked by large stylized curved horn handles, molded "G. ARGY-ROUSSEAU," ca. 1927, 4⅛" h..3,450.00

Dish, shallow sides w/two scrolled handles, the mottled amber body molded w/stylized flowers & leaves, signed in the mold "G. ARGY-ROUSSEAU," 8¼" l. 5,175.00

Figure of Tanagra, the woman clothed in flowing classical drapery in shades of grass green streaked w/emerald green & spring green,

Figure of Tanagra

ground & polished, signed "A Walter
- Nancy," ca. 1925, 8" h.
(ILLUS.) 2,070.00

Lamp, table-type, "Feuillage Exotic,"
the oviform shade & fitted lower dish
w/silver grey ground molded w/lav-
ender, mauve & deep purple stylized
flower petals about the top & middle,
raised on a wrought-iron base
w/circular foot, both shades signed
in the mold "G. ARGY-ROUSSEAU,"
ca. 1925, 12½" h.........................16,100.00

Lamp base, cylindrical, grey mottled
w/amber, green, red & black,
molded in low-relief w/stems of
roses, w/wrought-iron textured foot
& top, molded "G. ARGY-
ROUSSEAU," ca. 1919, 7½" h. 9,200.00

Paperweight, figural, cast in full-relief
as a green frog seated on a mottled
brown & green round base, modeled
by Henri Bergé, inscribed "A Walter
- Nancy - Berge Sclt.," ca. 1925,
2" d...3,450.00

Paperweight, figural, cast a stylized
mouse lying spread-eagled on a
circular base, in grey mottled
w/rose, purple, ochre & green,
molded factory mark "DECOR-
CHEMONT," inscribed "D352,"
ca. 1950, 4" d., 2¼" h...................1,840.00

Pendant, rectangular w/slightly
outcurved sides, grey body molded
in low- and medium-relief w/a
pendent pine cone & needles in
emerald green & chocolate brown,
molded "G.A.R.," 1921, w/original
silk cord, 2¼" l...............................1,495.00

Tile, hexagonal, molded w/a large
crab & various yellow seashells &
grasses, marked on side "A Walter
Nancy," 7" w. (ILLUS. left) 920.00

Pate de Verre Tile & Vide Poche

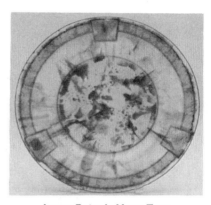

Large Pate de Verre Tray

Tray, thick walled circular plate in
clear w/brilliant & pale pink, amethyst & purple mottling, orange &
black accent coloration, molded leaf
border design w/persimmon fruits,
molded signature "G. Argy-
Rousseau," three small chips at
edge, 12¼" d. (ILLUS.) 1,320.00

Vase, 2¾" h., cupped body molded in
low-relief beneath the rim w/a band
of roses, grey shaded w/olive, pink
& green, signed "G. ARGY-
ROUSSEAU," molded "11948,"
ca. 1921 ....2,875.00

Vase, 5½" h., simple ovoid body
w/closed rim, press-molded &
carved, amethyst & frosted clear
decorated w/three black & green
molded crabs w/pincher claws &
red eyes surrounded by naturalistic
seaweed, impressed at center "G.
Argy-Rousseau" & w/"France" on
the base (ILLUS. top next
page)..5,500.00

Pate de Verre Crab Vase

Vase, 6½" h., ovoid body tapering to a wide flaring rim, grey mottled w/purple & violet, molded around the lower half w/furling spotted leaves in green & cobalt blue, molded "G. ARGY-ROUSSEAU" & "18025," ca. 1925 ....4,025.00

Vase, 7½" h., cylindrical body w/everted rim, mottled amber ground molded w/the heads of three long-haired maidens in colors of Tuscany red, brown & silver grey, signed in the mold "G. ARGY-ROUSSEAU," ca. 1928..............16,100.00

Trumpet-Form Pate de Verre Vase

Vase, 7¾" h., trumpet-form body, grey streaked w/rose, violet & crimson, molded in low-relief w/lappets & a lower band of various decorative devices, molded "G. ARGY-ROUS-SEAU," ca. 1927 (ILLUS.)...........11,500.00

Vase, 8½" h., flaring cylindrical body molded w/overlapping triangles & a patterned rim & foot, in grey mottled & streaked w/deep cobalt blue & turquoise, molded "G. ARGY ROUSSEAU," ca. 1925.................8,625.00

Pate de Verre 'Lions' Vase

Vase, 8¾" h., expanding cylinder, grey mottled w/ochre, pale yellow, brick red & charcoal grey, molded in low-relief w/three striding lions between borders of highly stylized scrolling foliage, molded "G. ARGY-ROUSSEAU" & "FRANCE," ca. 1926 (ILLUS.) 35,650.00

Vase, 9½" h., ovoid body tapering to a slightly flared wide mouth, molded w/stylized diaphanously draped maiden within an apple orchard above a band of stylized Greek key design, mottled shades of violet, aubergine, pale red, pink & dusty grey, signed in the mold "G. ARGY-ROUSSEAU - FRANCE," ca. 1926 ....55,200.00

Vase, 11¾" h., "Libation," ovoid, two portraits of an Egyptian woman carrying a water jug, w/broad frieze of repeating geometric devices between, executed in warm shades of orange, yellow & brown, impressed in mold "G. Argy-Rousseau" 38,500.00

Veilleuse (night light), ovoid grey shade streaked w/purple, amber & emerald green, cast in medium-relief w/three grotesque masques between zigzag borders, above a brickwork ground, in shades of raspberry, chocolate brown & black, simple wrought-iron mounts, signed "G. ARGY-ROUSSEAU," ca. 1923, 7½" h...6,325.00

Veilleuse (night light), ovoid body in grey mottled w/amber & streaked w/purple & green, molded in low-relief w/bands in charcoal enclosing flowerheads in crimson, fitting onto a circular wrought-iron base raised

on three ball feet, fitted w/a cap of
wrought-iron w/chiseled flowerheads & a hammered ball knob,
molded "G. ARGY-ROUSSEAU,"
ca. 1925 ....5,750.00

Vide poche (figural dish), irregular
contour, cast in low-, medium- and
high-relief w/oak leaves & acorns, a
beetle cast in full-relief at the center,
in shades of lemon yellow, lime
green, ochre, avocado & rust,
signed in intaglio "DAUM - NANCY"
w/cross of Lorraine, ca. 1920,
8¼" l. 3,450.00

Vide poche (figural dish), an
elongated shell-form shallow dish
applied at one rim w/a figural hermit
crab, in naturalistic colors w/green &
yellow predominant, molded marks
"A Walter, Nancy" & "Berge Sc.,"
9" l., 4" h.......................................2,530.00

Vide poche (figural dish), a shallow
oblong dish w/a realistic cockatoo
perched on one end, naturalistic
yellow coloring, molded mark "A.
Walter, Nancy" & "Berge Sc," 6½" l.,
6½" h. (ILLUS. right, with tile) 2,760.00

PEACH BLOW

*Originally inspired by a Chinese
porcelain vase with a "Peach Bloom" glaze,
the glass called Peach Blow was produced
in several versions by a half dozen
glasshouses beginning in the 1880s.
Hobbs, Brockunier & Company, Wheeling,
West Virginia made a plated ware that
shaded from red at the top to yellow at the
base and is called Wheeling Peach Blow.
The Mt. Washington Glass Company made
a homogeneous ware shading from rose
pink at the top to a pale blue below and
their version is the rarest type. The New
England Glass Company called their
version "Wild Rose" and it shaded from
deep rose at the top to creamy white at the
base. A somewhat similar ware was made
at the Steuben Glass Works, the Boston &
Sandwich factory and, in England, by
Thomas Webb & Sons and Stevens &
Williams. The English types are two-
layered glass. In the early 1950s the
Gundersen-Pairpoint Co. reproduced some
Mt. Washington Peach Blow.*

*A similar single-layer shaded glass was
brought out early this century by the New
Martinsville Glass Mfg. Co. which they
called "Muranese." Collectors today call
this line "New Martinsville Peach Blow."*

GUNDERSEN - PAIRPOINT

Butter dish, cov. $250.00

Compote, 4½" d., 3" h., paper label....150.00

Cup & saucer, glossy finish 250.00

Toothpick holder 350.00

MT. WASHINGTON

Peach Blow Creamer & Sugar Bowl

Creamer & open sugar bowl, lightly
mold-ed ribs, satin finish, applied
satin handles, one of the items sold
at the Libbey exhibit at the 1893
World's Fair, sugar bowl bears faint
trace of that decoration, 2½" h., pr.
(ILLUS.) 850.00

NEW ENGLAND

Tumbler with Satin Finish

Bowl, 5¼" d., 2½" h., scalloped rim 300.00

Celery vase, bulging cylindrical form
w/pie crust crimped rim, 3½" d........545.00

Rose bowl, bulbous, seven-crimp top,
satin finish, 2¾" d., 2⅝" h. 300.00

Tumbler, cylindrical, satin finish,
3¾" h. (ILLUS.) 475.00

Vase, 7" h., squatty bulbous base
tapering to a tall slender 'stick'
neck 239.00

WEBB

Small Webb Decorated Vases

Bowl, 4" d., 2½" h., squatty bulbous
shape, decorated w/heavy gold
prunus & pine needles & a gold
butterfly in flight, creamy white
lining, satin finish 300.00

Pitcher, tankard, 9" h., signed.............385.00

Rose bowl, miniature, decorated
w/gold flowers & butterfly, 2¼" d......385.00

Vase, 3¼" h., 2¾" d., baluster-form,
decorated w/gold prunus &
branches, creamy white lining
(ILLUS. right) 345.00

Decorated Webb Peach Blow Vases

Vase, 3⅜" h., 2⅝" d., low pedestal
base, globular body w/flared rim,
decorated w/heavy gold florals &
branch on front, reverse w/gold
butterfly, creamy white lining, satin
finish (ILLUS. right) 365.00

Vase, 3¾" h., 3¼" d., ovoid form
tapering to a short neck w/slightly
flaring rim, decorated w/silver
flowers & heavy gold leaves, glossy
finish (ILLUS. left, previous photo)...325.00

Vase, 5" h., 3½" d., ovoid body
tapering to a short flared neck,

enameled w/two-colored birds,
white flowers & gold foliage, creamy
white lining, propeller mark 495.00

Vase, 5⅛" h., 3¼" d., ovoid w/flared
neck, decorated w/heavy gold
leaves & silver flowers, creamy
white lining (ILLUS. left) 295.00

Vase, 6⅜" h., 3" d., bottle-form
bulbous body tapering to a 'stick'
neck, enameled w/gold leaves &
branches & silver flowers, glossy
finish, creamy white interior 245.00

Vase, 7½" h., 4" d., squatty bulbous
body tapering to a cylindrical neck,
decorated w/heavy gold prunus
blossoms, branches & pine needles,
creamy white lining, glossy finish.....325.00

Vases, 5" h., 2" d., cylindrical, applied
creamy blackthorn flowers, applied
clear frosted leaves & clear frosted
thorny base, creamy white lining,
pr...750.00

WHEELING

Wheeling Peach Blow Creamer

Creamer, globular w/tricorner top,
applied amber handle, glossy finish,
4¼" h. (ILLUS.) 785.00

Cruet w/original facet-cut amber stopper, ovoid body tapering to a small
cylindrical neck w/a high arched
spout, amber applied reeded
handle, 6¾" h. (ILLUS. top next
column) 1,085.00

Flask, tooled lip, glossy finish,
4½ widest w., 7" h. 750.00

Pitcher, 4½" h., wide ovoid body
tapering to a wide cylindrical neck
w/flaring four-cornered rim, applied
clear handle 785.00

Salt shaker w/original silver plate
top, spherical body, glossy finish,
2½" h..485.00

Wheeling Peach Blow Cruet

Tumblers, cylindrical, Drape patt.,
two w/satin & one w/glossy finish,
3¾" h., group of 3 ....460.00

Vase, 6½" h., 6½" d., bulbous, glossy
finish 850.00

Vase, 8" h., "Morgan vase," tall ovoid
body tapering to a slender ringed
neck w/flaring lip, glossy finish (no
stand) 770.00

Wheeling Peach Blow Bottle Vase

Vase, 9¼" h., bottle-form, bulbous
base tapering to a slender stick neck
(ILLUS.) 985.00

PEKING

*A variety of fine glass, often resembling
hardstones, has been produced in China
since the 18th century. Some of it is
overlay glass in one to five colors. Pieces
made for the Imperial court are the most
valuable.*

Bowl, 7¾" d., the ruby red lobed
body carved in relief w/seven

panels of jardinieres filled w/flowers,
each inscribed w/auspicious characters, Jiaqing period (ground rim
chips) $2,875.00

Condiment set, chrysanthemum-form,
consisting of an octagonal central
bowl surrounded by eight radiating
petal-shaped dishes, together w/a
fitted fabric & cardboard circular
box, 19th c., overall 18¼" d., the
set 2,875.00

Jar, cov., ruby red, carved on each
side w/scene of a horse & tree,
early 19th c., 4¾" h. 2,310.00

Peking Overlay Jar

Jars, overlay, ovoid, carved in green
w/birds soaring & perched amid
flowering prunus branches extending around the sides & issuing from
rockwork, all against a white ground,
minute chips, 6" h., pr. (ILLUS. of
one) 2,070.00

Peking Overlay Vase

Vase, 6" h., overlay, cylindrical body
w/waisted neck, deep yellow overlaid in deep red & carved w/long-
tailed phoenix & a pair of birds
among flowering chrysanthemum &

peony stems issuing from pierced rockwork encircling the base, a band of pendent *ruyi* lappets beneath the waisted rim, the base incised w/a four-character Qianlong mark (ILLUS.) 4,600.00

Vase, 7" h., baluster-form w/flaring cylindrical neck, carved w/confronting archaistic *chilong* divided by mock tasseled rings between descending leaf-tips & rising lappets, egg yolk yellow, late 18th c. 12,650.00

Vase, 8¾" h., bottle-form, the swelling sides incurving gently to the tall cylindrical neck in a rich amber tone, underside incised w/a four-character Qianlong mark within a square, 18th c. (footrim ground, neck possibly ground) 2,875.00

Vase, 9" h., ovoid body tapering to a tall narrow cylindrical neck, opaque camellia leaf green swirled w/other greens, underside w/four-character Qianlong mark within double square, late 18th - early 19th c. 1,725.00

Vase, 9½" h., two-color, yellow overlaid w/red & carved w/reserves of bird & flower design, 18th c. 1,045.00

Peking Bottle-Form Vase

Vase, 10¼" h., bottle-form, the globular body of dark emerald green supported on a thick ring foot, surmounted by a tall thick cylindrical neck, minor casting flaws, 18th c. (ILLUS.) 1,840.00

Vase, 12¾" h., bottle-form, finely carved through thick red to a snowflake white w/elegant ladies in palanquins followed by attendants & equestrian figures riding through a continuous landscape w/pavilions among rocky mountains & boldly

carved leafy trees & pine trees issuing from massive rockwork encircling the base, all below a *ruyi* collar around the shoulders, surmounted by a tall cylindrical neck vigorously carved w/pavilions & military figures in a rocky landscape w/large pine boughs extending up the neck, the lip rimmed in red, the underside w/a large well-carved four-character Qianlong mark within a double square, Qianlong period (minute chips) 54,625.00

Vases, 7⅜" h., overlay, baluster-form carved through the deep green over pink overlay to the white ground w/a phoenix & numerous birds perched & soaring amid flowering peony & prunus branches issuing from rockwork, the flared neck w/a band of keyfret & raised bosses, 19th c., pr. (chips, one w/ground rim) 3,450.00

Fine Peking Glass Vase

Vases, 8⅜" h., the yellow baluster-form body w/flaring rim carved in high relief w/songbirds perched among prunus & peony blossoms growing from rockwork formations, 19th c., pr. (ILLUS. of one) 920.00

PELOTON

This glassware was produced in Bohemia, Germany and England during the late 19th century. It features threads or filaments of colored glass rolled into a glass object to form random designs. Some pieces were further enamel-decorated.

Pitcher, 6½" h., bulbous ovoid body w/a cylindrical neck w/pinched spout, clear applied handle, the body w/clear threads interspersed w/pink, yellow, blue & white "coconut" threading.......................$137.50

Peloton Pitcher & Vase

Pitcher, 6⅝" h., 3⅝" d., squared bulbous body, round mouth w/pinched spout, clear applied handle, clear ground applied w/pink, blue, yellow & white "coconut" threading (ILLUS. left).......................165.00

Plate, 6" d., ruffled rim, clear ground w/white, pink, blue & yellow "coconut" threading............................95.00

Peloton Rose Bowl

Rose bowl, footed bulbous body w/rim drawn up to four points, white opaque body w/deep pink, blue, yellow & white "coconut" threading, 3½" d., 3¾" h. (ILLUS.) 295.00

Vase, 2¾" h., 3¾" d., bulbous body w/pinched, clover-shaped rim, embossed ribbed design, pinkish lavender w/pink, blue, yellow & white "coconut" threading 225.00

Vase, 3¼" h., 3⅞" d., bulbous body w/embossed ribbing & the top half pinched together to form two openings, shaded lavender to pink ground w/blue, pink, yellow & white "coconut" threading...........................265.00

Vase, 3½" h., 3" d., spherical body w/ringed neck & flat ruffled rim,

pinkish lavender ground w/white, pink, blue & yellow "coconut"' threading...195.00

Vase, 3¾" h., 4¾" d., squatty ribbed body w/folded over tricorner top, cased clear ground w/pink, blue, yellow & white "coconut" threading, white interior (ILLUS. right)..............295.00

Vase, 5" h., 4" d., ovoid body tapering to a trumpet-form crimped neck, pinkish lavender ground w/white, pink, blue & yellow "coconut" threading...245.00

Vase, 5⅜" h., 4⅛" d., ovoid body w/small molded ribs tapering to a crimped, flattened rim, white cased background w/pink, blue, yellow & white "coconut" threading 225.00

Vase, 6⅛" h., 3¾" d., ovoid body w/embossed ribbing tapering to a flaring neck w/crimped rim, shaded lavender to pink ground w/blue, yellow, pink & white "coconut" threading...275.00

Vase, 6¾" h., 5⅛" d., ovoid body w/embossed ribbing tapering to a flaring, crimped rim, cased clear ground w/royal blue "coconut" threading, white interior 225.00

Vase, 6¾" h., 5⅛" d., footed ovoid body tapering to a flat mouth, clear ground w/royal blue "coconut" threading...145.00

Vase, 6¾" h., 5⅝" d., footed ovoid body w/a wide shoulder & short, wide neck w/flat rim flanked by small square handles, clear ground w/green "coconut" threading............195.00

PIGEON BLOOD

Pigeon Blood Carafe & Cracker Jar

Its deep red color gives this type of glass its name. Popular in the late 19th century a number of mold-blown patterns were produced in this color.

Berry set: master bowl & three sauce dishes; Venecia patt., enameled w/wild rose decoration, 4 pcs.........$195.00

Bowl, 4½" d., 2⅝" h., Inverted Thumbprint patt.................................175.00

Bowl, 9" d., Torquay patt. w/resilvered silver plate rim..................150.00 to 175.00

Carafe, Beaded Drape patt., silver plate neck (ILLUS. left) 170.00

Cracker jar, cov., waisted form, Beaded Drape patt., silver plate rim, cover & bail handle (ILLUS. right)....195.00

Cracker jar w/original puffy lid, Torquay patt.....................................650.00

Cruet w/original stopper, Torquay patt....................................800.00 to 850.00

Cruet w/original stopper, Venecia patt.......................................650.00

Pitcher, water, Torquay patt.....................................375.00 to 395.00

Pitcher, water, Venecia patt................350.00

Salt & pepper shakers w/original tops, Bulging Loops patt., pr.....................185.00

Salt & pepper shakers w/original tops, Overlapping Petals patt., pr. 155.00

Spooner, Torquay patt.........................125.00

Syrup pitcher w/original metal cover, squatty form, Torquay patt..............425.00

Toothpick holder, Bulging Loops patt.....................................150.00 to 175.00

Tumbler, Optic Rib patt.......................125.00

Tumbler, Torquay patt., glossy finish..105.00

POMONA

Pomona Open Sugar Bowl

Pomona was another Art glass produced by the New England Glass Company under a patent received by Joseph Locke in 1885. This ware has a frosted ground on clear glass decorated with mineral stain, most frequently amber-yellow but sometimes blue. Pieces could be lightly etched with floral designs trimmed with staining. Two versions of Pomona were made. The first Locke patent was for a technique where a piece was covered with an acid-resistant coating which then was needle-carved with thousands of minute criss-cross lines. The piece was then dipped in acid thus cutting into the etched lines. A cheaper method was covered in a second Locke patent in 1886 and required that a piece be rolled in particles of acid-resistant material to coat it. It was then etched by acid which attacked areas not protected by the resistant particles. A popular etched design on Pomona is the cornflower.

Berry set: 8" d. master bowl & eight 4" d. sauce dishes; Inverted Thumbprint patt. w/turned in scalloped amber rims, 2nd patent, 9 pcs. $225.00

Bowl, 4" d., crimped & folded rim, 2nd patent...50.00

Bowl, 10" d., blue cornflower decoration, 2nd patent.....................225.00

Bowl, 10" d., 4¼" h., upright crimped sides, pansy & blue butterfly design, 2nd patent.......................................316.00

Celery vase w/ruffled rim & applied clear base, blue cornflower decoration, 1st patent, 6¼" h. 375.00

Creamer & open sugar bowl, squatty bulbous body w/Inverted Thumbprint patt., flaring ruffled amber rim & applied amber handles, 1st patent, pr. (ILLUS. of sugar bowl)................585.00

Cruet w/original bubble stopper, spherical body on applied crimped foot, applied handle, blue cornflower decoration, 2nd patent (ILLUS. top next column) 650.00

Finger bowl, crimped rim, 1st patent ..140.00

Finger bowl w/underplate: 3" d. bowl w/ruffled rim, 4½" d. underplate; blue cornflower decoration, 2nd patent, 2 pcs. 60.00

Finger bowls, amber-stained, signed, 1st patent, 4½" d., pr.......................345.00

Pitcher, tankard, 12¼" h., blue butter-flies & gold grasses, 1st patent........747.50

Punch cup, blueberry decoration w/honey amber stain on rim,

Pomona Cornflower Cruet

leaves & handle, 1st patent, 2⅝" d.,
2¾" h..175.00

Punch cup, blue cornflower deco-
ration, 2nd patent............................125.00

Pomona Toothpick Holder

Toothpick holder, cylindrical base
w/tricornered top, 1st patent
(ILLUS.) ....200.00 to 255.00

Toothpick holder, applied rigaree
band around the neck, 2nd patent...110.00

Pomona Cornflower Tumbler

Tumbler, cylindrical, blue cornflower
decoration, 2nd patent, 2½" d.,
3½" h. (ILLUS.) 145.00

Tumbler, water, Inverted Thumbprint
patt., blue cornflower decoration,
2nd patent, 2⅝" d., 3⅝" h. 145.00

Tumbler, blueberry decoration, 2nd
patent..165.00

Vase, 3" h., 6" w., fan-shaped
w/ruffled rim, blue cornflower
decoration, 1st patent 237.50

Vase, 5¾" h., 4½" d., crimped rim &
ruffled foot, blue cornflower deco-
ration, 2nd patent.............................480.00

Vase, 9" h., tri-cornered top, Diamond
Quilted patt., lily decoration, 2nd
patent...85.00

QUEZAL

Fine Quezal Decanter

In 1901 Martin Bach and Thomas Johnson, who had worked for Louis Tiffany, opened a competing glassworks in Brooklyn, New York. The Quezal Art Glass and Decorating Co. produced wares closely resembling those of Tiffany until the plant's closing in 1925.

Quezal

Quezal Mark

Center bowl, deep flaring wide-ribbed
bowl on a ribbed funnel base, blue
shading to purple w/overall golden
iridescence, signed, ca. 1900,
13⅛" d..$805.00

Decanter w/original pointed mushroom stopper, bulbous base tapering to a tall 'stick' neck w/flared rim, green & gold double-hooked feather designs on green, gold iridescent neck & stopper, designed by Martin Bach, marked "Quezal," 11½" h. (ILLUS.) 3,850.00

Taster, squared sides w/pinched dimples, gold iridescent interior & exterior, signed "Quezal" on base, 2¾" h..137.50

Vase, 6³⁄₁₆" h., floriform body on a low domed foot, opalescent decorated w/pulled green feathering w/amber iridescent interior, inscribed "Quezal - R - 858," ca. 1900 ....1,380.00

Vase, 7½" h., floriform, the opalescent sides decorated w/green striated feathering, the foot further decorated w/amber iridescent feathering, the interior in amber iridescence, inscribed "Quezal," ca. 1925.........1,035.00

Blue Iridescent Quezal Vase

Vase, 8" h., footed double-bulbed cylindrical body w/a short flaring neck, blue iridescent exterior, signed "Quezal" (ILLUS.).............................550.00

Vase, 8" h., swelled cylindrical shouldered body tapering to a trumpet-form neck, silvery & bluish green gold iridescent finish, signed on base 575.00

Vase, 9" h., footed ovoid body tapering to a slender 'stick' neck, Egyptian Revival style w/a creamy white body decorated w/a green zig-zag shoulder design above gold iridescent double hooked & pulled-feather design, by Martin Bach, foot inscribed "Quezal N.Y." (ILLUS. top next column) 2,300.00

Vase, 9¾" h., a cushion foot supporting a slender trumpet-form body w/a widely flaring & ruffled rim,

Decorated Quezal Vase

opaque white ground decorated on the exterior w/green & gold pulled-feather designs & a band of gold iridescent hearts around the neck, etched "Quezal 6" 1,265.00

Vase, 12¼" h., jack-in-the-pulpit type w/cushion foot, slender cylindrical body & wide rolled rim, purplish blue shading to golden iridescence, silver feathering on the foot extending into the body, signed 1,035.00

Vase, 13⅛" h., jack-in-the-pulpit form, the widely flaring ruffled rim above a slender stem & bulbous base in opalescent decorated w/finely pulled feathering in mint green & amber iridescence, the interior in amber iridescence, inscribed "Quezal," ca. 1920..4,600.00

Vase, 13½" h., jack-in-the-pulpit type, widely flaring top above a slender stem & squatty bulbous base, over-all amber iridescence w/the top tinged w/rings of pink & green, signed "Quezal - G646," ca. 1920..3,162.00

Quezal Jack-in-the-Pulpit Vase

Vase, 15" h., jack-in-the-pulpit type
w/cushion foot, slender cylindrical
body & widely flaring gently ruffled
rim, the exterior decorated w/green
& gold pulled-feather decoration,
iridescent gold interior, signed
(ILLUS.) 1,725.00

Vase, 16" h., jack-in-the-pulpit type,
the broad undulating mouth
w/crackled gold iridescence, issuing
from a slender stem & bulbous
cushion foot, elaborately decorated
w/gold & green pulled feather &
swirled designs, signed "Quezal M
702"...5,520.00

RICHARD

Richard Cameo Vases

*The Richard company of Lorraine,
France produced mainly two-layer,
commercial-grade cameo wares featuring
florals and landscapes. Their main
production was during the 1920s.*

Cameo bowl, 8" l., 4¼" h., oblong
bulbous lobed form, frosted clear
layered in amethyst & acid-etched
w/a band of horizontal leafy stem &
long-petaled blossoms, signed in
cameo on the side $550.00

Cameo vase, 13¾" h., elongated
teardrop-form body in grey mottled
w/pale orange, overlaid w/deep
forest green & cut w/a wooded
landscape w/towering conifers in
the foreground & distant mountains,
signed in cameo, ca. 1925
(ILLUS. right) 1,150.00

Cameo vase, 21¾" h., tapering
cylindrical body raised on a cushion
foot, grey streaked on the interior
w/amber, overlaid w/forest green &
cut w/a romantic Alsatian mountain
landscape, cameo signature, ca.
1925 (ILLUS. left).........................1,380.00

ROSE BOWLS

*These decorative small bowls were
widely popular in the late 19th and early
20th centuries. Produced in various types
of glass, they are most common in satin
glass or spatter glass. They are generally a
spherical shape with an incurved crimped
rim, but ovoid or egg-shaped examples
were also popular.*

*Their name derives from their reported
use, to hold dried rose petal potpourri or
small fresh-cut roses.*

Cased Glass Rose Bowl

Amber, Hobnail patt., scalloped rim,
three applied feet, 3" d., 5" h............$75.00

Amber, optic ribbing, the exterior
decorated overall w/enameled white
& pink daisies, red berries & green
leaves, ten-crimp top, 4¼" d., 4" h. ...110.00

Blue opalescent, Reverse Swirl patt.,
3½" d., 4½" h. 40.00

Cased, shaded heavenly blue Swirl
patt., creamy white interior, globular
w/eight-crimp top, 5⅞" d., 5¼" h.
(ILLUS.) 195.00

Cased, pink exterior decorated overall
w/heavy gold flowers & branches,
white lining, base marked w/enam-
eled red web & "E" (White House
Glass Works, Stourbridge, England)
on base, footed ovoid form, four-
crimp top, 3" d., 3" h.........................265.00

Cased satin, blue mother-of-pearl
Ribbon patt., white interior, six-crimp
top, 2½" d., 2" h. 210.00

Cased satin, blue mother-of-pearl Ribbon patt., white interior, nine-crimp top, 3¾" d., 4" h......................275.00

Rivulet Pattern Rose Bowl

Cased satin, rainbow mother-of-pearl Rivulet patt., white interior, three applied frosted clear feet, eight-crimp top, 5" d., 4" h. (ILLUS.) 695.00

Cased satin, rose red mother-of-pearl Ribbon patt., white interior, six-crimp top, 2¾" d., 2¼" h. 265.00

Cased Satin Rose Bowl

Cased satin, deep rose red mother-of-pearl Ribbon patt., white interior, frosted wafer foot, three-crimp top, 2⅝" d., 3" h. (ILLUS.) 225.00

Cased satin, deep rose red mother-of-pearl Herringbone patt., white interior, eight-crimp top, 3¾" d., 3½" h..195.00

Cased satin, shaded apricot mother-of-pearl Herringbone patt., white interior, eight-crimp top, 3¾" d., 4" h...195.00

Cased satin, shaded blue exterior, white interior, elongated melon-ribbed body, applied green petal-shaped feet, six-pointed top, 3¾" d., 4½" h...110.00

Cased satin, shaded heavenly blue exterior w/embossed flowers & leaves decoration, white interior, eight-crimp top, 3¾" d., 3¼" h..........125.00

Cased satin, shaded heavenly blue exterior decorated w/dainty white flowers & lacy gold foliage, white interior, applied frosted petal feet, eight-crimp top, 4¼" d., 5" h............135.00

Cased satin, shaded heavenly blue exterior decorated w/white morning glories & green foliage, white interior, egg-shaped, applied frosted petal feet, four-crimp top, 4½" d., 5" h..135.00

Cased satin, shaded heavenly blue mother-of-pearl Ribbon patt. exterior, white interior, eight-crimp top, 3⅞" d., 2¾" h............................225.00

Cased satin, shaded lemon yellow exterior w/embossed shell & seaweed design & enameled w/yellow & gold flowers & maroon leaves, white interior, eight-crimp top, 5½" d., 5⅛" h. 118.00

Cased satin, shaded peach mother-of-pearl Herringbone patt. exterior, white interior, six-crimp top, 3½" d., 3½" h..165.00

Cased satin, shaded pink exterior, white lining, bulbous body w/eight indented swirls, eight-crimp top, 5" d., 4⅞" h. 118.00

Cased satin, shaded pink exterior decorated w/small blue & white flowers & lacy gold decoration, white interior, applied frosted petal feet, eight-crimp top, 4⅛" d., 5" h.............135.00

Cased satin, shaded pink exterior decorated w/creamy white morning glory & green leaves, white interior, applied frosted petal feet, egg-shaped, four-crimp top, 4½" d., 5½" h..135.00

Cased satin, shaded pink mother-of-pearl Herringbone patt. exterior, white interior, egg-shaped, four-crimp top, 3½" d., 3½" h...................165.00

Cased satin, shaded rose pink exterior w/embossed flowers & leaves decoration, white interior, eight-crimp top, 3¾" d., 3⅜" h..........125.00

Creamy white, satin finish, decorated w/pink, blue & green maidenhair fern decoration & gold outlining, applied frosted wafer foot, eight-crimp top, 2⅞" d., 2⅝" h. 65.00

Creamy white decorated w/enameled lacy maroon flowers & green leaves, eight-crimp top, 5½" d., 5⅛" h..........125.00

Golden amber air-trap zipper pattern, twelve-crimp top, registry number on base, miniature, 2½" d., 2¼" h.........118.00

Golden amber air-trap zipper pattern, sixteen-crimp top, 4⅜" d., 4¼" h......150.00

Pink opalescent, egg-shaped, applied clear petal feet, eight-crimp top, 3½" d., 5" h. 195.00

Sapphire blue w/air-trap bubbles, egg-shaped, crimped top, engraved registry number, 2½" d., 2" h. 95.00

Sapphire blue, enameled w/small white flowers, red berries & green foliage, six-crimp top, 2¾" d., 2" h. 60.00

raised balls, the neck enameled w/scrolling coral edged in gilt & reserved against a strawberry ground, original paper label (ILLUS.) 5,775.00

Vase, 4" h., gold enameled griffin & scrolling against an orangish amber stained glass window ground........1,210.00

Vase, 6" h., double gourd-form, decorated w/colorful pansies & gold enameling on a frosted ground 1,210.00

ROYAL FLEMISH

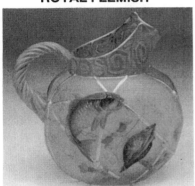

Royal Flemish Pitcher

The Mt. Washington Glass Co. produced this patented ware in the 1890s. It features very heavy enameled gold lines dividing the surface into separate sections which can be further decorated with colored stains and painted designs. Some pieces are marked "RF."

Cracker jar, cov., ovoid body, overall decoration of large Roman coins on stained panels divided by heavy gold lines, ornate silver plate cover, rim & bail handle, original paper label w/"Mt. W.G. Co. Royal Flemish," 8" h. $1,650.00

Pitcher, 8⅝" h., bulbous body w/a low cylindrical neck w/angled rim, applied rope twist handle, acid-finished, enameled w/two small fish swimming against a background of shells & marine plants in various shades of lavender, puce, deep emerald green, Chinese red, chocolate brown, & lemon yellow w/heavy gilt trim, reserved against a ground formed of irregular panels enameled in lavender & pale yellow between raised gold borders conjoined by

RUBINA CRYSTAL

Ornate Centerpiece Bowl

Rubina Crystal, sometimes spelled "Rubena," is a flashed glass shading from ruby to clear. Pieces can be enamel-decorated or left plain.

Centerpiece bowl, footed, Swirl patt., deep high pointed ruffles, mounted on ornate nickel-plated four-footed base w/cut-out leaf design, 10" d., 8" h. (ILLUS.) $225.00

Cologne bottle w/original facet-cut stopper, squatty bulbous body decorated w/cut-back band of leaves around the center, 3½" d., 4½" h. 110.00

Cologne bottle w/original clear facet-cut stopper, square w/a short cylindrical neck w/flared rim, overall Pineapple & Fan patt. cutting, 1¾" d., 6½" h. 75.00

Cologne bottle w/clear facet-cut stopper, cut-paneled cylindrical body, 2¾" d., 6¼" h. (ILLUS. right, top next page) 88.00

Cologne bottle w/original facet-cut stopper, cylindrical shouldered body w/a short neck & flared rim, overall

Rubina Cologne Bottles

lacy stippling, gold band trim on
shoulder & rim, St. Louis, France,
3" d., 7½" h. (ILLUS. left) 110.00

Condiment set: rectangular salt dip,
mustard pot & pepper shaker
w/original silver tops & ball-footed
silver plate holder w/angular handle;
overall cut design, 3⅝" d., 5¼" h.,
the set 195.00

Creamer, bulbous body tapering to a
flaring cylindrical neck w/pinched lip,
applied clear handle, embossed
threading design, gold trim, 2¾" d.,
2" h...85.00

Spooner, Venecia patt. 110.00

Sugar shaker w/original top, Hobb's
Optic patt. 195.00

Syrup pitcher w/original metal top,
Hobb's Optic patt. 235.00

Syrup pitcher w/original metal top,
Medallion Sprig patt. 265.00

Toothpick holder, scalloped beaded
rim, Beaded Heart & Star patt............28.00

Tumbler, flaring cylindrical form,
decorated w/yellow roses, blue
forget-me-nots & small yellow
flowers, 2¾" d., 3½" h. 55.00

Tumbler, Hobnail patt., 4" h. 65.00

Vase, 10" h., ruffled rim, decorated
w/h.p. enameled flowers & gold trim,
Hobbs, Brockunier & Co. 150.00

Vase, 10" h., 2⅛" d., slender trumpet-
form, decorated w/engraved fern-
type foliage 68.00

Water set: pitcher & two tumblers;
Hobnail patt., 3 pcs. 250.00

Water set: 9½" h., 5½" d. squatty
bulbous pitcher w/applied clear
reeded handle & six 3¾" h., 2¾" d.
tumblers; paneled sides enameled
w/yellow roses, white foliage, blue

Rubina Crystal Water Set

flowers & smaller gold flowers,
7 pcs. (ILLUS.) 550.00

RUBINA VERDE

Ornate Rubina Verde Vase

*Another flashed glass, Rubina Verde
shades from ruby to green or greenish-
yellow. Like Rubina Crystal, it was
popular in the late 19th and early 20th
centuries.*

Celery vase, decorated w/applied
rigaree & h.p. cherry blossoms &
butterflies, 6" d., 12" h. $265.00

Cruet w/original facet-cut greenish
yellow stopper, applied greenish
yellow handle, Inverted Thumbprint
patt., 7" h...485.00

Pickle castor, corset-shaped Inverted
Thumbprint patt. insert, w/ornate
footed silver plate frame w/matching
tongs, marked Tufts 395.00

Pitcher, water, Hobnail patt. 450.00

Syrup pitcher w/original metal top,
Inverted Thumbprint patt..................285.00

Tumbler, Inverted Thumbprint patt. 119.00

Vase, 8" h., 5½" d., jack-in-the-pulpit
form..245.00

Vase, 8¼" h., 1⅞" d., tall slender
waisted cylindrical form, decorated w/applied clear rigaree
spiralling trim around body, applied
clear petal feet (ILLUS.).....................95.00

Vase, 9¼" h., paneled, decorated
w/enameled daisies 75.00

SABINO

Sabino Opalescent Clock

*Ernest-Marius Sabino, a French Art
Deco glassmaker, began production of art
glass in the 1920s. He produced a wide
range of items in frosted, colored,
opalescent and clear glass in both blown
and pressed glass. The Parisian shop
closed during World War II and reopened
in the 1960s. Earlier works included
lamps, vases, figures and other items; after
1960 the production was primarily small
birds and nudes. In the 1970s a line of
limited edition plates was introduced.
Pieces are marked with the name in the
mold, an etched signature or both.*

Sabino
France

SABINO FRANCE

Sabino Marks

Clock, arched opalescent case cast
w/overlapping geometric devices &
molded festoons centered by a
circular chapter ring, molded
"SABINO," ca. 1925, 6⅛" h. $1,725.00

Clock, the domed opalescent case
molded w/a pair of lovebirds in
flowering branches, centering a
circular clock face, raised on a cast
gilt-metal base, unsigned, 10¼" h.
(ILLUS.) 1,438.00

Figure of a female nude, kneeling
& surrounded by three doves,
opalescent, engraved "Sabino
Paris," w/a paper label,
6¼" h. ....285.00 to 325.00

Figure of a draped maiden in contra-
posto w/a raised right arm, engraved
"Sabino Paris," opalescent, 7¾" h. ..880.00

Figure, "Suzanne," cast as the figure
of a nude dancer w/outstretched
arms holding an exotic cape, frosted
opalescent, unsigned, ca. 1927,
9" h..3,520.00

Figure group, nude woman kneeling
w/a cloth about her legs holding a
bird in her arms while other birds
nestle at her feet, opalescent,
signed in intaglio "Sabino - Paris,"
ca. 1925, 6⅛" h. 550.00

Sabino Luminiere

Luminiere, molded in full-relief as two
nude maidens draped w/scarves,
clear opalescent, minor chip,
w/illuminated wooden base, ca.
1930, 11¾" h. (ILLUS.) 2,013.00

Plaque, oval, molded in high-relief
w/an exuberant cherubic head, rich
opalescence, signed in the mold
"Sabino - France," together w/a
wooden stand, 17½" h. 2,640.00

Vase, 5½" h., deep squared
opalescent body molded overall
w/rows of rectangular thick blocks,
signed in the mold "Sabino France"
(chips at lower corners) 385.00

Vase, 6⅛" h., flaring square form,
molded w/raised smooth rectangles
alternating w/flush rectangles
decorated w/diagonal designs,
opalescent, stamped "SABINO -
FRANCE," ca. 1925 ....460.00

Vase, 12¼" h., ovoid body on a short
pedestal foot, molded overall
w/swirling clouds & bubbles, green,
from the 1925 Paris Exhibition,
incised "Sabino - France" (drilled)....690.00

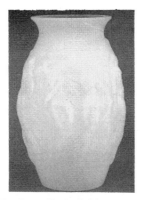

Art Deco Style Sabino Vase

Vase, 14⅛" h., "Gaieté," heavy walled
blown-molded opalescent ovoid
body decorated in the Art Deco style
w/eight semi-nude women in
exuberant postures of dance,
signed "Sabino Paris," late 1920s
(ILLUS.) 1,650.00

Wall sconces, three-sided frosted
design molded w/stylized flowers,
molded mark "SABINO FRANCE
4604C DEPOSE," 6¾ x 12", 5" h.,
pr..575.00

Wall sconces, ribbed diamond-shaped
frosted glass shade in grey molded
w/flowerheads at either side, fitting
onto a conformingly shaped
silvered-bronze support w/stepped
rectangular mounts, metal
impressed "Sabino Paris" & "MADE
IN FRANCE," 16" h., pr. (minor
chips to shades)............................1,870.00

St. Louis Cameo Atomizer

Cameo atomizer w/original silver plate
top, cylindrical vessel, cranberry cut
to clear, acid-cut flower & scroll
design, 3" d., 4" h. (ILLUS.) $135.00

Cologne bottle w/original clear facet-
cut stopper w/gold trim, cylindrical
body w/deep shoulder, a short
cylindrical neck w/flat flaring rim, red
cut to clear ground, decorated
w/gold stippled trim, 3" d., 7¼" h......110.00

Spill vase w/concentric millefiori
weight base, the flaring trumpet-
shaped clear bowl engraved
w/fruiting grape vines applied w/a
coral corkscrew cable within white
five-ply spiral threads to the rim
terminating to a faceted neck &
annulated collar, set on a clear base
composed of a white upset muslin
ground w/a garland of coral & white
elongated star canes, each w/a
periwinkle floret center alternating
w/lime green cogwheel canes lined
in white w/white floret centers about
a grouping of five cobalt blue &
white composite canes & a central
lime green, coral, blue & white whorl
& floret cane grouping, base 2⁹⁄₁₆" d.,
6¹⁄₁₆" h. (minor chips)....................3,680.00

Vase, 10" h., cranberry cut to opalescent iris blossoms decoration 450.00

ST. LOUIS

*The Saint Louis Glass factory in France
has been producing fine glass since the late
18th century. It is now known as the
Compagnie des Verrieres et Crystalleries de
Saint-Louis with showrooms in Paris.*

SATIN

*A very popular Victorian Art glass,
Satin glass features a soft matte acid-
treated surface which gives it its name.
Pieces are two-layered with the interior
white and the exterior a shaded pastel*

color. Mother-of-pearl satin is a special type where air-trapped designs between the layers form patterns like Herringbone and Diamond Quilted. A great deal of Satin was made in England and America but Victorian-style reproductions have been produced for many years. Also see ROSE BOWLS, STEVENS & WILLIAMS and WEBB.

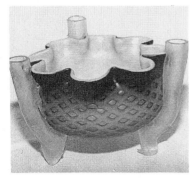

Unusual Satin Glass Bowl

Basket, flaring cylindrical base, rim pinched at middle forming a double lobed top, applied clear frosted handle, bridal white mother-of-pearl Herringbone patt., rich pink interior, 3 x 4¾", 5 ¾" h..............................$325.00

Basket, applied thorn handle, white mother-of-pearl Diamond Quilted patt., rose interior, 7¼" d., 8½" h. 795.00

Basket, bulbous base flaring to a fan-shaped crimped rim, applied frosted clear twisted thorn handle, applied clear edge trim, shaded heavenly blue mother-of-pearl Herringbone patt., white interior, 8¼" d., 9¼" h. ...550.00

Bowl, 6½" d., 4¾" h., gently rounded form w/ruffled top, three frosted thorny vases applied to sides & continue to form feet, shaded blue mother-of-pearl Diamond Quilted patt., white interior (ILLUS.) 450.00

Bowl, 7⅜" d., 3⅝" h., bulbous squatty body w/clover-shaped closely ruffled rim, tan to aqua Swirl patt. mother of pearl exterior, robin's egg blue interior, attributed to Stevens & Williams, England 850.00

Bowl, 9¼" d., 3⅜" h., footed, rounded sides w/turned-down ruffled rim, chartreuse mother-of-pearl Diamond Quilted patt., white exterior, applied frosted rim edging & three applied frosted thorn feet..............................425.00

Cracker jar, cov., ovoid body, shaded pink to white & decorated w/pink &

white carnation-like flowers & green leaves, resilvered cover, rim & bail handle, 5" d., 7½" h..........................225.00

Creamer, squatty bulbous base tapering to a wide cylindrical neck w/pinched lip, applied frosted blue handle, heavenly blue mother-of-pearl Raindrop patt., 3¼" d., 4½" h................................,....................225.00

Creamer, bulbous base tapering to a slightly flaring cylindrical neck w/pinched lip, applied clear frosted handle, shaded heavenly blue decorated w/dainty pink & cream flowers & small green leaves, white interior, 4¾" d., 6" h. 225.00

Creamer & open sugar bowl, bulbous w/crimped rims, the creamer w/pinched spout & applied frosted handle, heavenly blue mother-of-pearl Ribbon patt., creamer 3¼" d., 2¾" h., sugar bowl 3¼" d., 2¾" h., pr...395.00

Cruet w/original stopper, ovoid body tapering to a slender neck w/rolled rim, applied clear frosted handle, shaded apricot mother-of-pearl Diamond Quilted patt., white lining 1,450.00

Ewer, bulbous shouldered base w/a tall cylindrical neck w/a ring below the closely ruffled rim, applied frosted thorn handle, shaded blue mother-of-pearl Herringbone patt., white interior, 4" d., 6" h. 245.00

Ewer, footed ovoid shouldered base, flaring cylindrical neck w/tricorner rim, applied clear frosted handle, shaded pink decorated w/dainty blue flowers, creamy white water lilies & green leaves, white interior, 3⅝" d., 8⅜" h. 118.00

Ewer, footed melon-ribbed bulbous body w/a bulbous ring below the flaring pinched tricorner rim, applied clear frosted angled handle, shaded heavenly blue decorated w/three small birds in flight, green & brown leaves & three applied red jewels, white interior, 4⅛" d., 10¾" h. 145.00

Ewer, footed bulbous body tapering to a tall slender ringed neck w/crimped tricorner rim, clear frosted applied thorn handle, shaded blue mother-of-pearl Herringbone patt., 11½" h. (ILLUS. top next page)....................485.00

Ewer, applied clear rope handle, shaded pink mother-of-pearl Swirl patt., white interior, 15" h. 1,220.00

Herringbone Pattern Ewer

Decorated Satin Glass Ewers

top, shaded pink mother-of-pearl
Herringbone patt., white interior,
3" d., 3¼" h. 175.00

Mother-of-Pearl Rose Bowl

Rose bowl, globular, eight-crimp
top, Amberina-like shaded mustard
yellow to orange mother-of-pearl
Diamond Quilted patt., white interior,
3¾" d., 3¼" h.(ILLUS.) 485.00

Decorated Satin Ewers

Ewers, baluster-form body above a
cushion foot, tapering to a crimped
tricorner rim, shaded blue decorated
w/enameled white & yellow blossoms on orange scrolling branches
& leaves, clear frosted ropetwist
handle, 3½" d., 10" h., pr. (ILLUS.) ..225.00

Ewers, globular melon-ribbed
body w/narrow neck & flaring
ruffled rim, applied clear frosted
handle, shaded blue decorated
w/peach-colored flowers & lacy
foliage, white lining, pr. (ILLUS.
top next column) 475.00

Finger bowl, ovoid w/deeply crimped
rim, shaded pink mother-of-pearl
Diamond Quilted patt., white interior,
5⅜" d., 3" h. 245.00

Rose bowl, bulbous, eight-crimp top,
heavenly blue mother-of-pearl
Ribbon patt., white interior, 4" d.,
2¾" h..235.00

Rose bowl, egg-shaped, four-crimp

Small Satin Glass Rose Bowl

Rose bowl, squatty bulbous form, six-
crimp top, shaded peach mother-of-
pearl Herringbone patt., white
interior 3⅜" d., 3⅝" h. (ILLUS.) 165.00

Rose bowl, ovoid, six-crimp top,
shaded heavenly blue mother-of-

Herringbone Pattern Rose Bowl

pearl Herringbone patt., white interior 3¼" d., 4" h.(ILLUS.) 185.00

Rose bowl, bulbous, eight-crimp top, applied clear frosted petal feet, shaded heavenly blue enameled w/blue & creamy white flowers & tan buds, 4½" d., 4¾" h..........................135.00

Rose bowl, spherical body, six-crimp top, applied clear scroll feet, shaded rose Diamond Quilted patt. w/mold-blown ribbed body, white interior, 5½" d., 5½" h. 365.00

Rose bowl, egg-shaped, eight-crimp top, applied frosted petal feet, shaded blue decorated w/yellow buds, lavender leaves & orange & blue birds, 4" d., 6¼" h...135.00

Satin Basketweave Rose Bowl

Rose bowl, tall ovoid body w/overall embossed basketweave patt., six-crimp top, shaded rose, creamy white interior, attributed to Stevens & Williams, 4½" d., 6¼" h. (ILLUS.) 450.00

Salt shaker w/original top, shaded pink mother-of-pearl Diamond Quilted patt., white interior, 5½" h. 175.00

Exquisite Satin Glass Scent Bottle

Scent bottle w/sterling silver cap, spherical, bridal white mother-of-pearl Ribbon patt., flip-top cap engraved "Dora," collar stamped "CS," "FS," "STd" & "SILr," minor dents in cap, 4" d. (ILLUS.)..............535.00

Sugar shaker w/original silver plate top, blue mother-of-pearl Raindrop patt., white interior, 6¼" h. 415.00

Sugar shaker w/original top, shaded rose mother-of-pearl Diamond Quilted patt. exterior w/yellow "seaweed" coralene beading, white interior, 8" h....................................325.00

Sugar shaker w/original metal top, ovoid base w/short bulbous neck, heavenly blue mother-of-pearl Herringbone patt., white interior, 6¼" h...650.00

Satin Vase with Fan-shaped Top

Vase, 3½" h., bulbous w/fan-shaped piecrust crimped top, chartreuse mother-of-pearl Ribbon patt., white interior (ILLUS.) 285.00

Vase, 4¾" h., 6" d., squatty bulbous body tapering to a flaring three-petal rim, heavenly blue mother-of-pearl Ribbon patt., white interior 495.00

Diamond Quilted Pattern Vase

Vase, 5½" h., 3" d., teardrop-shaped
w/ruffled top, shaded pink mother-
of-pearl Diamond Quilted patt.,
applied frosted binding around top
ruffle, white interior (ILLUS.) 165.00

Ruffled Satin Glass Vase

Vase, 5½" h., 4" d., bulbous w/flaring
ruffled top, butterscotch mother-of-
pearl Diamond Quilted patt., applied
frosted binding, white interior
(ILLUS.) 195.00

Vase, 6" h., 3" d., ovoid body w/ringed
neck & flared & crimped rim
w/applied clear frosted rim edging,
heavenly blue mother-of-pearl Swirl
patt., white interior 195.00

Vase, 6½" h., 3¾" d., spherical body
tapering to a slender cylindrical
neck, shaded peach mother-of-pearl
Peacock Eye patt., white interior 235.00

Vase, 6⅝" h., 2⅞" d., tall ovoid-form
w/ringed neck & flaring crimped rim
w/applied clear frosted rim edging,
heavenly blue mother-of-pearl Wave
patt., white interior 195.00

Vase, 7" h., 4" d., ovoid body tapering

to a cylindrical neck w/flaring &
crimped rim, shaded heavenly blue
mother-of-pearl Diamond Quilted
patt., white interior 198.00

Vase, 7¾" h., 3¼" d., lily-form w/three-
petal crimped rim, rose mother-of-
pearl Ribbon patt., white interior, in
a silver plate footed pedestal base ..165.00

Vase, 8¼" h., 4¾" d., bulbous six-
sided form tapering to a flaring
cylindrical neck w/scalloped rim,
deep blue mother-of-pearl Raindrop
patt., white interior 225.00

Vase, 9" h., bulbous body, butterscotch mother-of-pearl Diamond
Quilted patt., decorated w/enameled
foliage, signed Webb 900.00

Vase, 9½" h., 4½" d., squatty bulbous
base tapering to a tall cylindrical
stick neck, shaded rose to green,
white interior, marked Webb 495.00

Large Decorated Satin Glass Vase

Vase, 11" h., 7" d., globular base
w/short neck & flared rim, Sandwich Peach Blow-like pink shading
to cream decorated overall w/gold
& lavender florals & foliage
(ILLUS.) 650.00

Vases, 7¼" h., 3¾" d., globular
base, slightly tapering ringed neck,
applied clear frosted angular side
handles, shaded rose pink to pale
pink decorated w/dainty white
flowers & gold flowers w/red "jewel"
centers w/green leaves, white
interior, pr. (ILLUS. top next
column) 195.00

Vases, 7¼" h., 4" d., cushion-
footed bulbous body w/ringed neck
taper-ing & flaring to a widely ruffled
rim, shaded pink mother-of-pearl
Herringbone patt., white interior,
pr..450.00

Floral Decorated Satin Glass Vases

Swirl Pattern Satin Glass Vases

Vases, 8½" h., 4⅝" d., ovoid body
   w/embossed Swirl patt., widely
   flaring ruffled rim w/frosted binding,
   heavenly blue, pr. (ILLUS.) 198.00

Diamond Quilted Satin Glass Vases

Vases, 10¼" h., 5⅜" d., ovoid w/short

ringed neck, pink mother-of-pearl
   Diamond Quilted patt., white interior,
   pr. (ILLUS.) 525.00

(End of Satin Glass Section)

SCHNEIDER

Schneider Bowl-Vase

*Charles and Ernest Schneider founded
their glassworks near Paris in 1908 and
produced a range of decorative glass.
Some of their cameo pieces are marked
"LeVerre Francais" (which see), and some
are signed "Charder."*

Schneider Mark

Bowl-vase, bulbous topaz body raised
   on a circular foot, etched w/a band
   decorated w/stylized leaves, applied
   w/two carved glass handles, etched
   "Schneider," 7¼" h. (ILLUS.).......$2,760.00

Cameo vase, 24" h., circular foot
   tapering in & then expanding
   forming a semi-ovoid body, mottled
   frosted body layered in polished
   pastel orange & etched w/a pendent
   berry design beneath a geometric
   band, candy cane mark on base...1,320.00

Compote, open, 8½" d., lime green
   opalescent molded ribbed bowl on a
   double knobbed amethyst base,
   signed 575.00

Compote, open, 12" d., 4¼" h., deep
   center w/a wide flattened rim, raised
   on a short knop pedestal & flaring

round foot, bubbled clear crystal w/bright pink mottling, bowl etched "Schneider," base signed "France" ..345.00

Ewer, spherical body w/a small, short neck w/a long pointed spout, applied angled handle w/crimped end, mottled purple to red layered, amethyst handle, signed "Schneider" at side, 6½" h. 489.00

Pitcher, 6" h., Art Deco style w/elongated spout on blue & orange spherical body w/angular applied amethyst handle, inscribed "Schneider" 302.50

Vase, 5¼" h., trumpet-form body w/flat flaring rim, on a thick disc foot, milky turquoise & green w/exterior splotches in maroon repeated on foot, inscribed "Schneider" on rim, "France" on the base 287.50

Internally-Decorated Schneider Vase

Vase, 10" h., bulbous body w/flared rim, internally decorated in mottled shades of amethyst, orange, pink & yellow, matte acid stamp "Schneider" (ILLUS.).........................495.00

Vase, 11¾" h., simple ovoid body tapering to a small molded neck, yellow cased to clear w/mottled brown & blue splotches between the layers, signed "Schneider" 402.50

Vase, 15½" h., footed baluster-form body w/a short neck & flared rim, mottled overall shading from purple to pink w/orange & yellow inclusions, dark amethyst foot, etched "Schneider" in block letters 1,210.00

Vase, 20" h., squatty bulbous body below a tall, slender stick neck, mottled pink cased to clear w/yellow streaks within, three applied nipple prunts on lower body, engraved "Schneider" urn mark at side 575.00

Vase, 23¾" h., squatty bulbous body below a very tall slender stick neck, bubbled orange w/brown striations & three applied brown prunts around the base, engraved in script "Schneider" w/vase mark 1,320.00

SILVER DEPOSIT - SILVER OVERLAY

Tall Silver Overlay Vase

Produced commercially in the U.S. and Europe since the late 19th century, Silver Deposit and Silver Overlay glass feature designs in silver deposited on the glass surface by various means, most commonly by electrolysis. Pieces with ornate Art Nouveau designs command the highest prices today and sometimes the silver is marked "Sterling" or "925". Also see LOETZ.

Bowl, 12¼" d., 3⅛" h., three-footed, clear w/silver overlay flowers & scrolls...$65.00

Flask, flat w/rounded shoulders, clear w/scrolling hallmarked silver overlay, hinged silver cover, 5" h...................275.00

Plate, 10" d., black w/silver overlay, marked "D. Rockwell Silver Co." 245.00

Tumbler, clear overlaid w/sterling silver bunches of grapes & leaves, 2¼" d., 3½" h., ...40.00

Vase, 5½" h., iridescent amethyst body applied w/angular Secessionist-style silver overlay bands, bands marked "Sterling," Austria, early 20th c. 440.00

Vase, 8" h., expanding cylinder

w/short flared mouth, rose red w/white lining, overlaid w/scrolling floral overlay, stamped "Sterling 680" (small bruise at side) 357.50

Vase, 9" h., semi-ovoid w/three buttresses running from beneath the rim to the base forming feet, cobalt blue decorated w/silver deposit floral medallions surrounded by overall foliate scrollwork, marked "sterling" 467.50

Vase, 10⅝" h., wide ovoid body tapering to a short & wide flaring neck, cobalt blue w/delicate overall floral silver overlay centered by a round reserve w/a floral bouquet, Europe, late 19th - early 20th c........467.50

Vase, 12" h., slender trumpet-shaped body on a thin round foot, green overlaid overall w/a silver spiderweb-style design 374.00

Vase, 13¼" h., tall flaring trumpet-form bowl in black amethyst atop a clear bubbled ball stem on a round pedestal foot, bowl & base overlaid w/stylized Art Deco silver florals, 1930s 546.00

Vase, 14" h., bulbous top w/wide flat mouth, the sides tapering to a slender body w/a cushion foot, dark green overlaid w/willowy carnations & interlaced leaves, marked on the base by the Alvin Mfg. Co., Providence, Rhode Island, ca. 1905 (ILLUS.) 2,760.00

Vase, 14" h., green overlaid w/silver cut in an Art Nouveau style floral design 1,155.00

SINCLAIRE

H.P. Sinclaire & Co., Corning, New York, operated from 1904 until 1928, turning out fine quality cut and engraved glasswares on blanks supplied by Dorflinger, Pairpoint, Baccarat, Steuben and other glassworks, Its founder, H.P. Sinclaire, Jr., had been associated with T.G. Hawkes & Co. from 1883, and had risen to a high position with that firm. Sinclaire showed a preference for engraved glass over deeply cut glass and this was to be the specialty of the firm that carried his name. From 1920 on, most of the crystal and colored blanks were of the company's own manufacture and, after 1926, engraving gave way to acid-etched designs.

Their trademark of an acid-stamped "S" within a laurel wreath interrupted by two shields was used on all perfect pieces but seconds were sold without the trademark from a special salesroom on the premises.

Bowl, 10" d., footed, cuspidor-shaped, amethyst $75.00

Candlesticks, slender candle socket, bobeche w/ten cut glass prisms, honey amber, signed, 9" h., pr.........295.00

Console bowl, amethyst, signed, 10" d., 3⅝" h. 135.00

Luncheon set: plate & wine goblet; Celeste Blue, signed, 2 pcs. 75.00

Perfume bottle w/original stopper, electric blue, signed, 6" h. 225.00

Plates, luncheon, Celeste Blue, signed, set of 8 ....160.00

Urn, Celeste Blue, 8" h. 150.00

Vase, 5" h., iridized blue, signed 175.00

Vase, 6" h., footed, No. 3374, cobalt blue 88.00

Vase, 7½" h., Celeste Blue................130.00

Wines, Celeste Blue, signed, set of 8...160.00

SLAG

Fluted Celery Vase

Slag glass, which original makers called "Mosaic" glass, was widely popular in the late 19th and early 20th century. It is sometimes also called "marble" or "agate." Slag glass is produced by mixing milk white and another color of glass to obtain a swirled design. Several colors were made including blue, green and caramel, but the rarest is 'pink slag,' made only in the Inverted Fan & Feather pattern for a brief period around 1900. Slag was made both in the U.S. and England and some reproductions have been produced, most notably by the Imperial Glass Corp.

Animal covered dish, Hen on nest
   w/lacy edge, rust, 8" l. $250.00

Bread tray, Tam O'Shanter patt.,
   purple 275.00

Celery vase, Fluted patt., purple
   (ILLUS.) 95.00

Jeweled Celery Vase

Celery vase, Jeweled patt., Atterbury,
   purple (ILLUS.) 95.00

Celery vase, Majestic Crown patt.,
   purple 95.00

Cruet w/original stopper, Inverted Fan
   & Feather patt., gold trim, pink......1,100.00

Mug, Bird in Nest patt., purple 85.00

Punch cup, Inverted Fan & Feather
   patt., pink 225.00

Salt dip, Inverted Fan & Feather patt.,
   pink 250.00

Sauce dish, Inverted Fan & Feather
   patt., pink 225.00

Pink Slag Tumbler

Sugar bowl, cov., Challinor's Flying
   Swan patt., butterscotch 185.00

Toothpick holder, Scroll with Acanthus
   patt., purple 125.00

Tumbler, cylindrical, Inverted Fan
   & Feather patt., pink, 2⅞ d.,
   4" h. (ILLUS. bottom previous
   column) ....350.00 to 375.00

Water set: 8" h. pitcher & six tumblers;
   Water Crane patt., blue, 7 pcs. 275.00

Whimsey, model of a thimble, purple ...75.00

SMITH BROTHERS

Floral-Decorated Syrup Pitcher

Originally established as a decorating department of the Mt. Washington Glass Company in the 1870s, the firm later was an independent business in New Bedford, Massachusetts. Beautifully decorated opal white glass was their hallmark but they also did glass cutting. Some examples carry their lion-in-the shield mark.

Smith Brothers Mark

Bowl, 5¼" d., 2½" h. melon-ribbed
   body, decorated w/purple violets ...$100.00

Cracker jar, cov., melon-ribbed body,
   decorated w/h.p. daisies, silver plate
   cover, signed 275.00

Pitcher, 8" h., decorated w/gold floral
   branch on glossy white ground 198.00

Powder box, cov., enameled floral

decoration w/beaded trim, lion
mark..275.00

Sweetmeat jar, cov., melon-ribbed
body, beige satin ground enameled
w/h.p. white daisies w/yellow
centers & green leaves, ornate silver
plate handled cover w/crown-
shaped finial, red rampant lion mark,
8" d., 4¾" h. 395.00

Syrup pitcher w/original silver plate
rim, cover & handle, bulbous melon-
ribbed body decorated w/soft pastel
florals, 4¾" h. (ILLUS.)....................685.00

Vase, 3¾" h., acorn-shaped melon-
ribbed body decorated w/enameled
florals & leaves w/enameled
beading on rim 145.00

Vase, 6¼" h., baluster-form,
embossed rope decoration around
rim, decorated w/delicate daisies &
leaves & heavy gold trim, rampant
lion mark 150.00

SPANGLED

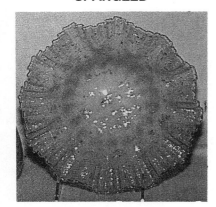

Spangled Glass Bowl

This decorative Victorian glass incorporated particles of mica or metallic flakes between layers of clear and colored glass, the casing being either transparent or opaque. The Vasa Murrhina Glass Company, Sandwich, Massachusetts, first patented this process in 1884 but other American and English firms made similar wares. This glass, like Spatter (which see), is sometimes erroneously called "End of Day."

Aventurine is a related glass which features a finely speckled design resembling gold dust on a solid color ground. Also see ART GLASS BASKETS.

Basket, spherical w/eight-crimp top,
applied clear thorn handle, rose
exterior w/mica flecks, white lining,
4⅛" d. 7¼" h. $195.00

Bowl, 8" d., 2¾" h., flattened ruffled
rim, shaded gold w/mica flecks
interior, white underside (ILLUS.) 95.00

Candlestick, hollow baluster-form
standard w/flared foot & downturned flared lip, black amethyst
w/ mica flecks, 18" h. 220.00

Creamer, cobalt blue w/silver mica
flecks, ground & polished pontil 110.00

Spangled Glass Creamer & Sugar Bowl

Creamer & open sugar bowl, hexagonal sugar bowl w/clear wafer
foot, ovoid creamer w/seven-sided
top, clear wafer foot & applied clear
handle, shaded pink to white
w/silver mica flecks, white lining,
creamer 2¼" d., 4" h., sugar bowl
3⅜" d., 2¾" h., pr. (ILLUS.)..............165.00

Ovoid Spangled Ewer

Ewer, ovoid body tapering to a cylindrical neck w/a three-petal rim,
cased orange ground w/mica flecks,

applied clear angled handle, white
interior, 4" d., 8½" h. (ILLUS.) 125.00

Spangled Ewer with Squatty Base

Ewer, squatty bulbous base w/tall
slender ringed neck, three-petal top,
all gold cased exterior w/mica flecks,
applied clear edging on rim, applied
clear angled handle, white interior,
5" d. 9¼" h. (ILLUS.) 145.00

Spangled Glass Pitcher

Pitcher, 4⅝" h., 3½" d., bulbous base
w/molded swirled ribs below a short
cylindrical neck w/pinched spout,
applied clear reeded handle, clear
cased heavenly blue w/silver mica
flakes (ILLUS.) 195.00

Pitcher, 8" h., melon-ribbed body
tapering to a cylindrical neck
w/ruffled rim, clear applied handle,
deep cranberry shaded to pink
exterior w/blue, pink, yellow &
black spatter & mica flecks, white
interior..295.00

Rose bowl, eight-crimp top, cased
rose exterior w/mica flakes in a coral
design, white interior, 3½" d., 3⅝ h.
(ILLUS.) 85.00

Spangled Glass Rose Bowl

Decorated Spangled Glass Scent Bottle

Scent bottle w/screw-on silver cap,
spherical body, shaded gold decorated w/enameled blue butterflies on
front, the reverse w/gold butterflies,
overall silver mica flecks, plain
domed silver cap, 3¾" d., 5" h.
(ILLUS.) 395.00

Tumbler, flaring cylindrical shape,
Inverted Thumbprint patt., peach &
white spatter, w/mica flecks, 2½" d.,
3½" h...45.00

Tumbler, tapering cylindrical form,
green w/mica flecks, 2⅝" d., 3⅞" h. 45.00

Vase, 5" h., 4¼" d., jack-in-the-pulpit
shape, green, brown & white spatter
w/silver mica flecks 79.00

Vase, 5" h., 4¼" d., spherical base
tapering to a wide cylindrical neck
w/fluted rim, pink, maroon, yellow,
white & blue spatter w/silver mica
flecks, white interior 65.00

Vase, 7½" h., 4½" d., bulbous base
tapering to a cylindrical neck
w/crimped, ruffled & rolled rim,
applied clear edging, pink, blue &
maroon spatter w/silver mica flecks,
white interior 115.00

Vase, bud, 8⅛" h., 2½" d., cylindrical

body, pink opalescent Swirl patt.
exterior w/mica flecks & applied
crystal spiral ruffled trim & five
applied crystal spiral feet 65.00

Spangled Glass Vase

Vase, 8⅞" h., 3½" d., ovoid body
tapering to a short cylindrical neck,
flared crimped rim w/applied clear
edging, cased pink exterior w/mica
flecks, white interior (ILLUS.) 110.00

Vase, 9" h., 4⅝" d., ovoid body
tapering to a cylindrical neck
w/crimped & rolled rim applied
w/clear edging, pink, yellow, blue &
maroon spatter w/silver mica flecks,
white interior 115.00

SPATTER

Spatter Glass Pitcher

*This multicolored glass is similar to
Spangled (which see), but without metallic
flakes. It features dots or swirls of color
cased on a clear, opaque white or colored
body. Widely produced in Europe and*

*England, it has been reproduced for
decades. Also see ART GLASS BASKETS
and JACK-IN-THE-PULPIT VASES.*

Basket, rectangular-shaped footed
bowl w/slightly ruffled edge, applied
clear twisted thorn handle, maroon,
white, green, blue & yellow spatter
exterior w/embossed Basketweave
patt., white lining, 4¼ x 5", 5½" h...$100.00

Basket, crimped & ruffled rim, applied
clear handle, pink, blue & white
spatter, white lining, 4¾" d.,
5¼" h...95.00

Basket, bulbous body w/eight-crimp
rim, applied clear branch handle &
clear leaf on the front, brown, blue,
white & pink spatter, white lining,
3½" d., 5¾" h.....................................110.00

Basket, flaring cylindrical body
w/crimped rim, applied clear twisted
thorn handle, embossed Hobnail
patt., cased blue & white spatter,
5" d., 6" h. 100.00

Basket, bulbous body w/closely crimped rim
& applied clear angular
handle, yellow, pink & white spatter,
white lining, 4½" d., 6½" h................165.00

Basket, bulbous w/star-shaped rim,
applied clear twisted handle,
embossed Swirl & Pinwheel Rosette
patt., maroon, white, yellow & green
spatter, white lining, 5⅜" d., 6¼" h...100.00

Basket, footed, flaring sharply ruffled
cylindrical body, applied clear thorn
handle, pink & gold spatter, white
lining, 5¾" d., 7¾" h. 155.00

Candlestick, baluster-form twisted
shaft w/clear applied crimped base,
pink & white spatter, 4" d., 9¼" h. 75.00

Candlesticks, baluster-form shaft
w/ringed base & clear applied petal-
shaped feet, amethyst & white
spatter, 4⅜" d., 8½" h., pr. 85.00

Candlesticks, baluster-shaped
w/cushion foot & w/molded swirled ribbing, maroon, green, blue,
yellow, white & pink spatter, 3⅞" d.,
8¾" h...135.00

Creamer & open sugar bowl: tankard-
shaped creamer w/clear applied
handle & petal-shaped feet, squatty
bulbous, open sugar bowl w/clear
applied petal feet; deep maroon,
blue, white, green & creamy spatter,
2⅝" d., 4½" h. creamer, 5" d., 3" h.
sugar bowl, pr. 88.00

Decanter w/original heart-shaped
clear stopper, ovoid body tapering

to a slender cylindrical neck w/petal-
shaped spout, applied clear handle,
blue & white spatter, 3½" d.,
8¾" h..135.00

Dresser box w/hinged cover, round
cylindrical sides w/fine molded
swirled ribbing, low domed ribbed
cover, white & color spatter
w/polychrome floral enameling on
the cover, brass fittings, late 19th c.,
4⅝" d...247.50

Ewer, pedestal cushion foot
supporting an ovoid body tapering to
a flaring neck w/tricornered rim,
applied clear handle, yellow & white
spatter exterior decorated
w/enameled yellow flowers & leaves
& a butterfly outlined in pale pink,
yellow interior, 3¾" d., 11" h. 118.00

Jam jar, cov., barrel-shaped, white
egg-shaped designs on green
spatter, crystal finial, white interior,
3¼" d., 6¼" h.....................................75.00

Jam jar, cov., cylindrical form w/green,
blue, white & tan spatter exterior,
white interior, silver plate frame &
lid, 3⅞" d., 7½" h. 105.00

Jar, cov., slightly domed cover
w/applied clear knob finial,
cylindrical sides w/applied clear
shell trim beneath rim, maroon,
yellow, blue & aqua spatter, white
interior, 3⅝" d., 5¾" h. 68.00

Pitcher, 6¾" h., 6" d., bulbous spherical swirled rib body tapering to a
short cylindrical neck w/pinched lip,
clear applied reeded handle, orange
& yellow spatter, yellow interior
(ILLUS.) 175.00

Sugar shaker w/original top, clear
cased cobalt blue, orange & white
spatter..145.00

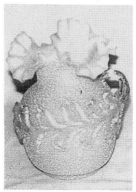

Ruffled Spatter Glass Vase

Vase, 6¼" h., 4" d., bulbous bottom
w/clear applied leaf across front,
ruffled rim, small clear applied
loop handle, yellow opaque
w/white spatter, plain yellow interior
(ILLUS.) 95.00

Vase, 7¼" h., 2¾" d., a bulbous shell-
molded top tapering to a cylindrical
neck, the base of the neck applied
w/three clear upright leaves forming
an apron & supported by petal-
shaped clear feet, yellow & white
spatter ground....................................50.00

Vase, 7¼" h., 5" d., cushion foot
supporting an ovoid body tapering to
a slightly flaring cylindrical neck,
clear applied angular shoulder
handles, clear cased yellow & white
spatter enameled w/purple & white
flowers, green leaves & a grey &
white bird decoration........................195.00

Vases, 11" h., 6½" d., footed, bulbous
base tapering to a cylindrical neck
w/flaring crimped rim w/clear applied
edging, sapphire blue & light blue
spatter, pr..395.00

STEUBEN

*The Steuben Glass Works was founded
in Corning, New York in 1903 and
continues to operate as a division of
Corning Glass. Glass genius Frederick
Carder helped the T.G. Hawkes firm
organize the factory which went on to
produce a beautiful array of colored art
wares until about 1933. Mr. Carder
devised many of the types of glass which
we list below*

AURENE

Steuben Marks

ACID CUT BACK

Vase, 6¼" h., oviform, the frosted
white ground overlaid in dark blue &
etched to depict three pussy willow
trees..$3,105.00

Vase, 9" h., bulbous ovoid body on a
small footring, the wide shoulder
tapering to a short cylindrical flaring
neck, greenish yellow ground overlaid in turquoise blue iridescence &
cut w/a band of stylized leaping

gazelles against stylized scrolling foliage, geometric rim & base bands, unsigned 4,400.00

Steuben Indian Pattern Vase

Vase, 9" h., footed expanding cylindrical body w/flaring rim, glossy black cut back to a frosted Alabaster ground in "Indian" patt. floral design (ILLUS.) 2,070.00

Steuben Acid Cut-Back Vase

Vase, 9¾" h., footed wide cylindrical body w/a wide shoulder to a short, flared neck, white overlaid in Jade green & acid-etched to depict styl- ized carnations (ILLUS.) 920.00

Vase, 10" h., tall flat hexagonal body, olive green opalescent ground overlaid w/turquoise blue irides- cence, cut w/a geometric stylized scene of a hunter w/drawn bow & a leaping gazelle in a jungle land- scape, unsigned, ca. 1925............4,675.00

Vase, 10¾" h., cylindrical body w/low foot & short neck, pale green cut to white w/three stylized figures in a landscape w/forest creatures, ca. 1925...2,013.00

Vases, 19½" h., footed cylindrical body tapering to a widely flared

neck, Jade green acid-etched w/oblong cartouches framing Oriental landscapes w/pagodas & flanked by stylized florals & mon, drilled & mounted as lamps on wooden bases, pr. 1,265.00

ALABASTER

Steuben Alabaster Decorated Vase

Vase, 5¾" h., double gourd-form, silky white decorated w/double hooked gold Aurene design on the shoulder & four green & gold pulled-feather designs around the base, shape No. 720, signed "Aurene 720" (ILLUS.) 3,335.00

AURENE

Aurene Candlestick & Punch Bowl

Atomizer, cylindrical w/spreading base, overall gold iridescent carved around the base w/a floral design, 9" h..115.00

Basket, gold iridescent finish, applied handle, 8" w., 8" h. 600.00

Bowl, 3¾" d., 1¾" h., upright sides w/flat rim, gold iridescence, shape No. 818 ....201.00

Bowl, 6" d., wide shallow rounded sides, overall fine blue iridescence ..275.00

Bowl, 12" d., shallow incurved sides, on three applied prunt feet, overall blue iridescence, shape No. 2586, engraved mark "Aurene 2586".........770.00

Bowl-vase, squatty bulbous body tapering to a short flaring neck, overall blue iridescence w/a central iridescent white chain applied band, shape No. 6178, signed, 5¼" h.....3,105.00

Candlesticks, ovoid candle socket w/flat flaring rim raised on a stem w/a rope twist upper section, on a circular foot, overall blue irides-cence, unsigned, 8" h., pr. 2,475.00

Candlesticks, ovoid candle socket w/flattened flaring rim raised on a stem w/a rope twist upper section, on a circular slightly domed foot, overall gold iridescence, signed "Aurene 686," 10" h., pr. (ILLUS. of one, left) 880.00

Candlesticks, ovoid elongated socket w/wide flattened rim, on a slender tapering stem w/a twist near the top, on a round foot, silvery blue irides-cence, signed "Steuben - Aurene 686," 10" h., pr. 1,380.00

Charger, silvery blue iridescence, signed, 14" d. 850.00

Cologne bottle w/original bulbous stopper, base decorated w/floral etching, blue iridescent finish, 8" h..800.00

Compotes, open, 4" d., 5¾" h., a wide shallow bowl w/upright sides raised on a slender swelled stem & disc foot, overall gold iridescence, shape No. 2642, signed, pr..............825.00

Compote, open, 6½" d., 6" h., shallow gently ruffled bowl on a slender stem twisted in the upper half, on a round foot, overall silvery blue iridescence, inscribed "Steuben - Aurene 367" 805.00

Cordial set: cylindrical decanter w/pointed stopper, four conical glasses & a round tray w/deep upright sides; gold iridescent finish, each piece signed "Aurene 2025," tray 6¼" d., decanter 8¾" h., the set (ILLUS. top next column) 2,860.00

Perfume bottle w/lobed mushroom stopper, spherical lobed body raised on three applied shell feet, overall blue iridescence, inscribed "Aurene - 2701," 4" h. 805.00

Perfume bottle w/tall pointed stopper, footed slender funnel-shaped body tapering to a short neck w/a flared,

Aurene Cordial Set

flattened rim, overall gold irides-cence, inscribed "F.Carder - Aurene - 1414," 8" h. 345.00

Planter, wide low round form w/in-curved sides, overall blue irides-cence, shape No. 2586, signed "Aurene 2586," 10" d. (some interior scratches) 517.50

Plates, 7½" d., round, crackled gold overall iridescence, set of 6 ....552.00

Punch bowl, deep rounded sides w/a flat rim, raised on a small, thick round foot, overall gold iridescence, shape No. 2852, signed "Aurene 2852," chips on foot edge, 12" d., 5½" h. (ILLUS. right w/candlestick)..605.00

Tumbler, overall gold iridescence, signed "Steuben Aurene 1044," 6" h..247.50

Vase, miniature, 1⅞" h., bulbous ovoid shouldered body w/a short flared rim, pinkish amber irides-cence decorated around the top half w/bands of striated scrolling lappets in olive green, the interior w/amber iridescence, signed "Aurene 651" 1,210.00

Vase, miniature, 2⅝" h., spherical body w/closed rim, tapering sharply toward the base, gold iridescent ground decorated w/trailed green hearts & vines & sprinkled w/white millefiore, marked "Aurene 609" ...1,320.00

Vase, 4⅜" h., footed ovoid body tapering to a wide, flat rim, rich turquoise blue iridescent ground decorated around the shoulder w/a band of striated scrolling lappets in pinkish amber iridescence, signed "Aurene 650" 7,370.00

Vase, 4¾" h., footed ovoid body tapering to a widely flaring rim, gold iridescent ground decorated w/green pulled looping around the shoulder, signed "Aurene 209" 1,210.00

Vase, 5" h., a tall slender cylindrical body w/flared rim set on a small knob & a wide disc foot, slightly paneled & decorated w/amber-pink iridescence trimmed w/spring green leafage & tendrils & millefiori blossoms, unsigned 1,100.00

Vase, 6" h., circular base supporting three cylindrical bases of tree trunk form, overall gold iridescent finish, etched "AURENE 2744" 690.00

Vase, 6" h., jack-in-the-pulpit type, a slender shaft on a round foot, the rim turned-up in back & ruffled around the edge, overall gold iridescence, signed "Aurene 2699" 1,610.00

Vase, 6¼" h., ten-ribbed flared ovoid body, strong blue iridescent lustre, inscribed "Steuben" 770.00

Vase, 7½" h., baluster-form body w/short flaring neck, the exterior in rich raspberry iridescence decorated w/five-petaled blossoms & scrolling vines & tendrils in rich pinkish amber iridescence, the interior w/bright amber iridescence, signed "Aurene 270" 12,100.00

Vase, 8" h., trumpet-form w/everted rim, strong gold iridescence, engraved "Aurene" & numbered, shape No. 1124 .... 522.50

Vase, 8" h., tall baluster-form shouldered body w/a short, bulbous waisted neck w/flat rim, olive green iridescence shading to grass green, decorated w/heart-shaped leaves & undulating tendrils in rich amber iridescence shading to silvery blue, the interior w/rich amber iridescence, signed "Aurene 255" 3,850.00

Vase, 8½" h., the flattened fan-shaped body w/smooth rim raised on a short knob pedestal on a disc foot, overall iridescent blue w/a delicate band of white vines & gold hearts near the rim, shape No. 2697, signed "Steuben Aurene 2697" (tooling blemish at both sides) 1,430.00

Vase, 9½" h., globular w/low foot & narrow neck w/flaring rim, deep cobalt blue decorated w/silvery blue iridescent trailings & leafage, the

neck & foot in amber iridescent, the neck decorated w/cobalt blue & white zigzags, alabaster lining, inscribed "AURENE," 1905-20 .... 18,400.00

Vase, 11½" h., bulbous spherical top w/flaring rim raised on a tall very slender stem above a domed disc foot, gold iridescent ground w/green heart & vine & white blossom inclusions around the top, inscribed "Aurene 578" 2,750.00

Vase, 12¾" h., shouldered tapering cylindrical body w/a cushion foot, a short flaring neck on the shoulder, overall strong gold iridescence, shape No. 2142, signed 1,150.00

Large Aurene Vase

Vase, 16½" h., classic baluster-form footed body, overall amber iridescence, inscribed "Steuben - aurene 3289," early 20th c. (ILLUS.) 5,175.00

BRISTOL YELLOW

Champagnes, shape No. 7336, 4" d., 8" h., pr. 170.00

Compote, open, 8" d. 100.00

Goblet, water, w/clear ball connector, shape No. 3140, signed 65.00

Nut dish, pedestal base, decorated w/black Jade threading, 3 x 5" 195.00

Pitcher, tankard, 9" h., quilted pattern body w/black Jade threading on the upper rim, shape No. 6829 .... 325.00

Vase, 8½" h., wide slightly flaring cylindrical body w/airtrap bubbles & applied random threading in brilliant yellow around the upper half, marked 220.00

BUBBLY

Bowl, 8" d., 4" h., clear w/blue
threading..200.00

Vase, 8" h., 7" d., cylindrical body
w/flaring rim, spinach green
w/threading at the rim 150.00

CALCITE

Bowl, 10" d., Calcite exterior, gold
iridescent Aurene interior,
No. 3200 ....375.00

Compote, open, 3¼" h., 8¼" d., widely
flaring shallow bowl w/lightly molded
ribbing, on cylindrical stem & disc
foot, gold iridescent Aurene interior,
shape No. 757 ....489.00

Console set: 10" d. bowl & pair of
6" h. candlesticks; bowl w/everted
rim w/blue Aurene interior & Calcite
exterior, candlesticks w/slightly
domed foot & wide rim in blue
Aurene w/Calcite upper stem,
candleholders shape No. 3581,
the set 1,870.00

Finger bowl & underplate, Calcite
exterior, iridescent gold Aurene
interior, 2 pcs. 335.00

Sherbet w/underplate, Calcite
exterior, blue interior, 2 pcs. 375.00

Vase, triple-bud, 12 ³⁄₁₆" h., a tall
widely flaring central trumpet flanked
by a pair of shorter slightly curved
trumpets w/elongated jack-in-the-
pulpit rims, all attached to a domed
disc base, overall iridescence, ca.
1920...1,375.00

CELESTE BLUE

Bowl, 12" d., acid cut-back dragonflies, shape No. 3200, signed "FC" ..950.00

Bowl,12" d., 5" h., signed....................295.00

Candlestick, ribbed candle socket
w/clear applied wafer foot, shape
No. 2596, 12" h. 150.00

Center bowl, round w/wide flaring
sides on a round tapering pedestal
foot, shape No. 7378, 14" d., 8" h. ...125.00

Cologne bottle w/original flower-
shaped stopper, square body,
signed "STEUBEN" 350.00

Compote, 8" d., 3½" h., shallow bowl
raised on a tapering cylindrical stem
on a domed foot, shape No. 1362 .....85.00

Console set: 12½" d. bowl & pair
8" h. candlesticks; the shallow bowl
w/wide flat rim raised on a low
funnel foot & molded w/optic ribbing,
the candlesticks w/large double-
knop stem tapering to a stepped
disc foot, candlesticks shape
No. 2596, 3 pcs................................489.00

Sherbets, signed, set of 6..................695.00

Vase, 8¼" h., pedestal base, folded
rim, shape No. 2907 ....225.00

CINTRA

Cintra Table Lamp

Cameo vase, 13¼" h., flattened ovoid
body, mottled green Cintra overlaid
w/Alabaster & acid-etched in
Carder's 'sculptured' chrysanthemum pattern below an Art Deco
border design, shape No. 6589,
large Steuben fleur-de-lis mark at
lower side.....................................5,462.50

Candlestick, lavender w/small bubbles
throughout, 10½" h. 1,425.00

Finger bowl, opal 110.00

Lamp, table model, green baluster-
form body overlaid in Alabaster &
acid-etched w/stalks of bearded
wheat & grasses, fleur-de-lis mark at
lower edge, mounted w/matching
wheat design gilt-metal base &
fittings & gazelle finial, 14½" h.
(ILLUS.) 1,210.00

Perfume bottle w/pointed stopper,
ovoid facet-cut body w/the black &
white Cintra interior veiled by
controlled air bubbles, cased in
heavy crystal, ca. 1925, 9" h.
(minor chips) 4,600.00

Vase, 8" h., widely flaring & ruffled rim
tapering to a swelled cylindrical
body, clear w/unusual robin's-egg

Ruffled Cintra Vase

blue colored suspensions throughout in the Sinter technique, fleur-de-
lis mark on the base (ILLUS.) 2,420.00

Engraved Cintra Vase

Vase, 15" h., tall footed ovoid body
tapering to a flaring funnel neck,
green Cintra overlaid in Alabaster &
acid-etched w/a stylized Art Deco
floral design, base drilled for lamp
mount (ILLUS.) 715.00

Wine, opal..385.00

CLUTHRA

Bowl & underplate, the hexagonal
bowl w/sharply tapering sides on a
matching round plate, both blue
shaded to white bubbled & mottled
crystal, tray 6½" d., bowl 2¼" h.,
2 pcs. 805.00

Plate, 6½" d., pink, signed 85.00

Underplate, pink, signed, 6" d............125.00

Vase, 7" d., 4½" h., bowl-form w/a
wide squatty body widest at the
middle & angling sharply toward the
flat rim & base, bubbly green top
shaded to white at the base 467.50

Vase, 9¾" h., 9¾" d., very wide
tapering ovoid body w/a deep
shoulder to the short neck w/flaring
rim, internal layer of bubbled,
mottled & swirled dark amethyst &
white cased in clear, acid-stamped
"Steuben" on base 825.00

Vase, 10¼" h., very wide tapering
ovoid body w/a deep shoulder to the
short neck w/a flaring rim, mottled
bubbly green cased in clear............825.00

Cluthra Handled Vase

Vase, 10¾" h., classic footed
baluster-form body w/a wide flaring
neck w/rolled rim, applied opal loop
handles at the shoulder, double-
cased crystal w/bubbled swirling
light amethyst between layers, base
stamped "Steuben" in script, shape
No. 2959 (ILLUS.) 1,870.00

Vase, 11½" h., very wide ovoid body
w/a wide rounded shoulder to the
short, flaring neck, pink bubbled
sides, signed 1,430.00

Acid-Etched Cluthra Vase

Vase, 13½" h., large baluster-form body w/short flaring neck, pink selectively mottled w/green overlaid in green & etched w/an Art Deco style figure of an archer w/drawn bow aiming at leaping gazelles w/clouds above & floral designs below, shape No. 7007, etched fleur-de-lis mark (ILLUS.)..............7,700.00

FLORENTIA

Steuben Florentia Bowl-vase

Bowl-vase, satin finish colorless body internally decorated w/six-petaled cinnamon-pink blossoms, applied lip wrap & necklace, shape No. 6781, signed "F. Carder - Steuben" w/fleur-de-lis, minor blemish at side, 5¾" h. (ILLUS.) 3,737.50

Florentia Center Bowl

Center bowl, rounded footed bowl w/a wide flat rim, internally decorated w/a large broad pink peach blossom & minute reflective particles, matte finish, 12" d., 4" h. (ILLUS.)...........2,200.00

GROTESQUE

Bowl, 4½" h., shaded green to clear, signed 325.00

Bowl, 8" l., 4¾" h., four-lobed, ruffled sides, amethyst shading to clear, shape No. 7276 ....425.00

Bowl, 10" l., 4¼" h., four-lobed, ruffled sides, ruby shading to clear, shape No. 7277 ....319.00

Bowl, 10" l., 5½" h., clear squared pillar-ribbed form, etched "Steuben"...220.00

Grotesque Bowl

Bowl, 11½" l., 6¼" h., four-lobed oblong ruffled sides in blue Jade, fleur-de-lis mark, minor interior surface wear (ILLUS.) 3,850.00

Bowl, 11½" l., 6¾" h., clear, signed 325.00

Bowl, 13" l., four-lobed, irregular scalloped rim, blue, shape No. 7537, signed 800.00

Bowl-vase, oblong flaring & randomly ruffled squared bowl w/four molded pillars on each side, clear, variant of shape No. 7435, signed on base "Steuben," 7 x 12", 6½" h. 287.50

Bowl-vase, oblong upright randomly ruffled form in green shading to clear, optic ribbing in sides, shape No. 7535, signed "Steuben," 7¼ x 12¼", 6½" h.............................374.00

Vase, 4" h., pedestal foot, trumpet-form w/scalloped rim, shape No. 7090..425.00

Steuben Grotesque Vase

Vase, 6½" h., 7 x 12" oblong Grotesque-form body, quatreform pulled & crumpled sides, silky iridized finish, shape No. 7277, signed "Steuben" 690.00

Vase, 7" h., 12" d., folded handkerchief form, ivory 575.00

Vase, 8½" h., domed foot supporting a fan-shaped bowl w/undulating rim, ivory (ILLUS. bottom previous column) 633.00

Vase, 11" h., paneled tulip-form raised on a pedestal foot, green shading to clear, shape No. 7090.....................475.00

INTARSIA

Steuben Intarsia Vase

Vase, 6¾" h., flaring cylindrical body w/applied double wafer stem & square black foot, clear w/internal midnight blue-black blossom decoration, inscribed "Fred'k Carder" (ILLUS.) 7,475.00

Vase, 9⅜" h., chalice-form, clear internally decorated w/stylized flowers in dark blue, raised on a hexagonal black foot, acid-stamped "STEUBEN" trade-mark, engraved "Fredk. Carder" signature, ca. 1929...9,775.00

IVRENE

Bowl, 10" d., 4¼" h., small foot supporting a deep & widely flaring body in iridescent white w/an unusual thin blue Aurene rim band 770.00

Centerbowl, twelve-ribbed flaring body, signed, 14" l., 6¾" h. 550.00

Vase, 5" h., flared rim, molded ribbed body, signed 225.00

Vase, 5" h., 4½" d., mushroom-shaped body tapering to cylindrical

neck w/flaring rim, polished pontil....110.00

Vase, 6" h., footed cornucopia-form, shape No. 7579 ....425.00

Vase, bud-type, 8" h., slender stick-form body w/a flared rim, on a small knop above a round foot, marked 302.50

Vase, 10" h., footed spherical base below a tall, widely flaring neck w/twelve molded ribs & a ruffled rim, shape No. 7565, marked 550.00

JADE

Plum Jade Bowl-Vase

Ashtray, green Jade, low round form w/incurved sides & three pulled cigarette rests, central applied scroll loop handle, marked, shape No. 7027, 5" w. 259.00

Bowl-vase, the wide squatty bulbous cased plum Jade body acid-etched in the Canton motif w/a scrolled etched ground, Alabaster lining, 8" d., 4⅛" h. (ILLUS.) 2,970.00

Bowl-vase, wide ovoid body w/flat closed rim, green Jade layered in Alabaster & acid-etched in Matzu floral decoration w/Japanesque trees & clouds in the Art Deco style, shape No. 6078, 8" d., 7" h. 805.00

Green Jade Candlesticks

Candlesticks, green Jade, baluster-
form standard below widely flaring
top centering a cylindrical candle
socket, on a round cushion foot,
intaglio-carved w/floral festoons &
garlands, one acid-stamped
w/Steuben mark, ca. 1930, 14⅝" h.,
pr. (ILLUS.) 1,610.00

Center bowl, widely flaring sides on a
small Alabaster footring, green
Jade, shape No. 5022, 12" d.,
4⅜" h..316.00

Center bowl, black Jade, embossed
ribbed design, shape No. 6890,
6½ x 12½" oval, 3½" h. 275.00

Center bowl, green Jade, broad
decumbent rim, shallow bowl,
15½" d...330.00

Steuben Yellow Jade Compote

Compote, 4" h., 10" d., translucent
"butterscotch" yellow Jade flaring
bowl on slender stem & circular foot,
shape No. 3234 variant (ILLUS.) ..1,265.00

Cup & saucer, green Jade, un-
signed 175.00

Pink Jade Dessert Set

Dessert set: 11½" d., bowl & eleven
8½" d. plates; pink Jade, each
intaglio-carved w/floral festoons
below a beaded border, plates
stamped "STEUBEN," 1903-33,
the set (ILLUS. of part) 1,840.00

Finger bowl w/underplate, green
Jade 145.00

Lamp, table model, slender baluster-
form body w/a widely flaring ruffled
neck, applied serpentine loop
handles down the shoulders, shape
No. 8002, 15" h. 350.00

Lamp base, green Jade tapering
ovoid shouldered vessel w/a short
cylindrical neck, deeply acid-etched
w/an overall design of chrysanthemum leaves & blossoms in the
'sculptured' pattern w/polished
finish, base drilled, 9¾" h. 489.00

Vase, 4" h., green Jade, baluster-
form, acid-etched Chang deco-
ration, shape No. 2112 ....4,900.00

Blue Jade Trumpet-form Vase

Vase, 5" h., ten pillar flared trumpet
form, brilliant cobalt blue Jade
vertically striped by internal design,
shape No. 7196 variant, fleur-de-lis
mark (ILLUS.) 1,495.00

Vase, 5½" h., 9" l., green Jade,
rectangular block form w/Alabaster
lion head medallions at each end,
shape No. 6381 ....357.50

Vase, 7" h., pedestal foot, classical
shape, light blue Jade, signed 950.00

Vase, 7" h., wide green Jade
cylindrical swirled body w/flaring rim,
fleur-de-lis mark on base 165.00

Vase, 9½" h., footed, ovoid body
flaring to short cylindrical collared
neck, green Jade 249.00

Vase, 10½" h., green Jade, applied
Alabaster handles, signed 955.00

MILLEFIORI

Steuben Millefiori Bowl

Bowl, 5½" d., 3" h., wide rounded sides resting on a small cylindrical foot, rich red infused w/millefiori in shades of ivory, grey, green & yellow, wide red rim band & red foot (ILLUS.) 3,450.00

Bowl, 6" d., 3⅛" h., composed of hexagonal sections of glass rods in shades of greenish turquoise & grey shading to cobalt blue at the upper walls & w/applied stringing at the rim in violet, engraved signature "Fredk Carder," 1915-20 ....19,550.00

Cigarette box., cov., rectangular clear base w/a silver-mounted rim, the hinged cover w/a silver rim enclosing a millefiori panel composed of blue, white, amber & deep red canes, signed in intaglio w/"FC" monogram, 3⅜" x 6¼", 2⅛" h. (crack in top) 2,588.00

POMONA GREEN
Bowl, 10" d., shape No. 3176, signed 125.00

Candlesticks, a tapering cylindrical socket w/a very wide turned-down flanged rim, tiny stem joins socket to flaring conical foot, clear green w/optic ribbing, shape No. 6466, 4½" h., pr. 201.00

Compotes, open, 7" h., shallow bowl w/flaring rim, raised on a hollow baluster-shaped stem & pedestal base, shape No. 7032, pr. 300.00

Console bowl, footed, 12" d................135.00

Goblet, pilsner-style w/crystal wafer foot..25.00

Urn, cov., tall tulip-form green optic-ribbed body on a funnel-form foot attached w/a wafer disc, the matching domed cover w/an applied figural pink & green pear finial w/blue stripes, shape No. 2996, fleur-de-lis mark, 12¾" h. 690.00

Vase, 6½" h., paneled trumpet-form body raised on a ringed, platformed base, green & topaz, shape No. 7188, signed................................95.00

Wine, w/crystal wafer foot....................20.00

ROSALINE
Cup & saucer, unsigned 175.00

Finger bowl & underplate, 4½" d. bowl, 5½" d. underplate, 2 pcs.........195.00

Goblet, Rosaline bowl on clear stem 30.00

Goblets, conical Rosaline bowl on applied twisted baluster stem & foot, 7" h., pr. 357.50

Vase, bud, 13½" h., Rosaline body on Alabaster base, shape No. 5228, signed 350.00

ROUGE FLAMBÉ
Bowl-vase, bulbous tapering ovoid body w/wide inverted flat rim, rich tomato red iridescence decorated around the shoulder w/a band of silvery blue iridescent threading vines & leafage, 4⅜" h. 16,500.00

Center bowl, 12" d. 6,000.00

SELENIUM RED
Candlesticks, Venetian-style, the brilliant red socket w/a wide flat flange applied to a central hollow clear disc stem wheel-engraved w/florals above a brilliant red domed disc foot, shape No. 7290, fleur-de-lis mark, 6¾" h., pr. 920.00

Candlesticks, short cylindrical socket w/flattened, flared rim raised on an ovoid standard, cupped pedestal base, shape No. 6626, 7" h., pr. 725.00

Plates, 8½" d., round w/twenty molded ribs, pr. 165.00

Vase, 7" h., footed cylindrical body tapering to a wide flaring neck, ribbed design, shape No. 6030........450.00

Vase, 12" h., tall slender lightly paneled ovoid body tapering to a flaring rim in deep red, raised on a low domed red foot, signed "STEUBEN - F. Carder," ca. 1920s 1,725.00

Wine w/twisted stem, signed 75.00

THREADED
Candlesticks, clear "controlled bubble" w/yellow threading overall, signed, 5" h., pr. 310.00

Compote, 6" d., 4½" h., clear "controlled bubble" w/yellow threading overall, signed..................165.00

Compote, 6¾" d., 5" h., clear con-trolled bubbles & a band of topaz threading...125.00

Compote, 7" d., 4½" h., controlled bubble stem supporting a clear bowl w/amber threading, unsigned 65.00

Dresser box, cov., cylindrical clear base w/applied Pomona green random threading, fitted low domed cover w/faceted & pointed green button finial, fleur-de-lis mark, 4¼" d., 4¾" h. 172.50

Vase, 5¾" h., 8" d., clear w/pink threading on the flared rim.................85.00

Vase, 7" h., footed wide cylindrical body w/slightly flaring rim, clear w/applied Rosa irregular threading around the top half, faint fleur-de-lis mark..230.00

Vase, 8" h., tapering form w/wide ruffled everted lip, clear w/green threading around lip, w/controlled air bubbles 121.00

Vase, 8⅛" h., 8¼" d., waisted cylindrical base w/flared fluted top, clear crystal, Inverted Thumbprint patt., w/irregular cranberry threading halfway down, ground pontil, fleur-de-lis on base 295.00

Vase, 10" h., 3" d., tall trumpet-form support on a pedestal base, clear w/green threading, shape No. 2163...95.00

TYRIAN

Rare Steuben Tyrian Disk

Disk, flattened surface w/leaf & vine decoration enhanced by raised iridescent threading applied over the greenish purple surface, 16" d. (ILLUS.) 16,100.00

Vase, 5⅜" h., tapering cylindrical footed body, shading from sea green at the neck to rich greyish blue at the base, decorated w/pinkish amber iridescent heart shapes & tendrils around the top half, signed "Tyrian" 2,750.00

Vase, 6⅝" h., baluster-form w/short wide neck, teal blue iridescent decorated w/silvery blue iridescent trailings & heart-shaped leafage, unsigned, ca. 1916 ....3,450.00

VERRE DE SOIE

Verre de Soie Console Bowl

Center bowl, 10½" d., 3¾" h., shape No. 3200, signed..............................165.00

Console set: 9¾" d. bowl & pair of candlesticks; the footed bowl in a diamond quilted design w/flat & widely flaring sides w/applied Pomona green threading around the top half, the matching candlesticks w/wide slanted rims w/applied Pomona green threading above deep flaring cylindrical sockets on short slender stems flaring to a wide round foot, strong iridescent finish, minute breaks in threading, candlesticks 4½" h., 3 pcs. (ILLUS. of bowl) 440.00

Perfume bottle w/original pinched & pointed teardrop stopper, squatty bulbous eight-lobe body tapering to a short cylindrical neck w/flared rim, w/full-length dauber, shape No. 2183, 5⅞" h. 402.50

Perfume bottle w/original stopper, melon-ribbed, clear w/Celeste Blue stopper, shape No. 1455, signed.....395.00

Perfume bottle w/original stopper, clear w/rose & Calcite stopper & dauber, shape No. 1455 ....325.00

Vase, 5" h., shape No. 618.................195.00

Vase, 10" h., baluster-form w/flared mouth, engraved overall floral decoration 357.50

MISCELLANEOUS WARES

Candlestick - flower arranger, six clear ribbed flaring leaves issuing from a central candle cup above an open base, shape No. 7516, 5½" l., 3" h., pr..230.00

Center bowl, crystal w/deep flattened oval sides tapering to molded brackets at the base, shape No. 8091, designed by Donald Pollard, 7¾ x 10¼", 7½" h. 316.00

Centerpiece, six tall clear triangular vases of various heights tapering down & conjoining on a circular foot, ca. 1925, unsigned, 15¼" h. 1,035.00

Cordial set: decanter w/stopper & six cordial glasses; crystal, the decanter w/a spherical body below a tall stick neck w/a tall tapering cylindrical stopper, small ovoid-form cordial glasses, each initialed "S," signed "Steuben," glass 2¾" h., decanter 12" h., the set....................................374.00

Figure of Buddha, clear, 8" h. 420.00

Goblet, crystal bell-shaped bowl w/black overlaid on the upper half, wheel-cut & engraved w/a feathery scroll design, slender waisted faceted stem & round foot, shape No. 7181, 9" h. 920.00

Goblets, cut crystal, the wide ovoid bowl cut w/the Finger Flute patt., ringed stem & round foot, engraved initial "S," shape No. 6268, Frederick Carder design, 5¼" h., set of 6 ....316.00

Steuben "American Heritage" Jars

Jars, cov., "American Heritage," clear crystal footed tapering cylindrical form, engraved w/an Indian, Trapper or Pioneer, w/conforming cover w/pointed knob finial, designed by Sidney Waugh, 1943, each engraved "Steuben," the latter two signed "Sidney Waugh" under portrait, 5¾" h., set of 3 (ILLUS.) ..2,860.00

Model of a pouter pigeon, molded crystal bird, uncut model, designed by Sidney Waugh, shape No. 7729, 7¼" l., 6" h..402.50

Models of pigeons, molded crystal bird w/cut feathers & features, shape No. 6824, signed "Steuben," 6½" l., 6" h., pr. (minor chips at wing tips) 1,725.00

"Salmon Run" Sculpture

Sculpture, "Salmon Run," tapering oblong crystal form engraved w/a school of salmon, masterwork designed by James Houston, engraved by George Thompson, number 14 of a series of 20, w/original red leather & velvet box, 18" l. (ILLUS.) 13,200.00

Sculpture, "Tree of Life," clear crystal in a stylized branched tree-form engraved & frosted w/real & surreal portraits, designed by Jacob Landau, executed by Donald Pollard, shape No. x3295, 14¼" h..16,500.00

Pheasant Table Ornaments

Table ornaments, models of pheasants, clear, each finely cut w/stylized patterns of feathers, each signed, ca. 1932, small chips to beaks of each, 11½" l., 6¼" h., pr. (ILLUS.) 2,588.00

Vase, 6¾" h., clear crystal, spherical body cut w/concentric facets, design attributed to Walter Dorwin Teague, unsigned, ca. 1930 ....1,495.00

Vase, 7¼" h., clear crystal, "Agnus Dei" patt., footed cylindrical body w/rounded base, engraved w/a stylized winged bull, shape No. 8207, marked on the base 467.50

Vase, 10" h., clear crystal, cylindrical body cut w/geometric patterns of lines & dots, designed by Walter Dorwin Teague, ca. 1930..............1,265.00

Vase, 10⅛" h., clear crystal, the footed bell-form vessel decorated w/geometric devices, designed by Walter Dorwin Teague, shape No. 7499, decoration T-108, acid-stamped "Steuben" 1,035.00

Vase, 13½" h., clear crystal, "Acro-bats," acid-etched scene w/stylized figures of two balancing acrobats, designed by Pavel Tchelitchew, from the series "Twenty Seven Contemporary Artists," dated 1939, signed "P. Tchelitchew," inscribed "Steuben 1939" 7,475.00

Vase, 13¾" h., "Lotus" model, crystal w/eight applied petals at the base of a flaring trumpet-form body, shape No. 7867, designed by George Thompson, signed "Steuben" 374.00

(End of Steuben Section)

STEVENS & WILLIAMS

Basket with Applied Decoration

A long-established English glassworks, by the mid-19th century the Stevens & Williams Company became known for its wide variety of lovely Art glass wares including Satin glass and appliqued wares sometimes called "Matsu-No-Ke." We list a sampling of their products here.

Basket, amber shading to opalescent pink, applied on one side w/a large ripe strawberry, clear green stem & three green leaves, crimped edge, thorn handle dividing into two twisted trailings at ends of the body & continuing to form four gnarled applied feet, 4½ x 6½", overall 6" h. (ILLUS.) $1,250.00

Basket, narrow ribbed body of clear cased pink w/mica flecks, the scalloped rim w/applied amber ribbon edge, applied twisted amber handle, 5" d., 7½" h..........................275.00

Bowl, 4¾" d., 3⅛" h., squatty bulbous body w/flaring & lobed rim, creamy

white exterior decorated w/applied amber rim edging & large applied amber ruffled leaves on each side, pink lining, applied berry prunt on base 145.00

Bowl, 6½" d., 1¾" h., shallow upright sides w/tightly ruffled rim, opaque pink & white stripes on clear, satin finish 245.00

Bowl, 7⅜" d., 3¾" h., satin glass, three-lobed clover leaf-form top w/tightly crimped rim, shaded gold to aqua mother-of-pearl satin Swirl patt., robin's egg blue lining 895.00

Cameo basket, pink on white w/intaglio-cut design of butterflies & flowers, thorn handle, hangs from its own stand of a matching inverted saucer base w/thorn crystal stem, overall 8¾" h. 965.00

Cameo mustard pot, cov., ovoid body in white overlaid w/deep pink & cameo-cut w/detailed flowers, leaves & vines, silver plate rim & cover, 1⅞" d., 3¼" h. 225.00

Cameo vase, 4" h., 1½" w., square w/applied opalescent scroll feet, pink layered in white & intaglio-cut w/flowers & fern 165.00

Cameo vase, 5" h., 3" d., squatty bulbous body tapering to a tall slender stick neck w/flaring ruffled rim, white overlaid w/pink & intaglio-cut w/leaves, grasses & dots, unsigned 295.00

Cameo vase, 5¾" h., 8" d., squatty bulbous body tapering to a ruffled rim, rainbow acid cut-back flowers & leaves in pink, blue, yellow, lavender & green on white opaque satin ground, ca. 1900..........................2,500.00

Stevens & Williams Cracker Jar

Cracker jar, cov., cylindrical off-white

exterior applied w/three leaves in green, amber & pink, pink lining, silver plate rim, cover & angled bail handle, 5½" d., 7½" h. (ILLUS.) 395.00

Creamer, bulbous body w/scissor-cut top & applied amber handle, creamy white exterior decorated w/applied blue flowers & green leaves, pink lining, 2¾" d., 2⅞" h. 275.00

Cruet w/original light blue bubble stopper, light blue bulbous body tapering to a cylindrical neck w/pinched spout, decorated w/overall white crackle design, applied angled blue handle, 4" d., 8" h. 145.00

Decanter w/original stopper, amber wafer foot supporting the tapering cylindrical amber body applied w/clear shell-shaped applique trim, amber stopper w/clear trim, amber & clear peacock finial, 5" d. 11" h. 495.00

Pitcher, 5" h., Hobnail patt., cranberry opalescent w/raspberry prunt 148.00

Rose bowl, spherical body w/box pleated top, shaded blue satin mother-of-pearl Diamond Quilted patt., white lining, 3¼" d., 3¼" h. 165.00

Rose bowl, satin glass, bulbous w/box pleated top, shaded heavenly blue mother-of-pearl Diamond Quilted patt. exterior, white lining, 4⅛" d., 3¾" h. 235.00

Stevens & Williams Rose Bowl

Rose bowl, spherical w/box pleated top, aqua shading to cream, creamy white lining, 5⅜" d., 4⅜" h. (ILLUS.) 195.00

Rose bowl, satin glass, egg-shaped w/box pleated top, blue opalescent w/alternating vertical stripes of frosted blue & opalescent blue, 4¼" d., 4½" h. 145.00

Rose bowl, satin glass, egg-shaped w/box pleated top, shaded brown

Stevens & Williams Rose Bowl

exterior decorated w/heavy gold enameled branches & flowers, creamy white lining, 3½" d.,4⅞" h. (ILLUS.) 450.00

Rose bowl, satin glass, ovoid body w/box pleated top, shaded pink mother-of-pearl satin Basketweave patt., creamy white lining, 4½" d., 6" h. 425.00

Sweetmeat dish, bulbous body w/fluted rim, blue, white & clear alternating swirled stripes, in footed silver plate holder w/handle, 4¼" d., 6" h. 100.00

Sweetmeat jar, cov., squatty bulbous body w/mold-blown vertical rib design, decorated w/alternating swirling stripes of chartreuse green, milk white & clear, silver plate rim, cover & bail handle, 5¼" d., 4" h. 195.00

Sweetmeat jar, cov., barrel-shaped, cranberry ground w/overall white crackle design, silver plate cover w/finial, rim & bail handle, 3⅜" d., 3⅛" h. 145.00

Vase, 4" h., 3¾" d., bulbous body w/widely fluted rim, milk white exterior decorated w/applied red cherries w/clear stems & leaves, pink lining 150.00

Vase, 4" h., 4½" d., globular body w/ruffled top, opaque off-white exterior applied w/large green & amber leaves on each side, amber edging around ruffle, pink lining (ILLUS. top next page)..115.00

Vase, 5¾" h., 3¼" d., bulbous body w/rolled rim pulled into four peaks, cream exterior w/applied ruffled amber, green & cranberry leaves, blue lining..145.00

Stevens & Williams Ruffled Vase

Vase, 6⅜" h., 3½" d., satin glass, pedestal footed squatty bulbous body tapering to a cylindrical neck w/flaring, scalloped rim, heavenly blue satin mother-of-pearl Swirl patt., white lining 195.00

Rubina Verde Swirl Mother-of-Pearl Vase

Vase, 6¾" h., ovoid w/corseted neck, rubina verde mother-of-pearl Swirl patt. (ILLUS.) 485.00

Vase, 6¾" h., 4" d., bulbous body tapering to a short cylindrical neck w/bulbous top w/eight-crimp rim, creamy white exterior applied w/a large striped green, cranberry & amber leaf, pink lining 165.00

Vase, 7⅛" h., 4⅞" d., bulbous baluster-form opaque white body w/a crimped & ruffled rim w/applied amber band around the pedestal & large amber applied leaves & amber bell-shaped flower decoration around the body..............................135.00

Vase, 7⅜" h., Silveria, clear w/silver foil inclusions, shaded in red, purple & green, further decorated w/green trailings, inscribed "S & W.," ca. 1900 (ILLUS. top next column) 1,380.00

Stevens & Williams Silveria Vase

Vase, 7½" h., 4½" d., ovoid creamy white body w/ruffled rim applied w/amber edging, the exterior applied w/three large ruffled leaves in green, amber & cranberry wrapping around the sides, deep rose lining 225.00

Vase, 8" h., 3½" d., white ovoid body tapering to a ringed center below the tall, flaring neck w/a squared rim, applied amber loop stem handle at center applied w/two amber plums w/pinkish amber leaves, pink lining 125.00

Vase, 9" h., peach blow ground decorated w/applied clear glass rigaree branches & leaves, satin finish, white lining............................275.00

Vase, double bud, 9¼" h., 6½" d., thorny trunk-form body, shaded lemon yellow decorated w/amber applied branch & leaves & two applied red cherries, white lining 175.00

Vase, 9¾" h., 4½" d., footed baluster-form body w/unevenly flared & ruffled rim, four applied pink & white flowers w/amber & green branches, applied amber loop branch feet & handles, deep rose shaded to paler rose exterior, white lining 795.00

Vase, 11" h., 4 ⅝" d., satin glass, tapering cylindrical body w/a flattened ring below the short flaring neck, shaded orange mother-of-pearl satin Swirl patt., white lining 245.00

Vase, 12" h., icicle design draped from neck, clear w/large figural turquoise salamander handles, brass footed stand 425.00

Vase, 12" h., 4" d., bulbous base

tapering to a wide cylindrical neck
w/scalloped rim, deep coral
decorated w/applied white opalescent rim edging & four large
ruffled leaves wrapping around the
body, creamy white lining 395.00

Unusual Stevens & Williams Vase

Vase, 13½" h., 8" d., novelty-type,
thorny clear feet & branches w/two
large pink opalescent flower-shaped
vases w/rows of clear applied leaves
(ILLUS.) 595.00

Stevens & Williams Enameled Vase

Vases, 10" h., footed tall trumpet-form
body in smoky amber applied
w/amber rigaree around the rim &
w/flattened amber prunts around the
sides, enameled w/stylized florals in
blue, red & green w/gilt trim, slight
gilt wear, pr. (ILLUS. of one) 247.50

Water set: pitcher & four tumblers;
Aventurine, 5 pcs. 1,050.00

(End of Stevens & Williams Section)

TIFFANY

Tiffany Cameo Vase

*Louis Comfort Tiffany established his
glassworks in Corona, New York in 1885
and went on to design and produce some of
the finest decorative glass ever made.
Tiffany was an outstanding designer of the
Art Nouveau era and many of his pieces
reflect this influence. Tiffany revived early
glass techniques and developed many new
ones. He sold his glassworks in 1928.*

Typical Engraved Tiffany Mark

Various Tiffany Marks & Labels

Bonbon, stretched bluish green
opalescence on ribbed bowl
w/internal herringbone decoration,
foot inscribed "L.C.T. Favrile
1700," 5" d., 3" h. $550.00

Bowl, 2¾" h., low bulbous body in
deep amber decorated w/applied
raised trailing devices in silvery-blue
iridescence against a deep purple
& dark blue iridescent ground,
inscribed "L.C.T. Q9917,"
ca. 1902 ....2,070.00

Bowl, 8" d., 3¾" h., footed, the deep body w/widely flaring sides & a flattened rim, overall gold iridescence, marked "L.C. Tiffany - Favrile 1848," w/a paper label 770.00

Bowl, 10" d., 3½" h., twelve-rib body w/stretched gold iridescent surface, wide slightly undulating rim, inscribed "L.C. Tiffany Favrile 1925"...412.50

Bowl, 12" d., shallow w/flaring rim, diamond quilted opalescent decorated w/bright pink giving a stretched effect at the rim, inscribed "L.C. Tiffany-Favrile 1561," ca. 1918-28...................................1,150.00

Bowl-vase, "Agate," squatty ovoid body tapering sharply to a flat base, the wide flat mouth slightly flared, red sides w/a pattern of diamonds in shades of mustard yellow, lime green, greyish green & wintergreen, marked "o6096," original company paper label, 4⅛" h. 5,225.00

Box, cov., bulbous base w/domed cover w/reticulated openwork at the top, blue iridescence w/the base decorated w/a stylized leaf & vine design, base signed "L.C. Tiffany - Favrile 7836D," 6½" h. 2,070.00

Cameo vase, 7" h., squatty bulbous gourd form in lemon yellow overlaid in butterscotch & deeply wheel-carved to depict overall woodbine leaves & vines, engraved "L.C. Tiffany Favrile 9815 A" (ILLUS.) ...6,050.00

Cameo vase, 14¼" h., shouldered ovoid body, clear decorated w/pale lime green & purple, finely cut w/clusters of grapes pendent from leafy vines, mounted within a conforming silver framework similarly cast w/clusters of grapes & leafage, w/vine-like handles continuing to the foot, silver impressed "TIFFANY & Co. MAKERS STERLING SILVER C.," ca. 1906.....................................11,500.00

Candlestick, the wide rib-molded & domed round foot supporting a squatty ribbed knob pedestal below the cylindrical socket w/wide, flat rim, overall white opal stripes in clear w/a pink stretched iridescent rim, marked "L.C.T.Favrile 1817," 4¼" h..440.00

Candlesticks, flaring socket above a bulbous tapering shaft on a disc foot, lustrous crimson red, inscribed

Tiffany Candlesticks

"L.C.T. Favrile," one w/partial paper label, 8¾" h., pr. (ILLUS.) 2,200.00

Candy dish, footed body w/ruffled rim, ribbed design, blue iridescent, 4" d..575.00

Center bowl, paperweight-type, the bulbous paneled clear body raised on a lime green foot, decorated w/rose-colored blossoms & opalescent green leafage & trailings, inscribed "L.C. Tiffany-Favrile 596T," ca. 1925, 4¾" h. 2,588.00

Center bowl, low foot, geometric floral devices within a diamond quilted pattern on the flared pastel aqua opalescent bowl, rim w/narrow stretched border, 11¼" d., 3½" h. 990.00

Center bowl, a shallow widely flaring bowl raised on a low pedestal foot, dark cobalt blue w/intense blue iridescence, marked "L.C. Tiffany Favrile P," 11½" d., 3" h. 1,045.00

Center bowl, wide, nearly flat sides around the small indented center, subtle herringbone leaf design in aqua green & opal white w/stretched iridescence at the rim, signed "L.C. Tiffany Favrile 1925," 12½" d., 3¾" h. 660.00

Champagnes, wide shallow bowl w/flaring rim raised on a thick, short & slightly flaring stem w/a widely flaring foot, overall gold iridescence, wheel-cut w/grapevine borders, each signed "L.C.T." or "L.C.T. Favrile," set of 12 ....1,870.00

Charger, circular, decorated w/radiating rays in medium-relief, the center decorated w/a floral pulled-feather design within concentric iridescent bands, in shades of purplish blue w/golden iridescence, inscribed "L.C.T. F1972," 17¾"d. 4,600.00

Compote, open, 3¼" h., footed vessel w/white leaf designs & blue iridescent finish, inscribed "L.C. Tiffany Favrile 1700" 418.00

Compote, open, 6¾" d., 4¾" h., a small shallow bowl w/a wide flat rim raised on a slender pedestal w/round foot, dark cobalt blue decorated w/overall stretched purplish blue iridescence, signed on base "L.C. Tiffany Favrile 1838".............880.00

Compote, 8" l. oval, 3¼" h., pastel green opalescence over clear lightly ribbed bowl, stem & foot, inscribed "L.C.T. Favrile 1919C" 385.00

Compote, 7⅜" h., paperweight-type, the shallow ribbed opalescent bowl decorated on the interior w/morning glory blossoms & trailing leaves in blue, pale green & lime green, the exterior w/irregular opalescent trailings raised on a ribbed stemlike standard above a circular base, inscribed "L.C. Tiffany-Favrile 3007P," ca. 1921 ....4,025.00

Cordials, small bell-shaped bowl raised on a paneled stem on a slightly domed foot, amber iridescent, inscribed "L.C.T.," 1892-1928, 4½" h., set of 10.........2,588.00

Cordial set: decanter w/stopper & four cordials; the footed decanter w/squatty bulbous body below a tall stick neck w/flared rim & tear-drop stopper, the gold iridescent body intaglio-carved w/a grapevine band, the matching cordials w/small bell-shaped bowls on tall slender stems also engraved w/grapevines, decan-ter marked "L.C. Tiffany Favrile," three cordials marked "L.C.T. Fav-rile" & one marked "L.C.T. Favrile 1229," decanter 9½" h., the set.............5,290.00

Creamer & sugar bowl, tankard creamer w/applied handle, squatty bulbous open sugar bowl; gold iridescent, signed "L.C.T.," creamer 1⅞" d., 2⅞" h., sugar bowl 3¼" d., 1⅝" h., pr. (ILLUS.) 750.00

Cup & saucer, squatty bulbous cup w/applied handle, wide dished saucer, overall gold iridescent w/tiny engraved leafy grapevine borders, signed "L.C. Tiffany Favrile 9776 E" 575.00

Tiffany Creamer & Sugar Bowl

Decanter w/original blown ball stopper, the footed inverted pear-shaped body tapering to a tall, slender stick neck, pale amber w/gold iridescent border decoration at the shoulder & below, base marked "L.C.T. N6560," 10¾" h. (some interior stain) 550.00

Tiffany Finger Bowl & Underplate

Finger bowl & underplate, gold iridescent finish w/engraved swag design, signed, underplate 6" d., bowl 2" h., 2 pcs. (ILLUS.) 475.00

Finger bowls & ice plates, the "Queen" patt., all w/amber iridescence, variously signed "L.C.T." or "L.C.T. Favrile," some numbered, 5" & 6" d., set of 12 ....8,800.00

Tiffany Flower Holder

Flower holder, the shallow circular vessel w/rolled rim in amber iridescent decorated w/deep olive

green leafage & trailings, the center
cylinder supporting a frog w/two tiers
of loops, bowl & frog inscribed "L.C.
Tiffany - Favrile 1131M," 11" d.,
4" h. (ILLUS.) 2,070.00

Goblet, the wide waisted bowl
w/flaring rim tapering at the base to
a small ring wafer above a tapering
slender stem on a slightly domed
round foot, overall gold iridescence,
signed "L.C.T. F1774," 8" h.............275.00

Goblets, wide flaring bell-form bowl
raised on a slender baluster-form
stem on a round foot, intaglio-carved
near the rim w/a grapevine band,
gold rainbow iridescent finish,
marked "L.C.T. Favrile," 4" h., set
of 6...3,680.00

Goblets, "Royal" patt., tall bell-form
bowl raised on a slender double-
twist stem & round foot, overall gold
iridescence, each signed "LCT,"
7¼" h., set of 8.............................2,530.00

Jar, cov., ovoid, brilliant amber
iridescent body intaglio-carved on
the lower section w/upright leafage
alternating w/ovoid panels, the
cushion-form cover faceted w/a
flowerhead, inscribed "L.C. Tiffany
Inc. Favrile," 1892-1928, 5½" h.....1,495.00

Tiffany Cypriote Lamp Base

Lamp base, "Cypriote," tapered urn-
form, iridized blue favrile Cypriote
shaft inscribed "Louis C. Tiffany
Favrile," fitted within a gilt-metal
foliate embellished mount impressed
"Cassidy Co. Inc. New York" on
base plate, glass shaft 9" h., to
socket 15" h. (ILLUS.) 1,495.00

Liqueurs, rounded base w/dimpled
surface, slightly flaring mouth,

amber iridescent, inscribed "L.C.T."
& numbered, 2" h., set of 12 ....2,588.00

Ornament, leaded glass, designed as
a moth w/outspread wings in shades
of green & amber mottled & striated
opalescent, unsigned, 1899-1928,
11¼" l. 2,300.00

Parfait glass, tall slender trumpet-form
body on a compressed knob &
round foot, pale aqua blue-green
w/opal stripes, signed "L.C. Tiffany
Favrile - 1873," 6¼" h. 440.00

Plate, 8¼" d., round w/slightly flaring
wide sides, opalescent w/the rim
decorated in cobalt blue & greenish
gold w/Egyptian Chain pattern
trailings, inscribed "L.C. Tiffany -
Favrile X77" 1,610.00

Plates, luncheon, 8⅞" d., circular
w/irregular edge in clear, internally
decorated w/mottled white radiating
streaks & edged in pale lavender,
inscribed "L.C. Tiffany Favrile,"
ca. 1925, set of 4 ....1,870.00

Sherbets, "Prince" patt., widely flaring
bell-shaped bowl on a short stem &
round foot, overall gold iridescent
finish, signed "L.C.Tiffany Favrile,"
3½" h., set of 6 ....935.00

Toothpick holder, gold iridescent body
w/solid blue iridescent base, signed,
1⅞" h...285.00

Tumbler, flaring cylindrical body, gold
iridescence w/applied gold lily pad
prunts, inscribed "L.C.T. - N8131,"
3⅜" h...165.00

Tumblers, barrel-shaped, gold
iridescent finish, two marked "LCT,"
3¼" h., set of 9 ....825.00

Tiffany Miniature Vase

Vase, miniature, 2¼" h., squat ovoid
body, amber iridescent decorated
w/heart-shaped leafage & trailings in
green, inscribed "L.C. Tiffany-Favrile
W1224," ca. 1905 (ILLUS.) 1,380.00

Vase, miniature, 2⅝" h., gently paneled ovoid body w/a short cylindrical neck, pale amber decorated w/loopings & trailings around the upper section, overall gold iridescence, w/original Tiffany Glass and Decorating company paper label, early 20th c. 690.00

Vase, miniature, 3½" h., a footed, waisted cylindrical body w/a sloping shoulder to a short cylindrical neck, opalescent amber w/pulled white zipper decoration around the sides & a hooked band around the neck, overall gold iridescence, marked "LCT °8604" 990.00

Vase, 4¼" h., paperweight-type, bulbous ovoid body, clear decorated w/pale olive green trailing & white petaled blossoms set w/millifiore centers, the interior in amber iridescence, inscribed "L.C.T. R2174," ca. 1902 ....5,463.00

Rare Tiffany Vase

Vase, 4⅜" h., wide ovoid body tapering to a wide gently flaring flat rim, clear overlaid w/ruby red on the body & decorated w/meandering fine-lined trailings in silvery grey iridescence, the upper rim in lemon yellow w/an applied random trailing along the juncture of the two colors, overall iridescence, signed "L.C.Tiffany - Favrile 9595Y," ca. 1905 (ILLUS.) 39,600.00

Vase, 4½" h., paperweight-type, the shouldered ovoid body in amber decorated w/pulled lappets in deep amber shaded w/emerald green & purple, the interior in amber iridescence, inscribed "L.C. Tiffany-Favrile 1843," 1892-1928..............3,850.00

Vase, 5¼" h., ribbed bulbous body w/widely flaring rim, raised on a low foot, ribbed opalescent infused

w/fuchsia pink, inscribed "L.C. Tiffany - Favrile 958P 1546," ca. 1921 ....920.00

Vase, 5¾" h., "Cypriote," inverted baluster-form, iridescent moss green textured surface decorated w/gold iridescent swags about the neck, inscribed "5781C L.C. Tiffany - Favrile".....................,.................5,175.00

Tiffany Opal Iridescent Vase

Vase, 6⅛" h., 6½" d., a widely flaring flattened rim above a short neck on a bulbous ovoid body tapering sharply to a small stem on a cupped applied foot, pale green w/stretched opal iridescent ribs, marked "L.C. Tiffany Favrile - 5-8689N - 1546" (ILLUS.) 880.00

Vase, 6½" h., trumpet-form bowl w/optic-molded white opal ribbing & shading from pale lavender at the top to white opal at the applied foot, signed "L.C.T. Favrile" 605.00

Vase, 7½" h., wide ovoid body tapering to a flared neck, clear encasing black decorated around the waist w/a band of deep turquoise cartouches w/white edging, signed "L.C. Tiffany Favrile 4077P," ca. 1921 ....3,575.00

Vase, 8" h., footed baluster-form body w/a cylindrical neck w/slightly flared rim, iridescent ruby red body w/black foot & rim band, engraved "1636 K L.C. Tiffany Favrile" 6,325.00

Vase, 8" h., paperweight-type, squared tapering body w/a gold iridescent ground decorated w/milky green leaves & stems w/white flower blossoms, engraved "L.C.T. 42232" (ILLUS. top next column) 3,850.00

Vase, 8½ h., ovoid body tapering slightly to a wide, flat mouth, internally-decorated, the ambergris body lightly molded w/21 ribs &

Tiffany Paperweight-Type Vase

decorated w/green, opal & brownish amethyst double hooked feathers, chains & zig-zag internal designs, overall iridescent finish, signed "L.C.T. A1634" 1,430.00

Tiffany "Tel el Amarna" Vase

Vase, 8½" h., "Tel el Amarna," the tall ovoid body w/small flat mouth & flaring foot, brilliant green cased to opal white w/the black shoulder decorated by green ribbon pulled over iridescent silvery blue controlled swirls, applied gold collar, rim & black cupped foot, marked on base "L.C. Tiffany Favrile 1347H" (ILLUS.) 4,950.00

Vase, 9½" h., floriform, pale transparent amber stem supports a slender trumpet-form peach opalescent ribbed bowl w/a widely flaring ruffled rim, applied iridescent foot, signed "L.C.T. M1142" 2,185.00

Vase, bud, 9¾" h., iridescent blue decorated w/silvery-blue swirls, inscribed "L.C.T. - G 83," ca. 1897 ....1,265.00

Vase, 10⅜" h., floriform, the waisted ribbed inverted bell-form bowl w/ruffled rim above a slender stem raised on a circular gently waisted domical ribbed base, overall amber iridescence, inscribed "L.C. Tiffany - Favrile 9359G," ca. 1912 ....1,380.00

Vase, 11¼" h., waisted floriform body w/everted rim, opalescent decorated w/pulled fine-lined green feathering, raised on a slender shaped stem above a domical foot further decorated w/green feathering, inscribed "L.C. Tiffany-Favrile V352," ca. 1904 ....2,588.00

Vase, 12" h., paperweight-type, cylindrical body w/flared base, the sides flaring to a bulbous top w/a wide, flat mouth, iridescent finish w/four internal upright spathaphylum flowers & long pointed leaves in white, yellow & dark brownish green, incised "3410 G L.C. Tiffany - Favrile" 23,000.00

Vase, 12½" h., cylindrical w/bulbous shoulder, striated amber opalescent decorated about the shoulder w/overlapping thick & thin pulled feathering in golden iridescence tinged w/violet, the whole in iridescence, inscribed "L.C.T. B413," ca. 1894 ....2,310.00

Tiffany "Vitro di Trina" Vase

Vase, 13" h., "Vitro di Trina," double gourd-form body w/rare internal geometric criss-cross design of blue, green & orange threads within the aquamarine body w/gold iridescence above, work attributed to Arthur Nash, signed on base "L.C.Tiffany Favrile 1540P" (ILLUS.) 2,860.00

Vase, 13¼" h., shouldered ovoid w/thick rolled rim, brilliant blue cased w/opalescent turquoise, decorated w/arrowroot leafage & trailings in amber iridescence

Tiffany Vase with Millifiore

& millifiore blossoms in white &
black, inscribed "Louis C. Tiffany
865N," ca. 1919 (ILLUS.) 16,100.00

Vase, 13⅝" h., floriform, the deep
ovoid widely flaring & ruffled bowl
w/lightly ribbed sides tapering to a
tall, slender knopped pedestal on a
round slightly domed foot, overall
deep amber iridescence, signed
"L.C. Tiffany Favrile 2448E" 2,750.00

Tiffany "Pulled-Feather" Vase

Vase, 14" h., waisted cylindrical body
in deep cobalt blue decorated w/a
green & white striped pulled-feather
design, engraved "L.C. Tiffany -
Favrile 07691" (ILLUS.) 2,860.00

Vase, 14¾" h., tall slender trumpet-
form body w/knob at the base & w/a
widely flaring ruffled rim, set on a
domed round foot, overall gold iridescence, engraved "L.C.T. W4584"
(ILLUS. top next column) 3,300.00

Vase, 15" h., paperweight-type,
baluster-form clear body internally
decorated w/tomato red poppies

Trumpet-form Tiffany Vase

w/variegated green leafage, the
interior in subtle iridescence,
inscribed "L.C. Tiffany-Favrile
3893G," ca. 1912 ....10,925.00

Vase, 17⅞" h., cylindrical w/bulbous
shoulder & slightly flaring base, blue
decorated w/an irregular band of
trailing heart-shaped leaves &
applied white flowerheads at the
shoulder, each wheel-carved, the
whole in silvery blue iridescence,
inscribed "L.C. Tiffany-Favrile
7235L," ca. 1917 ....5,500.00

Vase, 18" h., jack-in-the-pulpit style,
broad ruffled face above a slender
stem on a cushion foot, overall
golden amber iridescence, inscribed
"L.C. Tiffany - Favrile - 2058H" ...12,650.00

Vase, 18⅜" h., tall slender tapering
cylindrical body w/flaring rim, amber
iridescent, decorated w/thick applied
trailings & pulled damascene
feathering, inscribed "L.C. Tiffany -
Favrile 8232C," ca. 1908 (small chip
to trailing at base) 8,050.00

Vase, 22⅔" h., tall baluster-form
body w/a swelled ring below the
flaring rim, Cypriote finish, the cobalt
blue body decorated w/rainbow &
gold iridescent peacock feathers
w/green 'eyes,' signed "L.C. Tiffany -
F2888" 13,225.00

Vase, 23⅛" h., "Cypriote," cylindrical
tapering to a sloping shoulder,
opaque olive green decorated about
the shoulder w/a band of irregular
lozenges between borders of
damascene trailings in golden
iridescence, inscribed "L.C. Tiffany-
Favrile 2900G Exhibition piece,"
ca. 1912 ....37,375.00

Vase, 27" h., swelled cylindrical form

tapering slightly to a flat mouth, pale greenish amber iridescent ground decorated overall w/an iron brown iridescent swirling pulled-feather design, engraved L.C.T. E 138"..13,800.00

Wines, wide rounded slightly flaring bowl on a slender stem & round foot, gold iridescent finish, signed "L.C.T.," 6" h., set of 4......................968.00

Wines, shallow waisted bowl raised on a faceted stem & circular foot, brilliant amber iridescence decorated about the waist w/opalescent scrolling lappets, inscribed "L.C.T.," 1892-1928, 5" h., set of 12.......................................4,400.00

Wine set: footed ovoid decanter w/tall cylindrical neck & bulbous stopper & eight wines w/waisted cylindrical ribbed bowls on faceted stems; the decanter w/a cut band of wide oval facets around the middle, all pieces w/overall amber iridescence, decanter signed "L.C. Tiffany - Favrile," wines signed "L.C.T.," decanter 10¾" h., the set..............3,575.00

(End of Tiffany Section)

TORTOISE SHELL

Tortoise Shell Water Tumbler

This Victorian glass derives its name from its design of amber splotched with darker amber or brown which resembles real tortoiseshell. Made both in America and Europe, some Victorian-style pieces have been reproduced in recent years.

Bowl, 7¼" d., 3" h. $175.00

Bowl, 8½" d., 3½" h. 90.00

Decanter w/original stopper, square-shaped body, 10¾" h. 95.00

Pitcher, 8½" h., w/applied amber handle 125.00

Plate, 11¾" d., free-blown 82.50

Tumbler, water, swirl-molded, 2½" d., 3½" h. (ILLUS.) 125.00

Tumbler, cylindrical, alternating panels of mottled tan & maroon, 2¾" d., 3⅞" h. 125.00

VALLERYSTHAL

Established in the early 19th century in Vallerysthal, France, this factory operated until 1939. During World War II the factory was demolished. Today collectors look for their early pressed glasswares and the more modern cameo designs.

Vallerysthal

Vallerysthal Mark

Animal covered dish, rabbit, clear frosted, ca. 1899 ....$90.00

Vallerysthal Cameo Vase

Cameo vase, 7¾" h., tapering ovoid body w/a wide rim pulled-down in the front & pulled-up in the back, pale green acid-etched & overlaid in deep red & cut w/berried leafy branches, signed in intaglio, ca. 1920 (ILLUS.) 345.00

Cameo vase, 13¾" h., tall ovoid body w/a flattened rolled rim & the sides tapering to a round cushion foot, acid-etched clear overlaid in ruby red & amber & cut w/pendent berried branches, further decorated w/randomly-placed enameled florets, the whole trimmed w/gilding, signed in intaglio "Vallerysthal," ca. 1910..2,760.00

Vase, 6" h., baluster-form, clear overlaid in pink, acid-etched w/a leaf pattern, incised signature.............1,100.00

VAL ST. LAMBERT

The Cristalleries du Val-Saint Lambert was established in Liege, Belgium in 1825. A wide range of fine tablewares and Art glass has been produced since then and the factory continues to operate today.

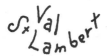

Val St. Lambert Mark

Bowl, 12" d., green ground w/applied frosted handles $200.00

Bowl, 12" w., circular fluted form in frosted olive green, molded w/lily pads & frosted scrolled handles, molded signature "Val St. Lambert - Belgique"..66.00

Cameo decanter & stopper, strongly tapering cylindrical form w/panel-cut neck & conforming stopper, the lower section cut w/pendent flowering leafage in cranberry red on a frosted ground, the neck & stopper in clear w/cranberry borders, signed in cameo, ca. 1900, 16⅜" h. 805.00

Val St. Lambert Cameo Ewer

Cameo ewer, tall slightly tapering cylindrical body, clear acid-etched overlaid in cherry red & cut w/sprays of wildflowers & leafage, signed in cameo, ca. 1900, 14" h. (ILLUS.).....920.00

Cameo vase, 12½" h., violet cut to frosted ground & enameled w/leaves & pendants......................................675.00

Coasters, clear, Zodiac patt., set of 12..215.00

Cologne bottle w/original clear facet-cut stopper, overlay, cranberry cut to clear w/cameo-style florals, signed, 5½" h..250.00

Compote, open, 3½" h., Amberina, a thin squatty bowl w/an upright rim flanked by applied loop handles, raised on a short pedestal w/flared foot, ruby rim above a mottled bowl, amber foot & handles......................165.00

Val St. Lambert Punch Bowl

Punch bowl, overlay, deep rounded bowl on an applied disc foot, brilliant red cut to clear w/a faceted circle & angled panel design, 12" d., 7¼" h. (ILLUS.) 431.00

Val St. Lambert Tumbler
Tumbler, tapering cylindrical form, upper portion decorated w/cranberry

bands, wide stippled acid cut-back clear band w/etched gold figures of classical women playing music & dancing, lower portion w/clear cut panels, gold trim, unsigned, 3⅛" d., 5¼" h. (ILLUS.) 225.00

Vase, 12½" h., baluster-form, acid cut-back decoration of stylized flowers, blue tint, etched "Val St. Lambert" in base.............................440.00

VENETIAN

Venetian Glass Candlestick

For over six centuries fine Venetian glass has been made on the island of Murano. Production continues today and Venetian glass, both ancient and modern, is very collectible.

Bowl, 17½" d., free-form scalloped rim, pale blue shaded to electric blue ground & decorated w/gold swirls..$245.00

Candlestick, two-light, a squatty bulbous top supporting two cylindrical candle sockets w/drip trays & raised on a cylindrical shaft above a domed foot, milky transparent enclosing white webs, applied black glass ring trim, finial & scrolling supports on the foot, designed by Ercole Barovier, Barovier Primavera, unsigned, ca. 1930, 9⅜" h. (ILLUS.) 7,475.00

Centerpiece, blown as a large reclining blossom & stem, moonlight blue opalescent leaves & clear corkscrew vines, 18" l. 65.00

Cordial set: baluster-form decanter & six goblets; smoke-colored, the decanter w/mermaid-form finial & interior white mermaid, the goblets w/mermaid-form stems, decanter 8½" h., the set..................................385.00

Dresser tray, rectangular, clear

frosted w/a raised twisted glass rod frame spaced w/ridged brass mounts, probably Seguso Studio, 10 x 16"...172.50

Epergne, three-lily, matching bowl, pink w/yellow, blue, white & gold latticino ribbons, 11½" d., 16½" h. ...725.00

Figure of a Flamenco dancer, composed of red, black, amber & opaque white blown glass, 15½" h..110.00

Figure of a gentleman, kneeling wearing an exotic costume w/flaring ruffled jacket & skirt above bulbous pantaloons, he carries a basket before him, clear w/black, pink, blue & gilt trim, ca. 1950, 10" h. 920.00

Figure of a maiden, the stylized female in pink-tinged iridescent standing & holding a garland of fruit & flowers above her head & draping down the front, the garland in shades of yellow, pink & green, raised on a clear domed base w/elaborate upturned ruffled rim, in the style of Napoleon Martinuzzi, unsigned, ca. 1935, 15⅝" h. 1,725.00

Figure of a sea nymph riding on a wave, clear w/gold accents, 10" h....330.00

Figure of a woman, dressed in a blue gown & large blue hat, hands & hair highlighted w/gold dust, 12" h. 265.00

Figures, a dandy presenting a red rose & a lady w/a fan, 9" h., pr........275.00

Figures of a man & woman, dressed in gold & white embossed swirl 18th century style court clothing, 11" h., pr...450.00

Venetian Glass Figures

Figures of black musicians & a dancer, two male musicians & a female dancer, each in black glass resembling humans but w/mouse like heads w/swollen red lips, fancifully dressed & mounted on circular bases in clear w/gold foil inclusions, each w/a pale green leaf at the base, unsigned, ca. 1930, 11¼" to 13" h., set of 3 (ILLUS.) ...2,875.00

Goblet, bowl w/embossed swirl design, clear w/gold flecks, on a dolphin-form stem 375.00

Model of a bird, white & blue, on clear pedestal, 8" h. 40.00

Model of a bird, green w/gold flecks, 15" h..75.00

Model of a duck, green w/spread wings & gold beak, 12" h. 75.00

Model of a duck, pink & gold, 12" h. 65.00

Model of a duck, green shaded to clear, 15" l. 150.00

Model of an elephant, blue, yellow & orange, 7" h. 31.50

Model of an elephant, gold & white, 8" l..31.50

Model of an elephant, turquoise, 10" l..40.00

Model of a fish, blue on clear base, 13" l..75.00

Model of a horse, blue, 4" l. 28.00

Model of a horse, blue, 10" l. 40.00

Model of a pheasant, clear w/blue accents, 15½" l. 135.00

Model of a ram, blue, 8" l. 35.00

Model of a squirrel holding a nut, brown, on base, 8" h. 30.00

Model of a squirrel, clear decorated w/red, green & silver dust accents, 11" 85.00

Model of a squirrel, amber decorated w/clear & copper accents...................50.00

Model of a swan, ruby Inverted Thumbprint patt. body w/applied gold flecked wings, tail & head, 4½" l. 65.00

Model of a top hat, free-blown clear wide slightly waisted cylindrical hat w/applied hat band & overall decorative 'crackling,' 8¼" h. 172.50

Models of ducks, turquoise w/gold flecks, 8" h., pr. 75.00

Models of roosters, orange & clear spangled, 7" h., pr...........................140.00

Models of sailfish, yellow & orange on white bases, 15" l., pr.......................100.00

Paperweight, figural pear, cased orange, 6" h. 60.00

Salt dips, model of a swan, amethyst ground w/gold flecks, 3¼", set of 6 ..150.00

Venetian Stemware Set

Stemware set: seven white wines & seven red wines; each w/a conical clear cup supported by a simple black opaque stem raised on a circular foot, decorated w/'fili applicati' in clear & black, signed "MVM - Cappellin - Murano," ca. 1925, 6¼" & 8" h., set of 14 (ILLUS. of part) 518.00

Stemware set: fourteen goblets, eleven wines, fourteen aperitifs & ten cordials; each w/ruby bowls etched w/grapevines & raised on a knopped stem & circular foot monogrammed "OMD," the set 825.00

Syrup pitcher, clear w/blue, green & white threading 350.00

Vase, 7" h., tapering cylindrical form, black w/green looped & trailed decoration w/gilt inclusions, signed 660.00

Vase, 7¾" h., tapering squared form, red cased clear decorated w/colorful millefiore canes, filligrana sections & ribbons in the Zanfirico technique 550.00

Vase, 10" h., slightly flaring cylindrical body w/flat rim, heavy-walled aquamarine internally decorated w/red & white spiral pinwheel medallions & gold inclusions, Murano Studio (some surface scratches) 632.50

Vase, 10" h., 9" d., clear w/controlled bubbles, attributed to Barovier & Toso...550.00

Vase, 10¼" h., simple ovoid body tapering to a short cylindrical neck w/flat rim, clear gold-flecked body w/swirled amethyst-mauve colored bands arranged as irregular 'window' panels overall, design attributed to Ercole Barovier for Barovier & Toso, unsigned (ILLUS. top next page)....................550.00

Vase, 11¼" h., flaring cylindrical body w/a widely flared & lightly crimped rim, gold-flecked clear inlaid w/two

Ovoid Venetian Vase

broad orange swirling stripes,
design attributed to Dino Martens for
Aureliano Toso, unsigned 550.00

Vase, 11¾" h., slightly flaring
cylindrical body w/a flat rim, heavy
walled green & aquamarine
internally decorated w/five colorful
fish, each emitting air bubbles,
Murano Studio, attributed to Gino
Cenedese 632.50

Vase, 12" h., paneled form, clear
w/brown & amber interior.................264.00

Vase, 12¼" h., "Il Burlesco," bulbous
blown body flanked by angled handles, trumpet-form neck, raised on a
trumpet-form base, clear decorated
w/black paste glass to depict a face,
designed by Pablo Picasso, blown
by Lado Bon, produced by Aureliano
Toso, Murano, signed "Picasso," ca.
1955..10,925.00

Vase, 14½" h., irregular gourd-form
w/elongated neck, clear w/enclosed
powders of red, royal blue, yellow,

Tall Cylindrical Venetian Vase

white & turquoise, latticine patches,
a large star-shaped murina & gold
foil inclusions, designed by Dino
Martins, from the 'Oriente' series,
produced by Aureliano Toso,
Murano, ca. 1948..........................7,763.00

Vase, 17" h., simple cylindrical form,
decorated w/a symmetrical patchwork of pale colors of blue, white &
salmon red, by Barovier & Toso
(ILLUS. bottom previous page).....2,990.00

Water set: 15" h. tankard pitcher &
four 6" h. footed tumblers; clear
ground decorated w/heavy gold
applique & h.p. florals, 5 pcs............320.00

Wine, twisted ball stem, golden
yellow..40.00

VENINI

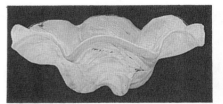

Venini Center Bowl

*A former lawyer, Paolo Venini, founded
this glass factory in Murano, near Venice,
in 1921. The firm soon developed a
reputation for its fine quality decorative
and tableware glass. A number of notable
designers have worked for Venini over the
years and many of their modernist designs
are highly sought-after. The factory
continues to operate today.*

Bottle w/original stopper, "Inciso," the
short ovoid vessel w/mushroom-
shaped stopper in clear cased in
red, designed by Paolo Venini,
unsigned, ca. 1956, 5¼" h. $575.00

Bowl, 5½" d., 3¼" h., "Pulegoso,"
heavy pale blue squared body
w/minute bubbles & gold foil inclusions, stamped "Venini Murano
Made in Italy" 467.50

Bowl, 5¾" d., 3¾" h., "Mezza
Filigrana," oval composed of pale
amber stripes alternating w/brown &
white latticino ribbons, stamped
"Venini Murano Italia".......................220.00

Bowl, 13¼" l., 3" h., "Filigrane," long

shallow leaf-form bowl composed of thread filaments in mauve, brown & apple green, tooled stem at the end, design attributed to Fulvio Bianconi, acid-stamped mark "Venini - Murano - Italia"..1,045.00

Cake stand, three-tier, each graduated tier composed of a flat circular dish w/upturned rim raised on a trumpet-form pedestal, the lower two tiers in powder blue opaque, the upper in bright yellow opaque w/central clear handle, each acid-stamped "venini - murano - ITALIA," top section w/portion of original paper label, 9½" widest d., overall 11" h. 1,438.00

Candlestick, pale smoky glass w/double baluster standard divided by a floriform section, on domed circular foot, w/a deep dished bobeche & a second extra bobeche, ca. 1930, 15½" h., the group............345.00

Center bowl, "Pulegoso," heavy walled emerald green oval w/overall iridescent surface, probably the work of Napoleone Martinuzzi, stamped mark "Venini Murano - Made In Italy," 1940s, 16½" d., 3" h..357.50

Center bowl, widely flaring deeply ruffled ribbed sides, clear & opaque white in a slumped form, base inscribed "Venini Italia," design attributed to Toni Zuccheri, 21" d., 7½" h. (ILLUS.) 550.00

Venini Centerpiece

Centerpiece, irregular form in olive green encased within corrugated clear & molded w/deep ridges resembling a large cabbage leaf, probably designed by Tony Zuccheri, inscribed "venini - italia," ca. 1966, 18" d. (ILLUS.) 920.00

Charger, large circular form w/clear reserve centered by an angry

orange eye, the rim in shaded green, probably designed by Carlo Scarpa, inscribed "venini - italia," ca. 1970, 19¼" d....................................460.00

Decanter w/stopper, "Vetro Battuto," ovoid body w/cylindrical neck, topaz w/a hammered finish, acid-stamped "venini murano ITALIA" & "BOTTLE MADE IN ITALY," 7¼" h. 748.00

Venini Glass Decanter

Decanter w/bulbous stopper, slightly swelled cylindrical body w/an angled shoulder to the short neck, deep purple cased in clear, the exterior carved w/a design of fine parallel lines, acid-stamped "venini - murano - ITALIA," ca. 1950, 10¾" h. (ILLUS.) 2,013.00

Decanter w/original stopper, "Inciso," the tapering triangular bottle w/domical stopper in clear cased in red, designed by Paolo Venini, unsigned, ca. 1956, 13⅝" h. 4,313.00

Venini Bottle-form Decanter

Decanter w/stopper, elongated bottle-form w/conical stopper in clear decorated w/vertical blue & yellow stripes, designed by Fulvio Bianconi, acid-stamped "VENINI - MURANO - ITALIA," ca. 1955, 17⅞" h. (ILLUS.) 3,163.00

Decanter w/original stopper, the waisted flattened cylindrical body w/tapering neck & large disk-form stopper in clear w/white & pink spiral striped decoration, signed & acid-stamped "venini - murano - ITALIA," ca. 1960, 21½" h. 1,380.00

Decanters w/original stoppers, squared bottle-form, one in marine blue decorated w/deep cobalt blue raised concentric trailing & flattened domical blue stopper, the other in bottle green decorated w/hot orange raised concentric trailing & flattened domical hot orange stopper, inscribed "venini - italia," the first acid-stamped "venini - murano - ITALIA," ca. 1962, 8¾" & 9" h., pr. 2,588.00

Display sign, opaque white lattimo rectangular plaque w/raised molded border on three sides & black Venini script logo in lower case letters, 4 x 6¼"..259.00

Figure of a gentleman, combining the "mask" & "patchwork" series, composed of black mask face, hat, trousers & shoes w/opaque white lattimo hair, beard, collar, stockings & gloves w/four fingers on the right hand & five fingers on the left, his coat of transparent red, blue & green pezzato squares, designed by Fulvio Bianconi, stamped on base "Venini Murano Italia," 14" h. 3,575.00

Figures, depicting a man & woman, each w/an amber head & arms, dressed in multicolored Renaissance costumes, designed by Fulvio Bianconi, each acid-stamped "venini - murano - ITALIA," ca. 1950, 13⅝" & 14" h., pr. 4,025.00

Hourglass, composed of two assembled pear-shaped containers, one cobalt blue, the other pale turquoise, 7¼" h. 230.00

Hourglass, of typical form w/one egg-shaped chamber in brilliant red-orange & the other in bottle green, supported by "zanfirico" canes around threaded glass rods w/circular wood bases, designed by Paolo Venini, w/original paper label "VENINI - MURANO - VENEZIA - N. 4901 - MADE IN ITALY," ca. 1957, 10½" h..1,438.00

Jar, cov., simple cylindrical body

w/fitted flat cover, opaque olive green w/amber cover, base stamped "Venini Murano Italia," w/Venini label, 4¾" h. 172.50

Venini Lamp Shades

Lamp shades, hanging-type, "Pezzato," each swollen elongated domical shade in clear w/patchwork decoration in pink, blue & purple, cased over white, designed by Fulvio Bianconi, unsigned, one w/paper label, ca. 1951, 13⅝" h., pr. (ILLUS.) 1,150.00

Light fixture, hanging-type, the shade in cased white decorated w/green, amethyst & red stripes, suspended from a simple rod standard, ca. 1955, 6" d..115.00

Mirror, table-type, the squared clear molded glass frame rope-twist design & wide rounded corners, on an easel support, impressed mark "VENINI - MADE IN ITALY," ca. 1930, 20" w., 22¼" h. 1,380.00

Model of a chicken,"Filigrano" glass, the clear curved tubular body w/white threading, a crimped tail & applied white comb & crimped white base, by Tommaso Buzzi, acid-stamped "venini - italia," ca. 1932, 7¼" h...1,725.00

Model of a cowboy hat, full-sized pinched "ten gallon" type blown in one piece, applied hat band, unsigned, 16¼" widest d., 7¼" h......440.00

Model of a shell, snail-type w/coiled end & open mouth at top, solid iridescent black amethyst w/raised dotted surface highlighted by gold leaf applications, polished base, unsigned, 4" h. 357.50

Models of birds, bulbous body pulled up at tail & beak, green "tessuto" cased w/iridescent clear, designed

Venini Glass Bird

by Tyra Lundgren, acid-stamped
"venini murano," 4⅞" h., pr.
(ILLUS. of one) 920.00

Venini Rooster & Hen

Models of chickens, whimsical rooster
& hen composed of lattimo &
multicolored swirled hollow cone-
form bodies w/applied black, red &
yellow detailing including wings,
comb, beaks, eyes & feet, on
platform bases, designed by Fulvio
Bianconi, stamped "Venini Murano
Italia," rooster broken-off & reglued
at ankles, 7¼" h., pr. (ILLUS.).......5,775.00

Venini Obelisks

Models of obelisks, conical top in
clear w/internal black & white spiral
threading, raised on faceted flaring
deep green base, acid-stamped

"venini - murano - ITALIA," ca.
1930, 10⅜" h., pr. (ILLUS.) 460.00

Cylindrical Venini Pitcher

Pitcher, 9" h., cylindrical body w/small
pulled rim spout, emerald green
decorated w/a single opaque lavender stripe up each side, designed
by Fulvio Bianconi & Paolo Venini,
ca. 1951 (ILLUS.)............................748.00

Toothpick holder, cylindrical, multicolored, acid-stamped mark, 3" h. 77.00

Vase, 4⅜" h., handkerchief-type, the
crimped & flaring body in deep red
cased over teal blue, designed by
Fulvio Bianconi, acid-stamped
"venini - murano - ITALIA," ca.
1948...2,185.00

Vase, 6" h., handkerchief-type, upright
randomly ruffled sides in turquoise
green cased to white, acid-stamped
mark "Venini Murano Italia".............345.00

Vase, 6¼" h., "Fazzoletto," slumped
handkerchief form, turquoise bluish-
green exterior, white interior, acid-
stamped mark "Venini Murano
Italia" 247.50

Teardrop-form Venini Vase

Vase, 6⅜" h., bulbous teardrop-form,
pale green iridescent body w/three-
ringed neck & applied side handles,
designed by Napoleone Martinuzzi,
acid-stamped "venini - ITALIA" &
enameled "5254," ca. 1930
(ILLUS) 690.00

(ILLUS) 690.00

Vase, 6½" h., widely flaring conical body in clear w/a green *summorso* layer below pale blue casing, finely ridged surface, base stamped "Venini Murano Italia".....................747.50

Vase, 7" h., spherical clear vessel w/slightly off-center internal wall in pea green, inscribed "venini - italia," ca. 1970 ....460.00

Vase, 8" h., bottle-form, spherical body tapering to a small neck w/flaring rim, amber mold-blown w/wavy indentations around the sides, acid-stamped "MADE IN ITALY," ca. 1930 ....92.00

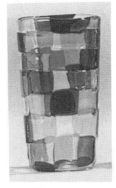

Venini Cylindrical Vase

Vase, 8⅝" h., "Vetro Pezzato Arlecchino," the cylindrical sides composed of patchwork squares in shades of lavender, citron yellow, chocolate brown & clear, designed by Fulvio Bianconi, acid-stamped "VENINI - MURANO - ITALIA" & w/original paper label & model number 4916, ca. 1955 (ILLUS.) ..6,325.00

Vase, 8¾" h., cylindrical clear body w/rolled rim, internally decorated w/two red tulips w/green leaves, possibly by Fulvio Bianconi, inscribed "venini italia" w/monogram, ca. 1951 ....1,093.00

Vase, 8⅞" h., the conical clear body w/applied emerald green rim & tooled handle rising from the base to the rim, acid-stamped "venini - italia," ca, 1930 ....575.00

Vase, 9⅛" h., "Pezzati," flaring cylindrical body, clear enclosing a pattern of blue, red, white, green & turquoise blue irregular squares, designed by Fulvio Bianconi, acid-stamped "venini - murano - ITALIA," ca. 1951 ....5,175.00

Vase, 9¼" h., handkerchief-type, of typical form in rose cased over white, designed by Paolo Venini & Fulvio Bianconi, inscribed "venini - italia," ca. 1950 ....805.00

Vase, 9½" h., the clear cylindrical body decorated w/spiral threading in gunmetal & violet above a deep brick red base, designed by Thomas Stearns, unsigned, retains original paper label, ca. 1962 ....2,875.00

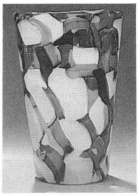

Venini Bianconi-Designed Vase

Vase, 10" h., "Vetro Pezzato Arlecchinó," slightly flaring cylindrical form w/undulating rim, clear, white, milky pale blue, blue, pale green, green & red in an overall patchwork design, acid-etched mark "venini murano ITALIA," designed by Fulvio Bianconi (ILLUS.).........................4,950.00

Vase, 11" h., handkerchief-type, the flaring irregular body w/undulating rim in pale slightly iridescent pink, designed by Fulvio Bianconi, acid-stamped "venini - murano - ITALIA," ca. 1948 ....1,840.00

Vase, 11⅝" h., handkerchief-type, "Fazzoletto," shaped as a rumpled handkerchief pulled into tall points, white cased w/black on the outside, designed by Fulvio Bianconi, acid-stamped "venini murano ITALIA," ca. 1950 ....1,495.00

Vase, 12" h., flattened baluster-form, bluish green w/an amber-colored base, acid-stamped mark "Venini Murano" 412.50

Vase, 12½" h., bulbous ovoid body w/a wide dimpled shoulder to a bulbous lobed short neck, grey shading to bluish green on the shoulder & neck, the surface acid-etched overall, probably designed by Carlo Scarpa, ca. 1935, unsigned 920.00

Vase, 13¼" h., "Messico," the lattimo cylindrical vessel w/rounded base & shoulder, in deepest amethyst w/random white trailing cased in clear, inscribed "venini - italia," w/original paper label, ca. 1970 ....1,438.00

Venini Tessuto Vase

Vase, 13½" h., "Tessuto," teardrop-form w/slender neck, half decorated in yellow & black vertical threads, the remainder in solid yellow, hammered surface, designed by Carlo Scarpa, ca. 1940 (ILLUS.) 7,475.00

Vase, 14⅛" h., "Pennellato," the waisted cylinder ascending to a cone, clear w/red, green & blue vertical lines, acid-stamped "Venini Murano ITALIA" 7,475.00

Vase, 15½" h., "Vetro a File," cylindrical tapering in slightly at top, milky 'vieus-rose' cased body internally decorated w/grey veining & purple raffia, stamped "VENINI MURANO ITALIA," attributed to Toni Zuccheri, ca. 1960 ....2,300.00

Vase, 17" h., bulbous blown body w/cylindrical neck & flaring rim, pale amethyst decorated w/two wraps at the shoulder, remnants of paper label "VENINI - MURANO - VENEZIA, NEW YORK - 125 E. 55th. - MADE IN ITALY," ca. 1950 ....1,725.00

(End of Venini Section)

VERLYS

Verlys originated in France in the mid-1930s and was produced by the French Holoplane Co. A branch, Verlys in

America, soon was opened in Newark, Ohio and produced wares similar to the French examples, but less expensive. Various Art Deco designs, some resembling Lalique glass, were blown or molded in clear, frosted clear and colors. Between 1955-57 the Heisey Company used some Verlys molds.

A Verlys France

French Verlys Mark

Ashtray, Birds & Bees patt., clear.......$45.00

Ashtray, clear w/leaf design.................20.00

Bowl, 6" d., Pine Cone patt., clear........50.00

Bowl, 6¼ x 10½", 4¼" h., Chrysanthemum patt., crystal etched, signed 295.00

Bowl, 11⅝" d., Birds & Bees patt., Directoire blue.................................400.00

Bowl, 14" d., Water Lilies patt., clear ..100.00

Bowl, 16" d., Pine Cone patt., clear......40.00

Bowl, 19" d., decorated w/relief-molded goldfish, clear.....................250.00

Box, cov., topaz w/chrysanthemum decoration, 5¼" d. 375.00

Charger, Birds & Dragonflies patt., 12" d., signed 89.00

Charger, Water Lily patt., clear, 14" d..145.00

Tassels Console Bowl

Console bowl, Tassels patt., clear, signed, 12" d. (ILLUS.)......................80.00

Console bowl, Water Lily patt., clear, signed, 15" d. 100.00

Console bowl, Water Lily patt., topaz, signed 300.00

Vase, 5" h., footed ovoid body tapering to a short cylindrical neck, molded overall w/flying butterflies, fiery opalescent, inscribed "Verlys" on base...172.50

Vase, 5" h., Lovebirds patt., clear.......150.00

Alpine Thistle Vase

Vase, 9½" h., Alpine Thistle patt.,
topaz (ILLUS.)....................................525.00

WAVE CREST

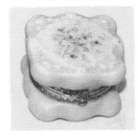

Small Wave Crest Box

This ornately molded and delicately decorated opal glass is the most famous line of the C.F. Monroe Company of Meriden, Connecticut. Wave Crest, and its related lines Kelva and Nakara (which see), were introduced in the early 1890s and continued to be popular until about 1910. Many pieces feature gilt-metal trim and fittings and some examples are lined with satin, especially popular boudoir accessories such as jewel boxes. C.F. Monroe Company closed in 1916.

WAVE CREST WARE

Wave Crest Mark

Bonbon w/silver bail handle,
decorated w/a network of vines,
leaves & blue flowers, deep lemon
yellow at top shading to white,
original label....................................$595.00

Box w/hinged lid, Egg Crate mold, lid
decorated w/central floral decoration
of pink & maroon flowers & green
leaves on a shaded light green
ground, 3" d., 2½" h. (ILLUS.)..........225.00

Box w/hinged lid, Egg Crate mold,
decorated w/red clover blooms,
3" sq...195.00

Box w/hinged lid, Helmschmied Swirl
mold, h.p. floral decoration on a
creamy white ground, 4½ d., 3" h. ..425.00

Box w/hinged lid, Egg Crate mold,
pink ground decorated w/clusters
of blue flowers, raised gold borders
surround floral groupings, wide
gilt-metal mounting, 4½ x 4¾" 550.00

Box w/hinged lid, Egg Crate mold,
decorated w/yellow & purple flowers,
5" sq...430.00

Helmschmied Swirl Box

Box w/hinged lid, Helmschmied Swirl
Mold, lid decorated w/dainty pink &
gold flowers & green leaves, shaded
blue to white ground, unmarked, no
lining, 5½" d., 3½" h. (ILLUS.)..........350.00

Box w/hinged lid, Baroque Shell mold,
decorated w/clover blooms on white
ground, 5½" d, ...195.00

Box w/hinged lid, Helmschmied Swirl
mold, overall decoration of nose-
gays of reddish brown florets on
ivory ground, matching new lining,
5½" d..375.00

Box w/hinged lid, Egg Crate mold,
w/enameled h.p. sprays of small
pink & white flowers & green

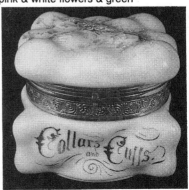

Wave Crest Collars and Cuffs Box

leaves, blue trim on a white ground, 3 x 5½" rectangle, 3" h. 495.00

Box w/hinged lid, Embossed Rococo mold, h.p. blue flowers on a pink ground, raised on an ornate gilt-metal footed base, 5" w., 6" l. 875.00

Box w/hinged lid, Egg Crate mold, enameled floral decoration on lid & "Collars & Cuffs" on side, 6" (ILLUS. bottom previous column) .850.00 to 950.00

Box w/hinged lid, round, the top decorated w/a courting couple in period costume, 6" d., 4½" h. 950.00

Box w/hinged lid, Helmschmied Swirl mold, decorated w/delicate flowers on the lid & sides, 6" d., 5" h. 400.00

Baroque Shell Box

Box w/hinged lid, Baroque Shell mold, top decorated w/blue, purple & grey flowers, green leaves & pink trim on a creamy white ground, 7" d., 4" h. (ILLUS.) 750.00

Box w/hinged lid, Egg Crate mold, decorated w/mauve to purple floral clusters, green ribbons w/enameled white dots & outlined in gold, 7" sq. 650.00

Box w/hinged lid, Helmschmied Swirl mold, lid w/h.p. peach, pink & white asters & moss green leaves, opaque white ground, ornate footed gilt-metal base, 7" d., 6½" h. 945.00

Box w/hinged lid, Embossed Rococo mold, decorated w/pink & white florals, 7¼" d., 5½" h. 695.00

Box w/hinged lid, Hexagonal mold w/embossed scrolling, top & sides decorated w/shaded pink florals & green foliage on a soft green ground, 8½" w., 6" h. 1,250.00

Card holder, upright rectangular form w/embossed frame design, gilt-metal rim, cloth lining, decorated w/delicate pink flowers & a blue border 310.00

Cigar holder, plain cylindrical body decorated w/h.p. florals, gilt-metal handled rim & scroll-footed base 250.00

Cigar humidor, cov., cylindrical, white opal body molded w/florals & h.p. w/"Cigars" in pink on the side over blue enameled forget-me-nots, the domed cover decorated w/an Indian on horseback, gilt-metal hinged mounts, red flag mark on base 660.00

Cologne bottle w/atomizer, squatty bulbous body, h.p. yellow floral decoration & enameled white dots on a white opal ground, nickel plate atomizer dated "1889" w/rubber bulb 265.00

Cologne bottles w/original scroll-molded creamy white stoppers, cylindrical body w/deep scroll-molded shoulder, a short cylindrical neck w/a flaring rim, enameled w/dainty blue flowers, green leaves & foliage & heavy gold scrolling on a creamy white ground, pr. 925.00

Wave Crest Cracker Jar

Cracker jar, cov., barrel-shaped, panels of yellow flowers w/pink centers & green leaves decorate a soft pink ground, resilvered rim, cover & bail handle, unmarked, 5½" d., 7¼" h. (ILLUS.) 350.00

Cracker jar, cov., barrel-shaped w/embossed scrolling, h.p. pink, blue & yellow pansies on a creamy white ground, resilvered cover, rim & bail handle, 5¾" d., 7¾" h. 295.00

Cracker jar, cov., Egg Crate mold, decorated w/h.p. lavender, green & tan florals on a white shaded to pale blue ground, 5" d., 9" h. 650.00

Cracker jar, cov., barrel-shaped body w/large embossed leaf design, shaded yellow to white ground decorated w/h.p. ferns, silver plate rim, cover & bail handle, overall 10½" h. 280.00

Creamer & cov. sugar bowl, decorated w/h.p. cupids & whimsical scrolling, creamer w/gilt-metal lipped rim & handle, sugar bowl w/gilt-metal rim, cover & bail handle, pr. ..100.00

Creamer & sugar bowl w/rope twist handles, decorated w/pink flowers on blue ground, pr............................150.00

Deck of cards holder, turquoise ground w/enameled large pink rosebud, white dotting on the front & back & similar decoration on both sides 325.00

Wave Crest Dresser Box

Dresser box., cov., short radiating molded ribs on the cover & around the base, cover decorated w/pink & blue florals, gilt-metal fittings, red banner mark, 4¼" d., 3¼" h. (ILLUS.) 287.50

Ferner, Egg Crate mold, decorated w/light pink spider mums, no liner, 7" sq...345.00

Glove box w/hinged lid, pink w/blue floral decoration, 4 x 8½" 875.00

Wave Crest Humidor

Humidor w/original brass cover & finial, cream & brown bulbous cylindrical body decorated w/three bulldog heads & "Three Guards-men," unmarked, 5⅛" d., 6½" h. (ILLUS.) 525.00

Jardiniere, bulbous nearly spherical body w/a wide, short cylindrical neck, the sides molded w/delicate scroll-bordered cartouches

decorated w/h.p. flowers, all on a pink ground, raised on a gilt-metal base w/scroll feet, 6½" h..................895.00

Mirror tray, embossed scrolls, decorated w/dainty blue flowers on a creamy white ground, ornate gilt-metal frame, 5¼" d..........................775.00

Photo receiver, Egg Crate mold, the body decorated w/clusters of pink & blue flowers & light green foliage on a creamy white ground, ornate gilt-metal rim 395.00

Salt dip, "tulip" mold, w/h.p. floral decoration 165.00

Salt shaker w/original top, embossed beaded foot, squatty bulbous body tapering to a cylindrical neck w/embossed beaded ring below the lid, decorated w/embossed scrolling & enameled w/two red-headed birds sitting side-by-side among yellow & brown foliage, 2¼" h. 68.00

Salt & pepper shakers w/original tops, hexagonal, Embossed Rococo mold, decorated w/h.p. florals, pr.....145.00

Salt & pepper shakers w/original metal tops, Erie Twist mold, decorated w/peach & blue forget-me-nots & daisies, pr. 145.00

Salt & pepper shakers w/original tops, embossed scrolling design, pink ground w/front & back blue floral decoration, pr...................................250.00

Sugar shaker w/original top, , Helmschmied Swirl mold, alternating panels of blue scrolls & yellow flowers 480.00

Sugar shaker w/original top, tapering cylindrical form, decorated w/h.p. daisies on front & back 195.00

Syrup pitcher w/original top, Helmschmied Swirl mold, white & beige swirls highlighted w/lavender & gold florals 295.00

Syrup pitcher w/original hinged top, paneled cylindrical body w/tapering shoulder, lacy transfer decoration & h.p. pink daisy-type flowers 165.00

Vase, 6½" h., footed, cylindrical body, embossed scrolling, beaded rim, decorated w/pink flowers 265.00

Vase, 7½" h., footed, bulbous body w/long cylindrical neck, embossed scrolling, decorated w/small red flowers 375.00

Vase, 8¾" h., squatty bulbous base

tapering to a tall cylindrical neck,
dark green lines bordering areas of
pink covered w/white dots & winding
over a background of blue forget-
me-nots, on gilt-metal base w/small
scroll feet 670.00

Vase, 9" h., pink shading to burgundy
w/h.p. floral decoration & raised gold
beading 1,950.00

Vase, 9" h., 1¼" rim d., squatty
bulbous body tapering to a tall
cylindrical neck, decorated
w/shaded pink to burgundy mums,
deep green enameled swags & a
deep green enameled rim w/white
dotting, footed gilt-metal base..........595.00

Vase, 12½" h., 4¾" d., cylindrical
body w/brass collar, decorated
w/pink wild roses on light blue
ground, ornate metal feet.............1,050.00

Vase, 13½" h., footed, burnt orange
ground decorated w/large purple
orchids on the front & back,
signed 1,095.00

WEBB

Webb Bowl with Applique

*Thomas Webb, an experienced English
glassman, opened his own glass factory in
1837 and from then on the firm became
known for its wide variety of fine Art glass,
including cameo, satin and Burmese. The
company continues to operate in Stourbridge, England making quality household
and decorative glass. Also see BURMESE,
ROSE BOWLS, PEACH BLOW and
SATIN & MOTHER-OF-PEARL.*

Bowl, 4" d., 2½" h., deep rounded
sides below the flat rim, ruby cut to
green in a floral wreath & swag
design, star-cut base $220.00

Bowl, 4½" d., 3½" h., squatty bulbous
rose bowl-form w/incurved six-crimp

top, pale aqua exterior decorated
w/swags of clear applied rigaree &
raised on applied clear reeded
scroll feet, creamy white interior
(ILLUS.) 245.00

Bowl, 4¾" d., 5" h., footed bulbous
form, garlands of clear rigaree
applied around the amber body, six
clear berry prunts applied around
the top edge, three applied clear
scroll feet 210.00

Webb Appliqued Cranberry Bowl

Bowl, 6⅛" d., 5½" h., spherical
cranberry body w/lightly molded
internal ribbing, clear applied heavy
scroll feet, three clear applied fan-
shaped devices & six berry prunts
around the flat mouth, applied
crystal berry pontil (ILLUS.) 265.00

Cameo bottle w/ornate sterling silver
cap & rim, cylindrical, red overlaid in
white & cameo-cut w/butterflies,
flowers & leaves, 5" h. 600.00

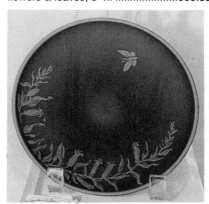

Webb Cameo Bowl

Cameo bowl, 6" d., 1⅛" h., deep blue
overlaid w/pale bluish white & cut
w/a curved branch of foxglove along
one side w/a butterfly near
the opposite edge, pontil incised
"1/6107" (ILLUS.) 875.00

Cameo decanter w/faceted stopper, clear w/a a bulbous flat-sided body w/a wide shoulder to the tall slender neck w/flared rim, a diamond patterned lower band, the sides w/three oval reserves overlaid in red & white & finely wheel-carved w/tulips & a bee, apple blossoms & leafage & hibiscus & a bee, ca. 1900, unsigned, 11⅛" h. (small chip to one reserve border) 1,150.00

Cameo flask, flattened oval shape, turquoise blue overlaid in white & cut w/stylized blossoms on leafy stems, hammered silver neck & round cap, unsigned, ca. 1900, 5⅜" l...1,840.00

Cameo inkwell, the thick domical body in deep teal blue overlaid in white & cut w/stylized blossoms & leaves, mounted w/a silver collar w/hinged bulbous lid engraved w/floral designs, unsigned, mount w/impressed hallmarks & "STERLING," ca. 1890, 4½" h...2,070.00

Cameo lamp, miniature, a tapering conical shade above an ovoid base, each in brilliant sapphire blue w/white cameo-cut blossoms, leaves & a butterfly in flight on the base & a morning glory vine on the shade, mounted w/a gilt-metal Silber Burner, four-sided medallion Webb mark on base, w/chimney, 8¾" h. plus chimney 3,300.00

Cameo mustard pot w/silver plate rim & lid, slightly compressed globular base, red overlaid in white & cameo-cut w/flowers & foliage, applied ring handle, 3½" h. 340.00

Cameo perfume bottle w/silver plate hinged cover, lay-down type, elongated ovoid form, chartreuse overlaid w/white & cameo-cut w/flowers & foliage, 4" l. 550.00

Cameo perfume flask, modeled as a swan's head, lemon yellow overlaid in white & finely wheel-carved, numbered "Reg. 11109," fitted w/a sterling silver neck & round cap stamped "GORHAM STERLING," ca. 1900, 5¾" l. 4,025.00

Cameo rose bowl, footed squatty bulbous body, eight-crimp top, creamy white overlaid in rich pink & cut w/bamboo branches, leaves & flowers, golden yellow interior, applied clear petal feet & flower prunt, 5⅝" d., 4" h. 795.00

Cameo scent flask, model of a fish, red overlaid in white & finely wheel-

carved, w/a sterling silver tail, glass marked "Reg. 15711," the silver w/English hallmarks, ca. 1885, w/original presentation box, 2 pcs. 5,175.00

Cameo vase, 5" h., gourd-form body, cranberry shading to amber cased over creamy opalescent white, overlaid in white & cut w/cyclamen blossoms, buds & foliage w/a butterfly & dragonfly in flight, unsigned, ca. 1890 ....1,840.00

Cameo vase, 5⅛" h., 3½" d., cylindrical, ivory opaque decorated w/carving of berries & leaves & brown staining trim, three frosted ball feet, hallmarked silver top band, signed "Thos. Webb & Sons Simulated Ivory" 795.00

Cameo vase, 6⅛" h., shouldered ovoid body w/everted rim, cranberry shading to golden amber cased over creamy opalescent white, overlaid in white & cut w/a spray of apple blossoms, buds & foliage w/a butterfly in flight, unsigned, ca. 1890..............2,300.00

Cameo vase, 6¼" h., footed ovoid body tapering to a short cylindrical neck, brown layered in white & cut w/a design of a large spotted lily blossom, a bud & leafy stems, linear neck & foot borders......................1,430.00

Cut & Cameo Webb Vase

Cameo & cut vase, 7¼" h., tapering ovoid body on a small footring, a waisted neck w/a widely cupped rim, clear cut w/an overall diamond point design, w/a diagonal inset panel at the side overlaid in pink & white & cut w/a branch of cherries & leaves, ca. 1890, unsigned (ILLUS.) 1,438.00

Cameo vase, 7½" h., wide ovoid body tapering to a short flaring neck, bright blue layered w/amethyst & overlaid in white, cameo-cut & carved intricately overall w/passion flowers w/broad leaves & tendrils, a trumpet vine cluster on the reverse, unusually detailed borders, marked "Thomas Webb & Sons Gem Cameo" 9,075.00

Cameo vase, 8" h., ovoid base tapering to a slender cylindrical neck w/flat rim, yellow ground overlaid in red & white & cameo-cut w/multi-petaled blossoms, buds & leafy stems, marked on base "Thos. Webb & Sons Cameo" 2,860.00

Cameo vase, 8" h., spherical body w/cylindrical neck, red overlaid in white & cut w/trailing apple blossoms & foliage & a butterfly in flight, signed in cameo "THOMAS WEBB & SONS - CAMEO," ca. 1890 ....2,300.00

Webb Scenic Cameo Vase

Cameo vase, 8⅝" h., "The Pet Parrot," cylindrical w/rounded base & low disc foot, low collared mouth, the medium blue sides overlaid in white & finely cut on the obverse w/a young maiden clothed in classical drapery seated on a stone coping, gazing at a parrot perched on her right hand, an urn & flowering leafage at her feet, between leaftip & flower borders & acanthus leafage, the foot further carved w/flowerheads, impressed "WEBB" & titled, ca. 1890 (ILLUS.) 31,050.00

Cameo vase, 9¼" h., globular w/short neck, red overlaid w/white, cameo-carved w/wild geranium leaves, blossoms & foliage, a butterfly reverse, linear borders 3,300.00

Cameo vase, 10" h., bulbous, citron yellow overlaid w/white, cameo-carved w/blossoms & foliage, a butterfly reverse, marked "Thomas Webb & Sons" 935.00

Webb Gem Cameo Vase

Cameo vase, 16" h., tall baluster-form body w/tall trumpet neck & raised on a knopped stem w/domed foot, dark amber overlaid w/white & finely cut on the obverse w/two acanthus-skirted angels decorating a large flower-laden foliate-mounted urn w/a festoon, the reverse w/a larger foliate urn w/bouquet, both between foliate-decorated borders, the whole further decorated w/scrolling acanthus & other leafage, designed & executed by the Woodall Team, ca. 1890, impressed "THOMAS WEBB & SONS - GEM CAMEO" (ILLUS.) 68,500.00

Cracker jar, cov., glossy cased peach blow w/engraved dia-monds & other geometric devices, sterling silver rim, cover w/ball finial & bail handle marked "Tiffany & Co. Makers," including finial 7¼" h. 935.00

Rose bowl, footed bulbous body, six-crimp top, heavenly blue satin exterior decorated w/gold prunus blossoms, a gold butterfly reverse, white interior, three applied gold enameled feet, 4" d., 3" h.................245.00

Rose bowl, ovoid footed body, eight-crimp top, creamy ivory decorated w/gold flowers & leaves, a gold butterfly reverse, applied clear feet, 2½" d., 3½" h. 95.00

Rose bowl, footed, squatty bulbous shape, eight-crimp top, rich pink exterior decorated w/three applied clear leaves w/stems extending down the sides & forming petal feet, creamy yellow lining, 4¼" d., 3½" h..145.00

Vase, 4¼" h., 2⅝" d., ovoid form w/short cylindrical neck, rich blue decorated w/gold flowers, branches & leaves, a gold dragonfly reverse, creamy white interior.......................225.00

Vase, 4¾" h., 4" d., wide ovoid body w/slightly flared rim, heavy gold flowers & branches decoration on shaded blue satin ground, creamy white interior, enameled red spider web & letter "E" on base, signed "E. Webb".......................................295.00

Vase, 4⅞" h., 4" d., ovoid form tapering to a short flaring rim, shaded blue satin ground decorated w/heavy gold florals, base marked w/red spider web & "E" 275.00

Vase, 5¼" h., 3⅜" d., footed, cylindrical w/rounded base, ivory ground carved w/berries & leaves & highlighted w/brown staining, hallmarked silver rim, three applied clear frosted ball feet, signed "Thomas Webb & Sons" 795.00

Vase, 5½" h., 4¼" d., footed spherical body w/short cylindrical rim, rich brown shading to creamy white decorated w/heavy gold leaves & flowers, white interior, applied creamy white wafer foot...................275.00

Webb Gilt-Decorated Satin Vase

Vase, 5½" h., 5¼" d., footed squatty bulbous body tapering to a wide, short cylindrical neck, shaded olive brown to yellow satin ground decorated w/heavy gold prunus branches & pine needles w/gold butterfly on the back, creamy white lining (ILLUS.) 550.00

Vase, 6⅜" h., 3½" d., bulbous body tapering to a tall cylindrical neck, decorated w/a gold butterfly in flight among gold prunus blossoms, satin golden yellow ground, creamy white lining 325.00

Vase, 7¼" h., 4½" d., conical shape w/shouldered neck flaring to a ruffled rim, shaded brown exterior decorated w/heavy gold floral decoration, salmon pink interior, satin finish, in a brass, bamboo-like tripod stand 495.00

Vase, 8" h., baluster-form body tapering to a double ringed neck & slightly flaring rim, oxblood ground w/raised fern decoration highlighted w/gold, white interior, signed 420.00

Vase, 9" h., 5" d., squatty bulbous body tapering to a tall cylindrical neck w/flaring folded over rim, dark brown shaded to cream ground decorated w/heavy gold flowers & leaves dropping down from the rim & a small gold dragonfly 325.00

Webb Satin Vases with Gold

Vases, 5½" h., 2¾" d., ovoid body tapering to a trumpet-form neck, shaded deep gold satin decorated w/heavy gold flowering vines & a butterfly, creamy white lining, pr. (ILLUS.) 550.00

Vases, 6⅝" h., 3⅜" d., ovoid body tapering to a wide cylindrical neck, overall heavy gold prunus decoration & a gold butterfly on a shaded brown ground, unsigned pr. 265.00

Vases, 7¼" h., 5" d., spherical body tapering to a short, cylindrical neck w/slightly flaring rim & applied angular bronzy handles, shaded orange decorated w/heavy gold maidenhair fern, small daisies & a gold butterfly on the back, white lining, pr. 495.00

(End of Webb Section)

GLOSSARY OF SELECTED
GLASS TERMS

Acid (or satin) finish - A matte finish on glassware which is achieved by exposing the piece to acid fumes during the finishing process. More rarely the finish is obtained by the use of a mechanical grinding wheel.

Applied - A handle or other portion of a vessel which consists of a separate piece of molten glass attached by hand to the object. Most often used with free-blown or mold-blown pieces but also used with early pressed glass.

Appliqued glass - A type of decorative glass which features hand-applied three-dimensional trim, often in the form of fruit or flowering vines. This glass trim is applied in the semi-molten state while the main object is still extremely hot so that the appliqué becomes an intregral part of the piece.

Art Glass - An umbrella term that refers to all types of decorative glasswares but most specifically to the expensive, specially patented lines produced during the late 19th century. Notable types of Art Glass include Amberina, Burmese, and Peach Blow, among many others.

Butter pat (or chip) - A very small dish, often round or square, used on Victorian tables to hold an individual pat of butter. Most often produced as part of china table services only a few types were produced in glasswares, most notably in cut glass.

Cameo glass - A glass composed of two or more layers of glass, most often of contrasting colors, which are then carved through the surface with decorative designs. This ancient Roman technique was revived by the English in the late 19th century and English examples usually feature a white outer surface cut through to expose a single color background. English cameo often featured classical and botanical designs whereas the slightly later French cameo often featured more abstract naturalistic and landscape designs in more than two colors. Cameo carving can be done either by hand or with the use of acid, the hand-carved examples bringing higher prices.

Cased glass - Glassware which is composed of two or more layers of colored glass. The inner layer may be blown into outer layers while the glass is still hot or a piece in one color may dipped into the molten glass of another color while it is hot. Cameo glass (see above) is a form of cased glass and Victorian satin glass is also often a cased.

Console set - A three-piece tableware set generally composed of a pair of candlesticks and a wide, low-sided center bowl. These sets in pressed and mold-blown glassware were especially popular in the 1920s and 1930s.

Cracker jar - Also sometimes referred to as a 'bisquit jar,' these are decorative Victorian counterparts of the modern cookie jar. Produced in various chinawares as well as Art glass, they are often rounded barrel-shaped pieces fitted with a silver plate rim, cover and bail handle.

Crimping - A method of decorating the rims of bowls and vases. The glassworker used a special hand tool to manipulate the nearly-molten pressed or blown glass and form a ribbon-like design.

Crosshatching - A term generally used in discussing Brilliant Period cut glass. It refers to a cut design of parallel or crossed fine lines.

Crystal - A generic term generally used today when referring to thin, fine quality glass stemware produced since the early 20th century.

Derived from the Italian term *cristallo* referring to delicate, clear Venetian blown glass produced since the 14th century.

Enameled decoration - A form of decoration used on many types of Victorian Art glass. White or colored enamel paints were generally hand-painted on a finished piece of glass which was then refired to bake-on the enamel decoration.

Epergne - A French term used to describe a special decorative vessel popular in the 19th century. It generally consists of one or more tall, slender trumpet-form vases centering a wide, shallow bowl base. The bowl base could also be raised on a pedestal foot. It sometimes refers to a piece with a figural pedestal base supporting several small bowls or suspending several small baskets. Also made from silver or other metals.

Etching - A method of decorating a piece of glass. The two main types are *acid etching* and *needle etching*. In acid etching a piece is covered with an acid-resistant protective layer and then scratched with a design which is then exposed to hydrofluoric acid or acid fumes, thus leaving a frosted design when the protective layer is removed. Needle etching is a 20th century technique where a hand-held or mechanized needle is used to draw a fine-lined design on a piece. Ornate repetative designs were possible with the mechanized needle.

Fire-polishing - A process used to finish mold-blown and pressed glass where a piece is reheated just enough to smooth out the mold seams without distorting the overall pattern.

Flashing - A form of decoration popular on various types of Victorian glass wherein a glass piece of one color is, while still very hot, dipped into molten glass of another color to form a very thin outer layer. Quite often this thin outer layer was then engraved with a naturalistic design

cut through to the base color. A similar effect could be obtained by applying a colored stain (often in ruby red or amber) and this staining was especially popular on late 19th century pattern glass whereas flashing was reserved for generally more expensive lines of glassware.

Handkerchief vase - A form of vase most often seen in 20th century Venetian glass where the sides of the piece are pulled straight up and randomly pleated to resemble a large handkerchief.

Iridescence - A type of shiny, metallic finish popular on late 19th and early 20th century glassware from makers such as Tiffany, Loetz and Steuben. The effect is achieved by spraying the still-hot piece with metallic oxides which deposit the shiny surface. Early 20th century Carnival glass utilized this finish on less expensive, mass-produced lines of pressed and mold-blown glass.

Jack-in-the-pulpit vase - A form of vase with the rim manipulated to resemble the wildflower of this name. Generally the back edge is curled up while the front edge is curled downward. Many types of late 19th century decorative glass featured vases in this form.

Knop - Another term for 'knob,' usually referring to a finial on a lid or a bulbous section on the stem of a goblet or wine glass.

Millefiori - An Italian term meaning "thousand flowers," in glass it refers to a design produced by combining small multicolored discs (or 'canes') of glass to form an overall design or to decorate the interior of a paperweight.

Mold-blown - A method of glass production where a blob of molten glass (called a "gather") is blown into a patterned mold and then removed and further blown and manipulated to form an object such as a bottle.

Novelty - A pressed glass object generally made in the form of some larger item like a hatchet, boat or animal. They were extremely popular in the late 19th century and many were meant to be used as match holders, toothpick holders and small dresser boxes.

Opal - Pronounced o-pál, this was the term used by 19th century glassmen to describe the solid white glass today known as milk glass.

Piedouche - A French term referring to a paperweight which is raised on a low, applied clear foot.

Pontil mark - The scar left on the base of a free-blown, mold-blown and some early pressed glass by the pontil or punty rod. The hot glass object was attached at the base to the pontil rod so the glassworker could more easily handle it during the final shaping and finishing. When snapped off the pontil a round scar remained which, on finer quality pieces, was polished smooth.

Rigaree - Applied ribbon-like crimped decoration which highlights some types of Victorian Art glass. It is a form of *appliqued* (which see) decoration.

Rose bowl - A decorative small spherical or egg-shaped bowl, generally with a scalloped or crimped incurved rim, which was designed to hold rose petal potpourri or small rose blossoms. It was widely popular in the late 19th century and was produced in many pressed glass patterns as well as more expensive Art glass wares such as satin glass.

Scalloping - A decorative treatment used on the rims of plates, bowls, vases and similar objects. It was generally produced during the molding of the object and gave the rim a wavy or ruffled form.

Serrated - A form of notching on the rims of glass objects which resembles the edge of a saw blade. Sometimes referred to as a *sawtooth* edge, it is quite often found on cut glass pieces.

Sickness - A term referring to cloudy staining found in pressed or blown glass pieces, especially bottles, decanters and vases. It is caused when a liquid is allowed to stand in a piece for a long period of time causing a chemical deterioration of the interior surface. Generally it is nearly impossible to remove completely.

Spall - A shallow rounded flake on a glass object, generally near the rim of a piece.

Stemware - A general term for any form of drinking vessel raised on a slender pedestal or stemmed base.

Teardrop - A deliberately placed inclusion in a piece of glass which is formed by a bubble of air. They are sometimes used to highlight the stopper of a bottle or decanter or in the stems of goblets, wines and other stemware.

Vesica - A cut glass term referring to a cut design in the form of a pointed oval.

Water set - A tableware set popular in all types of 19th and early 20th century glasswares. It usually consisted of a large pitcher and a set of six matching tumblers or goblets.

Whimsey - A glass or ceramic novelty item. Generally in Victorian glass it is a free-blown or mold-blown object, often made by a glassworker as a special present and not part of regular glass production. Glass shoes, pipes and canes are examples of whimseys.

APPENDIX I

GLASS COLLECTORS' CLUBS

Art & Decorative Glasswares

American Cut Glass Association
Sherry Linville, Membership Chair
36 Crosstie Lane
Batesville, IN 47006

Antique and Art Glass Salt Shaker
  Collectors' Society
2832 Rapidan Trail
Maitland, Fl 32751

Mount Washington Art Glass Society
Edith Lawson, Treasurer
60 President Ave.
Providence, RI 02906

Paperweight Collectors Association
P.O. Box 468
Garden City Park, NY 11010

The Whimsey Club
Jeff & Mary Waterhouse
4544 Cairo Dr.
Whitehall, PA 18052

Other Types of Glass

Akro Agate
  Akro Agate Art Association
  Joseph Bourque
  Box 758
  Salem, NH 03079

  Akro Agate Collector's Club, Inc.
  Roger Hardy
  10 Bailey St.
  Clarksburg, WV 26301-2524

Cambridge
  National Cambridge Collectors
  P.O. Box 416
  Cambridge, OH 43725-0416

Candlewick
  National Candlewick Collector's Club
  c/o Virginia R. Scott
  275 Milledge Terrace
  Athens, GA 30606

Carnival
  American Carnival Glass Association
  c/o Dennis Runk
  P.O. Box 235
  Littlestown, PA 17340

  Collectible Carnival Glass Association
  c/o Wilma Thurston
  2360 N. Old S.R. 9
  Columbus, IN 47203

  Heart of America Carnival Glass
    Association
  c/o C. Lucile Britt
  3048 Tamarak Dr.
  Manhattan, KS 66502

  International Carnival Glass Association
  c/o Lee Markley, Secretary
  R.R. 1, Box 14
  Mentone, IN 46539

  New England Carnival Glass Club
  c/o Eva Backer, Membership
  12 Sherwood Rd.
  West Hartford, CT 06117

Depression
  National Depression Glass Association
  P.O. Box 69843
  Odessa, TX 79769

  20-30-40 Society, Inc.
  P.O. Box 856
  LaGrange, IL 60525

  Western Reserve Depression Glass Club
  c/o Ruth Gullis, Membership
  8669 Courtland Dr.
  Strongville, OH 44136

Duncan
National Duncan Glass Society
P.O. Box 965
Washington, PA 15301

Fenton
Fenton Art Glass Collectors of America
P.O. Box 384
Williamstown, WV 26187

National Fenton Glass Society
P.O. Box 4008
Marietta, OH 45750

Findlay
Collectors of Findlay Glass
P.O. Box 256
Findlay, OH 45839-0256

Fostoria
The Fostoria Glass Society of America
P.O. Box 826
Moundsville, WV 26041

Fry
H.C. Fry Glass Society
P.O. Box 41
Beaver, PA 15009

Greentown
National Greentown Glass Association
LeAnne Milliser, PR.
19596 Glendale Ave.
South Bend, IN 46637

Heisey
Heisey Collectors of America
P.O. Box 4367
Newark, OH 43055

Imperial
National Imperial Glass Collector's Society
P.O. Box 534
Bellaire, OH 43906

Milk Glass
National Milk Glass Collectors Society
c/o Helen Storey
46 Almond Dr.
Hershey, PA 17033

Morgantown
Old Morgantown Glass Collectors' Guild
P.O. Box 894
Morgantown, WV 26507

Morgantown Collectors of America, Inc.
c/o Jerry Gallagher
420 1st Ave. N.W.
Plainview, MN 55964

Phoenix & Consolidated Glass Collectors
c/o Jack D. Wilson
P.O. Box 81974
Chicago, IL 60681-0974

Stretch Glass
Stretch Glass Society
c/o Joanne Rodgers
P.O. Box 770643
Lakewood, OH 44107

Tiffin
Tiffin Glass Collectors' Club
P.O. Box 554
Tiffin, OH 44883

Westmoreland
National Westmoreland Glass
   Collectors' Club
P.O. Box 372
Westmoreland City, PA 15692

Westmoreland Glass Collectors Club
c/o Harold Mayes
2712 Glenwood
Independence, MO 64052

Special Glass Clubs

Glass Knife Collectors' Club
P.O. Box 342
Los Alamitos, CA 90720

Marble Collectors' Society
P.O. Box 222
Trumbull, CT 06611

National Reamer Collectors
c/o Larry Branstad
Rt. 1, Box 200
Grantsburg, WI 54840

National Toothpick Holder
   Collectors' Society
c/o Joyce Ender, Membership
Red Arrow Hwy., P.O. Box 246
Sawyer, MI 49125

Pairpoint Cup Plate Collectors
P.O. Box 52D
East Weymouth, MA 02189

Perfume and Scent Bottle Collectors
c/o Jeanne Parris
2022 E. Charleston Blvd.
Las Vegas, NV 89104

General Glass Clubs

Glass Collectors Club of Toledo
2727 Middlesex Dr.
Toledo, OH 43606

Glass Art Society
Alice Rooney
1305-4th Ave., #711
Seattle, WA 98101-2401

Glass Museum Foundation
1157 N. Orange, Box 921
Redlands, CA 92373

Glass Research Society of New Jersey
Wheaton Village
Millville, NJ 08332

National Early American Glass Club
P.O. Box 8489
Silver Spring, MD 20907

APPENDIX II

Museum Collections of American Glass

Many local and regional museums around the country have displays with some pressed glass included. The following are especially noteworthy.

New England

Connecticut: Wadsworth Atheneum, Hartford.

Maine: Jones Gallery of Glass and Ceramics (June - October), Sebago; Portland Museum of Art, Portland.

Massachusetts: Old Sturbridge Village, Sturbridge; Sandwich Glass Museum (April-November), Sandwich.

New Hampshire: The Currier Gallery of Art, Manchester.

Vermont: Bennington Museum (March-November), Bennington.

Mid-Atlantic

Delaware: Henry Francis du Pont Winterthur Museum, Winterthur.

New Jersey: Museum of American Glass, Wheaton Village, Millville.

New York: Corning Museum of Glass, Corning; Cooper-Hewitt Museum, the Smithsonian Institution's National Museum of Design (by appointment), New York; Metropolitan Museum of Art, New York; New-York Historical Society, New York.

Pennsylvania: Historical Society of Western Pennsylvania, Pittsburgh; Philadelphia Museum of Art, Philadelphia; Westmoreland Glass Museum, Port Vue.

Southeast

Florida: Lightner Museum, Saint Augustine; Morse Gallery of Art (Tiffany glass), Winter Park.

Louisiana: New Orleans Museum of Art, New Orleans.

Tennessee: Houston Antique Museum, Chattanooga.

Virginia: Chrysler Museum of Norfolk, Norfolk.

Washington, D.C.: National Museum of American History, Smithsonian Institution.

West Virginia: The Huntington Galleries, Inc., Huntington; Oglebay Institute - Mansion Museum, Wheeling.

Midwest

Indiana: Greentown Glass Museum, Greentown; Indiana Glass Museum, Dunkirk.

Michigan: Henry Ford Museum, Dearborn.

Minnesota: A.M. Chisholm Museum, Duluth.

Ohio: Cambridge Glass Museum, Cambridge; Milan Historical Museum, Milan; National Heisey Glass Museum, Newark; Toledo Museum of Art, Toledo.

Wisconsin: John Nelson Bergstrom Art Center and Mahler Glass Museum, Neenah.

Southwest and West

California: Los Angles County Museum of Art, Los Angeles; Wine Museum of San Francisco and M.H. de Young Museum, San Francisco.

Texas: Mills Collection, Texas Christian University, Fort Worth.

SELECTED BIBLIOGRAPHY

Art Glass - General

Grover, Ray and Lee. *Art Glass Nouveau*. Rutland, Vermont: Charles E. Tuttle Company, 1968.

Grover, Ray and Lee. *Carved & Decorated European Art Glass*. Rutland, Vermont: Charles E. Tuttle Company, 1970.

Lee, Ruth Webb. *Victorian Glass, Specialties of the Nineteenth Century*. Rutland, Vermont: Charles E. Tuttle Company, 1985.

Pullin, Anne Geffken. *Glass Signatures, Trademarks and Trade Names from the seventeenth to the twentieth century*. Radnor, Pennsylvania: Wallace-Homestead Book Company, 1986.

Revi, Albert Christian. *Nineteenth Century Glass - Its Genesis and Development*. New York, New York: Thomas Nelson, Inc., 1971.

Chocolate Glass

Measell, James. *Greentown Glass - The Indiana Tumbler & Goblet Company*. Grand Rapids, Michigan: The Grand Rapids Public Museum, 1979.

Custard Glass

Heacock, William. *Encyclopedia of Victorian Colored Pattern Glass, Book 4, Custard Glass from A to Z*. Marietta, Ohio: Antique Publications, 1976.

_____. *Fenton Glass - The First Twenty-five Years*. Marietta, Ohio: O-Val Advertising Corp., 1978.

Heacock, William and James Measell and Berry Wiggins. *Harry Northwood - The Early Years - 1881-1900*. Marietta, Ohio: Antique Publications, 1990.

_____. *Harry Northwood - The Wheeling Years - 1901 - 1925*. Marietta, Ohio: Antique Publications, 1991.

Cut Glass

Boggess, Bill and Louise. *American Brilliant Cut Glass*. New York, New York: Crown Publishers, 1977.

_____. *Collecing American Brilliant Cut Glass, 1876-1916*. West Chester, Pennsylvania: Schiffer Publishing, Ltd., 1992.

Farrar, Estelle Sinclaire, and Jane Shadel Spillman. *The Complete Cut & Engraved Glass of Corning*. New York, New York: Crown Publishers and The Corning Museum of Glass, 1979.

Pearson, J. Michael and Dorothy T. *American Cut Glass For the Discriminating Collector*. New York, New York: Vantage Press, 1965.

Pearson, J. Michael. *Encyclopedia of American Cut and Engraved Glass (1880-1917) Volumes I, II and III.* Miami Beach, Florida: self-published, 1975, 1977 & 1978.

Revi, Albert Christian. *American Cut and Engraved Glass.* New York, New York: Thomas Nelson, Inc., 1972.

Wiener, Herbert, and Freda Lipkowitz. *Rarities in American Cut Glass.* Houston, Texas: The Collectors House of Books, Publishing Co., 1975.

English Glass

Grover, Ray and Lee. *English Cameo Glass.* New York, New York: Crown Publishers, 1980

Hadjemin, Charles R. *British Glass - 1800-1914.* Woodbridge, England: The Antique Collectors' Club, 1991.

Manley, Cyril. *Decorative Victorian Glass.* New York, New York: Van Nostrand Reinhold Company, 1981.

Wakefield, Hugh. *Nineteenth Century British Glass.* London, England: Faber and Faber, Ltd., 1982.

French Glass

Garner, Philippe. *Emile Gallé.* New York, New York: Rizzoli International Publications, Inc., 1976.

McClinton, Katharine Morrison *Introduction to Lalique Glass.* Des Moines, Iowa: Wallace-Homestead Book Company, 1978.

Percy, Christopher Vane. *The Glass of Lalique, a collector's guide.* New York, New York: Charles Scribner's Sons, 1983.

Libbey Glass

Fauster, Carl U. *Libbey Glass Since 1818 - Pictorial History & Collectors' Guide.* Toledo, Ohio: Len Beach Press, 1979.

Mary Gregory

Truitt, R. & D. *Mary Gregory Glassware, 1880-1990.* Kensington, Maryland: self-published, 1992.

Moser Glass

Charon, Mural K. *Ludwig (Ludvik) Moser - King of Glass.* Hillsdale, Michigan: Charon/Ferguson, Division of Ferguson Communications, Publishers, 1984.

Opalescent Glass

Heacock, William. *Encyclopdia of Victorian Colored Pattern Glass, Book II, Opalescent Glass from A to Z.* Marietta, Ohio: Antique Publications, 1975.

_____. *Fenton Glass - The First Twenty-five Years*. Marietta, Ohio: O-Val Advertising Corp., 1978.

Heacock, William, and William Gamble. *Encyclopedia of Victorian Colored Glass, Book 9, Cranberry Opalescent from A to Z*. Marietta, Ohio: Antique Publications, 1987.

Heacock, William and James Measell and Berry Wiggins. *Harry Northwood - The Early Years - 1881-1900*. Marietta, Ohio: Antique Publications, 1990.

_____. *Harry Northwood - The Wheeling Years - 1901 - 1925*. Marietta, Ohio: Antique Publications, 1991.

Pairpoint Glass

Avila, George C. *The Pairpoint Glass Story*. New Bedford, Massachusetts: The New Bedford Glass Society, 1978.

Padgett, Leonard E. *Pairpoint Glass*. Des Moines, Iowa: Wallace-Homestead Book Company, 1979.

Paperweights

Flemming, Monika and Peter Pommerencke. *Paperweights of the World*. Atglen, Pennsylvania: Schiffer Publishing Ltd., 1993.

Hollister, Paul. *Glass Paperweights of the New-York Historical Society*. New York, New York: Clarkson N. Potter, Inc., 1974.

Steuben Glass

Gardner, Paul V. *The Glass of Frederick Carder*. New York, New York: Crown Publishers, Inc., 1971.

Tiffany Glass

Koch, Robert. *Louis C. Tiffany's Glass - Bronzes - Lamps, A Complete Collector's Guide*. New York, New York: Crown Publishers, 1971.

_____. *Louis C. Tiffany - Rebel in Glass*. New York, Crown Publishers, 1964.

McKean, Hugh F. *The "Lost" Treasures of Louis Comfort Tiffany*. New York, New York: Doubleday & Company, 1980.

Wave Crest

Cohen, Wilfred R. *Wave Crest - The Glass of C.F. Monroe*. Paducah, Kentucky: Collector Books, 1987.

Grimmer, Elsa. H. *Wave Crest Ware - An Illustrated Guide to the Victorian World of C.F. Monroe*. Des Moines, Iowa: Wallace-Homestead Book Company, 1979.

AMERICAN & EUROPEAN
DECORATIVE & ART GLASS PRICE GUIDE

INDEX